Rights *for a* Season

Rights *for a* Season

The Politics of Race, Class, and Gender in Richmond, Virginia

Lewis A. Randolph and Gayle T. Tate

The University of Tennessee Press

Knoxville

This book is printed on acid-free paper.

Library of Congress Cataloging-in-Publication Data

Randolph, Lewis A.
Rights for a season : the politics of race, class, and gender in Richmond, Virginia /
Lewis A. Randolph and Gayle T. Tate.—1st ed.
   p. cm.
Includes bibliographical references (p.) and index.
ISBN 1-57233-224-7 (cl.: alk. paper)

   1. African Americans—Civil rights—Virginia—Richmond—History.
   2. African Americans—Virginia—Richmond—Politics and government.
   3. African Americans—Virginia Richmond—Social conditions.
   4. Civil rights movements—Virginia—Richmond—History.
   5. Social classes—Virginia—Richmond—History.
   6. Sex role—Political aspects—Virginia—Richmond—History.
   7. Richmond (Va.)—Race relations—Political aspects.
   8. Richmond (Va.)—Politics and government.
   9. Richmond (Va.)—Social conditions.
   I. Title.

F234.R59 N473 2003
323.1'1960730755451'09046—dc21   2002152529

To the memories of

Louis H. Randolph & Emmett Ward II

and to

the descendants of
the Randolph slaves,
the Willie family, and the
Bethlehem Baptist Church
of Richmond, Virginia,

For Keeping Faith

Contents

Illustrations

FIGURES

MAPS

Tables

Foreword

Why has the mobilization of black voters in U.S. cities in the post–civil rights era not resulted in significant improvements in social-welfare services, funding for public education, the availability of moderate and low income housing, or the overall quality of life for black residents in inner-city neighborhoods? Why have black elected officials been unable (or unwilling) to facilitate the redistribution of social and economic resources in American cities from the white business and corporate elites and wealthy professionals to the working and lower-class African Americans whose votes put them in office? How did a black "conservative" political and economic agenda emerge over the last two decades to challenge the "progressive" political positions assumed by black leaders in the NAACP, National Urban League, and other civil rights organizations on issues of social welfare, public education, and changing family structures?

Lewis A. Randolph and Gayle T. Tate's *Rights for a Season: The Politics of Race, Class, and Gender in Richmond, Virginia* provides detailed and well-researched answers to these important questions. Beginning with an examination of race, class, and gender issues in Virginia during the era of American slavery, and taking their story through the divisive and controversial political campaigns in Richmond in the 1970s and 1980s, Randolph and Tate present a comprehensive analysis of the complex interplay of social, economic, and cultural factors that help to explain African American political behavior and mass mobilization.

Political and economic affairs in post-colonial and antebellum Richmond were dominated by a planter aristocracy and mercantile elite that rose to power and influence on the basis of the economic wealth produced by enslaved African and African-American workers. While enslaved Africans in the Tidewater and Chesapeake regions cultivated tobacco and other farm products for the domestic and international markets, enslaved workers and free blacks were hired by merchant and industrial capitalists who opened factories in Richmond to produce processed tobacco goods for local and national consumption. Richmond's enslaved and free black workforce was instrumental in the formation of the distinct social and cultural institutions that emerged in the African American community before the outbreak of the Civil War. The practice of "hiring out" slave laborers to industries in Richmond, Norfolk, and other southern cities created networks of communication that allowed the plotting of revolts, insurrections, and other forms of black resistance and "collective insurgency." These urban "free spaces" were also filled with social and fraternal organizations and religious institutions that emerged and cultivated a distinctive African American culture and value system that served as an alternative to the world the slaveowners made.

Following Emancipation and the end of military action, the African American churches in Richmond became the most visible sites of social and political mobilization, and in the postbellum reconstruction campaigns religious leaders and free black property owners were instrumental in forging the community's political and social agenda. At the same time, African American women played an indispensable role within the churches and the community at large and contributed immensely to campaigns for social and economic advancement. And although they were denied the vote, African American women participated in the movements for social change, including the organized protests against the "pass system," which required that African Americans carry passes while moving around the city, the sit-ins to end discriminatory practices on the city's streetcars, and the labor strikes initiated by stevedores and other workers demanding higher wages. In the 1870s black male Republicans were gradually being replaced by white "Conservatives" and Democrats in the Virginia assembly and in local governments. This process culminated in the restoration of white supremacy in state politics after 1883, following a systematic campaign of violence, fraud, corruption, and intimidation of black voters. During these years African American church women were victimized by forms of "ecclesiastical sexism" in the institutions to which they had devoted considerable time, talent, and treasure. Unfortunately, gender issues split black church congregations at a time when solidarity within the African American community was the best defense for maintaining the momentum in the collective struggle for black social, political, and economic advancement.

Although Republican attorney John Mercer Langston was ultimately victorious in his campaign to serve as U.S. Representative from Virginia's Fourth Congressional District in 1890, by the end of that decade black Richmonders had come to realize that self-determinist economic activities in the educational, business, and financial arenas would be the primary vehicles for individual and collective advancement. "Race enterprises" began to flourish in black Richmond in the 1880s and 1890s, including the Savings Bank of the Grand Fountain United Order of True Reformers, opened in 1888; the Southern Aid and Life Insurance Company, opened in 1893, one of the first black insurance companies; and the Saint Luke Penny Savings Bank, opened the same year by Maggie Lena Walker, who became the first woman bank president in the United States. Walker was a truly impressive figure who promoted numerous business and philanthropic enterprises, particularly among African American women in Richmond and throughout the state.

Despite the "lily-white" pretensions of the state Republican Party, thirty-three black Republicans were elected to the Richmond City Council in the late nineteenth century, representing the predominantly black district of Jackson Ward. However, conservative Democrats, through the Walton Act in 1894 and the suffrage provisions included in the state constitution in 1901–2, succeeded in disfranchising the vast majority of black Virginians through age, literacy, and residency requirements, poll taxes, and other measures. Although African Americans challenged these voting requirements through the judicial system, they lost in the state and federal courts. In an attempt to register their opposition to lily-white Republicans, independent black Republican candidates ran for state and local political offices in 1906 and 1921. Unfortunately, when black conservative leaders refused to support these candidates in 1921, this unsuccessful bid for political support and recognition prefigured the emerging ideological divisions among African Americans in Richmond and throughout Virginia.

The political machine controlled by Democratic politician Harry Byrd dominated Virginia politics from the 1920s until his death in 1966. Considered by some "a kinder, gentler white supremacist," Byrd opposed overt displays of racial hostility and violence, but was equally committed to maintaining black subordination in all aspects of social and political life. While African Americans remained wedded to the party of Lincoln, southern and northern white Democrats could ignore them. When African Americans began shifting their political allegiance to the Democratic Party and Franklin D. Roosevelt's New Deal in the 1930s and 1940s, however, white Democratic politicians encouraged the formation local of black "sub-machines" in Chicago, New York, Philadelphia, and other northern cities controlled by the new black Democratic (formerly Republican) politicians. The creation of jobs in separate black programs within the National Youth Administration (NYA), Works Projects Administration (WPA), the Public Works Administration (PWA), and other New Deal agencies was used to draw black voters into local Democratic political machines. Unfortunately, in Richmond, as Randolph and Tate demonstrate, during this period black residents who could vote had no alternative to Byrd's Democratic machine, and they received few benefits from their political allegiance. In the post–World War II period, when black Democratic politicians such as William Dawson in Chicago, Adam Clayton Powell Jr. in New York City, and Charles Diggs in Detroit were consolidating their political bases, African American leaders in Richmond organized the Richmond Civic Council (RCC), whose major objective was to increase black voter registration in the city. Spurred by the city charter reform movement headed by the white-led Richmond Citizens Association, the political mobilization in the black community culminated in the 1948 election of the first African American, attorney Oliver Hill, to the Richmond City Council in the twentieth century. However, Randolph and Tate describe the swift decline of the RCC and its lost of political legitimacy by 1952, when the organization was split over which of two black candidates, Rev. William L. Ransome or life insurance executive David C. Deans, to support for city council. The result was that no black was elected to the city council in 1952, and by 1954 the RCC had vanished from Richmond's black political landscape.

In the wake of the Supreme Court's *Brown v. Board of Education* decision in May 1954 declaring legal segregation in public education, southern Democratic politicians, led by Virginia's Sen. Harry Byrd, launched a campaign of "massive resistance" to the implementation of public school desegregation. Randolph and Tate present detailed information on the response of Virginia's political establishment to the *Brown* decision and trace the origins of Richmond's most important civil rights organization, the Richmond Crusade for Voters (RCV), to the opposition generated in the black community to a local referendum designed to prevent the desegregation of Richmond's public schools. Initially involved in voter registration drives, the RCV soon moved into electoral politics and nonviolent direct-action protests. Organized by physicians William S. Thornton, William Ferguson Reid, and other middle-class black professionals, Randolph and Tate contrast the era of "quiet integration" of the police department and municipal agencies in the 1950s with the civil rights activism beginning in 1960, especially the year-long boycott against Thalhimer's department store.

In recounting the story of the civil rights movement in Richmond, Randolph and Tate focus on gender and class issues, and particularly the significant contributions of black women activists. They use extensive interviews with former civil rights activists Janet Ballard, Ethel T. Overby, Ruby Clayton Walker, Ora Lomax, and others to describe and document the sexist and male chauvinist beliefs and practices within civil rights organizations. Their analysis of working-class black activist Curtis Holt's struggles to get Richmond city officials and upper-class black leaders to support the installation of a traffic light at a dangerous intersection in a poor black neighborhood clearly demonstrates the negative impact of class biases on the black campaigns for social advancement. While the black elites who dominated the RCV were successful in gaining political influence through the endorsement of winning black and white candidates (including some RCV members), class and gender divisions allowed black conservatives, doing the bidding of the white corporate establishment, to sow seeds of dissension and division within the RCV and African American community.

As the proportion of black voters in Richmond increased in the 1970s, white corporate and political elites, with the help of black conservatives, attempted to annex predominantly white suburban areas to the city in order to dilute black voting strength. This strategy proved unsuccessful, and when the courts finally allowed an election for city council members to be held in 1977, it resulted in a black majority for the first (and only) time in Richmond's history. Henry Marsh was elected by the council as Richmond's first African American mayor.

While the city council elections in 1977 represented a major political victory for black Richmonders, it was short-lived. The new progressive black politicians who came to power attempted to address the pressing social welfare needs of the city's poor and working-class residents. However, conflicts soon arose between the council's black majority and white business elites over "Project One," a major downtown development project. Randolph and Tate make it clear that the confrontation over Project One served as the springboard for political challenges launched by black conservatives in the elections of 1982. Black conservatives, led by L. Douglas Wilder and others closely aligned with the city's corporate elite, attacked the black liberals on the city council and were successful in unseating Willie Dell, a progressive black woman politician. Randolph and Tate reveal how black conservatives made use of sexist attitudes and class biases among African Americans to defeat Dell's bid for re-election. In the years after the election of 1982, biracial conservative coalitions have dominated political and economic decision making in Richmond and have served to thwart black political advancement and the implementation of progressive policies aimed at improving the social and educational conditions for the city's poor and working class residents.

Rights for a Season is a welcome addition to the expanding literature on urban politics in the United States. Based on extensive scholarship and oral interviews, Randolph and Tate describe the complex interplay of racial, class, and gender issues in explaining political continuity and change in the capital of the former Confederacy. In the post–civil rights era, white conservatives' desire to maintain political power, as well as class, gender, and ideological divisions among African Americans, proved to be important factors in the defeat of progressive black politicians interested in improving the social conditions for Richmond's poor and working-class residents. In *Rights for a Season* Randolph and Tate argue convincingly that biracial coalitions of progressive leaders and organizations, and the political mobilization of the urban poor and working class, will be needed to challenge conservatives' domination of the urban and national political landscape.

V. P. Franklin
Teachers College
Columbia University

Acknowledgments

In so many ways the decade that we spent working on *Rights for a Season: The Politics of Race, Class, and Gender in Richmond, Virginia,* represents a major "season" in both of our lives. Our research on Richmond politics has led us down many roads, from a more comprehensive examination of the multifaceted roles that race, class, and gender played in challenging the entrenched white power structure to critical new insights of the historical and political spaces that black Richmonders recontextualized for themselves in their mobilization efforts. Along the way, as we spun this collective endeavor into whole cloth, we incurred tremendous debts of gratitude to many individuals who helped make this project a reality. First and foremost, we owe thanks to Adriane M. Livingston, who suggested that we do the project and for nurturing its evolution. Our thanks to Lionel C. Newsom, who contributed valuable information during the early stages of the project on the southern civil rights movement and its impact on black political development in the post-civil rights era. We are deeply indebted to Willie Dell, who not only provided us with a wealth of information about Richmond politics, but also granted us unlimited access to her personal papers and documents of key and lesser-known individuals who were instrumental in shaping the local political arena. Special thanks are owed to Chris Silver and John Moeser for their depth of knowledge on Richmond's history and politics and for introducing us to major black political leaders, including Willie Dell. We are also grateful to Roland Otey, Schwanna Otey, Jody Allen, and Anthony Keitt for graciously opening their homes and providing emotional sustenance during our initial research endeavors.

There were a number of people whose contributions helped us formulate our analytical approach to the city's local civil rights movement. A special thanks to Alice Clarke Lynch, Naomi Morse, and Vergie Binford for providing insightful information on Ethel T. Overby and her role as a social activist. We owe never-ending thanks to Ora Lomax and Ruby Clayton Walker for their personal recollections of the civil rights struggle and to Alto Mae Holt for providing the additional archival materials on her late husband, Curtis Holt. We are indebted to Bob Brickhouse for providing us with a picture of Curtis Holt. We also owe a very special thank you to the late Janet Jones Ballard and Alma Barlow, who provided us with a firsthand analysis of the intrinsic components of race, class, and gender embedded in the city's black politics in particular and the larger political arena in general.

Other individuals who gave unselfishly of their time so that we would "get it right" include Peter Bailey, Roland Turpin, George Lee, Clarence Towns, Martin Jewell, Michael P. Williams, Saad El-Amin, R. Allen Hays, Francis Foster, Elsa Barkley Brown, Wendell T. Foster, Franklin Gales, William Thornton, Bill Harris, Oliver Hill, Benjamin R. Murray, William J. Jones, Marie Hashgawa, Marietta L. Matthews, Mary Wise, Francine Wise, Arthurine Hampton, and Harmon Buskey.

We are grateful to the individuals at a number of institutions who provided us with assistance and archival materials for this project. They include Greg Kimble, the staff of the Library of Virginia, and especially Audrey Johnson and the picture collection branch; Teresa Roane and the photographic services of the Valentine Museum; Celia Suggs of the Maggie Lena Walker National Historic Site for the photo of Maggie Lena Walker; Katrina Boston and The Newsome House Museum and Cultural Center for their assistance; Charles Saunders of the *Richmond Times-Dispatch* and the Research Library for obtaining critical black-and-white photos for the book; Suzanne K. Durham of the L. Douglas Wilder Library at Virginia Union University; the staff at the Prints and Photograph Division and Photo Duplication Services of the Library of Congress; Dan Williams in providing advice on the photos for the jacket design; and the tireless efforts of Ray Bonis of the Special Collections and Archives of the Cabell Library at Virginia Commonwealth University.

We want to thank especially Sheila Jean Walker and Michael Rupright for their excellent editing of the manuscript and C. Ann Gordon for checking our numerical calculations and tables that appear throughout the text. We were ably assisted by Barbara Jo Mitchell, secretary of Rutgers University's Africana Studies Department, who painstakingly coordinated a great deal of our research efforts with her vast knowledge of computer software. Janice Gray also provided numerous services on behalf of the project. We owe a special debt of thanks to Michael Mumper, chair of the Department of Political Science at Ohio University at Athens, for his consistently positive responses to funding requests at critical stages of the book and, similarly, to Joyce Kohan, former assistant dean of the College of Arts and Sciences of Ohio University at Athens, who also provided financial support for the project. The steadfastness of our editors, Jennifer Siler and Scot Danforth, as well as the University of Tennessee Press editorial staff, especially June Hussey, moved the project smoothly through its final stages.

Over the past decade we have benefited from a number of scholars who informed the project, either with an analysis of black politics, a close reading of portions of the manuscript, through sharing their work with us, or by critical commentary on southern politics; of course, many colleagues patiently listened while we talked incessantly about the project. Our thanks to James Jennings, Georgia Persons, William E. Nelson, Hanes Walton Jr., Robert E. Weems Jr., Marcus Pohlmann, Todd Swanstrom, Charles V. Hamilton, Frances Fox Piven, Akasha (Gloria) Hull, Randall Ripley, and the late Robert Mier. We deeply appreciate the thoughtful criticism of Charles Jones and Oscar R. Williams who read the entire manuscript. In the same vein, we owe a tremendous debt of gratitude to V. P. Franklin, who not only meticulously read the manuscript and gave us invaluable criticism but graciously consented to write the foreword for the book.

We've been blessed with a group of loving supporters who constantly encouraged us to stay the course by providing encouragement, a sounding board, archival materials, current newspaper clippings, and source materials, and in the process they made innumerable sacrifices on our behalf. We thank Ernest M. Tate Jr., Eartha Tate, the late Lucille Carter Tate, Alyce Cobbs, Ruth Ernestine Tutler, Charles Tutler, Adah Ward Randolph, Andrew Clifton, Desmond Randolph, Devin Randolph, Kenya Tate-Dewdney, Rosalind White, Melva D. Burke, Katherine Burke Williams, Violet Matanzo, Bella Alonzo, Harry Wynn, Estelle Crocker, Phillip Crocker, the late Juanita T. Glasgow, the late George L. Glasgow, the late Ethel L. Willie, Olive Ramos, Peter J. Randolph, Mary Ann Randolph, Zella Mae Randolph, Clemmie Ward, Patricia Wright, Sandra Wright, Tia Miller, the late Harriet Taylor, the late Rozella Gregg, Gloria Harper Dickinson, Geraldine Pemberton-Diallo, Lillie Johnson Edwards, Gwen Parker Ames, Donald Ames, Atiba Parham, Gwen Parham, Charles Hughes, Essie Hughes, Kenneth B. Boyd, Marsha F. Boyd, P. Eric Abercrumbie, Elona Boykins, and Yolanda S. Robinson.

Rights for a Season

Introduction

Theoretical Perspectives on Black Political Mobilization

The South is confronted today with one of the most difficult political problems in the Western world—the adjustment of racial relations. Out of this race problem has developed a political system widely misunderstood and widely misinterpreted. But "Southern politics is no comic opera. It is a deadly serious business that is sometimes carried on behind a droll facade."

V. O. Key, *Southern Politics in State and Nation,* 1949

As black Richmonders moved toward electoral power in the late nineteenth and twentieth centuries, their mobilization efforts were often thwarted by the external hegemony of the white power structure as well as intragroup conflicts over race, gender, and class. This book posits that the dynamics of race, class, and gender and their collective impact on urban and black politics are dominant variables in altering the political landscape and in determining collective political responses and their subsequent outcomes (Randolph and Tate 1995, 137). This is a political science case study of (1) black political mobilization in Richmond, Virginia, as blacks moved from protest and politics to electoral power, and (2) the dynamics of race, class, and gender and how these evolving variables affect urban and black politics in a medium-sized city.

Richmond was chosen for study so that we might add to the rich and growing body of literature that is currently developing on southern cities and their unique brand of local politics. In addition, we wished to illuminate the complexities of the politics of the city itself, spanning several decades of race relations, political mobilization, and an entrenched class structure. This research contributes to regional analysis by providing examination of another southern city that can be used for future comparative urban studies. Relative to other southern cities, Richmond boasts a benign racism, a reality that offered few opportunities for black incorporation into city politics until the adoption of a nine-seat single-member district system in 1977. Throughout its history, however, black Richmonders have struggled to be included in every phase of the city's political development. This black political independence emerged soon after the Civil War, when newly freed men and women evinced a high degree of political mobilization, threatening the restored government of Virginia and, ultimately, the white elite power structure. This racial polarization, in which blacks are diametrically opposed to whites while simultaneously depending on the internal cohesion of both racial groups, became the centrifugal force of the city's politics. The intertwining variables of race, class, and gender exacerbated past political tensions and drives much of contemporary mobilization efforts.

We argue, utilizing a historical and political framework, that the dynamics of race, class, and gender undergird Richmond's political history of slavery, disfranchisement, segregation laws, racist customs, and gender bias, all under the guise of "southern gentility." In contemporary politics, we argue that these interlocking variables create theistic cleavages in the political structure, forcing the realignment of political factions as well as a superficial inclusion of those formerly excluded from politics. As with other southern cities in the midst of racial turmoil and upheaval, where segregation was being displaced by more inclusive governmental structures, Richmond's history of racism, elitism, and sexism was a background against which blacks mobilized for social change.

There are four themes that appear throughout this book. First, we contend that race, class, and gender must be in the foreground in analyzing racial politics in Richmond. Although race is the precipitating factor and often the dominant variable in racial tensions between blacks and whites, class cleavages and gender animosity play salient roles as well. Further, if the political stakes involved are high enough, and relatively complex, internal and external class cleavages and sexism become germane to the political conflict.

While the race, class, and gender issues, with race predominating, have overtly defined the city's racial politics, the internal aspects of these variables within the black community have also been significant. All of these variables, prevalent within Richmond's early African American community, were immediately apparent after the Civil War and intrinsic as a fact of life thereafter. During the civil rights movement (CRM) in Richmond, the dynamics of race, class, and gender were instrumental in the movement's success, but they also contributed to the failure of the 1977 black majority on city council.

Isolated from the rest of the body politic, black Richmonders constituted an aggrieved population, and in mobilizing to address their grievances, relied on indigenous grass-roots black political leadership (Tilly 1978, 72; McAdam 1985, 15). The second theme of this book, political reliance on African American leadership, remains a critical issue in the political development and mobilization of Richmond's African American community. The third theme involves the exploration of the historic political alliance between African American and white conservatives in Richmond. On balance, this alliance has created a political climate in which it is increasingly difficult for a progressive opposition to emerge and challenge the city's economic power structure. Finally, the fourth theme of this study is that most development projects offered by black politicians are rejected out of hand, unless they primarily enrich Richmond's white elites (with blacks receiving only token economic benefits) and are totally controlled by white elites. White leaders in Richmond might perceive their city as representing a New South, but this study posits that although Richmond's brand of local politics is unique, the former capital of the Confederacy is very much a part of the hegemonist Old South.

RACE AND CLASS IN BLACK POLITICS LITERATURE

This study assessed the subfields of urban politics and black politics and found that, across these two fields, race, class, and gender are significant variables. Although class and race have been addressed in prior studies, the complexities of race, class, and gender have not been fully explored. Consequently, if we are to assess the impact of the three intertwining variables on Richmond's black body politic, and its urban political and policy arenas, an examination of these two subfields is required for situating our case study within the literature.

Race

In an article in the *National Political Science Review,* Hanes Walton Jr., Leslie B. McLemore, and C. Vernon Gray classified by subfields what they deemed the premier works on black politics (Walton, McLemore, and

Gray 1990, 196–218). Their subfields ranged from electoral politics to pressure politics. Walton, McLemore, and Gray revealed that of the ninety-two books on black politics, six were written by African American political scientists and eleven by European American political scientists. The remaining seventy-five books were written by nonpolitical scientists (199). Most of the texts on black politics were written by European and African American historians, sociologists, journalists, and former African American elected officials (199). In addition, only one book cited examined local protest politics in a southern city (201–11). Prior to 1962, two works on urban politics written by political scientists encompassed the African American political experience (204–211). The subfield of race or white supremacy so dominates the interpretation and understanding of southern politics that studies by V. O. Key Jr. and Everett C. Ladd on southern politics focused almost exclusively on race and overlooked class and gender issues within the African American community (Key 1948; Ladd 1969). Until recently there was no recognized subfield on gender. Race was not accepted by the political science mainstream as a possible subfield until 1996, when a new subfield, race and ethnicity, emerged. The article revealed that the study of racial matters was analogous to the subfield of black politics. If someone was studying race and politics, it was understood during that era that he or she was simply examining black politics. The race variable has been introduced into political science, and the current subfield of black politics addresses the issue of race.

Race is both an important and divisive issue in shaping relationships between and among political and social groups. The influence of race in the politics of Chicago, Atlanta, Los Angeles, Philadelphia, Boston, and other major cities is well documented (Sonenshein 1993; Grimshaw 1992; Keiser 1990, 49–72, 108–24; Pinderhughes 1987, 1–318; Jennings and King 1986; Preston 1987; Jones 1978a, 1990b; Gosnell [1935] 1969). Research on race in black politics has generally aligned it with other political phenomena, such as race and machine politics, race and coalition politics, race and regime politics, and race and ethnic politics.

As a variable, race was first introduced by political scientists examining its relationship to machine politics. The pioneering work of Harold F. Gosnell, *Negro Politicians: The Rise of Negro Politics in Chicago* (1935), explained why African Americans during the mid-1930s remained loyal to the Republican party, while most white Americans were aligning themselves with the Democratic party. William J. Grimshaw, in *Bitter Fruit,* reiterates Gosnell's position: "Gosnell argued that black political behavior was culturally rooted in the unique experience of slavery and emancipation. In this way, the Republican party was more akin to a religious institution, as the 'party of Lincoln, the emancipator,' than a political party" (Grimshaw 1991, 8).

Grimshaw's text was the next major attempt to explicate race and its relationship to Chicago's political machine. Grimshaw emphasized the class cleavages within Chicago's African American community and revealed that poor, but not middle-class blacks, were vulnerable to the machine of Democratic city politics. Thus, the black class cleavages in Grimshaw's analysis of the machine and its relationship to blacks provides an effective explanation of why blacks supported an organization that consistently subjugated and exploited them. Grimshaw reveals that blacks supported the machine when popular political sentiment went from the right to the left on the political spectrum, and they abandoned the machine when opinion shifted from left to right. Blacks supported the machine when it suited their interests and opposed the machine when it was not congruent with their interests (Grimshaw 1991).

However, the relationship between race and political machines in northern urban communities is an insufficient frame of reference for our analysis. For instance, unlike Chicago, Richmond is a medium-sized southern city not historically dominated by a powerful political machine. Moreover, Richmond is not ethnically and racially diverse like Chicago, and consequently, Richmond's blacks cannot form coalitions with other ethnic groups and they generally protest and oppose Richmond's white power structure alone. Chicago, like most of its northern and midwestern counterparts, has a checkered past in the area of race relations. Chicago's race relations were shaped by its history of de facto segregation, which in turn shaped white and black sociopolitical relationships throughout the city's history. In Richmond, however, racism is clearly an intrinsic part of the political landscape and social fabric because of the city's endemic history of de jure segregation. Thus, Chicago's race relations were shaped by de facto segregation, whereas Richmond's race relations were fabricated by customs that were deeply rooted in the southern slavery, history, and cultural experience. Furthermore, blacks in Chicago could vote and a few held political office. In Richmond, a variety of exclusionary measures following slavery, such as the poll tax, literacy tests, white primaries, the grandfather clause, and the understanding clause, excluded blacks from local electoral politics.

Blacks in Chicago and Richmond are divided by class, but class is a more salient issue in Richmond's African American community. Thus, the incorporation of machine politics in the subfield of black politics does not fully take into account the impact of class and the southern Jim Crow system that not only governed more rigidly white and black relations but also excluded blacks from the political process. Applying the political machine analogy to Richmond would not adequately interpret Richmond's politics, and especially the city's black politics, because such important concerns are liable to be slighted. Other political scientists have studied race and coalition politics through such phenomena as biracial and multiracial coalitions. Dominant in coalition politics are Browning, Marshall, and Tabb's *Protest Is Not Enough;* Raphael Sonenshein's classic analysis of multiracial coalitions, *Politics in Black and White;* and James Jennings's *Blacks, Latinos, and Asians in Urban America* (Browning, Marshall, and Tabb 1984; Sonenshein 1993; Jennings 1994). These books exemplify the broad spectrum of literature and viewpoints in the study of race and coalition politics.

Protest Is Not Enough examines the significance of race in terms of black political empowerment by situating race in the context of coalition politics. Browning, Marshall, and Tabb assert that white and liberal coalitions are critical to the political incorporation and success of blacks and Hispanics in the political arena because liberal coalitions tend to be more responsive to the needs and interests of minorities (1986, 242–62). Thus, the authors postulate that race as a divisive issue can be overcome through political coalitions that include white liberals. Their analysis of the importance of a liberal-dominated biracial coalition to the success of black political empowerment at the local level is relevant to those situations in which a biracial coalition is possible. However, where there are no liberals and the prospects of a coalition between whites and blacks is remote, then the authors' emphasis on forming a biracial coalition may not be realistic for whites and blacks in a southern community enthralled by racially polarizing politics.

Another interpretation of race through coalition politics is through the phenomenon of multiracial coalitions. The most effective advancement of this perspective was offered by Raphael Sonenshein in *Politics in Black and White.* Sonenshein submits that "biracial politics are still alive" (1993, xv). His treatment of race in the backdrop of Los Angeles' multiracial coalition leads him to contend that if blacks are to achieve black political empowerment, they will have to attain it through "a unified model [which] accepts that black mobilization and white liberal support are core factors in the success of black incorporation" (272). Sonenshein "is convinced that [no] candidate or group can pursue its objectives citywide without at least one partner in another community . . . [because]

the city is becoming more complex, more international, and more politically attuned" (267–68). He presents a compelling argument; however, while Los Angeles is a multiracial and multiethnic community, Richmond is not. Class and gender divisions within African American politics are much more evident in Richmond than in Los Angeles. Sonenshein's multiracial model would not sufficiently address class and gender in Richmond, where the dominant racial groups are blacks and whites, bipolar opposites for centuries.

Another explanation of race through coalition politics is offered by James Jennings in *Blacks, Latinos, and Asians in Urban America*. Jennings's model differs from the Sonenshein and Browning, Marshall, and Tabb interpretations. For Jennings, a major problem confronting urban America in the future will be the capability of blacks, Latinos, and Asians to form viable political coalitions at the local level for the betterment of their communities:

> The nation's major "racial" urban eruptions in the last fifteen years have powerfully raised the issue of relations between communities of color. This was a key issue emerging from the Liberty City rebellions in Miami in the early 1980s, as well as those in Washington, D.C., in 1990, New York City in 1991, and Los Angeles in 1992. There were other factors associated with these urban rebellions, but the political and social impact of the particular relations among blacks, Latinos, and Asians also emerged as a critical question in all of these events. (Jennings 1994)

Jennings's assertion is appropriate for urban communities with large diverse racial and ethnic communities, though it does not fully assess the importance of race in Richmond's social fabric, nor the impact of race, class, and gender on black political development in the city's politics.

Class

Although not a recognized subfield in political science, class as a variable has frequently appeared in research studies involving urban politics and, especially, the black urban experience. Until recently, studies focusing exclusively on class concerns were the domain of sociologists, political economists, urban historians, urban political geographers, and a few political scientists in the subfield of urban politics. Research studies conducted by political scientists have generally involved a multidisciplinary approach to analyzing the dynamics of race and class. Few studies conducted by political scientists have focused exclusively on race and class, and most of them have appeared during the last ten years.

In the subfield of black politics, the discussion of class as an explanatory variable has been featured exclusively in the literature along with
the race variable as an explanatory factor when examining a new political phenomenon. Consequently, the discussion of race and class has generally appeared in a small number of book chapters and articles, and
even fewer journal articles. For instance, the first article written by a
political scientist exclusively discussing race and class did not appear
until 1994. Ricky Hill's seminal article "The Study of Black Politics: Notes
on Rethinking the Paradigm" (Hill 1994) argues that class is the missing
link in black politics:

> The missing links of American politics exist because of ideological and polit-
> ical formations that are nontraditional and dominated have never been gen-
> uine alternatives to dominant-class politics. Communist, socialist, and social
> democratic formations have been unable to confront, or compete within and
> for, dominant-class power. They have thus never received full attention in the
> leading analyses of American politics. The research questions have always
> centered on the politics of Democratic and Republican parties. (Hill 1994, 12)

Hill believes that future studies involving race and class should examine
(1) the political strategies used by blacks to generate demands of the
dominant population; (2) through historical analysis, the influence of
political ideology in "shaping the black experience in the United States"
(1994, 16); and (3) new concepts that explain the black political experience and provide a more comprehensive political analysis of black political development in America. Thus, Hill appears to be suggesting two
important points. First, the subfield of black politics should be heuristic
in terms of its approach to analyzing persistent political problems that
beset America's black citizens. Second, future studies in the subfield of
black politics should engage the discipline by providing descriptive
analyses of and prescriptive solutions to the problems that continue to
exploit a subgroup because of its race and class.

Two additional articles address the issue of race and class within the
subfield of black politics: "An Anatomy of the Black Political Class," by
Martin Kilson and "The Black Underclass as Systemic Phenomenon," by
Mack Jones. Kilson's and Jones's articles explain the polarizing affect of
class on the black body politic. Kilson, for example, contrasts the transformation of white immigrant group political leadership in urban areas
with the transformation of the black political leadership class arguing
that the minor influence of the black political leadership class in the
Democrat and Republican parties over time may have contributed to current class cleavages within the black body politic.

In his comparison of the black political leadership class with that of most white ethnic immigrant groups, Kilson explains that the

> Type I politicization persona for the black political class from the early 1900s to 1960s performed a unique constitutive and systemic task that the Irish Type I persona did not have to perform—namely, to incorporate blacks into citizenship social contract. The Irish protest persona, by contrast, performed the task of articulating cultural and class interests of a subproletariat that was culturally alienated from WASP-hegemonic America but that had citizenship status by virtue of being white. Surmounting the ethnic illegitimacy attached to blackness was, then, a Sisyphian function of the black protest persona that no white ethnic bloc protest persona confronted. (Kilson 1996, 16)

According to Kilson, class cleavages within the black body politic have been exacerbated over the last thirty years because black political leaders have provided significant tangible benefits to the black bourgeoisie. "The federal government's affirmative action policies," he notes, "expanded the black middle-class occupational ranks from 13 percent of employed blacks holding such occupational in the early 1960s to 45 percent by 1983" (Kilson 1996, 19). The adoption of fiscally conservative public policies during the Nixon-Ford and Reagan-Bush administrations rendered black political leaders incapable of providing significant tangible benefits to working-class and poor blacks. For example, black leaders failed to "generate a quantum-leap expansion of initiatives around blacks' policy needs" and were unable to provide "viable education systems for black children from working-class and poor households sections of the community" (18). The perception that black leaders were either weak or indifferent to the needs of working-class and poor blacks may have contributed to the class cleavages currently within the black body politic.

Kilson argues that the polarizing effect of class within the contemporary black body politic had an impact on the black political leadership class. A vacuum in credible black political leadership occurred after the death of Martin Luther King Jr., Malcolm X, and other prominent black leaders during the period from 1960 to 1980, Kilson asserts. The new black political class failed to design and articulate a political agenda that could "focus on that massive crisis of poverty and societal disarray —an increasingly internecine cycle of crime and violence—that has stunted modern mobility among 30–40 percent of black American households" (Kilson 1996, 20). Their failure widened the gap between the black political leadership class and their working-class and poor black constituencies. The gap widened even further when these groups

supported alternative leaders (mostly at the local level) whom they perceived as demonstrating more empathy with their social, political, and
economic plight.

The "Million Man March" illustrates that disparate classes of black
men were frustrated with the national black leaders' political and social
agenda. These groups were eventually motivated and mobilized by individuals not associated with the traditional black political leadership class.
The political frustration of blacks at local levels enabled the rise of such
political mavericks as Al Sharpton in New York, and other urban community activists throughout the United States, to assume the role of
community activist/leaders. In spite of the vacuum in the current black
political leadership class, and the gap between black political leaders
and their working-class and poor black constituents, these groups still
support representatives of the national black political leadership class
(for example, Jesse Jackson). Although minister Louis Farrakhan of the
Nation of Islam has garnered wide support among disparate classes of
blacks, he has yet to seek elected office (Kilson 1996, 30).

Kilson's article contributed to the subfield of black politics a plausible explanation of how the class issue emerged as a "wedge" issue within
the contemporary black politics. Moreover, Kilson's research has particular relevance to our Richmond study. For instance, a thesis of Kilson's
article is that black political leaders generally distribute public policy
benefits unevenly to the haves at the expense of the have-nots. Some of
our key participant-observers representing working-class and poor blacks
stated clearly that only the black middle class, not the poor, benefited
from the election of the black majority on city council. This particular
political allegation was consistently echoed in public by two grass-roots
leaders, the late Curtis J. Holt Sr. and the late Alma Barlow. Holt and
Barlow, leaders in Richmond's poor black communities, frequently criticized the black middle-class leadership on Richmond's city council during the late 1970s. Kilson also identified the same black political schisms
based on class that were prevalent in Richmond's black political history
before and after the election of the black majority to city council. These
same political class divisions still plague contemporary Richmond's African American community.

The second article and the book that address class and race are Mack
Jones's "Black Underclass as Systemic Phenomenon" (see p. 8) and
Michael C. Dawson's *Behind the Mule: Race and Class in African-American
Politics* (1994). Jones and Dawson employ a multidisciplinary approach
(for example, integrating social policy literature with political science lit-
erature) to consider whether class or race is dominant in explaining black

politics. The Jones article and the Dawson text are significant to this discussion because the authors present their cases by challenging William J. Wilson's underclass thesis presented in his text *The Declining Significance of Race* (1994). Jones rejects the cornerstone of Wilson's thesis—that a black underclass is new in most urban areas—arguing instead that the emergence of an urban underclass is not a new phenomenon but simply a byproduct of the white racism that has always permeated the American political economy.

Wilson argues that class is a major determinant of the quality of life for blacks and that the black middle class benefited the most from the CRM. For Dawson, however, race is still the dominant factor in determining the quality of black life, though class is becoming increasingly significant. Despite class divisions, Dawson contends, the political attitudes of poor and middle-class blacks reveal a commitment to group solidarity based upon a belief in "linked fate" that "racial group interests take precedence over class interest for many blacks" (Dawson 1994, 8, 58). Dawson illustrates his "linked fate" concept using the Chicago mayoral election of Harold Washington in 1983: "Both Kleppner and Alkalimat and Gills studies of Harold Washington's first successful campaign for mayor of Chicago vividly illustrate how the perception of a single racial group interest overcame long-standing ideological and class divisions within the black community and how the campaign itself helped reinforce African American group consciousness" (58). Dawson urges the use of a multidisciplinary approach to completely understand and explain a particular black phenomenon (13). His linked fate concept was used by Richmond's black elite during the campaign to elect the first black majority to city council. It informed and mobilized Richmond's black community, suggesting that there was a threat to the well-being of all black Richmonders should a black majority not be elected. As Dawson states, the linked fate concept is periodically used as a ploy by black elites to "perpetuate the perception that racial group interests take precedence over class interests for many blacks" (58). During the election, blacks were frequently urged by Richmond's black political elites to put aside their political differences in order to elect blacks to city council.

Mack Jones offers another explanation of how the variable of class explains the current political divisions within black politics and provides a counter-explanation of Wilson's underclass thesis. While Wilson argues that the rise of an urban underclass stemmed from "the malfunctioning of the American economy" or the social pathology "of members of the underclass" (Jones 1992, 54–55), Jones suggests that poor health care, poor education, poor housing conditions, and institutional racism led to the emergence of an urban underclass. Although Jones differs with Wilson on the causes of the emergence of the urban underclass, they share a similar outlook on the future of this population. Jones, like Wilson, contends that if a national program is not enacted to address their specific problems, the "underclass will become increasingly impoverished" (64). Jones maintains that, given these dire circumstances, black political leadership will continue to come from the middle class, arguing that they are successful because of hard work and achieve their success by merit. Middle-class blacks would also claim that poor blacks have no one to blame for their poverty but themselves (64). If black political leaders are predominately conservative, the black underclass will receive very little empathy. However, if the black political leadership class perceives the existence of an underclass to be a systemic issue, then, according to Jones, "it may force a public debate on the dialectical relationship between poverty and wealth, between affluence and decadence and between privilege and deprivation. Such a point of departure would at least stimulate a national debate on the systemic character of the problem of the underclass" (65).

Jones's research is part of a growing body of work by political scientists who adapt concepts from sociology, such as the underclass, and apply them to explain the political and policy implications of a particular political phenomenon. A second trend is the influence of social policy researchers on political scientists examining race and class in African American politics. In *Behind the Mule: Race and Class in African-American Politics* (1994), for instance, Dawson reveals that his research on race and class is modeled on current research used by psychologists to explicate "how psychological processes are critical for the formation of social identity. Particularly the work of Turner is used to help develop a theory of African-American group interests that explains the continued political homogeneity of African Americans and describes the conditions under which African Americans will begin to display political diversity" (Dawson 1994, 10). Dawson finds that social psychology methods can be applied to analyzing black politics on a micro level. Jones, Kilson, and Dawson all use race and class as variables important to students of black politics.

RACE AND CLASS IN URBAN POLITICS LITERATURE

Just as race and class have been well documented in black politics literature as polarizing concerns, urban politics scholars such as Stone, Parenti, and Bachrach and Baratz have documented the influence of race and class in Atlanta, Baltimore, Newark, New Jersey, and elsewhere (Stone 1989, Parenti 1973, Bachrach and Baratz 1970). The treatment of race and class as explanatory variables in most urban politics literature can be traced to community power studies and black mayoral research studies.

The dominant approach used by political scientists during the 1950s and 1960s to explain the political dynamics and processes of most urban political communities involved political participation (Randolph 1990). The type of study that dominated early urban literature was the community power inquiry. Debates over the distribution of power produced three schools of thought: pluralist, elitist, and antipluralist. The leading scholars and spokespersons for these groups were Robert Dahl (pluralist), Floyd Hunter (elitist), and Michael Parenti, Peter Bachrach, and Morton Baratz (antipluralist) (Carson 1977). The proponents of the elitist theory believed that power and policy making in most urban communities were controlled by economic elites. Advocates of the elitist theory equated wealth with power and political influence (Hunter 1953).

Pluralists rejected this argument because they believed that decision making was highly fragmented and that power was decentralized because the democratic process enabled individuals or groups to freely compete in the political market (Dahl 1961). Antipluralists countered that the most important decisions in the policy process were those involving nondecisions. According to Parenti and other antipluralists, nondecisions are essential to understanding the distribution of power in communities because as a result of the mobilization of bias, certain groups' interests were included or excluded from the policy-making process (Carson 1977).

Debating the distribution of power, scholars tried to explain urban politics/policy making from a narrow perspective. Elitists equated wealth with influence and believed that political variables had no impact on the process. Pluralists, on the other hand, believed that politics mattered but that economic variables had no significant influence on the process. Antipluralists believed that attitudes of decision makers were of primary importance. Researchers suggested that either economics, attitudes, or politics alone was the deciding factor in explaining policy outcomes. Focusing on one specific aspect of the problem, they failed to produce a clear understanding of the relationship between elected officials and the different racial concerns within a specific city, and how these concerns were addressed in the urban political and policy arena. Debates between the different schools of thought (especially between pluralist and elitist) were generally about whose research methodology was superior. Missing from these discussions were explanations of how the influx of racial minorities, and poor citizens in particular, had an impact on the balance of political power between blacks and whites. In his study of Atlanta, Georgia, for instance, Hunter does not discuss the political ties between established black elites and white elites. But a political arrangement between black and white elites is well documented in Moeser and Silver's text *The Separate City,* and in Stone's *Regime Politics: Governing Atlanta, 1946–1988* (Moeser and Silver 1995; Stone 1989). Hunter's research on Atlanta is relevant to our Richmond research because both were controlled by oligarchical elites. The presence of an oligarchical elite was revealed in Moeser and Dennis's text *The Politics of Annexation: Oligarchic Power in a Southern City* (1982). Moeser and Silver's *Separate City* establishes the presence of an elite class but also reveals a weak political relationship between some black ministers and white elites over a period of time. The political ties between black ministers and white political elites were never formalized.

Although Dahl's pluralist model fails to take into account how the issue of race can influence urban politics in a pluralistic democratic process, the pluralist model was not always applicable to Richmond. First, the exclusion of blacks from Richmond's political system prior to the CRM is well documented. For example, although Oliver Hill, a black, was elected to city council in 1948, he was the first black elected to council since 1898. Moreover, a second black, B. A. "Sonny" Cephas, would not be elected to council until 1960 (Moeser and Silver 1995, 82). Two blacks served on city council from 1898 to 1960, but the majority of blacks during that period were excluded from Richmond's political process because of disfranchisement after Reconstruction and, later, by Virginia's use of the poll tax in federal, state, and local elections. Second, black Virginians who identified themselves as Democrats and Republicans were excluded from affiliating with state and local political organizations because neither the state nor the local parties welcomed black participation (Randolph and Tate 1995). Furthermore, even though blacks were active participants at the national level in the Democratic and Republican parties, they exercised very little influence with their parties at state and local levels.

Since the 1977 election of a black majority on Richmond's city council, the pluralist model can be applied in some instances to the city's political arena. However, an oligarchical elite did exist. Moeser and Silver state that "Richmond's political power prior to 1977 rested with the city's white upper class. . . . Unlike the Atlanta model, however, Richmond's white leadership never cultivated a partnership with the black middle class except when it was necessary during elections to garner some black votes to win at-large seats on city council (1995, 12). The pluralist model prior to 1977 was not always applicable to Richmond. Moeser and Silver's research appears to corroborate our position that Richmond's exclusionary politics prevented blacks from sharing the political and social resources of a pluralistic society. For instance, they note that "characteristic of Richmond's power structure, indeed the power structure of Virginia, was the dominant role of a white aristocracy. Like the upper classes of both Atlanta and Memphis, Richmond's blue bloods had an instinctual aversion to the lower classes, believing that power should be exercised by those with sufficient levels of education and with the proper blood lines" (12).

After the passage of the 1965 Voting Rights Act and the Twenty-fourth Amendment, which outlawed poll taxes in state and local elections, the number of black political organizations began to increase in Richmond. The emergence of these different black political organizations eventually led to frequent political skirmishes between the organizations competing for dominance over the city's black body politic, but this competition was an indication that the black political scene in Richmond was becoming increasingly pluralistic.

Although both the pluralist and elitist models inadequately address the issue of race and its impact on politics, one community power model does address the concerns of race and class—the antipluralist model. For instance, Parenti's research on Newark, New Jersey, and Bachrach and Baratz's research on Baltimore's social programs during the War on Poverty era of the 1960s clearly attempt to address the issue of race and class. Bachrach and Baratz contend that "non decisions" explain why certain racial and class groups' interests are consistently channeled out of political and policy making arenas while other groups' interests are consistently allowed to proceed (1979, 80). Bachrach and Baratz's research not only reveals the class divisions within Baltimore's African American community but also provides illustrations of how blacks in Baltimore through social programs and black power were able to slightly alter the city' political process (103).

Similarly, Michael Parent's classic study, "Power and Pluralism: A View from the Bottom" (Parenti 1973, 246–55), explains how and why minority groups such as blacks during the late 1960s were locked out of Newark's political and policy-making decisions. For example, Parenti attributes the exclusion of blacks to problems of organizing and mobilizing working-class blacks and to lack of political knowledge on the part of blacks about the operation of the political system (1973, 258). Protest alone is insufficient, Parenti argues, when an oppressed population attempts to unseat an unresponsive and insensitive city government. As an example, Parenti illustrates how a protest demonstration surrounding the installation of a traffic light at a dangerous neighborhood corner did not lead to a positive outcome for the black protesters (ibid., 246–55). Our Richmond study reveals some findings similar to those of Parenti in Newark. For example, our research revealed that poor black Richmond neighborhoods were also ineffective in having traffic lights installed at a dangerous intersection. Our conclusion is that with the exception of the antipluralist literature, community power literature demonstrated limitations in explaining the impact of race and class on urban politics and policy.

RACE AND CLASS IN BLACK MAYORAL STUDIES LITERATURE

The next approach that emerged from the urban politics subfield to address the issues of race and class was that of the black mayoral study. The chief black mayoral studies in southern cities are Clarence Stone's *Regime Politics: Governing Atlanta 1948–1988* (1989); "Atlanta and the Limited Reach of Electoral Control," a study coauthored by Stone and Carol Pierannunzi (1997); and Marcus Pohlmann and Michael P. Kirby's *Racial Politics at the Crossroads: Memphis Elects Dr. W. W. Herenton* (1996). Clarence Stone's pioneering research on Atlanta explains the historical development of Richmond's black body politic and reveals the ties connecting white and black elites. Additionally, Stone's study meticulously traces and explains the process by which Atlanta's regime began the process of politically incorporating the city's black middle class. The incorporation of the black middle class in Atlanta's governing coalition enabled black mayors and their black political allies to avoid the political challenges of a black insurgency movement between the black middle class and working-class and poor blacks. Stone's research appears to corroborate an argument in William E. Nelson Jr.'s study "Cleveland: The Evolution of Black Political Power" (1987). According to Nelson,

> Since the publication of my original article in 1982, additional evidence has
> come to light that allows us to comment more precisely on the impact of the
> new black politics on the social and economic transformation of the black
> community. This evidence suggests that the upsurge in the election of "new

breed" black politicians to public office has been most effective in the promotion of the social and economic interests of upwardly mobile, elite sectors
of the black community. (Nelson 1987, 172)

For Stone, the black middle class was undeniably the primary beneficiary
of the black political incorporation that occurred in Atlanta. This conclusion indirectly supports our research findings. In Richmond, Richmond's white political elite lacked a politician with Atlanta mayor
Hartsfield's political astuteness to orchestrate the incorporation of Richmond's black middle class into the governing coalition. Richmond's
white political elite was not willing to listen, compromise, or even consider sharing power, even on a junior partnership level, with blacks.

Pohlmann and Kirby's research on Memphis, *Racial Politics at the
Crossroads,* is significant to urban politics and provides an in-depth
analysis of a key mayoral election in one of the most racially polarized
cities in the South. The authors demonstrate how a black mayoral candidate in Memphis was able to effectively organize a coalition of blacks
and white moderates to become the first black mayor of Memphis.
According to Pohlmann and Kirby, biracial coalitions are difficult to
achieve, especially after a city reaches a certain level of racial tolerance or
a "point of racial reflexivity." Memphis, having reached a certain level of
racial tolerance, found it extremely difficult not only to elect a black
mayor but also to develop and maintain a progressive biracial electoral
coalition.

Pohlmann and Kirby's research is relevant to our Richmond study
because it explains how whites, even when clearly in the minority, still
operate decisively to select the kind of black mayoral candidate that
shares similar political views and interests. For instance, if the candidates
for mayor are all black, and if blacks comprise over 60 percent of the
population and whites comprise 20–30 percent of the population, then
white voters can determine the outcome of the election, especially if the
black vote is divided. Whites can affect the outcome of a local mayoral
election by performing the role of "whites as moderators." White voters
perform this role when they perceive one black mayoral candidate as
either too liberal or too militant in terms of their political interests. If the
black vote is divided, the minority white voters can function as a swing
vote to prevent an extremely liberal or "militant" black mayoral candidate from winning.

The "whites as moderators" phenomenon occurred in Richmond
during the campaign of Willie Dell, when she ran for reelection in 1983.
Dell was perceived by most conservative white voters as a "militant"

black candidate. Her opponent, on the other hand, was a black conservative who was perceived by white voters as someone whose values and views were more congruent with their own. Thus, when the campaign became a tightly contested, a small number of white conservative voters, along with some additional factors such as the presence of a highly organized black conservative political organization in the political arena and the presence of a possible political coalition between conservative black Republicans and Democrats, contributed to Dell's defeat.

The black mayoral studies of Stone, Stone and Pierannunzi, and Pohlmann and Kirby are relevant to our research because of similarities to our Richmond study.

GENDER RESEARCH AND POLITICAL PARTICIPATION

Just as we use the effects of race and class in this study to explore the political behavior of African Americans in Richmond, Virginia, so we will use sex-based interpretations to shed light on black women's political participation amid broader political, economic, and social forces: on the complex interplay between black men and women in organizational structures for social change, and on the dimensions of patriarchy that existed in the local CRM and the emerging arena of electoral politics in Richmond. Belinda Robnett, in her book *How Long? How Long?: African American Women in the Struggle for Civil Rights,* argues that the complexities, such as emotions and spontaneity, of black political leadership in social movements would add more substance to the theoretical development of movement leadership. In the past, scholars have focused more on the rational, planned political behavior than on those elements that may determine female leadership in the broader structures of the movement. Robnett writes, "Aside from the fact that race, class, gender, and culture shape who does what for the movement, analyses of only formal leaders and their organizations have led to an oversimplified understanding of the internal dynamics and structure of specific movement organizations, as well as among movement organizations in the overall movement sector" (1997, 22–23).

In the past three decades, historical retrievals have surfaced that place the struggles of African Americans not only in the national context of social movements but also in the larger framework of linking their cultural struggles to the international black diaspora. Within this ongoing research, the growth of research on black women, illuminating their political and social roles, has contributed immeasurably to our understanding of the political forces that shape black female political leadership. Before the late 1960s, history was relatively silent about the political, economic, and social roles that black women played in the African American struggle for social justice.

Expansion of the research has provided us with a framework for understanding varied historical and political interpretations for undertaking a cogent analysis of black women's experiences in American society. Primarily, scholars have followed three major research directions. One direction involves the historical interpretations of black women and the dialectical nature of their role in society at different historical moments. Some of the works in this field are Gerder Lerner's *Black Women in White America* (1973); Jeanne Noble's *Beautiful, Also, Are the Souls of My Black Sisters* (1978); Paula Giddings's *When and Where I Enter* (1984); Darlene Clark Hine's *Black Women in White* (1989); Evelyn Brooks Higginbotham's *Righteous Discontent* (1993); Stephanie J. Shaw's *What a Woman Ought to Be and Do* (1996); and Deborah Gray White's *Too Heavy a Load* (1999). Another direction focuses on black women's critical roles in African American families and the state-market collaborations of racism, politics, and economics that affect family structure. Some of the revisionist work on the black family include Andrew Billingsley's *Black Families in White America* (1968); *The Black Family,* by Robert Staples (1971); *The Strengths of Black Families,* by Robert Hill (1972); Joyce Ladner's *Tomorrow's Tomorrow* (1971); Noralee Frankel's *Freedom's Women* (1999); *The Black Family in Slavery and Freedom,* by Herbert Gutman (1976); and Bonnie Thornton Dill's article "The Dialectics of Black Womanhood" (1990). The third direction emphasizes the political consciousness, resistance, and activism of black women in protest movements and their transformative shifts to the electoral arena. This direction is integral to this book, and works by these scholars will be incorporated into the following discussion.

The point of departure for most scholars concerned the position that black women occupied in American history and the American political system. Mae C. King, in her article "Oppression and Power: The Unique Status of the Black Woman in the American Political System" (King 1975), posits that black women's unique status in the American political structure was engendered by enslavement, by the racial oppression that transcended enslavement, and by gender discrimination. The convergence of these three variables relegated black women to a stationary position in the caste system. Of these three variables, King argues, race is the major determinant in the oppression of black women, in defining her subordination from slavery to the contemporary period:

> While racism was institutionalized by the slave system, this ideology assumed a value independent of the particular system under which it flourished. Consequently, when the plantation slave structures were destroyed, the oppression of the black woman and other blacks, which was now justified on a racial basis, continued in other institutional forms. . . . As a result, the emergence of economic, social and political structures in the aftermath of slavery perpetuated the fundamental functional power relationship between blacks and whites. (King 1975, 116)

Some scholars utilize a more interactive model in exploring the terrain of black women's oppression. For example, Deborah K. King, in her article "Multiple Jeopardy, Multiple Consciousness: The Context of a Black Feminist Ideology" (1988) views race, class, and sexism as producing "multiple forms of discrimination" resulting in the subordination of black women. "The modifier 'multiple' refers not only to several simultaneous oppressions but to the multiplicative relationships among them as well," she notes. "In other words, the equivalent formulation is racism multiplied by sexism multiplied by classism" (1988, 270).

Like King, scholar and political activist Angela Y. Davis, in her book *Women, Race, and Class*, notes the simultaneous oppressions of race, gender, and class that black women confronted during slavery. "If the most violent punishments of men consisted in floggings and mutilations, women were flogged and mutilated, as well as raped," she states (1983, 7). In a similar context, Bonnie Thornton Dill argues that black women, in negotiating their social roles, are reacting to "multiple forms of oppression" that they confront in their daily life experiences. For Dill, the "attitudes, behaviors, and interpersonal relationships . . . were adaptations to a variety of factors, including the harsh realities of their environment, Afro-American cultural images of black womanhood, and the sometimes conflicting values and norms of the wider society" (1979, 547).

Black women's oppression in Virginia was determined by the intersection of capitalism and patriarchy from their enslavement to the modern period. Because the caste system was pervasive and permeated every aspect of society, critically placing race as paramount in the superordinate-subordinate relations that determine southern society and "etiquette," it diverted attention away from the other inherent components of the caste system, which included the sexual exploitation of black women by white slaveholders and the elitism propagated by the ideology of white supremacy. Subsequent to the emancipation of African Americans in Richmond on April 3, 1865, the simultaneous forces of oppression—"race, class, gender, and cultural determinants"—though intricately complex, produced a multiplying effect on black women's lives. Indeed, the "multiplier" effect of gender, race, and class may be identified as one layer within the multilayered "multiple hierarchies" (Crenshaw 1993, 114) of societal arrangements.

Black women come to political activity with preexisting experiences of the "multiple forms of oppression" determining their lives. Living in a world of power and privilege that has excluded them all of their lives, they are already disadvantaged in the home, the workplace, the community, and the public arena. A growing political consciousness means that they have identified the dominant configurations of power and control in the private and public spheres and seek self-consciously to alter the control of these state-market collaborations over their lives. In the process, they simultaneously change the effects of these oppressions in the private sphere as well. Patricia Hill Collins posits in her work *Black Feminist Thought* that the material reality that informs black women's lives simultaneously provides the framework for a unique black feminist consciousness to emerge: "Black women's work and family experiences and grounding in traditional African-American culture suggest that African-American women as a group experience a world different from that of those who are not Black and female. Moreover, these concrete experiences can stimulate a distinctive Black feminist consciousness concerning that material reality" (1991, 24).

Until the 1960s, most of black women's political activity had been nonelectoral in nature. Although black women voted and ran for elected offices after the passage of the Nineteenth Amendment, black women in the South were soon disfranchised, nullifying their hopes for political equality (Terborg-Penn 1998, 136–58). Since the Voting Rights Act of 1965, there has been a marked increase in black women's political participation in the electoral arena as both voters and officeholders. In examining the two modes of black women's political participation during four historical periods—enslavement, Reconstruction, from post-Reconstruction to World War II, and the post–World War II era—Jewel L. Prestage posed three contentions: (1) there is a connection between the continuous political activity of black women and the broader social processes that determine their material realities, (2) black women seek empowerment as women and as African Americans, and (3) black women's political activity has shifted over time from an emphasis on nonelectoral activity to a significant emphasis on electoral participation (Prestage 1991, 89).

In much of the historical period before the civil rights movement, black women's political activity was informally structured through communities, churches, and women's organizations, although black female activists honed their political leadership skills in the antislavery and suffrage movements as well. Similar to those of white women, black women's political activities included political forums and debates, fundraisers, political campaigns, lecturing, and persuading men to agree with the women's views on important issues concerning the plight of African Americans and women. In the antebellum era, black women, including Maria W. Stewart, Mary Shadd Cary, Frances E. W. Harper, Sojourner Truth, Sarah Parker Remond, and the Forten-Purvis women of Philadelphia, were shaping the political debate around abolition, women's rights, free produce, temperance, and emigration, all issues that affected the black community. Historian Willi Coleman, in her study "Architects of a Vision," notes that "women were willing and able to plead their own cause for equality within the earliest attempts to create a unified and mass political agenda among African Americans" (1997, 30).

After emancipation in Richmond, black women simultaneously participated in the emerging Republican party and in the social mobilization of the community, seeking the eradication of laws and customs that had been instituted during slavery and reactivated immediately after emancipation. Elsa Barkeley Brown, in her article "Negotiating and Transforming the Public Sphere," states that by the 1880s black women in Richmond were still fighting to establish their political voices in the nonelectoral arena of community activism as well as in the electoral arena of party politics:

> In the immediate post–Civil War era women had voted in mass meetings and Republican Party conventions held at First African, thus contradicting gender-based assumptions within the larger society about politics, political engagement and appropriate forms of political behavior. Now, women sitting in the same church were petitioning for the right to vote in an internal community institution, couching the petition in terms designed to minimize the request and avoid a challenge to men's authority and position. (Brown 1994, 107)

By the dawn of the twentieth century, black women had not only engaged in local struggles to alter state and local laws that determined their lives but also participated in the larger suffrage movement for women's voting rights. Black suffragists such as Sojourner Truth, Frances

E. W. Harper, Hattie Purvis, and Sarah Parker Remond had participated in the campaign for decades, and others, such as Caroline Remond Putnam, Charlotta Rollin, and Josephine St. Pierre Ruffin, joined the movement later (Terborg-Penn 1998, 18–35, 42). In local struggles, black female activists were also instrumental in galvanizing black women around the significance of their voting rights. Certainly, Sarah Dudley Pettey shaped black women's political culture around the suffrage campaign in New Bern, North Carolina, with her "Woman's Column," and Maggie Lena Walker, founder and president of the Saint Luke Penny Savings Bank in Richmond, was equally effective in mobilizing the local suffrage campaign (Gilmore 1996, xv–xvii; Brown 1990, 179). Despite these prodigious efforts, however, as Rosalyn Terborg-Penn in her book *African American Women in the Struggle for the Vote, 1850–1920* poignantly concludes, "The Nineteenth Amendment victory was a shallow one for Black women, an anti-climax especially for those in the South who had dared to believe that winning the vote could enable them to participate in the electoral process. With these bitter lessons behind them, Black women redirected their energies toward other—race-centered— political goals" (1998, 12).

The rise of the Byrd machine in Virginia, from the 1920s to the 1960s, effectively disfranchised African Americans in Virginia. Under segregation, black women honed their leadership skills and organizational expertise in black churches, civic organizations, the early women's club movement, and sororities, many of which became vehicles for covertly protesting against segregation. These groups, in effect, paved the way for black women's roles as "bridge leaders," connecting the goals of the community with those articulated by the black leadership during the Richmond civil rights campaign in 1960. Although the local movement was successful in dismantling segregation in the 1960s, the power elite still maintains economic control, as well as exercising political control through representatives on the city council, of the city. There was no takeover of local institutions until 1977, when Richmond's city council —a council on which few black women have served—gained a black majority. Since Willie Dell failed to regain her council seat in 1982, few black or white women have ventured into Richmond's electoral arena.

Certainly, some of the larger questions that should be posed are raised by Gloria J. Braxton in her article "African-American Women and Politics: Research Trends and Directions." First, "Should African American women view their relationship to politics as other groups in America?" Second, "What is the best strategy for achieving maximum power?" (1994, 282–84). Other scholars have offered answers to those questions.

In her book *Feminist Theory,* bell hooks states that women must engage in a feminist revolution and in that struggle seek a cultural transformation that will reconstruct notions of power. "Our emphasis must be on cultural transformation: destroying dualism, eradicating systems of domination" (hooks 1984, 163). Similarly, Shelby Lewis, in her study "A Liberation Ideology: The Intersection of Race, Sex, and Class," viewed black women's struggle against oppression in an international context. Black women must wage a global struggle against capitalism and imperialism, liberating all people from oppression (1988, 38–44). For our case study, the question of how black women envision, mobilize, and reconstitute power may tell us a great deal about the nature of their struggle.

BLACK POLITICAL MOBILIZATION

Although various theorists offer a partial view of black political behavior, this book is more aptly situated in political mobilization. That allows an exploration of race, class, gender, and cultural determinants that affect the political struggle for social change in Richmond as well as an analysis of blacks mobilizing for redistributive power and resources over disparate periods of development. "Mobilization," Morrison notes, "is defined as the collective activation and application of community or group resources toward the acquisition of social and political goods" (1987, 9). In the black experience, racial consciousness, political and social isolation, perennial powerlessness, and cumulative grievances against the white power structure are primary factors in the collective activation and insurgency of black communities. Often, there are organizational stages of development, regional and local, that institutionalize struggle and social change. At other times, there are intense periods of mobilization when communities galvanize for social justice that will ultimately lead to the redeployment of political and social resources and the control of local institutions. The process of black political mobilization that took place in Richmond was a complement to the broader phenomenon of social and political change that was activated in the South as blacks struggled for civil rights and the reallocation of political and social resources. Underlying this study is acknowledgment of the pervasive racism that shapes the southern political environment where much of the collective activity takes place.

Black political mobilization in Richmond had three identifiable processes: (1) the community's longstanding resistance to racial sub-ordination that spurred sporadic mobilization efforts in the past; (2) the contemporary regional and local crises that politicize the community around common concerns, providing impetus for collective activation; and (3) the establishment of new organizations, the assumption of power of venerated political institutions that legitimizes the new phase of struggle in the community, facilitating its transformation from protest into electoral politics, and the acquisition of political and social resources.

Although this book focuses on the social and political forces that shaped the CRM in Richmond, followed by the subsequent rise and demise of the black majority council from 1977 to 1982, the city offers a compelling portrayal of three periods of evolutionary change: resistance, social mobilization, and political mobilization (Morrison 1987, 6–8). Dialectically, each period contained elements of a subsequent period of social change, and the black community was undergoing minor but significant transitions that prepared it for the next phase of its struggle. Historically, the first period is characterized by the sustained resistance of the slaves from 1619 to the emancipation of the slaves in Richmond on April 3, 1865, by federal troops (see chapter 1). Defining this period, at one end of the sociopolitical spectrum was the construction of a slave society and the socioeconomic hegemony of the white planter elite that endured for approximately 250 years. At the other end of the sociopolitical spectrum, defining the underpinnings of the era, was the enslavement of African peoples, the development of a slave community, and the creation of a transatlantic slave culture that sustained their survival and resistance until freedom. And "women, the principal exponents of African culture, were at the forefront of that struggle" (Okihiro 1986, 5). Within this "culture of survival and resistance," slaves collectively mobilized plantation and urban resistance (Collins 1991, 10).

The forging of the dialectical relation of oppression and resistance, advanced in *The American Negro Slave Revolts,* by Herbert Aptheker, provides a theoretical framework for exploring the process of collective mobilization (1983, 374). The political environment, created by the planter elite, was altered by the slaves in their quest for freedom. As slaves engaged in this struggle, the forms and methods of plantation and urban resistance activated the process of collective mobilization. Whether they were forms of daily resistance or the more dramatic method of episodic rebellions or the galvanizing of the community to preserve its worship traditions, they were all "defensive mobilization" tactics and strategies to undermine the system.

The critical function of "defensive mobilization" strategies is that in altering the political environment of hegemonic rule, they simultaneously activate political resistance by the powerless. As Charles Tilly notes, this "defensive mobilization" process is often employed by the powerless in seeking empowerment (1978, 73). Slaves were defensively mobilizing their limited resources—that is, labor power, the ability to sabotage farm equipment, knowledge of the terrain, and an emerging racial conscious-ness—to change their material circumstances. These defensive mobiliza-tion efforts, according to Tilly, are made when "a threat from outside induces the members of a group to pool their resources to fight off the enemy" (ibid., 3). Within this era of sustained resistance, there were already incipient forms of collective mobilization by the slaves.

Although plantation resistance has been widely documented, partic-ularly Nat Turner's rebellion in Southampton County, Virginia, urban resistance in Richmond, albeit in disparate forms, also was prevalent and provided opportunities for group mobilization. Richmond's unique sys-tem of industrial slavery facilitated urban resistance. Under this system, surplus slaves came in from the surrounding Tidewater plantations to work in the city's tobacco factories, in flour mill factories, on railroad and canal construction, in iron foundries, and as domestic servants on ships and in white households (Rachleff 1984, 5–6; Wade 1964, 28–29, 33–36; O'Brien 1978, 511). Placed on an annual contract basis, sometimes nego-tiated by the slaves themselves but most frequently by slave-hiring bro-kers in Richmond, slaves undergirded the city's industrial expansion (Eaton 1960, 664–66; Wade 1964, 48–50; O'Brien 1978, 513–14).

But industrial slavery, vastly different from plantation slavery, also created semi-autonomous slaves. "In addition to being able to choose their masters among the various factories," Eaton notes, "they were given a small sum of money . . . to find their meals and sleeping quarters" (1960, 669–70). Many slaves preferred living in urban areas for the mod-icum of freedom they provided and found an economic incentive in earning overtime monies that were paid directly to them. Both male and female factory workers were able to earn extra monies for themselves and, working alongside free black laborers and living in already segre-gated communities, facilitated a community cohesiveness, intermarriage between slaves and free blacks, and the institutional development of Richmond's black community (O'Brien 1978, 520–35; Jackson 1942, 161–63; Wade 1964, 166–67, 172).

Richmond's industrial expansion was the catalyst for disparate forms of urban resistance. As the city's industrial development expanded in the antebellum era, it drew on an aggregate population of slave labor for fac-tory commodity production, ultimately weakening the slave system. Unable to maintain the rigid de jure infrastructure of slavery, the city enforced de facto segregation of the races to maintain white hegemony (Wade 1964, 277–78). As Richard C. Wade notes, "Thus, even before slavery had been abolished, a system of segregation had grown up in the cities" (1964, 277). As the city was being transformed, so were the slaves who were then experiencing a restrictive "quasi-free" status and desired the complete freedom enjoyed by other workers.

One form of urban resistance was the large-scale rebellions planned by the Secret Keepers in 1793 and the Gabriel Prosser conspiracy in 1800, where hundreds of slaves and free blacks organized across disparate seaport cities in Virginia, with Richmond as the base of operations, for a slave uprising. Although both efforts were discovered and aborted, they exacerbated the racial tensions in the city, leading to further restrictions on black mobility. Another form of resistance, far more prevalent, were the slave runaways, a perennial problem in Richmond until the Civil War. In the 1830s, for example, "in a single weekend, more than a score of blacks disappeared" (*Richmond Enquirer,* Nov. 26, 1833). A more subtle form of resistance employed by slaves and free blacks was the founding of five antebellum black churches in Richmond and several "secret societies" that appeased the dictates of the white elite on the surface but served as forums for protest against slavery and as "communications centers" for runaway slaves (O'Brien 1978, 529–30, 534–35). All forms of antebellum urban resistance in Richmond laid the foundation for the social mobilization that occurred after emancipation.

The second period, from the emancipation of Richmond on April 3, 1865, by federal troops to the total disfranchisement of black Richmonders under the new state constitution in 1902, was characterized by intense inchoate efforts of social mobilization and a more protracted period of political mobilization (see chapter 2). In this case, social mobilization is aptly described by Karl Deutsch, who argues that it is a transformation process taking place as groups move "from traditional to modern ways of life" (1961, 493). Deutsch observed this phenomenon in "substantial parts of the population in countries which are moving from traditional to modern ways of life. It denotes a concept which brackets together a number of more specific processes of change, such as changes of residence, of occupation of social setting, of face-to-face associates, of institutions . . . and finally of personal memories. . . . Singly, and even more in their cumulative impact, these changes tend to influence and sometimes to transform political behavior" (1961, 493).

For black Richmonders, though the incipient process of change began with building the community's infrastructure during the antebellum era, the more massive changes took place after emancipation. Seeking political inclusion after gaining their new status, blacks found that freedom did not readily alter most of the de jure segregation that was in place; nor did it change the de facto environment that still prevailed. One political venue was the emerging Republican party, in which black Richmonders hoped not only to effect their social and political status but also to mobilize the community around the common grievances that still plagued their lives. In actuality, black Richmonders were engaging in social mobilization, an acquisition of their civil rights, as well as political mobilization, seeking a redistribution of political, social, and economic resources while the federal troops were there to provide a modicum of safety. This dual mobilization effort employed strategies of civil disobedience that politicized the community while preparing blacks for political participation.

In June 1865, two months after emancipation, black Richmonders created the conditions for their social mobilization efforts. Minion K. C. Morrison emphasized the fact that "it is protest activity that marks the early mobilization campaign" (1987, 11). Protest was the principal thrust of Richmond's mobilization initiatives as blacks sought to transform the powerlessness engendered by their enslavement into autonomy and self-determination. What followed was an intense two-year period (1865–67) during which black Richmonders seized control of their churches; organized the community to fight the odious "pass system," which had been reactivated to limit black mobility; established a plethora of voluntary associations to stabilize the community; created independent Emancipation Day celebrations; and organized a "sit-in" on the city's streetcars, successfully integrating the system in 1867. Because military Reconstruction was short-lived in Virginia (ending in 1870, when the state was readmitted to the Union) and because the alliance between the northern occupation forces and the restored antebellum leadership of the Richmond junta of planter-industrialists was very strong, black Richmonders received marginal support for social resistance initiatives.

As already mentioned, coexisting with these social mobilization efforts was black Richmonders' political mobilization program, through which masses of black men and women flocked to the Republican party, determined to participate and shape, in conjunction with their new white Republican radical allies, the party's future agenda. This black-white Republican alliance would remain a checkered affair until its dissolution in the early 1900s. But because race is endemic to Virginia politics, the Democrats' tarnishing of the Republican party (and frequently vice versa) with race-baiting rhetoric would endure. Every local, state, and national election, circumscribed by race, would subsume political and social issues of larger importance. Over the long haul, Republicans would strive to shake their "cultural baggage" as diligently as the Democrats pinned it to them in every election. Despite their erstwhile white allies, however, black Richmonders participated in the constitutional convention and were atypical in the post-Reconstruction era in sending elected representatives to both houses of the Virginia General Assembly and to Richmond's city council until 1898, although they were limited in their effectiveness by the prevailing racism and the domination and control of the Democratic party (Rachleff 1984, 41–42; Jackson 1942, 81; Chesson 1982, 191).

Despite these prodigious political efforts, the rise of the Conservative-Democratic party after its victory in the 1869 state election began the process of the disfranchisement of blacks that was ultimately successful in 1902. Seeking to control black political activism as well as all of the elections, the Conservative-Democrats created Jackson Ward, by siphoning off parts of the city's other five wards, to house the majority of the black population. Dubbed the "black belt" or "the ward," Jackson Ward was noted for its intense black political activism throughout much of the nineteenth century and still holds the key to the city's political mobilization. Its initial creation, however, was designed to supplant the emerging activism and ensure white Democrats' victory in close city, state, and national elections, maintaining white hegemony in Virginia. "The gerrymandering of Jackson Ward," Chesson states, "insured white control of the five other wards and of the city government" (1982, 192–93).

Internally, Jackson Ward became the center of black political activism in Richmond. By the 1880s, however, after the massive labor organization of the 1870s, Richmond's black community was showing signs of being factionalized by class and gender cleavages retarding its leadership potential. These cleavages would result in a decided shift in ideological perspectives as well. There had always been a tiny black elite during the antebellum era, and they emerged as leaders after emancipation, but the male and female working-class leadership dominated postbellum organizations as well as the community's social and political mobilization efforts. This latter group was now being supplanted by "new issue Negroes," who were born after the Civil War, were educated, were most often professionals, and generally possessed more moderate views than those of working-class blacks on racial progress (Chesson 1982, 202).

The rising black elite of the 1880s also perceived black women in middle-class traditional terms and chafed even at their volunteer participation in church organizations, societies, and national clubs, much less at the front lines of political discourse. This gender schism constrained the black community's political viability because black women's independent political voices had been muted. Although black women created other venues for their social and political participation, particularly the early black women's club movement, the gender schism in the black community, paralleling the divisions in white society, never healed. At the same time that black women's political voices were being muted in the 1880s and 1890s, so was black political participation, both concomitant with the restoration of white supremacy.

In the efforts of black Richmonders to combat disfranchisement, their political mobilization took on the incipient trappings of a mass movement. According to Doug McAdam, "Social movements would appear to be collective phenomena arising first among segments of the aggrieved population that are sufficiently organized and possessed of resources needed to sustain a protest campaign" (1985, 15). Full of resentment against the erosion of their civil rights and the rapidly dimming prospects of freedom, black Richmonders staged a boycott against the then-segregated streetcars. Targeting the Virginia Passenger and Power Company, which operated the streetcars, black Richmonders believed that they would once again be successful at eliminating segregation on the transportation system. Black Richmond protesters were in concert with other protesters resisting the Jim Crow system inasmuch as similar consumer boycotts were simultaneously taking place in twenty-five other southern cities (Meier and Rudwick 1969, 758).

Historian Robert E. Weems Jr. argues that consumer boycotts by African Americans are economic retaliatory measures to force social change: "As the turn-of-the-century boycott of 'Jim Crow' streetcars demonstrates, African-Americans, because of humiliating differential treatment based upon race, have withheld economic support of European- American businesses" (1995, 73). This mass consumer boycott in Richmond was so effective that the Virginia Assembly, in efforts to curtail the movement, introduced legislation to eliminate appropriations for black schools, causing the protesters to shift political ground. With scarce political resources and a paramount concern about its children's future, the community could not wage a battle on two fronts and the boycott began to unravel.

Although the Richmond black community continued its collective activation—evinced in the 1917 NAACP legal suit against the city for residential segregation ordinances and by its adoption of the 1921 "Republican ticket" fielding a slate of black Republican candidates to register their independence and voting potential to the Republican party —the Jim Crow system was a harsh reality. By the late 1920s, the rise of

Democrat Harry F. Byrd (first state senator, then governor in the 1920s, and finally U.S. senator from the 1930s until his death in 1966), the principal architect of the massive resistance (MR) campaign in Virginia in the 1950s and 1960s, enforced the segregation system until the civil rights movement in Richmond. During this period, the Byrd machine was consolidated, with Byrd at the helm of the Democratic party in Virginia, promoting such segregationist policies as the poll tax, the understanding clause, the literary test, and white primaries to cripple the black electorate. Although a marginal group of blacks continued to vote and black candidates ran in most elections, voting restrictions and fear of the violence and intimidation of the Ku Klux Klan (KKK), particularly in the 1920s and 1930s, had a cumulative effect on the black community. "For example," notes Buni, "in Richmond in June 1925, when a delegation of colored citizens inquired of the Richmond Democratic Committee why they were not allowed to vote, they were told simply that it was against party rules" (1967, 117).

By the 1940s, there was a resurgence of racial pride and political activity in the Richmond African American community as well as in other southern cities. This awakening spurred a mobilization shift to the establishment of political organizations, training grounds for leaders (in addition to black ministers), to emerge, and to a stronger interconnection between the black church and political and social organizations. Undoubtedly, this new resurgence was fueled, in part, by black soldiers returning home from World War II. Having experienced a new sense of freedom abroad, they were determined to change the racial subordination of blacks at home. Another contributing factor was an increase in the size of the black middle class and its press for the elimination of the segregation system. In their study *Participation in America* (1972), Sidney Verba and Norman H. Nie showed that the development of racial consciousness is concomitant with political participation. Katherine Tate's work *From Protest to Politics* identifies racial pride and black organization development as two of the collective resources that blacks employ in their move toward electoral participation (1993, 76–81). In this pre-CRM era, southern communities were already shoring up their cultural and political infrastructure.

Initially, the mobilization efforts of black southern moderate leaders in Richmond and other southern cities were pronounced. "Mobilization," William Gamson notes, "is a process of increasing readiness to an organization or a group of leaders" (1975, 15). As moderate black leaders began integration meetings with white southern moderates seeking to establish mechanisms that would abolish the segregation system, they aroused the concern of black Richmonders as well as the ire of white seg- regationists. Although they met until 1954, a period of eight years, their inability to garner any concessions from white southern moderates led to their being politically discredited in southern black communities and negatively viewed as accommodationists. Although this "failed alliance" met with marginal success, it lent its voices to the period of "quiet inte- gration" (1946–57) that took place in several southern cities.

In Richmond, quiet integration, or "easy integration," although it included voluntarily desegregation of the buses in Richmond owing to the Supreme Court decision favoring the Montgomery bus boycott movement, consisted generally of token representation of blacks in fire, police, and other city services. In reality, the Supreme Court decision in *Brown v. Board of Education of Topeka, Kansas,* I and II (1954–55) and the gathering storm of marching feet of more-militant blacks turned the tide. This growing political awareness in Richmond facilitated the develop- ment of a number of protest organizations.

The NAACP, the Richmond Urban League (RUL), and the Richmond Civic Council (RCC) formed the core of the black community's "defen- sive mobilization" strategy (see chapter 3). In pursuit of its goals of political participation, as Charles Tilly indicates, the group utilized "preparatory" tactics for mobilizing existing resources against a pervasive condition (1978, 73). The RCC organized in this period, was an umbrella coalition of civic associations, fraternal organizations, and religious groups, largely dominated by black ministers, and had a highly placed emphasis on voter registration. The RCC believed that increased voter registration would lead to greater black electoral participation and ulti- mately to black representation on the city council. The strategy led to the successful election of Oliver Hill, the well-known NAACP lawyer, to the city council in 1948, but RCC's failed political alliance with a white citizens group, the Richmond Citizens Association (RCA), to garner biracial support and allegations of financial collisions with the white power elite led to the organization's demise. Supplanted by a new group of activists, the Richmond Crusade for Voters (RCV), who vowed to be independent of the city's elite, the community was now poised for increased political activism.

The RCV, founded in 1956, coalesced a generation of insurgency. In the South, black resistance to de jure segregation had ranged from the NAACP activism and litigation that culminated in the *Brown* decision (I and II) to the establishment of local movement centers, the intrastate integration efforts of the Congress for Racial Equality (CORE), and the Montgomery bus boycott—all of which had received international attention. In Richmond, as in all southern cities, blacks had to contend with the massive resistance of white segregationists against desegregation. The RCV, with an early emphasis on voter registration, rekindled defensive mobilization strategies in the black community and emerged as an independent political voice providing an effective challenge to the Byrd machine.

Premobilization activities by black women were essential to the CRM in Richmond (see chapter 5). Janet Ballard, Ethel T. Overby, Ruby Clayton Walker, and Ora Lomax were some of the early civil rights activists instrumental in defining areas of individual and collective protest, and all of them emerged as "bridge leaders," that is, leaders of the civil rights movement who, as mentioned earlier, occupy the informal "free space" connecting the goals of the community with those articulated by the black leadership (Robnett 1997, 19). Ballard's leadership in desegregating Thalhimer's department store's beauty salon and Overby's undermining of the white educational administration's efforts to get black parents to sign pupil placement sheets in support of segregation alerted the community to the vulnerability of the segregation system (Ballard interview 1993; Overby 1975, 32). Doug McAdam sees these early efforts as cognitively liberating because they "signify to insurgents that the political system is becoming increasingly vulnerable to challenge" (1982, 48–49).

The sit-ins by students from Virginia Union University on February 20, 1960, in Woolworth's department store on Broad Street sparked Richmond's CRM. Sit-ins by the students were also staged, simultaneously, at six other downtown lunch counters. It was the arrest of the students, however, on February 22, at Thalhimer's in front of five hundred supporters, and their demand for a boycott of the department store, that mobilized the community and launched the movement. The subsequent arrest of community elder Ruth Tinsley, a senior advisor to the Richmond NAACP Youth Group, as she was waiting to be picked up by a friend, was the political spark that unified the movement for the two-year boycott. Although the black press placed greater emphasis on this boycott, primarily owing to its middle-class origins, Harmon Buskey simultaneously led a similar boycott by working-class participants, who had formed the East End Neighborhood Association (EENA), against Springer Drug Company, a major local drugstore chain, which was successfully desegregated seven months before the agreement was reached in the Thalhimer's boycott on August 30, 1961 (Williams 1990, 48). As the movement progressed, it dismantled de jure segregation and, at the same time, it exacerbated the existing class and gender cleavages in the community.

In the process of the community's transformation from protest to politics, organizations such as the Richmond Crusade for Voters, gearing up for the complexities of electoral politics and black political participation, were facilitated by new federal laws. The Twenty-Fourth Amendment to the U.S. Constitution in 1964, which outlawed the use of poll taxes in federal elections, the passage of the Civil Rights Act of 1964, the Voting Rights Act of 1965, and the federal courts banning the use of poll taxes in state and local elections in 1966 legitimized the black struggle for political enfranchisement (see chapter 5). As the RCV shifted from a crisis-oriented to a franchise-oriented organization, becoming an intermediary between the white political elite and Richmond's black community, other more conservative groups such as the Voters Voice (VV) and the People's Political and Civic League (PPCL) would emerge, creating political schisms in the black community (Holton 1987, 85). Now that the critical battle had been fought to dismantle de jure segregation, competing progressive and conservative ideologies surfaced, jockeying for a political power base in the electoral arena. Simultaneously, as political alignments, realignments, and tenuous biracial coalitions were forged, they threatened the fragile racial solidarity in the black community.

Class, gender, and racial cleavages began to define Richmond's political landscape after the CRM. By 1970, the white elite, fearing that the black majority population would create a black majority council, annexed nearby Chesterfield County, a suburb of forty-seven thousand white, middle-class residents, to dilute the voting strength of the black electorate (Holt interview 1997; Moeser and Dennis 1982, 143–44). Curtis Holt, a grass-roots organizer and already a potent voice in the working-class community, became a major force in the annexation controversy and ultimately changed the face of Richmond's politics. When the RCV's "grand strategy" of uniting with whites who also were opposed to the annexation, believing that their combined voting strength would defeat the white power structure in the 1970 election, collapsed, blacks suffered an 8 percent dilution in voting strength. Holt, believing that the annexation diluted the political inclusion of blacks, filed a lawsuit against the City of Richmond.

Holt's legal challenge to the annexation question, combined with the prodigious efforts by RCV to politically challenge the white establishment, dealt a major blow to Richmond's white power structure. In

Richmond v. United States (1974), the U.S. Supreme Court ruled that the city's annexation of land in Chesterfield County, coupled with an at-large council system, was evidence of the city's attempt to dilute the voting strength of blacks in Richmond (Moeser interview 1991). In *Richmond v. United States* (1977), the U.S. Supreme Court accepted a proposed compromise to change the city's representation from an at-large system to a single-member ward, or district, system to ensure African American representation on the city council (Moeser and Dennis 1982, 159–88). Holt's legal challenge and RCV's efforts to increase black representation were

Fig. 1. Curtis J. Holt Sr., August 1970. Courtesy of Robert Brickhouse.

augmented by the adoption of a nine-seat single-member district system in 1977, which increased black representation on the city council and led to a special councilman election on March 8, 1977 (Moeser and Dennis 1982, 174–78). This special election enabled the RCV's representatives to have an African American majority on the city council and to elect the city's first African American mayor, Henry Marsh.

White intransigence to the African American community's emphasis on political leadership and inclusion, as well as the class-gender schisms on the city council that paralleled similar divisions in the black community, foreshadowed the demise of the black majority council. Another significant factor contributing to the council's demise was the resurgence of black conservatives who would form biracial alliances that ultimately shifted political power back to the white established elite. The black majority council's brief five-year history (1977–82) was marred by philosophical and policy differences between blacks on the city council and the city's white elite, who had controlled the political and economic power for centuries.

This historical division escalated during the 1978 deliberations about the selection of a hotel for the proposed Project One convention center and office complex strongly favored by the business community. When that community selected the Hilton Hotel chain and the African American majority council recommended the Marriott Hotel, the conflict was finally resolved when the Hilton chain sued the city and won a $5 million lawsuit for racial bias. The city's loss of credibility triggered the existing class and gender tensions in the black community that led to the 1982 defeat of Willie Dell, a liberal African American female member of the city council. In essence, she became the sacrificial lamb of the controversy (some believed that Dell's detractors were really aiming at Mayor Henry Marsh), and her defeat paved the way for the election of Roy West, a black conservative, as councilperson and, ultimately, mayor of Richmond. With this election, the progressive agenda of the black majority council ended (see chapter 6).

Willie Dell's prodigious efforts in mobilizing her predominantly lower-working-class constituency to seek institutional benefits to enhance the quality of their lives garnered her a reputation as a "radical" on the city council (see the Conclusion). Likewise, among her supporters and detractors, she was known as an outspoken leader for the disfranchised, and her initiatives to remedy the lives of the "poor, blacks, elders, and women" drew both praise and criticism (Marsh 1984). Although she was

Fig. 2. Willie Dell speaking at the Cannon Creek Nature Area, July 1980.
Courtesy of Willie Dell.

viewed with disdain by black upper-class women who believed that she was not a southern "lady" by their standards, it was widely speculated that her growing popularity would make her a likely candidate to succeed Mayor Marsh and thereby become the first black female mayor in the city's history. As a result, many conservatives viewed her ascendancy with considerable dismay. One white conservative informed Dell that she was considered too black by white conservatives, and they searched for the whitest black person they could find to capture her council seat (Dell interview 1993).

The redrawing of Willie Dell's district boundaries, presumably to protect a more vulnerable councilman, was a major factor in Dell's defeat. In addition, the inattentiveness of the black majority council to the effect that these changes would have on Dell's election may be due to sexism as well as political shortsightedness, given her reputation. Whereas formerly her constituents were working-class blacks, in the redrawn district her constituents were 69 percent working-class blacks and 31 percent whites (Lynch interview 1993). There were decided class and ideological shifts as well, with more middle-class and upper-class blacks and conservative whites in the redrawn district. Dell's campaign was also marred by hostile audiences, and speculations abound that her detractors were going full tilt to get her conservative opponent, Roy West, elected. Personal attacks on Dell's character soon emerged, such as "she was looking for a man" and that she was "wearing the pants" in her household, both comments revealing the gender bias of the campaign as well as the desperation of her opponents. The inability to mobilize her constituency, low voter turnout, and the support of Roy West by upper-class blacks and white conservatives were all contributing factors in her defeat. The election of West to the council and eventually to the office of mayor foreshadowed the destabilization of Richmond's black political majority on the city council, and the hiring of new public officials solidified the new conservatism.

In the course of studying and analyzing the political landscape in Richmond, several questions have guided this case study. The central question has been, Can the fundamental commitment by blacks to social change and political participation and a redeployment of political and social resources precipitate social and political mobilization? Do the complex, intertwining factors of male and female leadership, racial solidarity, and different classes thwart or facilitate community mobilization? If black women's political voices are critical to the struggle for social equality, and we believe that they are, will the local institutional takeovers by black men thwart overall community development? What force does black conservatism have in facilitating progress for African Americans? Finally, if racial solidarity and longstanding resentment at the political structure are among the key variables that spark political protest, are they also critical variables in sustaining institutional power and resource acquisition? We hope that the following chapters will provide answers to these and other questions.

"The Bitter Cup of Slavery"
Construction of a Slave Society

Remember that we are one, that our cause is one, and that we must help each other, if we would succeed. We have drunk to the dregs the bitter cup of slavery; we have worn the heavy yoke; we have signed beneath our bonds.

Frederick Douglass, 1847

THE COLONIAL ERA

Long before the incorporation of Richmond in 1742, its city charter in 1782, or, indeed, its becoming the state capital in 1779, blacks were fully intertwined into the history, culture, and economy of Virginia. Richmond was shaped as much by the confluences of slavery, cash crop commodity production, and the white planter aristocracy as it was by being located in a temperate climate that was conducive to tobacco cultivation. The city, containing 60.1 square miles (County and City Data Book 1988, 800), was built on the fault line of the James River, was the transition point between the Piedmont region of the west and the Tidewater region of the east, and would soon gain a reputation for its canals, trade, and commerce. Typical of many southern cities, the die had already been cast: by the time Richmond emerged as an urban center, the construction of Virginia's slave society had been in progress for more than a century and would shape the city's future.

Shaping much of the state's character were the racially subordinate caste of blacks, on one hand, and the rising oligarchy of the planter elite on the other. These groups formed polar opposites that would, over time, coalesce in a political struggle. Much of this struggle would be manifest for more than two centuries in the construction of a slave society, followed by a brief respite of freedom for blacks subsequent to emancipation, and then social segregation and political disfranchisement until the mid-twentieth century. In all phases of this turbulent history, frequently perceived as bucolic by Virginia's aristocracy, blacks would be combative, at times overtly and at other times covertly, thwarting the oppression that circumscribed their lives.

The construction of Virginia's slave society was determined by a complex array of factors as the colony legalized slavery in the period from 1619 to 1705. Certainly, the importation of African slaves was predicated on such factors as European colonization and the global slave trade that enveloped the New World, as well as the popular local and European consumption of sweet Virginian tobacco. But it was also predicated on such pragmatic realities as the growing paucity of labor in the colonies and the avarice of the state's tobacco planters (Kerr-Ritchie 1999, 13; Harding 1981, 5–6; Boles 1984, 10). As historian Philip D. Morgan notes in his *Slave Counterpoint: Black Culture in the Eighteenth-Century Chesapeake and Lowcountry,* by the last half of the seventeenth century, Virginia had already taken on the trappings of a plantation society but needed a slave labor force to stimulate its economy (Morgan 1998, 1). As Virginia legalized slavery, the legal status of blacks declined, going from indentured servitude to slavery and finally to economic commodity. Concomitantly, the pivotal roles that African slaves played in tobacco and cereal grain production fueled Virginia's market economy, the enduring wealth of the planter elite, and, ultimately, Richmond's industrialization.

The importation of Africans to the Virginia colony was initiated when a Dutch man-of-war arrived and sought provisions in exchange for twenty Africans. Thrown into the turbulence of the slave trade, these twenty African captives arrived in Jamestown, Virginia, in August 1619. Although historically perceived as slaves, these early Africans were in fact indentured to the colonial administrators. In that sense, their labor was similar to that of the white indentured, who were also a part of the growing laboring classes in the colony. These Africans eventually gained their freedom and some even rose to the status of property owners. Andrew Johnson, one of the more widely recognized free blacks of the period, owned property, had indentured servants, and held slaves (Breen and Innes 1980, 7–18; Russell 1969, 25; Morgan 1998, 13). Blacks experienced an initial fluidity in the colony, where their legal status as indentured could be elevated to free status. Forming a small part of the colony's population, for "several decades, indeed, blacks in Virginia and elsewhere had a status within the laboring classes that varied from indentured apprentice and servant to free man and free woman" (Harding 1981, 26).

Yet the presence of blacks was a harbinger of things to come, and already there were signs that the initial ambiguity of the colonists regarding blacks was changing. The English aversion toward Africans was initially evinced in the 1624 and 1625 censuses. The 1624 census indicates, for example, that there were twenty-two blacks in the colony, but the count hinged on how blacks and whites were recorded. Each white person was identified by his or her full name in both the 1624 and the 1625 census reports, whereas most of the blacks have no names at all or are recorded simply as "one negro" or "Negro woman" or, in one instance, as six blank lines followed by the word "negro." The 1625 census shows a slight improvement in that one black has a complete listing and five blacks have almost complete listings (*Historical Statistics of the United States* 1976, 1153). Because indentured servants used this data source to measure their entry into the colony and the duration of their servitude, this data source proved critical in their gaining their freedom. Just as important, as these early census reports show, the English had already begun to perceive blacks as inferior to whites. Several scholars have contended that the racial attitudes of the colonists toward Africans, in most instances, predated their arrival on American shores, facilitating their enslavement.

In the early 1600s, the colonists in the Virginia General Assembly began to put the planks in place that would eventually consolidate the power and hegemony of the planter class. The tobacco boon of the early 1600s, the dearth of labor, and the necessity for land cultivation, as well as the planters' visions of wealth, provided impetus for the institutionalization of slavery. Serving as colonial administrators, planters were in the critical position of effecting the status of blacks by shaping colonial statutes and rendering judicial decisions to legitimize the slave system. One of the early judicial decisions of the colonial administration was to thwart the growing alliance of black and white laborers by driving a wedge between the two groups, whose future cooperation would threaten slavery's survival and, consequently, the planters' emerging elitism.

The first colonial case that would have a major effect on the laboring population was the Hugh Davis case of 1630. This case marks the inchoate stage of judicial decisions that would delineate black from white laborers, foster a prevailing political environment of racial attitudes in regard to blacks, and posit black women as social pariahs: "Hugh Davis to be soundly whipped before an assembly of Negroes & others for abusing himself to the dishonor of God and the shame of Christianity by defiling his body in lying with a negro which fault he is to act [*sic*] Next Sabbath day" (Higginbotham 1978, 23).

As A. Leon Higginbotham notes in his book *In the Matter of Color: Race and the American Legal Process: The Colonial Period,* Hugh Davis was probably a white indentured servant and, because the black woman received no known punishment, she was more than likely a slave (1978, 23). The intent, however, of the Hugh Davis case was to signal a warning to both blacks and whites regarding the immorality of interracial cohabitation and to more subtly denote that any other forms of interracial bonding also would be perceived as criminal acts. But more important, the case formed the underpinnings of what would later emerge as the "Jezebel" thesis: that black women driven by passion and uncontrollable lust for white men would cause these men to commit acts of sexual transgressions for which the women should and must be punished. With this early identification of black women as immoral and degrading, they would eventually be stigmatized as lascivious and vulnerable to white male sexual exploitation (White 1985, 27–46; Giddings 1984, 35–36; Morton 1973, 1–13).

By 1640, the colonial environment was becoming increasingly hostile for the three hundred blacks who were in Virginia. A decade after the Hugh Davis case, the Virginia General Assembly passed a statute relegating all blacks to slave status. The shift in the legal status of blacks in that year was due to the colonists' growing interest in slavery and the need to augment as well as circumscribe its labor force. Blacks not only plummeted from indentured servitude to slavery, but all blacks entering the colony were now treated as slaves. Scholar Paula Giddings notes that "no African man or woman who set foot in Virginia after 1640 had the benefit of indentures or the hope that their 'service' would be anything but lifelong" (1984, 36).

The John Punch case of the same year reinforced blacks' new legal status. Punch, a black indentured servant, and two white indentured servants escaped in a skiff to Maryland, were captured, and were returned to Virginia for punishment. Although the two white indentured servants received as punishment four additional years of service, Punch received slavery (Higginbotham 1978, 28–29; Russell 1969, 29–30). The racial cleavages are evident in the disproportionate sentencing of blacks and whites for the commission of the same crime, but what is also apparent is the redefinition and further denigration of black men's legal status. Although the Robert Sweat case of the same year, in which a white man who impregnated a black woman was to do penance and the black woman was to receive a whipping, suggested a "pocket of grace," the issues of disproportionate sentencing for the same offense, the already declining status of black women for more than a decade, and the belief that the black woman was already enslaved, have merit (Higginbotham 1978, 23–24; Guild 1969, 21).

For the remainder of the seventeenth century, the Virginia Assembly passed a flurry of statutes and codes to solidify the perplexing problems of enslavement. Undoubtedly, the vicissitudes of closing all the legal loopholes as the colony institutionalized an oppressive system created myriad legal issues. Subsumed under the creation of this legal infrastructure of slavery were the colonists' intense struggle to obtain wealth and power and their perennial land speculation while they simultaneously engaged in the dehumanization of African peoples. "The fact that so few masters felt compelled to justify their behavior even as they actively participated in the construction of a slave society suggests the extent to which human inequality was simply taken for granted," notes James Oakes (1982, 5).

The statutory recognition of slavery that came in 1661 created a permanent pool of African male and female laborers and their progeny, principally captured from the Senegambia and the Bight of Biafra regions, to work in the tobacco fields. For black women, the statute of 1643, which relegated them to the fields, and the statute of 1662, that all children born in the colony shall follow the condition of the mother, inextricably linked them and their children to slavery (Higginbotham 1978, 42–44; Kulikoff 1978, 230–31; Giddings 1984, 37). For black women, the 1643 statute, though clearly an indication that the colony needed more agriculturalists in tobacco production, meant that they would perform all of the labor intensive tasks associated with cash crop commodity production. The later statute of 1662 made black female slaves increasingly vulnerable to sexual exploitation because they bore the double duty of intensive labor production as well as being the reproductive nexus of the labor force.

The colonists' perennial problem of separating black and white indentured had not abated by the end of the seventeenth century. Whereas the original focus of thwarting interracial liaisons was directed at black women and white male indentured in the Hugh Davis case of 1630, the colonists now turned their attention to the relationships between white women and black men. The colonial statute of 1691, which forbade interracial relationships and marriages between white women and black men, had several purposes. Although the initial intent was to discourage white woman from having "bastard child(ren) by a Negro," an additional reason for the law was to stop the practice of slave-holders who, in their zeal to increase their labor forces, were fostering these relationships. Giddings states that "white womanhood notwith-standing, so many masters purchased White women for the explicit pur-pose of marrying them to their Black slaves, thus making slaves out of them that it had become a scandal" (1984, 38).

While planters were in the throes of stabilizing a labor force for the commodity production of tobacco, they were also apprehensive about the slaves' religious life. Even though some were not interested in reli-gion at all, seeing it as a waste of time, others were not opposed to the baptism of slaves, believing that Christianity might make their slaves a more tractable labor force. The statute of 1667 addressed some of their concerns. Slaves could be baptized as Christians, but baptism did not alter their slave status. By 1670, another statute established that all non-Christians who came by sea would be enslaved (Higginbotham 1978, 37–38; Russell 1969, 39–40; Guild 1969, 44). Both statutes sought to address the religious status of slaves who were either in transit within the colonies or coming to the colonies through the international slave trade.

Although the commercial interests of planters predominated in the importation of African slaves and the legal institutionalization of slavery, there was growing apprehension in the colony concerning these devel-opments. In an effort to control slaves' entire working lives and perhaps to stifle criticisms of the increasing presence of blacks, the slave code was developed to reinforce the existing statutes. And that slave code, note Franklin and Moss, "borrowing heavily from practices in the Caribbean and serving as a model for other mainland codes, was comprehensive if it was anything at all" (1988, 55). Slaves had to travel with passes at all times, restricting their interplantation mobility and escape attempts, and corporal punishment was applied for all minor infractions. For theft, a major offense, "slaves were to receive sixty lashes and be placed in the pillory, where their ears were to be cut off." For the more serious offenses, slaves paid with their lives. "Slaves found guilty of murder or rape were to be hanged" (ibid.).

Despite the statutes, codes, and increasingly circumscribed oppres-sion of blacks, tension in the colony grew as whites became more fearful of slave retaliation. Some whites still complained of slaves' resentment of being forced to labor for others and their growing intractability. Governor Edmund Andros, by 1694, believed that the slave code was inadequate and that slaves had become unruly and unmanageable (Franklin and Moss 1988, 55). The tension was undoubtedly exacerbated by individual instances of manumission. In 1684, for example, John Farrar of Henrico County stipulated in his will that his slave, Jack, be manumitted (Court Records of Henrico County, 1677–1692, 299). Scholar John H. Russell notes that by "the year 1690 the free negro class had become an object of suspicion and fear" and a law was quickly passed in 1691 to stem manumissions by individual slaveholders (1969, 51). But for several decades there had been a growing collusion in the colony between enslaved blacks, free blacks, and white indentured, and the notions of resistance and freedom had already been planted.

By 1705, blacks were designated as chattel property in Virginia, foreshadowing or paralleling events in other southern colonies that were constructing the legal parameters of their slave societies. "All Negro, mulatto, and Indian slaves within this dominion shall be held to be real estate and not chattels and shall descent unto heirs and widows according to the custom of land inheritance" (Higginbotham 1978, 52). In one generation, Africans had gone from indentured servitude to slavery to chattel property. These statutes were also "public declarations that blacks were, by virtue of their being black, slaves for life, and that their status was that of laborers held as property" (Oakes 1982, 27). Dehumanized to an economic commodity, blacks were now capital assets that could be passed from generation to generation. All African laborers, whether free or bond, were now synonymous with slavery, degradation, and an odious caste system. This stigmatization of blacks would be one of the more enduring legacies in Virginia.

The tremendous increase in African importation to the colony in the later decades of the seventeenth century put the final plank in place in the developing slave society. To be profitable, the commercialization of cash crop commodity production depended on a gang labor force for every step of the production cycle. Historian Allan Kulikoff notes that "African slaves began to be imported directly from Africa for the first time around 1680; from 1679 to 1686, seven ships with about 1,450 slaves arrived in Virginia from Africa" (1978, 230). The influx of Africans to the colony continued unabated in the eighteenth century as the plantation culture began to define the southern region. Approximately forty thousand Africans came into the colony, most directly from Africa, between 1700 to 1740 (Donnan 1931, 172–74; Kulikoff 1978, 230). This gang labor force, essential to tobacco and cereal production, increased the region's export commodities and vastly expanded the colony's economy. Plantation and slave fever, viewed as sure signs of future wealth and prosperity, defined all classes of whites in society—those who had slaves and were seeking to augment their numbers and those who were working to get their initial complement of slaves—and characterized southern popular attitudes.

A Three-Tier Slave Society

Characteristic of the legitimatization of this slave society was one "Virginia landowner [who] advertised eight hundred acres of "good plantable Land" for which he would accept "ready Money, or young Negroes" (Oakes 1982, 26). A three-tier social structure, this slave society was dominated by the planter elite, whose patriarchal power rested on their possession of land and slaves, and the colony's political and legal apparatus in Virginia's assembly. By the mid-eighteenth century, the consolidation of the Tidewater planter aristocracy would dominate politics, the region's economy, land speculation, the possession of slaves, the number of plantations, and southern traditions for the next two centuries. At its core, this elite not only instituted a slave society but also created oligarchical rule of white supremacy that still prevails. V. O. Key Jr., in examining twentieth-century Virginia politics in his *Southern Politics in State and Nation,* traces Virginia's oligarchical structure to this period: "Withal, the Virginia machine is an anachronism. With its cavalier and aristocratic outlook, it can boast, quietly, of an eighteenth-century tone" (1949, 19–20).

Slavery, the slave trade, and the marketing of slave products were integral to the nascent capitalist system, and a discernible interactive economic pattern emerged between southern planters and northern financiers that, ironically, aided in rigidifying the oligarchical structure. Planters, having grown accustomed to the profits derived from the southern ecosystem of involuntary labor, created an idyllic environment in which their domination and authority over slaves and slave commodity production became integral to a flourishing southern market economy, providing linkages to northern merchants, the Caribbean, and Europe. Northern shippers, financiers, factors, brokers, and merchants, as well as southern planters, farmers, and workers, were all engaged in plantation management, and slave commodity production and distribution, deriving economic gain from the system (Foner 1941, 1–14). The planter elite, then, though they were inextricably tied to northern capitalism, realized that their tenuous power and hegemony pivoted on their control of both the politics and the economics of Virginia.

The middle tier of this slave society was composed of moderate slave-holders and farmers who were constantly moving westward, seeking more land and slaves in order to prosper. Oakes notes the difference between the planter elite and the middle-class slaveholders: "What distinguished the planter aristocracy from the slaveholding middle-class was not any lack of accumulation but a lack of struggle" (1982, 65). The planter elite had been stabilized for generations, accumulating wealth and prosperity, whereas middle-class slaveholders frequently had two careers as they migrated westward to seek their elusive dreams of wealth. Rapid soil exhaustion from tobacco production and the lack of crop rotation with cereal grains to replenish the land caused many slaveholders to pack up family, slaves, and furniture and move to another location. Oakes also comments on this continuous cycle of "slave fever": "For as long as there were land and slaves enough to keep their society 'uninterruptedly prosperous,' exuberance would overwhelm the slave holders' fear of failure. It was no wonder that every piece of new land was looked upon as the site of future wealth and greatness" (1982, 129).

Arguably, most moderate slaveholders and farmers, like their elite counterparts, were so indebted to northern financiers and their constant land speculation and slave purchases, increasing their indebtedness annually, that they could not easily extricate themselves (Foner 1941, 10–13). Consequently, New York City financiers owned southern plantations and slaves, charged exorbitant rates of annual interest, and ensured that their monies and profit margins were deeply interwoven in the Virginia plantation system. This financial relation between the North and the South contributed both to the construction and maintenance of the slave system and to the lack of abolitionist support for the emancipation of the slaves by northern businessmen.

At the bottommost tier of this slave society were the slave laborers (men, women, and children), agriculturalists who specialized primarily in tobacco production and secondarily in the export economy of cereal grains. The slave community was centered on the pattern of labor production, the specificity of the cycles of tobacco, corn, or wheat cultivation, the purchase and sale of friends and family members, and plantation management. Former Virginia slave Matilda Henrietta Perry recalls the rigid regimen maintained for tobacco cultivation: "Tobaccy? Use to get sick of seein' de weed. Use to wuk fum sun to sun in dat old terbaccy field. Wuk till my back felt lak it ready to pop in two. Marse ain' raise nothin' but terbaccy, ceptin' a little wheat an 'corn for eatin', an' us black people had to look arter dat 'baccy lak it was gold'" (Perdue, Barden, and Philips 1976, 223–24). Former Virginia slave Frank Bell remembers the gender-specific tasks associated with wheat cultivation on John Fallons's Virginia plantation: "John Fallons had 'bout 150 servants an' he wasn't much on no special house servants. Put everybody in de field, he did, even de women. Growed mostly wheat on de plantation, an' de men would scythe and cradle, while de women folks would rake and bind. Den us little chillun, boys an' girls, would come along an' stack" (ibid., 26).

The intensity of labor production was exacerbated because slave-holders sought to save money by furnishing slaves with worn out tools. Despite this handicap, slaves were still expected to plant, cultivate, and harvest the crops and ready them for transport to international and domestic markets. Some slaveholders would cultivate all three export crops, allowing wheat and corn to replenish the nutrients in the soil that were lost during tobacco production. Former Virginia slave Archie Booker was a slave on a plantation where slaves were responsible for the culti-vation of all three crops: "Dem day dey raise co'n, wheat an' terbaccy an' give ye rations fur a week at a time. We wuk fum sun to sun. All de slaves wuk. Onlies speshul slave dey had wuz a man whut blow de ho'n fur us to go to wuk an' to come home at night" (Perdue, Barden, and Philips 1976, 53).

Slaves' cohesiveness around labor production facilitated strong kin-ship ties and racial solidarity in the slave quarters. Eugene Genovese argued persuasively that the social bifurcations in society generated by slavery made these blacks victims of class exploitation (1974, 3–4). Sev-eral scholars have identified class and race as major components shaping the forces of slavery; the inevitability of blackness made these laborers slaves, and, correspondingly, an active racism on the part of white soci-ety in their domination of all blacks made slavery a racial caste system (*North Star,* June 13, 1850; Robertson 1996, 16; Escott 1979, 97–99).

Slave Culture, Community, and Resistance

The slave community in the Tidewater and Piedmont regions was created by African male and female laborers who interwove disparate African tra-ditions and New World cultural influences, the mode of agricultural pro-duction and the exigencies of slavery, and the yearning for dignity and freedom into a diasporic slave culture. In this creative process, slaves drew on their historical memories of an African homeland, an emerging class consciousness, and a racial solidarity born out of the southern caste system that circumscribed their lives. These Africans were not "communities of people at first, and they could only become communities by processes of cultural change. What they shared at the outset was their enslavement; all—or nearly all—else had to be created by them" (Mintz and Price 1976, 9). Forging kinship and fictive kin ties, bonds, and connections that enabled them to withstand a common oppression, slaves from disparate groups and areas of the African continent became a people.

As the influx of African slaves increased toward the end of the eighteenth century, the Virginia slave community possessed a rich heritage of African traditions and values. Scholar Sterling Stuckey notes that "with the slave population of Virginia at 187,000 in 1770, slaves formed 40 percent of the inhabitants; by 1790, nearly 60 percent of slaves in the United States resided there and in Maryland. Since the overwhelming majority of the slaves brought into Virginia until the end of the trade were African born, they provided the foundation of values from which slave culture was erected, New World experience being interpreted largely from the African point of view" (1987, 31).

African retention among the slaves was facilitated by the colony's use of gang labor forces for crop production and the creation of slave quarters to house the slaves. By the 1750s, all of the medium-sized and large plantations of fifteen or more slaves had slave quarters, facilitating community life. Within the slave community, a quasi-autonomous space for the slaves away from the prying eyes of whites, the amalgamation of disparate African religious systems, traditions, and values inculcated with the pragmatism of the New World environment gave rise to a new transatlantic slave culture. Slaves created a culture that contained components of African religious belief systems, African traditions and values, folklore, music, dance, food, evangelical Christianity, and protest and resistance—all serving as a bulwark against the forces of oppression.

Religion forged the fundamental character and spirit of slave culture. Whether it was the retention of disparate African religious belief systems or evangelical Christianity making its appearance in the slave quarters by the mid-eighteenth century, it eased the transplantation process of Africans to the New World. Despite "the juggernaut of evangelicalism" in the Chesapeake region in the 1740s, however, many slaves never came in contact with evangelical missionaries, and of those who did, some still favored the retention of their African forms of worship and sought spiritual comfort in a fragmented world with the wisdom that had bonded their people for centuries. Even with those who took on the trappings of the new religion, it was still tentative for "the fires of revival that initially swept most of the British North American colonies in the 1740s flared up intermittently during the 1780s and 1790s particularly in the Chesapeake region of the upper South" (Raboteau 1997, 92) made it a gradual, uneven process of acceptance. Converting mainly to the Baptist and Methodist faiths because of their popular appeal, slaves embraced this emancipation of spirit while reinterpreting Christianity from an African prism (Raboteau 1978, 212–88; Wilmore 1983, 15–28; Stuckey 1987, 30–43). As historian and folklorist Charles Joyner notes, "To underestimate the Africanity of African-American Christianity is to rob the slaves of their heritage" (Joyner 1994, 19).

African Christianity, as well as African religious worship, coexisting in the slave quarters and frequently in the same persons, provided stabilizing influences in the slave community, respite from their earthly woes, and well springs of hope and redemption. The development of slavery, concomitant with successive waves of evangelical Christianity, led formerly resistive antebellum planters to gradually embrace Christianity in order to foster tractability in their slaves. But slaves shaped an African Christianity with an emphasis on human dignity, self-esteem, justice, protest, and spiritual and material freedom. In fact, notes Raboteau, "runaway slave advertisements in Virginia and Maryland newspapers complained that blacks were being ruined by the 'leveling' doctrines of Baptist and Methodist sectarians" (1997, 93). In the dichotomization of the soul and the spirit, slaves created parallel realities, one of the inner sacred self that communicated with the Supreme Being, and, the other, the material self whose focus was on freedom.

Evangelical Christianity, principally packaged for slave obedience by planters, was juxtaposed to the redemptive qualities of African Christianity sustained in the slave community. Understanding the religious ploy of their masters, slaves were nevertheless empowered by their new-found God to question the primacy of being owned by anyone but the Supreme Being. As theologian Gayraud Wilmore contends, "Even though they [slaves] adopted the outward appearance of Christian conversion, they took from it only what proved efficacious for easing the burden of their captivity and gave little attention to the rest" (1983, 11). Slaves believed that if their God was of hope and divine retribution, He would soon save them from their oppressors.

Although African religious worship and African Christianity were the driving forces behind the survival and resistance of the slave community, these dominant cultural factors were reinforced by the folktales, the work songs and spirituals, the socialization of children, the respect of the elders bearing wisdom, and African and New World music traditions. Slave women played a pivotal role in nurturing this "culture of survival and resistance" by their extensive female labor collectives, by their gender-specific tasks of voluntary labor in the slave community, and by encouraging their children to escape whenever possible (Jones 1985, 29–32; White 1985, 119–41; King 1995, 120–21). The creation of this "culture of survival and resistance" was an oppositional force in the slave community.

Oppositional Force of Resistance

As far back as 1663, two years after the official recognition of slavery, blacks were creating their "culture of survival and resistance." As slave plots, uprisings, and rebellions were uncovered, some colonists became increasingly agitated. Slaves were quickly becoming adept at utilizing meetings or special occasions to plan subversive activities. Although funerals for Virginia slaves were times for celebration because many believed that the slaves for whom the funerals were held were returning to Africa, it was also a time to collectively mobilize around escape activities (Morgan 1998, 640–41). Franklin and Moss note that "in 1687, while a funeral was taking place, a group of slaves in the northern neck planned an uprising, but the plot was discovered before it could be carried out" (1988, 54). Despite the law of 1670, indicating rewards for runaways, and the 1680 statute in which "the frequent meetings of considerable numbers of Negro slaves under pretense of feasts and burials is judged of dangerous consequence" (Guild 1969, 45), black resistance was becoming integral to slavery in the colony.

Once the political environment of resistance was activated, slaves could employ various modes and means of resistance to spontaneously challenge oppression on a daily basis, provide cover for planned strategies of resistance, or participate in planned, episodic uprisings and rebellions. Daily resistance took various forms, including poisoning the masters, mysterious arson, truancy, abortion, crop spoilage, the destruction of equipment, feigning illness, work slowdowns, and confrontational slaves. Frequently extreme acts of violence against the slave community, such as rape, murder, or physical brutality, were met with retaliation. In those instances, historian Peter H. Wood tells us in Kelley and Lewis's work, *To Make Our World Anew,* that "overseers were beaten to death by angry work hands in the fields; masters and their families were poisoned by desperate servants in the kitchen. Setting fires also became a favored act of defiance, since arson, like poisoning food, was difficult to prove and easy to deny" (Kelley and Lewis 2000, 91).

Outlyers and other runaways fed the "culture of survival and resistance." Defying the slave institution, these fugitives dealt a symbolic and material economic blow to the system. As historian Allan Kulikoff reports, "Almost as soon as Africans landed, they attempted to run away together." There were two outlying runaway communities in the Chesapeake region, one in Lexington, Virginia, and the other in Maryland, in the 1720s (1978, 238–39). Symbolically, they represented freedom to the slave community, and the runaways were considered heroic whether they were captured or remained free; myth and folklore grew up around their efforts. Economically, their escapes resulted in a financial setback to slaveholders, the loss being the expenditures and profit associated with purchase and expected slave productivity. Despite the laws and the rewards for their recapture, black fugitives became integral to the slave institution.

Frank Bell, a former Virginia slave, reflects on runaways whom he witnessed as well as a quasi-successful organized effort of slave resistance: "Well, I come on out an' got in the wagon an' ole Marser drove me down to the 7th Street Wharf, to ole Joe Bruin's omnibus where they had them. Uncle Moses was standing there chained up with 40 or 50 other slaves what had been sold along with him. They all was runaways, there was a gang of them what had tried to get to Canada. All but ten had been caught, including Uncle Moses" (Perdue, Barden, and Philips 1976, 27).

The larger hemispheric black resistance also provided impetus and inspiration to Virginia slaves. The Haitian Revolution, which began in 1791 as a slave uprising on the island of St. Domingue and culminated in the founding of a black independent republic in 1804, sparked dramatic resistance in the slaves' struggle for freedom in Virginia and throughout the Americas. Virginia slaves had initially been receptive to the French because French soldiers, though they labored valiantly beside the Americans in their fight for independence, were widely believed to have given safe harbor to black runaways during their stay in Virginia. This forced Governor Benjamin Harrison into the dubious position of thanking the French for their assistance while simultaneously asking "the French commander to allow Virginia masters to search for their human property among the blacks traveling with the troops" (Sidbury 1997, 535). This contradictory pattern was also evinced by Thomas Jefferson (and his Jeffersonian party, which dominated Virginia's Assembly), who supported the French Revolution and advocated democratic-republican ideals throughout the world but would not recognize the new Haitian Republic and steadfastly supported plantation slavery.

However, in spite of the contradictory pattern established by planters of who should be free and who should be enslaved, slaves gathered information from black sailors; newspapers, particularly the *Virginia Gazette and General Advertiser;* private conversations; and newly arrived black Haitian refugees that inspired their resistance (*Virginia Gazette and General Advertiser,* Mar. 14, 1792, June 2, 1802; *Liberator,* Sept. 17, 1831; Bolster 1997, 144–57; Sidbury 1997, 537–39; Hunt 1988, 115–21). Virginia slaves were politicized by the Haitian rebellion with a new sense of diasporan consciousness. "During the 1790s," Sidbury notes, "Virginia slaves responded to the inspiration of the Haitian Revolution by discussing attempts to forge links with enslaved people of African descent in other parts of the New World" (1997, 534). Several plots of slave unrest in Virginia in the 1790s were linked to the Haitian rebellion (Hunt 1988, 115–16; Frey 1991, 229–30). This idea of resistance and the notion of freedom on the part of urban slaves and their free black counterparts would form the underpinnings of Richmond's industrial slavery.

Richmond, Industrial Slavery, and Resistance

The development of industrial slavery was triggered by Richmond's rising industrialization, which needed an aggregate of cheap laborers, and the surplus of slave labor on some plantations where there was a shift away from staple crop production to a more diversified economy. Although the hiring of slave labor was always integral to interplantation life, industrial slavery placed blacks into an urban milieu where the bonds between master and slave were weakened and, in some instances, tangential. Over time, increased pressures from urban slaves who broadened the parameters of their bondage, runaways, who underscored the slave struggle for freedom, and abolitionists, who conspired with slaves in planning escapes in Richmond, all served to weaken the system.

Richmond's urban environment transformed the lives of free black and slave laborers coming from surrounding rural areas to work in the city's artisan shops and factories. Slaves, both skilled and unskilled, were "hired out" by their masters on an annual contract basis and came into the city from a slave culture rich in African traditions and from the regimentation of plantation labor with the inspiration of the Haitian rebellion and an eagerness to experience this new quasi-independence. Blacks, bond and free, went to work in artisan shops, tobacco factories, flour and iron mills, building and construction, on railroads, and in stone quarries. Other blacks were hired as domestic servants for white Richmonders who did not want to purchase slaves and be subjected to Richmond's tax levy.

In the "hiring out" process, planters often relied on intermediaries to conduct the business arrangements. Although the contract for slave labor was generally between the planter and the industrialist for a fixed annual fee, as slave-hiring brokers entered the negotiations, the system became more flexible, distancing the planter from the transaction as well as his control of his property (Eaton 1960, 664; Wade 1964, 42–43). As historian Richard C. Wade states, "The border cities and Richmond relied more on private agencies to bring employers and available bondsmen together. Brokers for the purpose grew up, much like the 'Intelligence Offices' in the North, and even appeared where public facilities were available" (1964, 42).

Within the "free space" of negotiations, some slaves were able to not only loosen the constraints of their bondage but also move up to a tenuous quasi-free status in the city. At the beginning of the year, some slaves were able to negotiate their own contracts as long as the master received the agreed-on fee for their labor. Other slaves were able to negotiate a fee over and above the price desired by the master. "Despite abuses," Eaton notes, "hiring was often a form of upgrading of slave labor and of loosening the bonds of servitude" (1960, 669). Slaves who worked in factories could receive wages for overtime work as well as a stipend for room and board in the city. Although slaves were initially forced to live in the master's "compound," which was "the urban equivalent of the plantation . . . provid(ing) a means of social control as well as of shelter," this system soon broke down and some of the physical and social control of the slaves was lost (Wade 1964, 61). "Living out" meant that slaves sought rented rooms, basements, back alleys, or sheds where a modicum of privacy and freedom could be provided (ibid., 66–67). Although there was diligent effort on the part of Richmond to curb slaves' behavior with restrictive slave codes, the inability to control blacks in the urban environment, as well as blacks seeking to expand their freedom at every turn, weakened the urban slave system.

Just as Richmond's urban landscape created the impetus for quasi-independence for some slaves, it also changed the context and strategies of black resistance by enabling the incorporation of more free blacks into rebellion efforts. Urban resistance also included the participation of slaves and free blacks from several towns and cities, an extensive network of communication, and heavy reliance upon black seamen and other blacks who were mobile and harboring a clear resentment against the planter elite and the mercantilists. Free blacks were pivotal in these efforts because of their resources in addition to their symbolic presence among the slaves: "As residents of the city, exempt from many of the restrictions slavery imposed on other blacks, the freedmen excited envy among the slaves and contributed to their disquiet" (Wade 1964, 225). Before 1793, most forms of black resistance were initiated in rural areas; after 1793, urban resistance and plantation resistance were tributaries to the overall black struggle for freedom.

In 1793, the Secret Keepers conspiracy involved insurrectionists in Richmond, Norfolk, and Charleston who planned a revolution to overthrow slavery (Sidbury 1997, 540; Hunt 1988, 115–16). Although the Richmond rebels were the leading conspirators, there were linkages through Gowan Pamphlet, a free black minister, and undoubtedly some seamen, who conveyed news and information to other seaport cities. Historian James Sidbury states that in a letter (the original of which was lost) from Pamphlet to the "Norfolk Keeper," Pamphlet revealed the essence of the plans, which were rumored to have several thousand participants: "The Richmond Keeper, who was clearly the dominant figure among the insurrectionists in Virginia, told the Norfolk Keeper to 'hold' himself in readiness to strike, and pledged to send 'orders' when he 'hear[d] from Charleston again.' The conspirators, he promised, would 'be in full possession of the hole [sic] country in a few weeks'" (Sidbury 1997, 540).

Although the conspiracy was discovered and aborted, it engendered fear in white southerners, leading to increased societal proscriptions for blacks. But the rise of industrialization in Richmond was hampered by the city's restraints on its slave laborers. Slave hirelings who were working in the city and mingling with free workers resented their slave status. By 1800, Gabriel Prosser, a blacksmith on the Prosser plantation in Brookfield, a few miles from Richmond, inspired by the Haitian rebellion, planned a revolt. As a slave hireling, Prosser spent several days a month in Richmond working for skilled artisans. Encouraged by the schism between the Democrat-Republicans and Federalists in Richmond and fueled by his resentment of his enslavement, Prosser crafted a careful retaliatory plan: "Several hundred men would make a surprise midnight attack on Richmond to capture arms, burn warehouses, and perhaps take the governor as hostage, thereby inspiring a general uprising among thousands of Africans" (Harding 1981, 55; Egerton 1990, 194–95).

Although it was primarily an urban plan, Gabriel Prosser and his brothers, Solomon and Martin, recruited slaves from nearby plantations, as well as slaves and free blacks in the port cities of Richmond, Petersburg, Charlottesville, Suffolk, and Norfolk. Black seamen were recruited for specific assignments. "Black boatmen along the James had long been the carriers of information and runaway slaves as well as goods for merchants; now several were involved as couriers," states Egerton (1990, 198). Prosser, evincing a religious radical resistance, shored up his followers' courage with stories of the successful Haitian rebellion and God's rescue of the children of Israel from bondage. On August 30, 1800, the day of the planned uprising, a terrible storm in Richmond spoiled the attack strategy. Before Prosser could reassemble his troops, the plot was betrayed and eventually all of the conspirators were rounded up. Prosser went to his death silently.

The Nat Turner rebellion in Southampton County in August 1831, three decades after the aborted Prosser rebellion, signaled the continuity of black resistance into the antebellum era. Although it was a southern slave rebellion, it promoted fear in whites, who then imposed greater restrictions on blacks as far away as Philadelphia (Winch 1988, 130–31). For Turner, a black slave preacher, the time was at hand for black redemption. Like Gabriel Prosser, Turner was imbued with a religious radicalism that shaped his early maturational years, believing that a fierce resistance to oppression was a part of God's holy war. As he sought the heavens for signs of his "calling" or "mission," Turner fervently believed that he had been anointed by God with divine power.

The portentous eclipse of the sun in February 1831 was a sign favorable to Turner's mission, and he was already poised to wreak havoc on white slaveholders and deliver his people from bondage. Within the slave community, Turner was emerging as a leader, having already distinguished himself among his peers with his spontaneous exhortations at black Baptist meetings as well as his knowledge of pottery, gunpowder, and mystical healing practices (Harding 1981, 78). "Where slaves' meetings were prohibited and, therefore, held secretly in the woods or slave quarters, the charisma of the slave preacher was known only to those whom he led" (Becker 1997, 181). Thus, an acknowledged indigenous leader of the slave community, Turner was able to draw around him a small band of slave rebels who had expressed a commitment to an uprising for liberation and were in concert with Turner's belief that once the rebellion was underway, they would receive mass support from other slaves who were waiting for an opportunity to strike a blow against the system. Turner decided on July 4, 1831, as the day of liberation for its ironic symbolism: slaves would finally receive freedom on the day that white Americans celebrated their independence from Great Britain.

Turner's illness on the day of redemption forced a change in plans, and he once again awaited a sign from the heavens. Finally, "in the dark hours of the morning of August 22, Nat Turner's God pressed him forward at the head of his band of black avenging angels, drove him in search of what seemed the ultimate justice" (Harding 1981, 95). Moving systematically from house to house, starting with his owners, the Travises, the group, numbering about sixty and armed with hatchets and axes, slaughtered all whites in their path. Turner's plan to march to Jerusalem, where they hoped to get a cache of weapons to use in their struggle, was soon halted by a county-wide alarm. Once the alarm spread and militia and vigilante groups were organized in hot pursuit, the slaves, outmanned and outgunned, retreated to the woods to regroup. In the days that followed, all of the slave rebels were captured, except Turner, who remained at large until October 30, 1831. On November 11, 1831, Nat Turner went to the gallows silently, leaving slaves inspired by his heroism and his oppressors to reinterpret this slave uprising as a demonic anomaly instead of a struggle for justice and freedom.

These plots and uprisings denoting urban and plantation resistance were incipient forms of "collective insurgency" that slaves and free blacks used to actualize their goals of freedom. Since the colonial era, there had been a long history of plots, conspiracies, and aborted and real uprisings in Virginia, creating a politically charged atmosphere and acrimonious relations between slaves and masters. Whereas the planter aristocracy chose to deny the exploitation of the slave labor that created and sustained their wealth, slaves recognized and resented their material conditions. Despite the rhetoric of proslavery apologists, slaves perceived the slaveholding class as the enemy standing between them and freedom. In episodic resistance, these resisters, as Anthony Oberschall argues, "shared targets and objects of hostility held responsible for grievances, hardship, and suffering" (Oberschall 1973, 119; McAdams 1985, 41–44). The long-standing resentment and grievances of slaves against the system were accumulative and needed a political spark (such as an event typified by the Haitian rebellion; a material condition which was the enslavement of Africans; and indigenous leadership, which the Secret Keepers, Gabriel Prosser, and Nat Turner provided) to mobilize free and slave resistance.

THE ANTEBELLUM ERA

Two centuries of white supremacy in Virginia, buttressed by the emerging oligarchy in the early 1800s in Richmond, laid the foundation for the superordinate-subordinate relations between blacks and whites characteristic of the antebellum era while creating a vehicle for black political mobilization. V. O. Key Jr. describes Virginia's oligarchical structure, which dominated the state's political apparatus: "Political power has been closely held by a small group of leaders who, themselves and their predecessors, have subverted democratic institutions and deprived most Virginians of a voice in their government" (1949, 19). This politically entrenched planter-industrialist class of judges, editors, and bank presidents (dubbed the "Richmond Junta") shaped not only conservatism in Richmond's politics and immigrant antipathies but also their pseudo-aristocratic superiority toward their urban slaves and free blacks (Chesson 1981, 20).

By the 1840s, Richmond was considered the major industrial city in the South. Although mercantilists had possessed visions of making the city the center of trade and commerce connecting Europe, the North, and the South, Richmond's commercialism was gradually being replaced by a growing industrial economy. This industrial development by the old established mercantile elite was gradually being infiltrated by new industrialists with more-progressive ideas regarding the city's development and, ultimately, political and economic leadership. Although the alliance between the established elite and new entrepreneurs would be an uneasy one at times, both classes were cut from the same cloth in their aristocratic pretensions and support of southern slavery. Before the antebellum period, the city's mercantile, trade, and transportation classes had shaped the city's growth and prosperity through their political leadership on Richmond's civic council and control of the dominant economic initiatives. But the new entrepreneurs, just as businessmen had done in northeastern cities, were soon supplanting the old elite with new ideas and technology. Touting regional self-reliance and progressive internal improvements to shore up Richmond's infrastructure, these entrepreneurs were carving their place in Richmond's history. Men such as Joseph R. Anderson provided the indigenous leadership to this group: "Joseph R. Anderson typified this group; manager of the Tredegar Iron Works and director of the Richmond Branch of the Farmers' Bank of Virginia, he was also a major stockholder in two internal improvements companies and a member of St. Paul's Episcopal Church, the House of Delegates, the Richmond City Council, and the executive board of the Richmond Board of Trade" (Rachleff 1984, 4).

The investment of borrowed northern capital in modern industrial equipment and the advantage of the state's resources in tobacco and pig iron soon transformed the Virginia capital into a southern industrial center. Aided by the James River and the Kanawha Canal, as well as the five railroads that terminated in the city, entrepreneurs developed factories that would export finished products to international and domestic consumers. Richmond's factories depended on the raw materials of Virginia's agricultural production of tobacco; the expensive pig iron from the Trans-Allegheny region and the more costly Virginia metal; the cheaper northern pig iron, equipment, parts, and financing; a pool of German and Irish immigrant laborers; a low-cost urban slave and free black labor force for processing and exporting materials to the United States and Europe; and federal government contracts that frequently led to plant expansion and stability of the labor force.

This growing industrialization created an acute need for an aggregate labor force. That need was filled in part by the large influx of white Irish and German immigrants who came to Richmond seeking jobs and who, just as they did in northeastern cities, solidified their positions as wage laborers in industrial production. However, notes Dey, "northern and European ironworkers were reluctant to settle in slave states and could only be lured south by premium wages" (1966, 22). These immigrants were particularly noticeable in the iron trade, where "a large force of Irish and German workers formed the bulk of the Tredegar's ordinary working population" (ibid., 28). The other part of the industrial need for labor was remedied by the slave and free black labor force. Quickly understanding southern racial attitudes and American racial relations, Irish and German laborers refused to work alongside black menial laborers and, instead, were trained for the semiskilled and skilled jobs in industrial factories. Frequently, they filled the overseer and supervisory positions over slaves and free black laborers, although there were usually no discernible differences in their skills.

Slavery was the connection between the agricultural production of plantations and the manufacturing and shipping processes of the industrial cities. Black laborers, mostly slaves, although some blacks were free factory workers, were primarily trained for the unskilled and semiskilled positions with the primary exception of tobacco factories, where they were also trained as skilled laborers. Just as there were intraclass tensions between the old established elite and the new industrialists, there were working-class tensions between black and white laborers. As more slaves poured into Richmond's factories, their presence exacerbated the apprehensions of white laborers, who failed to form coalitions with black workers. When white workers, despite their working-class status, bought into the ideology of white supremacy maintained by the elite, they also believed that black workers were their enemies and that slave laborers would be used to undercut their wages and their overall position in the labor market.

Richmond's fifty-two tobacco factories, of which forty-nine produced the popular chewing tobacco, relied almost totally on slave labor ("Federal Industrial Manuscript Census"). Just as slaves worked in the cash crop production of tobacco, black men, women, and children were at the manufacturing and processing end as well. "By the mid-1850s," Rachleff notes, "3,400 slaves worked in the city's tobacco factories" (1984, 6). The growth in the number of slaves in factory production continued, and, as John O'Brien notes, "tobacco factories in 1860 employed 3,364 men and boys, most of whom were slaves, and in this year the entire male slave population of the city stood at 6,636" (1978, 511). If we consider the larger role that slaves played in tobacco factories, approximately 12,843 slaves worked in these factories in Richmond, Lynchburg, and Petersburg, primarily employed in processing "plug," "twist," and smoking tobacco for domestic and European consumption (Kerr-Ritchie 1999, 19).

In the main, two types of tobacco-processing factories utilized the bulk of slave laborers. One type treated and repackaged tobacco for European shipment. Slaves in these factories worked as steamers, prizers, pickers, and shippers; here they dried the tobacco, removed the midrib sections, made the leaves more pliable by moisturizing them, redried them, and finally placed them in the hogshead for shipment (Rachleff 1984, 6–7). The second type of tobacco processing was for "plug" and "twist" chewing tobacco. Although the processing was very similar to that of the first type, here slaves flavored the tobacco leaves with licorice, sugar, and rum and then dried them. This process was then followed by the skilled process of "lumping" the tobacco into uniform rectangular shapes or "twisting" it into rolls. Slaves were also responsible for running the hydraulic presses that pressed the "plugs" into uniform size, firmness, and appearance, and slave women, usually employed as steamers and pickers, were also assigned to affix the labels and package the final product (Rachleff 1984, 6–7).

The seventy-seven iron foundries in Richmond, machine shops, forges, and rolling mills also utilized a great deal of slave labor, which ultimately contributed to the industry's expansion. As Joseph R. Anderson, head of Tredegar Iron Works, began to develop his iron establishment, he realized that slave laborers were essential to lowering his production cost, enabling him to compete with northern and European manufacturers. Although Anderson as well as other iron foundry owners employed northern and immigrant skilled laborers, their high labor costs cut into the profit margins of these manufacturers, who were at a serious disadvantage when competing with northern and European manufacturers for government and business contracts.

In 1842, Anderson solved his problem by purchasing and hiring slaves as skilled laborers. As Anderson sought to introduce slaves in the skilled positions of puddlers, heaters, and rollers, in the rolling mills formerly reserved for white employees, a labor dispute arose between Anderson and his white workers. White laborers, believing that Anderson would eventually replace them with slave labor and already racially antagonistic to black workers, went on strike on May 22, 1847. The workers' goal was "to prohibit the employment of colored people in the said Works" (*Richmond Times and Compiler*, May 28, 1847). Anderson met the challenge of his white laborers by claiming that they had "fired themselves," forcing him to bring in skilled black laborers in the Tredegar and Armory rolling mills.

The southern and northern press quickly took sides in the growing dispute. The southern press, led by the *Richmond Enquirer* on May 29, 1847, rallied behind Anderson and supported the right of masters to do whatever they desired with their property or slaves would be rendered "utterly valueless." The northern press, circumventing the race and slavery issues, focused instead on the class question concerning the white workers and Anderson. According to the northern press, because the southern aristocracy viewed all laborers as inferior, it failed to realize that these wage laborers feared the loss of their jobs, the humiliation of working alongside black workers, or being replaced by them. While the southern press centered on the question of slavery and the rights of slave owners and northerners focused on the class issues, both denied their own racism and elitism as well as that of the white workers.

With the support of the southern press as well as other members of the planter-industrialist elite, Anderson broke the strike and purchased and employed black male and female workers in the foundry for ten-hour shifts. The incentive for slave men, women, and children who worked in the tobacco, flour, and iron industries was that they could earn overtime wages for themselves. Charles Dey's *Ironmaker to the Confederacy: Joseph R. Anderson and the Tredegar Iron Works* indicates that slave labor reduced Anderson's production cost by 12 percent (1966, 30). By the early 1850s, "the Tredegar and Armory works employed 100 slaves in a labor force totaling approximately 250 men" (26).

Despite a growing apprehension on the part of some of Richmond's leaders of the increasing use of slave labor in the city's factories, by the late 1840s slaves and free blacks were integral to the city's economy. And

Richmond, sparked by the increasing emphasis on industrialization, was becoming more ethnically diverse. From 1820 to 1860, the large influx of white immigrants combined with the slaves and the free black population tripled the total population of the city. By 1860, the white population had increased from 6,445 to 23,635; the slave population underwent similar growth, increasing from 4,387 to 11,699; and free blacks increased from 1,235 to 2,576 (Wade 1964, 327–30; O'Brien 1978, 511).

By the 1850s, Richmond was developing the race and class tensions typical of most industrializing cities. In a city already marked by the competition between mercantilists and industrialists vying for political and economic power was the prevailing tensions between black and white workers. There was the perennial fear among Irish and German immigrants, working in the same tobacco factories and iron foundries as free blacks and slaves, that blacks could always be used by the employers to displace white workers. As they had learned in their strike against Tredegar Iron Works, there was no support for the white working class against the industrial elite in Richmond, leaving them in a weak bargaining position for wages and job-related grievances.

The city's fathers, on the other hand, fearing black and white workers' solidarity, sought to empower working-class white males by granting universal white manhood suffrage in Virginia's new constitutional system of 1851. As elites were forming racial and political alliances with white working-class laborers, they stifled working-class consciousness between blacks and whites. If black and white workers coalesced around common concerns that they had as workers, they would challenge the planter-industrialist elite who controlled their lives. For the city's elite, as well as the rest of Virginia's aristocracy, their power and hegemony rested on the division of black and white workers and the racial subjugation of blacks. The political enfranchisement of white male workers came at the critical juncture when these workers were pressing the elite for economic gains, posing a threat to the class system. As historian Leon F. Litwack notes, "In several states the adoption of white manhood suffrage led directly to the political disfranchisement of the Negro" (1961, 75). In Virginia, the granting of universal white male suffrage when a majority of the white males in the state were not slaveholders thwarted solidarity between black and white workers and contributed to the inferior status of both free and enslaved blacks.

In 1852, the Jordan Hatcher case exacerbated the underlying tensions in the city. Jordan Hatcher, a seventeen-year-old slave, was employed as a steamer, separating the harsh midrib from the tobacco leaf, in the Walker and Harris tobacco factory. Having already been warned earlier in the week that he was keeping dirty stems on his workbench, his second warning cost him a whipping from his nineteen-year-old overseer, William P. Jackson. When Hatcher's entreaties failed to stop the beating, he began to resist. What both young men understood was that "the lash in the white hand on the black back was a symbol of bondage recognized by both races" (Wade 1964, 186). Jackson, perceiving Hatcher's resistance as impudence and a threat to his authority, gave Hatcher another cowhide whipping determined to put him in his place. "In the ensuing scuffle, Hatcher struck Jackson on the head with an iron poker that was close at hand and then fled the scene, hiding out for three days in a nearby stable before he was apprehended" (Link 1998, 622). After Jackson's death several days later, due in part to the doctor's failure to provide appropriate medical attention for his wounds, Hatcher was tried and convicted of first-degree murder and sentenced to be hung on April 23 of that same year.

During the period of case review by Governor Johnson, the city polarized into factions. Some of Richmond's business community members who shared the widespread sentiments of the Virginia Colonization Society that blacks should be removed from the state to West Africa advocated a commutation of Hatcher's death sentence to sale and transportation to the Deep South. Others, mostly tobacco manufacturers, sought the death penalty, believing that Hatcher's death would set an example for other blacks and curb their growing insubordination in the factories and in the city. On May 7, 1852, two thousand white male workers protested the governor's decision to commute Hatcher's death sentence and sell him to Louisiana. On the surface, the workers were proclaiming that Jackson's murder had not received adequate punishment, but their underlying reason was that "these apprentices competed for jobs with Richmond's hired slaves, and many of the young men in the mob were probably factory overseers—like the slain William Jackson—who felt threatened by the erosion of their authority over slaves" (Link 1998, 627). The Hatcher case crystallized existing racial and class tensions on one hand, and, on the other, the resistance to white authority by the growing number of blacks in the city.

The Antebellum Black Richmond Community

The utilization of a large population of free black and slave labor in Richmond's industrializing process created the material conditions for several emerging factors: (1) the coexistence of urban and plantation resistance until emancipation, (2) an embryonic working-class consciousness among blacks that took root in the antebellum era and flowered in the 1870s, and (3) the development of the critical institutions of family, church, and mutual benevolent societies—"secret societies"—in the antebellum free black community that laid the foundation for their freedom immediately after the liberation of the slaves by northern troops in Richmond in April 1865.

Although slave workers were integral to the city's industrial development and experienced a tentative independence vastly different from their plantation counterparts, they still resisted their enslavement in various ways. As slave workers became urbanized and more familiar with the city of Richmond and the various systems of transportation, established contacts in the grogshops and other neighborhood shops, and were able to choose where they wanted to live, they gained considerable independence. In addition, "shops also grew up that catered to Negroes. Sometimes these were run by free colored, sometimes by whites, and even occasionally by slaves" (Wade 1964, 134). Most slaves saw this new independence as leading to freedom. Either individually or through the Underground Railroad, many urban slaves became runaways and were a significant part of black urban resistance. "In Richmond," Wade notes, "they used hackney coaches and the railroads, in the river towns steamboats provided handy escapes; and everywhere bondsmen, feigning errands, took wagons and drays as getaway vehicles" (215).

This loss of slave property frequently created a ripple effect, and masters became increasingly alarmed as other slaves were emboldened to make a break for freedom. One Richmond master saw slave escapees "not only in the loss of property, but in the effects [they] perceptively ha[d] on those who remain behind" (*Richmond Enquirer,* Nov. 26, 1833). Southern newspaper editors, in their advocacy of the slave system, invariably saw free blacks or white abolitionists in their midst as responsible for encouraging slave runaways. In the 1830s, when more than twenty slaves disappeared in a single weekend, the editor of the *Richmond Enquirer* commented that "there is a regular system for removing them. Depend on it, some infamous whites are concerned in it" (*Richmond Enquirer,* Dec. 26, 1833). Abolitionist agitation gained momentum in the 1850s, and slave fugitives kept apace. One Richmond editor, also of the *Richmond Enquirer,* was convinced of an organized network of agitators in the city. "There is little doubt that there are agents in this city who are in communication with the North and have every facility for running off slaves," he declared (*Richmond Enquirer,* Feb. 15, 1855).

Proslavery apologists were in a bind as they sought to deal with the growing number of slave fugitives. On one hand, they touted the docility and contentment of slaves, and on the other, they castigated the abolitionists for creating slave restlessness that led to the growing numbers of escapees. In the former instance, if slaves were happy with their lot, there would be no reason to escape, and in the latter instance, if they were escaping in increasing numbers, this fact belied their contentment. Regardless of which leg they stood on, proslavery apologists could not escape the fact that slave escapes required planning, organization, and courage, all attributes that were supposed to be in short supply among slaves. Their rationale notwithstanding, proslavery apologists were unable to stop this growing internal problem, and it was threatening to destabilize the system. Unwilling to examine slavery and the horrors it engendered, slaveholders were consistently forced to place the blame for slave fugitives elsewhere.

Although one white woman saw slave resistance as a product of outside agitation, she nevertheless described the escape method employed by domestic servants:

> There was unquestionably an underground agency to decoy away our negro servants, or to assist any who meditated flight from their owners. Thefts of the most provoking character were everywhere perpetrated, usually under circumstances which pointed to family domestics as the perpetrators. . . . The store room or pantry of the citizen, or a gentleman's or lady's wardrobe would be plundered and the articles mysteriously disappear and all efforts of the police to discover the thief or the destination of the missing goods would generally prove unavailing, to be followed in a short time by the singular disappearance of one or more of the domestics of the robbed establishments, to be heard of no more in Richmond. (Rachleff 1984, 10)

William Still of Philadelphia, dubbed the "father of the Underground Railroad," recorded the circumstances that led Miles Robinson, a slave hireling in Richmond, to contact an agent on the Underground, plan his escape, and arrive at Still's home:

> Hearing that he was to be sold, he conferred not with his mother, brothers, or sisters (for such he had living as slaves in Richmond) but resolved to escape by the first convenience. Turning his attention to the Underground Rail Road, he soon found an agent who communicated his wishes to one of the colored women running as cook or chambermaid on one of the Philadelphia and Richmond steamers, and she was bold enough to take charge of

him, and found him a safe berth in one of the closets where the pots and other cooking utensils belonged. (Still 1970, 563)

Whereas some slaves protested against their slave status by running away, others resisted the system by circumventing the laws that circumscribed their existence. Because whites feared the camaraderie between slaves and free blacks, there were statutes that prohibited their association. Such associations were difficult to control in the city, enabling slaves, seeking a family life, relationships, and enduring ties, to move into Richmond's free black community. The "bonus" or "overtime" monies received by urban slaves working in factories contributed to the vitality of the free black community in innumerable ways. Many slaves rented rooms or spaces from other blacks, purchased provisions in the community, patronized the grogshops, became affiliated with one of the black churches, or belonged to one or more of the community's "secret societies," sustaining the community's growth and development.

Capital accumulation by both slaves and free blacks led to the founding of the critical institutions of family, church, and "secret societies." With the steady income gained from overtime work, many slaves were able to purchase themselves and family members. Even though Richmond slaveholders manumitted 352 slaves in the antebellum era, from 1831 to 1860, most slaves gained their freedom by running away or through self-purchase. Subsequent to gaining their freedom, some former slaves sought to accumulate real estate, often with the legal title resting in some white person's name (Jackson 1942, 174, 181). "By 1860 seventy-one free Negroes in Richmond held property of a minimum value of $1000. . . . Fifteen of these, by frequent purchases of real estate, accumulated property worth $4000 or $5000" (151).

The purchase of real estate by blacks in Richmond led to the black community's expansion and development. This small group of free property owners would form the core of Richmond's black elite after emancipation. Slave and free artisans and entrepreneurs had easier access to property accumulation than did factory workers. As skilled workers, artisans and entrepreneurs had managed to get a modicum of informal or formal education, thereby creating more opportunities for themselves. Whereas owners of livery stables proved the most lucrative in purchasing real estate, barbers, shopkeepers, restaurant proprietors, confectioners, contractors, and some tobacco factory workers also were successful in buying property. Although black men bought more real estate than did black women, black female seamstresses, nurses, tobacco steamers and washerwomen also purchased urban property (Jackson 1942, 155–58).

Families and churches were the cornerstones in Richmond's black community. Many slaves attempted to have some semblance of a family life and married other slaves or free blacks as they lived with the tentativeness of black life in Richmond. The fact that the city was known for its lucrative slave markets, free blacks frequently being fair game as well, made blacks even more determined to have a family life. Within the family constellation, children were socialized in the African American culture of survival. Circumventing the tight restrictions preventing slaves from learning to read and write, many urban slaves learned to read and were able to pass their knowledge on to their children. Very rarely was formal education possible, but free and recently freed blacks strove to acquire a rudimentary education even impressing missionaries coming into the city two weeks after emancipation (Rachleff 1984, 11).

By the 1840s, Richmond's black community began to purchase their own churches, and this assertion of independence and leadership contributed more than any other factor to the community's stability. Black churches were the instruments of black leadership development. Church members could determine elements of the worship service, handle administrative and financial affairs, and establish considerable independence from their denomination, particularly those of the Baptist faith, which encouraged independent churches. Before the 1840s, blacks had wanted to purchase a church, but whites thwarted the initiative, seeing black churches as an opportunity for free blacks and slaves to plan escapes and rebellions. "The Nat Turner revolt greatly heightened the suspicion that religion was a primary factor in slave uprisings," Wilmore notes (1983, 32). Recent memories of Nat Turner (the slave preacher), the Secret Keepers conspiracy that many believed was spearheaded by Gowan Pamphlet (the free black preacher), and the Denmark Vesey rebellion of 1822 in Charleston, South Carolina, were all intertwined in independent black religious worship.

But by the 1840s whites were becoming increasingly uncomfortable in the integrated First Baptist Church in Richmond and were forced to reevaluate their prior stance on black church development. The popular conversion of blacks to the Baptist faith brought these new worshipers to the services at First Baptist in increasing numbers. As the numbers of black church members continue to grow, so did the frustrations of white parishioners. On the one hand, blacks outnumbered whites and were demanding a more energetic worship service, and on the other, white church members feared that this strong black presence thwarted the drive for new white church membership. White members, perceiving black members to be an obstacle to increased white participation, recanted their former stance on black churches and moved expeditiously to clear all of the legal hurdles for blacks to purchase the church for $5,902.08 (Jackson 1942, 161). In 1841, the prominent First African Baptist Church was founded with the legal stipulation that the supervising overseers and minister, Reverend Robert Ryland, had to be white.

Although the church's infrastructure was designed to placate white apprehensions, the all-black board of deacons that handled all church administrative matters gave blacks considerable independence. The disputes among members, marriage counseling, financial planning, internal church improvement, and the induction of new members were handled by the deacons (O'Brien 1978, 523–29; Jackson 1942, 161). Because the white overseers provided sporadic supervision at best and the minister was advised as often as he gave advice to the congregation, the influence of the black deacons was pervasive. Although there was valid criticism among slave members that only free blacks were given broad administrative duties in the church, the First African Baptist Church and all subsequent black churches created opportunities for the development and honing of the leadership skills of black men. As the authority of black deacons spread in the community, the black church became recognized as a training ground for black male leadership. With the establishment of the hierarchy of black male leadership, directly under the white minister, black women found it difficult to gain influential positions in the black church. In the postbellum era, tensions around the ecclesiastical sexism of black men, as black women sought decision-making positions, would erupt in one of Richmond's churches (see chapter 2).

The growth of First African Baptist Church precipitated black church institutional development in Richmond. Undoubtedly, the worship service, the Bible classes, the benevolent societies, the choir, which was already gaining a broad reputation, and the "liberating atmosphere" were contributing factors. By the late 1850s, slaves and free blacks swelled the membership rolls of the church to more than three thousand members. This overcrowding led to the founding of Second African Baptist Church in 1847 and Ebenezer Church in 1856 (O'Brien 1978, 526–27; Jackson 1942, 161). "Separate black churches—mainly Baptist due to the congregational independence of that denomination—sprang up not only in the North, where emancipation gave blacks more leeway to organize institutionally, but also in the South, where an increasingly entrenched slave system made any kind of black autonomy seem subversive" (Raboteau 1997, 92).

Because all southern whites remained chary of black churches, these churches were forced to navigate the tenuous terrain of placating white society while creating a subtle black resistance to oppression. These churches were forced to take on the outward manifestations of compliance while shaping their activities and programs to meet the needs of the community. These black churches provided a covert forum for slaves and free blacks to criticize slavery. "Mirroring the communities they served, the churches enabled blacks to celebrate themselves as a collectivity, and they provided the protective space whereby each could contend with the other about common concerns" (Gravely 1997, 140). Black Richmonders were interested not only in criticizing slavery but also in utilizing their resentment against the system to create covert paths of support for slaves and resistance.

Richmond's black churches also provided covert sanctuaries of support for resistance. Runaways were not expelled from the church, as they were in integrated churches, perhaps sending subtle encouragement to other slaves who were contemplating a bid for freedom. Reverend Ryland, the white minister of First African Baptist Church, established a mailing system for runaways to remain in contact with other church members as well as to provide them with details of the best escape routes to freedom (O'Brien 1978, 534–35). There were other elements of resistance as well. Ryland himself circumvented the 1831 law against black literacy and preaching by distributing Bibles and religious materials among church members, establishing a lending library, and allowing black ministers to preach by calling on them to "pray" (532). Overt resistance had tentative ties to the church as well. Jane Williams, a slave woman who murdered two members of her master's family, was an active member of the First African Baptist Church.

Black churches expressed solidarity and independence by purchasing freedom for its members, creating networking and financial assistance to churches in other cities, and establishing charitable societies to aid the poor. In Richmond, black churches collectively pooled their resources to purchase the freedom of the "slave deacon Thomas Allen and the slave families of two free-black preachers to enable the three to embark on missionary work outside the South" (O'Brien 1978, 531). The First African established a broad-based network of contact and financial support with fledgling Virginia churches and other black churches as far away as Canada (O'Brien 1978, 531; Raboteau 1997, 93). Black Baptist churches in Richmond also supported the missionary work in Africa led by Reverend Lott Carey, a slave minister from Richmond (Wilmore 1983, 105). In this way, Richmond's black churches stayed connected to both the northern and the African churches during the antebellum era, which facilitated their transition to freedom after the Civil War.

Black Richmonders, who had few social outlets, founded "secret societies" that facilitated the transition to urban life and strengthened the coping mechanisms needed to navigate the daily labyrinth of racial discrimination, slavery, and social ostracism. These societies provided for those crises in community members' lives and would greatly expand their purpose, type, and functioning in the late 1860s. In the 1850s, the Poor Saints Committee of the First African Baptist Church contributed more than two thousand dollars to assist both slaves and free blacks in the community. Frequently, these societies were ancillaries of black churches and provided another form of mobilization and resistance to domination and control in Richmond's black community. The plethora of secret societies that flourished immediately after the Civil War suggests that a majority of them were founded during the antebellum era.

The colonial era marked the beginning of the African presence in Virginia. Within a decade of their arrival, the construction of a slave society had been implemented. The combination of laws, statutes, the global slave trade, the paucity of labor, fertile land, and the avarice of the colonists for wealth and prosperity were all factors in the enslavement of Africans. Slave labor stimulated Virginia's economy ultimately sustaining a planter elite as well as the subsequent antebellum industrializing process in Richmond and other Virginia cities. The preponderance of slave labor in Richmond's factories transplanted many slaves from plantation to urban slavery and, ultimately, one step closer to freedom.

But Africans brought more than their agricultural labor to the Virginia colony. Their protracted resistance to enslavement, their challenge to oppression, and their conspiracies and rebellions shaped the colony as much as their agricultural expertise did. Whereas the American Revolution did little to alleviate the plight of Virginia slaves, and indeed led to plantation expansion, the Haitian Revolution inspired free-black and slave resistance. Resistance evolved into disparate forms, taking place on plantations and urban centers, as blacks transplanted their struggle for freedom wherever they found themselves. In Richmond, where the rigid plantation codes of behavior were no longer applicable, "race became more important than legal status; and a pattern of segregation emerged inside the broader framework of the peculiar institution" (Wade 1964, 266). In the efforts of blacks to stem the tide of slavery and social segregation, they drew on religion, which had sustained them in the fields, as a catalyst for resistance in the urban center.

"Blow Ye the Trumpet, Blow"

The colored people from all parts of the state was crowding
in at the capital, running, leaping, and praising God that
freedom had come at last. It seems to me that I can hear
their songs now as they rung through the air: "Slavery chain
done broke at last; slavery chain done broke at last—I's goin'
to praise God till I die."

Rev. Peter Randolph, 1893

CHURCH, SOCIETIES, AND COMMUNITY

For the majority of blacks, emancipation brought the first taste of freedom on America's shores. Now, following nearly 250 years of enslavement, black men and women could reclaim their hope and dignity,
search for loved ones who had been lost in the slave system, establish
familial and community relationships, and take on the mantle of
freedom. In spite of the fact that the Emancipation Proclamation had
been signed by President Lincoln, freeing slaves on January 1, 1863, slavery did not end in Richmond until the city fell to the Union troops on
April 3, 1865. Nevertheless, freedom brought indescribable joy to the
oppressed. Fannie Berry, a former slave from Virginia, recalled those early
moments of freedom: "The colored regiment came up behind and when
they saw the colored regiment they put up the white flag-Yo' 'member
fo' dis red or bloody flag was up—Now, do you know why dey raised dat
white flag? (No, tell me why.) Well, honey, dat white flag wuz' a token
dat Lee had surrendered" (Perdue, Barden, and Philips 1976, 38).

Another black woman, hearing the news on a plantation in nearby
Yorktown, Virginia, waited to express her joy in secret away from the
prying eyes of whites:

I jump up an' scream, "Glory, glory, hallelujah to Jesus! I's free, I's free! Glory to God, you come down an' free us; no big man could do it." An' I got sort o' scared, afeared somebody hear me, an' I takes another good look, an' fall on de groun', and roll over, an' kiss de groun' for de Lord's sake, I's so full o' praise to Masser Jesus. He do all dis great work. De soul buyers can nebber take my two chillen lef' me; no, nebber can tak 'em from me no mo'. (Haviland 1881, 414–15)

The joy of black Richmonders was coupled with the determination to create family life while they simultaneously solidified and expanded their cultural institutions. This proved to be a herculean task as they now confronted a hostile and war-torn city. Richmond was economically devastated following the burning of its business district, and overall the southern market economy was making slow recovery. There were already signs that black progress would be thwarted and compromised by the former Confederate soldiers and officials who lost the war. The very hierarchical racial structure upon which slavery rested was in total disarray. For centuries, the credo of wealth, property, and slavery were pseudo-aristocratic trappings that shaped the lives of industrialists, slaveholders, and the old established planters. Nor could one easily escape the psychological superiority that white supremacy afforded southerners who no matter what their social status could dominate and control blacks. Now, this life-style, in most instances their raison d'être, was undergoing transition and transformation. To have lost the war and your future generations fighting in a lost cause was humiliating enough, but to daily confront "free blacks" who were demanding equality and political inclusion galled these ardent southerners.

The doctrine of white supremacy in Richmond had to be transformed so that white southerners could still maintain domination and control over blacks while they exploited their labor in order to resuscitate the southern economy. Black Richmonders, who wanted to preserve their newly won freedom, had to engage the system on political terms, demanding participation and inclusion into the body politic. By reconstructing and expanding their antebellum cultural institutions, black Richmonders were able to use their churches, fraternal organizations, mutual benevolent societies, and secret political unions to spearhead the political and social mobilization of the community. Gamson informs us that "mobilization is a process of increasing the readiness to act collectively by building the loyalty of a constituency to an organization or a group of leaders" (1975, 15).

The incipient political mobilization of Richmond's African American community following emancipation rested upon the black leadership and cultural institutional formation achieved in the antebellum era. This tiny black elite group of antebellum leaders purchased their freedom or were free-born, were self-employed or slave artisans, and were able to accumulate property during the period from 1840 to 1860 (Jackson 1942, 142, 145). Lott Carey, a black slave minister from Richmond, was typical of this group. Through Carey's work "as foreman in a tobacco factory he was able to buy first his own freedom and later that of the members of his family. During this process he also bought a small farm on the outskirts of Richmond for $693" (145). Through the coalition of slaves and free blacks and the collective pooling of their resources, African Americans in Richmond reestablished and expanded black churches and societies that survived the antebellum era, slavery, and the Civil War.

In the decade following emancipation, class alignments became more pronounced. Members of the rising middle class were self-employed, had some education, and had accumulated property either in the antebellum era or soon after emancipation. This tiny black elite was in marked contrast to the masses of black laborers who worked in Richmond's factories, flour mills, quarries, and foundries, and in households of the increasingly affluent whites. As more native Richmonders returned after the war and other blacks migrated to the city seeking opportunities, and still others were on a perennial search for family members, the expansion of the black community's church and societal affiliation broadened the base of middle-class and working-class leadership. A leadership base was usually established by gainful employment, membership and position of influence in one of the local black churches, membership in one or more of the societies, and strong community activism for progressive change.

Black women's base of leadership was most often tied to the family, church, work, and community activism. Black women's experiences and leadership paths were very different in slavery and proved very different in the transition to freedom. Doug McAdam reminds us that there were differential experiences of male and female activists in the later civil rights movement and one must deconstruct them in gaining an understanding of gender differences (1992, 1140–1211). Black female Richmonders gained influence by exhibiting strong moral character, providing a cohesive family unit, and being a working member of the church and generally affiliated with several church and community societies. Most, if not all, black women worked as household domestics or factory laborers to augment family income. Since most families were either extended families or had taken in boarders to supplement house-hold income, women performed the double duty of caring for both the home and the boarders. Black women who were held in high esteem in church and societal associations, and often participated as grass-roots organizers, found that their influence paved the way for the rest of their "family unit" in church and community affairs. From the beginning moments of freedom, black women defined the community as an exten-sion of their homes and believed that race and gender struggles were inseparable.

The black church provided the institutional framework for the spiri-tual and secular mobilization of Richmond's black community. Having survived the ordeal of slavery and the trauma of the Civil War, Rich-mond's black churches were a beacon of light to slaves, particularly as the war entered its last desperate stages. Aiding in the resettlement of blacks, the churches provided a sense of community, unity, and purpose. By fusing race consciousness, religion, and politics, the black church became the bulwark against oppression as it promoted unity among its followers. "The independent church movement among blacks, during and following the period of the Revolutionary War," Gayraud Wilmore states, "must be regarded as the prime expression of resistance to slav-ery—in every sense, the first black freedom movement" (Wilmore 1983, 78). Richmond's black churches, five of which were founded during the antebellum era, laid the foundation for black spiritual, social, and polit-ical development.

After emancipation, the churches grew and expanded to service the tremendous influx of blacks coming in to the Richmond area for jobs, looking for "a church home," searching for family members, and hoping to rekindle former ties with long-lost friends. In the midst of the chaos and confusion, blacks had a profound need for spirituality and to thank God for their "deliverance." Freedom reinforced blacks' belief in biblical redemption, that "He had brought them through the storm." It was this "sacred view" of the cosmos, sustained over centuries of enslavement, that caused the black church to remain at the center of community life, providing sanctuary for a weary people. Thus, black Richmonders giving praise on Sunday morning that included sermons, prayers, songs, spon-taneous exhortations, camp meetings, and revivals, all affirmed their long journey to freedom.

The church served a multiplicity of functions in the black commu-nity. For urban slaves in Richmond, working primarily in the tobacco factories, quarries, flour mills, iron foundries, artisan shops, and nearby small farms, the black church concretized their new freedom and independence in family and community life. One of the church's primary functions was to strengthen black family life by encouraging the mass wedding ceremonies that took place as slave couples reaffirmed their informal marital commitment to each other. These relationships played a pivotal role in family development, the socialization of children, and securing the foundation of community life.

As the black church became institutionalized in the postbellum era, it quickly grew into an autonomous institution with a clear mission to the community. Blacks "seized control of their churches by June 1865, named new pastors, and used church buildings for schools, employment offices, and staging areas for organizing public protests and celebrations" (O'Brien 1978, 535). Embedded in this institutionalization process was the construction of a black male hierarchy. Black men assumed the leadership roles in the church—not only the clergy but also the two dozen or more deacon positions in each church. The men who took these positions were the most influential and prominent members of the community and were perceived as the moral arbiters of church and community life. They arbitrated disputes among church members, settled questions after hearings on marriage and divorce, determined membership admission procedures, expelled backsliders, and decided on the readmission of repentant sinners (O'Brien 1978, 528–30). Although the ministerial leadership had to have broad-based church and community support, they effectively regulated church policy and social and legal disputes for people who were reluctant to engage the legal system.

Utilizing the meager revenues that came from the weekly contribution of members, periodic fund-raisers generated by black women, and fees charged for political meetings, forums, and debates, the black church created a secular program that touched every aspect of the community's social, political, and economic life. Some of the larger black churches in Richmond maintained independent schools for children and adults to raise the literacy level in the community and foster self-improvement. Since former slaves were hungry for education, these schools were usually overcrowded. As missionaries arrived in Richmond under Union occupation, they supplemented a "literacy campaign" that had been in existence since the 1840s. Missionaries quickly noted this campaign: "The colored people of Richmond are far more intelligent and thrifty than any I have met with in the South—and though the laws against learning have been so strict, many can read and a large portion know their letters and can spell a little" (Swint 1966, 155).

Churches believed their role was not only to provide for the immediate community's spiritual needs but also to spread the gospel. The missionary work of evangelical Christianity was threefold: to provide for those in dire need in Richmond, to promote hunger programs abroad, and to spread the gospel worldwide. Africa inspired a missionary crusade for the most resolute missionaries. Although "African fever" would infuse the black church in the 1880s, missionary work to Africa had long inspired black Richmonders. Reverend Lott Carey, a native slave minister of Richmond who took emigrants to Liberia in 1821 under the auspices of the African Baptist Missionary Society and the General Baptist Missionary Convention, had inspired many who saw a way to maintain an African connection while spreading the gospel. "Carey founded churches that were supported by the Baptists of Richmond," Wilmore notes. "In 1815, he had organized the original African Missionary Society of Richmond and raised seven hundred dollars for its work. . . . The Baptists of Richmond, with whom he kept in close contact, were stirred by the prospect of missionary emigrationism in Africa" (1983, 105–6).

The black church had a salutary effect upon the development of African Americans' political and social consciousness. They fostered political activity in the community by providing political forums to educate the masses, held protest meetings to collectively mobilize the community around key issues, and held political debates to galvanize support around a common agenda. In the transition from slavery to freedom, the African American community was being transformed into a political and social entity.

As former slaves picked up the fragments of their lives, and as most acquired jobs they had held during slavery, they quickly realized that freedom and struggle were intertwined. The more they struggled for political inclusion, the more elusive freedom became. Their initial demands for the repeal of slave laws that hampered their movement, and their subsequent political inclusion, pitted them against the occupied forces and the rapidly reconstituting southern elite under the new Conservative party. Already there were signs that blacks were being segregated into Jackson Ward, which would be legally done in 1871, to marginalize their voting power and affect the city's and state's electorate.

Mutual benevolent societies, fraternal orders, social organizations, and incipient labor and political unions served as the social and economic ancillaries of the black church. This intricate, latticed network of organizations that permeated the community laid its economic foundation by providing club members with mutual assistance as well as support for the medically indigent and impoverished. "As Richmond's most prominent church, the First African Baptist generated the greatest number of such secret societies," notes Rachleff (1984, 15). Despite the hue and cry raised by the *Richmond Enquirer* and *Norfolk American Beacon* over the proliferation of these "secret societies" during the antebellum era, there were hundreds of them in the postbellum period (*Richmond Enquirer,* June 3, 1854; *Norfolk American Beacon,* Apr. 21, 22, 25, 1854). In the decade following emancipation, "black Richmond was honeycombed with more than 400 such societies, which reached into its every corner and touched every sphere of activity" (Rachleff 1984, 25).

Black Richmonders, who had few social outlets, found that these voluntary associations facilitated their transition to urban life as well as strengthened the coping mechanisms needed to navigate the treacherous terrain of racial discrimination, social ostracism, and potential disfranchisement. Such societies provided for crises in members' lives, such as sickness, economic distress, and, in case of death, funeral expenses and widows' benefits. The vibrancy of these societies came to the attention of the white press when one benevolent society, the United Sons of Love, conducted an elaborate funeral possession for one of its members a year after emancipation (*Richmond Republic,* Jan. 22, 1866). The economic umbrella that these societies provided not only mitigated the harshness of members' lives but financed significant funeral rituals, believed by some of these former slaves to take their spirits back to Africa.

Watkins argues that black voluntary associations were critical in providing a stabilizing influence in black communities undergoing the socioeconomic shifts in society (Watkins 1990, 51–56). For Richmond's black community, these societies offered tranquility in the seismic political and economic chaos engendered by the Civil War. In conjunction with the black church, these societies reduced the alienation associated with urban living, particularly for newcomers or those returning to the area following the war. Members also responded to the camaraderie, the sharing of resources, the debates on prominent contemporary issues, and the establishment of enduring social ties, which was, in many instances, reflective of the extended kinship network system typical of many African and former slave communities.

Church-related societies such as the Christian Union Aid Society, the Pilgrim Travelers, Soldiers of the Cross, and the First Star of Jacob were affiliated specifically with one of the local churches and focused on church maintenance and charity work. Although some of these societies were "promiscuous," including both males and females, just as many were gender-based. Black women's church organizations such as the Female Soldiers of the Cross, the Female Star of Jacob, Daughters of the Golden Rod, and Daughters of Jerusalem, served as women's auxiliaries or female societies. Even where there were mixed-gender societies (such as the prominent Golden Rule Society, founded by members of the First African Baptist Church in 1872) and men filled some leadership positions, women clearly played the dominant role in fund-raising activities (Records of the First African Baptist Church; Records of Freedman's Savings Bank). In fact, black women dominated fund-raising activities for both church and community.

The growth of many of these societies depended on the organizational expertise of blacks who had worked as slaves or free labor in antebellum Richmond, had been members of a black church and a "secret society," had survived the traumas of war, and had directed the expansion of these affiliations after the war. The Secret Sons of Love, United Daughters of Love, and Mutual Benevolent Society were beneficial societies that provided death benefits for widows and children and funerals for the deceased. True Laboring Class, No. 1; the National Laboring Club; the Railroad Helpers; the Bailey Factory Hands; Combined Industrial Society, No. 35; and Laborer's Association, No. 55 functioned as both benevolent and trade-union associations, furnishing sickness and death benefits as well as unemployment benefits. Membership in these organizations was trade-specific, and meetings were held on job conditions and work-related activities.

Philip Banks, for example, was an officer in the National Laboring Club. He had been a slave in Richmond during the 1840s and joined the First African Baptist Church as a youngster. Following the war, Banks, still living with his family, became a tobacco factory worker. Although John Henry Dixon had been born free in antebellum Richmond, his experiences were similar to those of Banks. Dixon's family were also members of the First African Baptist Church, and he and his brother, George, became tobacco factory workers following emancipation. While John moved into the tobacco trade society, his brother, George, joined the politically oriented Union Bengal Aid society and became active in the Republican party (Rachleff 1984, 28).

Political societies were vital to sustaining the freedom of the African American community by placing the community's political grievances before the Richmond City Council, the Virginia General Assembly, and the Republican party. Predominantly strivers and activists, these groups held a fair number of the rising black middle class among its members. Bandleader and carpenter Elijah W. Dabney, for example, was an officer in the Union Liberty Protective Society, and by the 1870s he had purchased a home in Jackson Ward (Rachleff 1984, 31). The Rising Sons of Liberty, the Rising Daughters of Liberty, and the Rising Sons of America were among the political societies that spearheaded political awareness in the community. Most of these societies had ties to the Republican party, whose radical wing initially courted black male voters, although the relationship would steadily deteriorate over time.

While black women were denied suffrage, it did not exclude them from political participation, and they made their mark on the political spectrum in campaigning for candidates, educating the community around the issues, organizing political fund-raisers and voter mobilization, and bridging the gap between political, benevolent, and church societies. Black women also participated in all of the mass political activities in the Richmond community, including protest marches, the rescue of prisoners from the police, and the integration of the city's streetcars. In the formal arena, black men, women, and children participated in the constitutional convention deliberations of the Republican party in 1867, which shaped the Underwood constitution of 1869.

EARLY MOBILIZATION EFFORTS

The early mobilization efforts of Richmond's black community was around the common grievance of the "pass system." The "pass system," which had been a slave law to limit their mobility, was now reinstated for Richmond's free black citizens and perceived clearly as a law of racial subordination. Its resurgence emphasized the economic and political collusion between the federal occupying forces, state legislators, and white employers who wanted to control this pool of available cheap labor. Morrison notes that the response of blacks to "restrictive elements" is collective because the stigmatization is against the entire group: "Blacks, more often than not, do not have the option to act individually, since the assertion of inferiority is collective" (1987, 5). Tilly argues that groups "defensively mobilize" when they perceive "a threat from outside (that) induces the members of a group to pool their resources to fight off the enemy" (1978, 11). In protesting against the pass system, blacks were seeking to eradicate the law and create an influential base in the body politic.

The pass system was an egregious affront to the entire black community, yet it was especially acute for former slaves who were searching for family members, self-employed contractors who frequently moved about the city, or common laborers going to and from the city's factories and workshops. Workshops and factories were frequently inspected for system violators. Citizens caught without passes were arrested, imprisoned in the "negro bull pen," or hired out as common laborers in the city. Even black citizens visiting Richmond experienced the same fate. John Oliver, a black visitor from Boston, stopped to look at the "bull pen" and found himself on a perilous journey of arrest and imprisonment:

> We stopped to look at it, when I was hailed by a Provost Guard, who without asking for a pass, demanded to know why I was walking in the street. I told him I came to see Richmond. Then he said you will stop here with me. I asked him how long? "Longer than you think for," he replied. He continued to address me in vulgar and abusive language. I showed him my protection from Massachusetts, which I told him "ought to protect me in any part of the world." But he said he did not care for that, and contemptuously spurned it. (Rachleff 1984, 37)

The political spark that galvanized the black community came on June 7, 1865, two months following emancipation, when eight hundred men, women, and children were arrested by the federal occupying forces and local police for failure to carry passes. Community leaders quickly seized the moment to forward a letter of protest to the *New York Tribune* citing two interlocking problems which threatened to disfranchise the community. The larger problem was the restoration by the federal military of the antebellum Richmond oligarchy. Led by Mayor Joseph Mayo, his administration, and his police force, this group, which had diligently enforced the slave system, kept alive the war conflict and abused Union prisoners, was the same group that now terrorized blacks with the pass system. "For a long series of years he has been the Mayor of Richmond," the letter noted, "and his administration has been marked by cruelty and injustice to us, and the old Rebel police now again in power have been our greatest enemies. It was Mayor Mayo who in former days ordered us to be scourged for trifling offenses against the laws and usages; and his present police, who are now hunting us through the streets" (*New York Tribune*, June 17, 1865).

The community quickly mobilized with additional participants so as not to lose the momentum. On June 8, as information was quickly disseminated to the community, additional activists joined the initial leaders in drafting a petition to President Johnson protesting the pass system:

> A number of men who have been employed upon plantations have visited Richmond in search of long—lost wives and children, who had been separated by the cruel usage of slavery. Wives, too, are frequently seen in our streets, anxiously inquiring for husbands who had been sold away from them, and many of these people, who ignorantly supposed that the day of passes had passed away with the system which organized them, have been arrested, imprisoned, and hired out without their advice or consent, thus preventing the reunion of long estranged and affectionate families. (*New York Tribune,* June 17, 1865)

The group continued their mobilization efforts on June 10 with a mass meeting for the entire community at the First African Baptist Church, where a committee was selected to visit President Johnson to present their grievances. Other community members bore the responsibility of raising travel funds for the committee by appealing to black churches. This mobilization effort proved successful, and thus mobilization became a viable strategy that the community employed for other grievances. In this instance, Mayor Mayo was removed from office; Gen. Alfred Terry, a more moderate Union army officer, was put in charge of Richmond, and Terry abolished the pass system and extended an olive branch to the black community. In turn, the black community was empowered by this broad-based strategy of utilizing the northern press to strengthen their case, presenting grievances to officials for redress, and, at the same time, disseminating information and generating mass community support through mass meetings at local black churches.

Emancipation Day celebrations proved to be another vehicle for the black community to demonstrate their growing independence and militancy. While the celebrations became increasingly more political and exhibited ties to the radical wing of the Republican party, the community steadfastly maintained its independent political strategies as a vehicle to mobilize their constituency and pressure the system. Although city officials and white Republican party stalwarts frequently pointed to January 1 as the legitimate day of emancipation, black Richmonders chose April 3, the actual day they were liberated from bondage, as the day worthy of celebration. As the community planned a huge parade of several thousand participants, including many celebrants from out of town, they incurred the wrath of whites. On the day before the parade, a mysterious blaze burned down the Second African Baptist Church, the center of parade activities. The community resolved that they would carry on the parade as planned and would rebuild the church (*Richmond Dispatch*, May 22, 1866; Dec. 28, 1966). The festivities concluded on this first celebration, April 3, 1866, with white radical Republican party leaders led by Reverend J. W. Hunnicutt, and black community leaders, jointly calling for racial equality.

With the impending Reconstruction and anticipated suffrage, the second Emancipation Day celebration, on April 3, 1867, was decidedly more political. "The day before, General Terry had suspended all local elections because Congress was going to assume control of Reconstruction," Rachleff notes. "Blacks were now confident that the right to vote would soon be theirs" (1984, 41). Following the parade, local white radical Republican party leaders Reverend Hunnicutt and Burnham Wardwell and black popular leaders Peter Randolph and Lewis Lindsay spoke on the rights and responsibilities of suffrage and urged black voter registration. Lindsay, a bandleader and very active in the Republican party, cautioned black men on "ballot-box etiquette": "Wait until you get to the ballot-box before you proclaim your political sentiments. Then vote for a good man without regard to color. But whatever you do, don't cast your vote for a rebel" (*Richmond Dispatch*, Apr. 4, 1867).

Although blacks in Richmond were active in the Republican party, they continued to demonstrate their independence beyond the sanction or knowledge of party leaders. Increasingly, as the Republican party's structure became more formalized, it excluded black issues and limited general participation. This new formal framework, which was removing the white radical Republican leaders, was also alienating mass political participation, particularly that of black women and children, who had been diligent participants in the electoral process. In subtler ways, it was also excluding those who were community activists outside of the formal party structure. The Republican party, with its new formal structure, had more control over the political process and black voters.

By the third Emancipation Day celebration, April 3, 1868, blacks had resorted to their direct-action strategy to air a longstanding grievance. The community found particularly irksome the toll footbridge, established by former mayor Joseph Mayo, that separated Richmond's and Manchester's black communities. Resolved to make a symbolic statement of the problem, as the community parade neared the bridge, two hundred black activists separated from the larger group, crossed the bridge and refused to pay the toll (*Richmond Dispatch*, Apr. 7, 1868). This was, in many ways, a turning point in the direct-action strategies of black Richmonders and their hopes for social change. Already the reorganization of the Republican party was underway; black issues and ideas were not only being contained, but these strategies failed to elicit a response.

Politics of Inclusion

Black Richmonders entered electoral politics via the Republican party's state convention in Richmond in April 1867, where two-thirds of the 210 delegates were black. Lewis Lindsay, the bandleader; John Oliver, the newcomer from Boston who had been imprisoned in the negro bull pen; Joseph Cox, a tobacco factory worker; Fields Cook, a barber; and Cornelius Harris, a shoemaker, were all recognized community leaders who were elected delegates to the convention. Thousands of black Richmonders actively participated in the deliberations. The contested issue that would frame the upcoming constitutional convention was the confiscation of the property of former Confederate officers. While Cook, for example, urged moderation, Harris argued for the redistribution of the confiscated property to blacks to establish their independence (Rachleff 1984, 41–42; Morton 1973, 35). Many blacks believed that following the confiscation of the property each black would be given forty acres and a mule.

Coinciding with the convention deliberations, blacks continued their mass political action by staging a sit-in on the city's streetcars (*Richmond Dispatch,* Apr. 12, 1867). Inspired by a successful sit-in that had occurred in Charleston the month before, black Richmonders constructed a two-pronged approach: the initial challenge to the system, with the anticipation of arrests, followed by continued provocation, more arrests, and organized mass action. The initial challengers, four community activists, paid their fares, took seats inside that were normally reserved for whites only, and refused to move. The arrest of these protesters galvanized community support for further political action. Later in the month, three more challengers tested the system, one claiming that "he had paid his money and he'd be damned if he wouldn't ride." All three were arrested (*Richmond Dispatch,* Apr. 24, 1867). The second arrest precipitated the organized mass community action. As the police arrived, "negroes were seen flocking from every direction to the point, and before the car had reached the place where the arrest was made, a large crowd, numbering several hundred, had collected." The quick mobilization of the crowd, proving that "they were ready for any emergency," the organizational strategy of the protest, and following the police to the station house undoubtedly contributed to the black community's winning access to the city's streetcars one week later (ibid.).

That same month, blacks stepped up their political action in an effort to settle labor disputes when the Stevedore Society of Laboring Men of the City of Richmond struck for higher wages on the city docks. Although the strike had strong community support, the high rate of unemployment and migrant workers coming into the city were contributing factors in its failure. Despite that failure, and the replacement of the laborers by black and white strikebreakers, the strike inspired a black coopers' strike one month later. But the coopers, who struck for higher wages, were replaced by white strikebreakers (*Richmond Dispatch,* May 16, 1867). Race, the chaos of war, impoverishment, and the economic flux of the state's economy thwarted the development of biracial coalitions and working-class consciousness across racial lines.

The political action of black Richmonders seeking to eradicate all of the social barriers to racial subordination, and the black alliance with white radical Republicans, was catalytic in bringing northern Republicans to Richmond for the constitutional convention. Holton notes that "blacks first served in public office in Virginia in 1868 when twenty-five blacks were elected to the post–Civil War constitutional convention" (1987, 1). Under military Reconstruction, the convention delegates were required to draft a new constitution to be approved by both Congress and Virginians in order to gain readmittance to the Union. Blacks, white radical Republicans—the "ultras," whose power base rested largely on black support—and moderate Republicans hoped to carve out their influence in the new legal document.

While clearly the ultras, led by Reverend Hunnicutt, Judge John Underwood, and James Morissey, dominated the convention's proceedings, Lewis Lindsay and Joseph Cox reflected the black community's independent political agenda. Lindsay and Cox were supported by thousands of blacks who attended the session, closing down factories, mills, sections of iron foundries, and creating disruption in white households as they participated in the deliberations. While blacks were dubious about ever achieving social equality in Virginia, political equality that centered around the issues of land, education, suffrage, and racial discrimination were tantamount to their freedom, citizenship, and material progress.

Blacks were in full support of the disfranchisement of former Confederate officers and saw the confiscation of their property as a means of land redistribution. They also advocated a heavy tax on the properties of former slaveholders in order to force them to sell parcels of their farmland to black sharecroppers. Pressing their claims for equality and integration, blacks argued that suffrage should be guaranteed for black men and women (*Richmond Dispatch,* Jan. 2, 4, 14, 23, 1868; Feb. 15, 1868; Apr. 3, 25, 1868). Undoubtedly, this was in recognition of how critical black women's activism was to the community's quest for political equality and progressive change. Seeking to wed their direct-action protest strategies to the formal mechanisms of inclusion, blacks argued that discrimination on public accommodations and conveyances should be illegal ("Debates and Proceedings" 1868, 150–51). Despite encouragement from a strong gallery of black supporters, black delegates' proposal was defeated on school integration. Although white radicals were widely acknowledged as black "allies," they joined with moderate Republicans in defeating the proposal for school integration. Blacks were largely unsuccessful during convention deliberations; their progressive agenda on school integration, land redistribution, and suffrage for women would not be included in the new Underwood constitution (appropriately named because of his leadership at the convention). Indeed, the questions of school integration and suffrage would not be settled until the middle of the next century.

By the time of the Republican party's nominating convention in Petersburg in the spring of 1869, the shifting political winds were already brewing as radical Republicans began to distance themselves from their black constituency. There were already party factions, and the hostilities between the moderates and ultras were readily apparent. What was also in evidence was the rise of the Republican party machine under the aegis of William Mahone, James Humphreys, and William Wickham, and that this tightly organized moderate GOP faction would supplant the ultras' leadership and black participation would be placed on an "as needed" basis. With such political apparatus as ward committees, precinct captains, convention delegates, independent political campaigns determined by the party leadership, and the disfranchisement of women, party politics was essentially a white male preserve.

Governor Henry Wells was the gubernatorial candidate, backed by both the radical faction of the Republican party and the black delegates. Gen. William Mahone, a Confederate officer during the Civil War, feared that Wells would thwart his attempts for the consolidation of the railroads, party leadership, and the distancing of the radicals from the party's power base (Wynes 1961, 4–5; Morton 1973, 70–79; Buni 1967, 1). When

Lewis Lindsay, a black Richmond delegate, nominated J. D. Harris, a black delegate from Hampton, Virginia, for lieutenant governor, Mahone's followers seconded the nomination—a gambit that lulled blacks and radicals into a false sense of complacency. Following the convention, however, moderate Republicans formed an opposition caucus and created a "True Republican" slate, nominating Gilbert C. Walker for governor and John T. Lewis for lieutenant governor. To induce the support of the Conservative party, which had fielded its own ticket headed by Robert F. Withers, the True Republicans extended an olive branch to the former by supporting the Underwood constitution minus two objectionable clauses: the disfranchisement of the Virginia elite and the barring from public office of all former Confederate officers and those who had provided them with aid and comfort during the Civil War.

The Conservative party, formed in 1867 from loose coalition of Democrats, former Whigs, industrialists, and planters, was willing, begrudgingly, to accept the constitution, but it wanted the clauses that would disfranchise them eliminated. The party reached a compromise with the federal government in which they agreed to accept black suffrage in return for separating the clauses from the constitution. The constitution would then be approved, blacks would gain suffrage, and the restrictive clauses would be voted on separately, guaranteeing them certain death by white Virginians. This plan was supported by the moderate Republicans.

This political alliance between the Conservatives and the moderate Republicans resulted in both factions accepting Walker and Lewis as their party candidates. The fusion of the two groups crystallized the political issues into a racial one. Using a race-baiting tactic that would become the hallmark of the Conservative party, they raised the specter of "Negro rule" to gain the votes of white Virginians. The tactic was successful, and the Walker ticket defeated the Wells ticket in the July 1869 elections by a vote of 119,535 to 101,204 (Wynes 1961, 5). The Conservative ticket even won, by a slight margin, in Richmond. The fusion ticket enjoyed other victories as well, with an overwhelming majority in the Virginia General Assembly. Although there were six black state senators out of 43 members and 21 black house delegates out of 137 members elected, the Conservative party was in power. The approval of the constitution and the defeat of the restrictive clauses were also Conservative victories.

Thus, in two years, Virginia went from the dismantling of military Reconstruction, which restored some stability to the state, to a Conservative party government composed of those rebels who had initiated the chaos in the first place. The antebellum aristocracy of industrialists and planters as now restored to its former position of prominence. Unlike some other southern states, there was no prolonged period of military occupation by federal troops in Virginia. Nor did Virginia have a period of "black reconstruction" in which blacks assumed some of the mantle of leadership. In Virginia, there would be brief spurts of black progress, but blacks would always be undermined by both Republicans and Conservative-Democrats, and periods of brief political promise were always more smokescreen than actual political gain. It comes as no surprise, then, that in the next decade, Conservatives would be on a relentless crusade to reestablish white supremacy. As John Hope Franklin states in examining this period in the South, "White Southerners expected to do by extralegal or blatantly illegal means what had not been allowed by law: to exercise absolute control over Negroes, drive them and their fellows from power, and establish white supremacy" (Franklin and Moss 1988, 226). In Virginia, the suppression of African Americans by the Conservative party was the law.

The isolation of the ultras, the erosion of black political power to mute their political protest, and the rise of white supremacy was a fact of life in Richmond following the election of 1869. James Humphreys of the Mahone faction, serving as local party chair, sought to minimize black political power by establishing "secret ballots," so that votes could be manipulated and counted by party regulars who had already predetermined the outcome. Black "co-optation" was also practiced, with some political activists, such as Joseph Cox and Lewis Lindsay, given menial jobs in attempts to quell the black political leadership's independence and protest. As the Conservative party began to establish its hegemony, the black popular movement began to frazzle, and many black Richmonders sought greener pastures in the lower South.

Over the next several years, in various forms of political actions and strategies, Richmond's black community would attempt to counter the encroaching political isolation that was designed to minimize their potential voting power. One political action came in March 1870 when Governor Walker appointed a new white conservative city council for Richmond which, in turn, elected Henry K. Ellyson as mayor. When Chahoon, the chief of police, refused to let Ellyson's administration take over, a confrontation developed between the two forces. Chahoon appealed to the black community for support. Black activists, such as Ben Scott and others, mobilized the black community, believing that once Ellyson's administration gained control, blacks would bear the brunt of his conservative administration. On two separate occasions, black crowds came out, attacked the police, and were later dispersed. To end the growing confrontation, General Canby, the federal commander, decided that the entire matter should be relegated to the courts.

The Conservative legislature of 1871 moved quickly to begin the process of disfranchising blacks. Having established the specter of Negro rule, they could now declare it a reality and pass laws justifying the oppression of blacks. By April 1871, Jackson Ward was gerrymandered to include most of the black population to control and limit their role in Richmond politics. Since each ward could elect three members to serve on the board of aldermen and five representatives to serve on the city council, the plan was that these eight black representatives from Jackson Ward, out of a forty-eight-member council, would be ineffective. But the other side of this political and social segregation was that Jackson Ward would ultimately develop into a black stronghold of activism and politics. While blacks were also living in Marshall, Jefferson, and Clay Wards, they were not in significant numbers to alter the election of white Conservative-Democratic candidates. The legislature also required that separate lists of black and white voters be kept, and the list of black voters could conveniently be misplaced at election time.

By 1873, the Conservative party was solidified enough to campaign solely on its race-baiting tactics. Wrapping themselves around the mantle of white supremacy, the party had the support of native white Virginians and the predominantly white, conservative press. The *Richmond Daily Dispatch,* most often serving as a tool of the conservative causes, reinforced the campaign rhetoric by declaring, "Shall the whites rule and take care of the negroes, or shall the negroes rule and take care of the whites?" (*Richmond Dispatch,* Mar. 4, 1873). As the campaign wore on, the press grew more truthful and bolder and engendered more fear in white Virginians. "The Conservative party," it declared, "is the white man's party, and the Radical party is the negro party. The former proposes to keep all the offices in the hands of the whites, and the latter is forced to divide the offices with the negroes" (*Richmond Dispatch,* Apr. 28, 1873).

With the sweeping victory gained in the state elections of 1873, and the overwhelming majority gained in state assembly, the Conservative party enacted a series of amendments to the Underwood constitution. The amendments, designed to continue the disfranchisement of blacks, were targeted specifically at black strongholds in places like Jackson Ward. A poll tax, for example, was established as a prerequisite for voting; petit larceny was grounds to disqualify voters; and the reduction of house delegates from 137 to 100 would ultimately allow more gerry-mandering of black communities (Wynes 1961, 12–13). Additionally, black schools were closed for lack of operating capital. "Driven from the polls by intimidation in the forms of violence and economic reprisal, and by legal measures such as the poll tax and disfranchisement for conviction of petty theft," Charles Wynes notes, "the Virginia Negro by the end of the 1870's was in despair" (14).

As black Richmonders saw their political gains eroding, they became increasingly disillusioned with Republicans, whom they viewed as their erstwhile "allies" but who were rarely supportive. The more Conservatives gained control of the government, the more tenuous became blacks' political and social status. Black activists, like John Oliver and Lewis Lindsay, both strong Republican party supporters, agreed with the new group of working-class community activists who believed that blacks could not function effectively within the party machine. Instead, they had to create an organizational vehicle that would pressure the formal political channels for their political and social rights. Their salvation remained in building an independent political force upon the existing social and cultural institutions in the black community. These activists found in the Colored National Labor Union (CNLU) a vehicle of political expression.

The Colored National Labor Union established a local chapter in Richmond in 1870 that emphasized racial solidarity as well as interracial cooperation among workers. Politically, a new group of black working-class activists had matured in Richmond. These laborers had deepened their racial and class consciousness through maintaining societies in the community, the cross-fertilization of ideas from participating in national labor organizations, and spearheading strikes in Richmond to mitigate their common plight. They realized that in order to struggle successfully against the industrialists they had to combine forces with whites, who were potential strikebreakers and links to national and international unions for support, information, and biracial struggle.

In 1870, an interracial coopers' union was established as a local chapter of this international organization (Rachleff 1984, 63–64). As well organized as they were, the CNLU demand for better working conditions, rights to public accommodations and conveyances, and municipal services drew no response from Conservative party leadership. Other community grievances were also falling on deaf ears in the city's administration. The community's perennial problem of police brutality, exacerbated by the "arrest of a female, who was seized without a cause, [and] shamefully dragged through the streets" (*New National Era,* Nov. 3, 1871), elicited complete indifference from the city council. The movement petered out in 1871, not for lack of effort or enthusiasm but because their political power had been circumscribed.

By the late 1870s, political disfranchisement had taken its toll on the black community and much of the grass-roots activity of the prior decade had quelled. Black Richmonders were also coping with the economic reversals of the depression of 1873–78, which only now were showing evidence of abatement. Blacks were slowly recovering from the loss of jobs, severe wage cuts in the public and private sectors, and the sickness, destitution, and death that resulted from the ravages of winter weather, unemployment, and drafty old houses. The tobacco manufacturing sector, which blacks had long relied upon for steady income, was now being mechanized, and skilled laborers, such as lumpers and twisters, were being supplanted by automation (Rachleff 1984, 86). The expanding cigarette manufacturing industry, which should have absorbed most of the displaced workers from the tobacco factories, were only giving jobs to white working-class women. Black working-class women, the majority of black women in Richmond, held the same jobs they did before slavery in the tobacco factories, in flour mills, and as household workers for white families. Many of these workers, as well as their children, lost their jobs during the economic depression of the 1870s or were forced to take severe wage cuts that rendered them destitute.

The crisis of the depression in Richmond's black community was compounded by the failure of the Freedman's Savings and Trust Company Bank, which held the entire savings of individuals as well as the community's four hundred societies. The bank's failure was apparent long before its final demise in April 1874 due to inaccurate bookkeeping, sloppy management, and financiers speculating and unloading bad loans on the bank. When Frederick Douglass was made president of the bank, he was unaware that the speculators had drained its capital resources then deserted, leaving blacks to take the fall. Desperately trying to rebuild the bank's credibility and a sound fiscal management policy, Douglass invested his own money as a stopgap measure while appealing, unsuccessfully, to the U.S. Senate Finance Committee for investment capital to save the institution (Franklin and Moss 1988, 215–16). The closing of the bank wiped out black Richmonders' entire collective fortune of $140,000.00. Thus, their disfranchisement and the loss of their economic support system made the problems of black Richmonders especially acute.

The Conservative party split of 1879 was politically and economically fortuitous for blacks, who now comprised a third of the electorate and held the balance of power between the short-lived Funder and Readjuster parties (Moore 1975, 170). Coming on the heels of the depression, as well as a decade of labor organizing, politicized by the black bricklayers strike in 1874 and the strike of black and white coopers in 1877, some workers were still seeking an independent political voice. While on balance there was no great enthusiasm for the greenback movement which emerged in the same decade, because it evinced no black concerns, black Richmonders still gained from their local chapter a more broadly defined working-class movement. Thus, the statewide convention held in Richmond in March 1879 to access their relationship to the Republican party found the huge crowd of blacks in attendance circumspect at best.

The Funder-Readjuster controversy centered on the $46 million, loan plus interest, that the state owed its creditors from the antebellum era. The Funders, largely planters and industrialists who had plowed the money into internal improvements during the 1840s and 1850s, hoping to rejuvenate industrial development, insisted that they had a moral obligation to pay their bondholders even if it meant higher taxes and lower school allocations. Readjusters, on the other hand, opposed this approach, favoring tax reform, increased public school expenditures, and a downward adjustment of the debt. Many poor white Virginians who had been in dire straits since the war wanted lower taxes and increased school resources and saw the debt repayment plan link to an industrial-planter class alliance. Blacks, although cautious, supported the Readjusters since the debt occurred during slavery, and they were strongly in favor of tax reform, better schools, and an end to the caste system. One scholar notes the pragmatic relationship between the Readjusters and blacks: "The Readjusters said to Negroes, 'Put us in office and we will keep your schools open, pay your teachers, provide for your higher education, abolish the whipping post, and remove your insane from jails to a well equipped asylum.' And they did it. These were the motives controlling the Negroes when they went to the polls in 1879" (Johnston 1929, 255).

The black-Readjuster alliance garnered a vote of nearly 82,000 to 61,000 in favor of the Readjusters, giving them control, with the support of black legislators, of the Virginia General Assembly. The Readjusters captured 41 of the 100 Virginia House of Delegates seats and half of the 40 Virginia Senate seats. Twelve blacks were elected to the state house and two to the state senate (Rachleff 1984, 90; Moore 1975, 172; Buni

1967, 4). Although blacks held the balance of power in the legislature, gains would be slight until the 1881 gubernatorial election. Yet "this Readjuster-Negro axis dominated the legislature until its adjournment in March 1880. Black votes provided the margin of victory on roll call after roll call, electing dozens of white insurgents to state offices and county judgeships" (Moore 1975, 172). Immediately following the election, and under the watchful eye of Ross Hamilton, a black house delegate member for the last decade, blacks such as R. A. Paul and Richard Forrester were appointed to minor patronage jobs in Richmond, such as the Richmond School Board. This new influence enabled them to put pressure on Judge Christian, who in the past had been unresponsive to their demands, to place blacks on juries and revitalize the school system. The first black jurors were appointed in March 1880, and by the end of that year, black schools had nearly doubled in Virginia.

Following the Readjusters poor showing in the 1880 presidential elections, and the unwillingness of blacks to support a neutral ticket and endanger Republican control of the White House, William Mahone realized that the black vote was critical in the upcoming 1881 gubernatorial election. In Richmond, blacks asserted their political independence in the presidential election by voting for James Garfield for president and John S. Wise for Congress, thereby creating a split ticket conceived by the community. Determined to elect the Readjuster candidate, Governor William E. Cameron of Petersburg, Mahone began to diligently court what he dubbed the black Republican "phalanx" with a more inclusive political agenda. As the coalition congealed, Richmond's black politicians issued a call for a black state convention to endorse the new alliance. At the same time, the convention consolidated the demands of blacks upon the new machine in power.

The Funders countered the growing biracial coalition with a massive campaign of race-baiting tactics and strategies designed to pull white Virginians back into the fold. Since race played a major or minor role in almost all elections until the early 1900s, and thereafter whenever Republicans proved to be a threat, Funders simply configured the racial tactic to address the present political context. Native Virginia aristocrats who led the Funders took advantage of the underlying fear of white Virginians of black retaliation for slavery as well as their own beliefs of their innate superiority. White Virginians were also apprehensive of exaggerated reports of so-called Negro rule from their southern sister states. Feeling alienated over the new political and economic transitions in their lives, and the new social status of blacks, white Virginians readily believed the Funders' propaganda that black visibility and militancy meant that black rule was imminent.

Race-baiting campaign tactics were already proving to be a time-honored strategy to rally white voters, and, supported wholeheartedly by a white southern press, the Funders argued that a "pure white Saxon government" was at stake. Indeed, white Anglo-Saxon civilization was hanging in the balance: "It is not the principle of the debt, but the principle of pure white Saxon government that we stand for; it is not the interest of the debt, but the paramount interest of our State and race that is now wavering in the balance" (*Richmond State,* Sept. 27, 1881). In 1881, however, despite an intensive racial campaign, the Readjuster-black coalition won the election by a twelve-thousand-vote margin. With William E. Cameron elected as the new governor, the coalition was now in complete control of the state legislature.

Although blacks had regained political influence, and grass-roots activity in black communities was going full tilt, it was the first time since emancipation that state legislators and administrators in local areas improved the quality of black lives. The state tax code was revised and the back taxes of wealthy citizens were collected. The poll tax was abolished along with the whipping post (previously, anyone who receive a whipping was disfranchised) (Jackson 1942, 81; Wynes 1961, 22; Holton 1987, 5). Virginia Normal and Collegiate Institute, a state institution of higher learning for blacks, was established at Petersburg; a black mental health facility was opened; and the public schools were reopened. Black representatives, who were mainly concerned with issues of civil rights and lynching, were also concerned about issues such as travel on common carriers, landlord-tenant relations, and jury service for all citizens.

Richmond's black community was reenergized by the Readjuster-black alliance, and the militancy of the period resulted in the surfacing of internal and external tensions. One source of internal gender conflict was the ecclesiastical sexism that formed the authoritative framework of the black church. At the helm of Richmond's black church institutional structure was the First African Baptist Church, and, by the Spring of 1880, parishioners were questioning its male-dominated leadership. Susan Washington, recognized as a church and grass-roots organizer in the community as well as a pro-Readjuster militant, presented a petition signed by two hundred black women who wanted to participate and vote in the major decision-making deliberations governing church affairs. This was coupled with the charge of Henry Buford, a lay minister, that Reverend Holmes should be removed for "unchristian like conduct" toward some of the black female parishioners (Records of the First African Baptist Church, May and June 1880). Both issues escalated into serious bones of contention that finally led to hundreds of parishioners leaving First Baptist to found Fifth Baptist Church.

Pro-Readjuster militants also fought to displace the local Republican party leadership that was in control of local ward committees. Most of the white ward leaders were not supportive of the Readjuster movement and were attempting to exercise more Conservative control in local areas. For black Richmonders, that meant that local patronage jobs, city council influence, and candidate selection for city council would come under their umbrella. This could possibly siphon off some of their best leadership or, at worse, not allow black leadership to emerge at all. Blatant or subtle forms of "co-optation" were always prevalent in the party machine, and blacks feared that patronage appointments always ran the risk of alienating appointees from the community. While R. A. Paul, former Richmond School Board appointee and later appointed personal messenger for Governor Cameron, did not become alienated from blacks, his new position removed him from daily contact with his community power base.

But the Readjuster-black alliance was devoid of a theoretical and praxis construct of political and social equality, and its tenure was brief in the body politic. Already the Readjusters' political agenda had lost most of its steam before the general election of 1883, partly due to lacking a cohesive liberal agenda, as well as internal corruption and feuding over future party leadership inside the Mahone faction. However, it was external forces that sealed its fate. The Funders, equally as corrupt and dishonest, and intending to recapture the assembly, had launched a vigorous campaign focusing on race as the dominant issue. One of the messages, "And now for the fight this fall! We must beat the 'niggers' and their allies," was bold and blunt enough to rally white Virginians to the Funders-Democratic party (Wynes 1961, 46). This time their "race-baiting" campaign tactics were aided by the "Danville riot" of November 4, 1883, a few days before the election. The riot was precipitated when a black man jostled a white man on the street and the ensuing melee escalated into a fight and the killing of one white and four blacks.

The Danville riot was made to order for the Democratic campaign. Since Danville had a sizable black population that held a majority of the town's council seats, and four of their nine policemen were black, as well as the superintendent of the public market, Democrats touted that the riot was the result of "black domination." What was missing from this observation was that the mayor, judge, the commonwealth's attorney, the constable, the chief of police, and the commissar of revenue were white and that blacks were participating in the town's administrative affairs (Buni 1967, 5; Morton 1973, 119–21; Moore 1975, 181–82). But the riot kept blacks, fearful of retaliation, from the polls and, simultaneously, encouraged whites to go to the polls to halt the encroaching black menace. Virginia voted in the aftermath of the riot, giving the Democrats a major victory of 67 percent of the seats in the state legislature. Moreover, this victory signaled the end of the Readjuster party and any notions of equality for blacks. One scholar observes the significance of this election: "The Confederate tradition began to assume the proportions of a cult, and the pressure of the race issue rapidly increased. As far as the Negro was concerned, the stage was set for reactionary measures which paved the way for his final disfranchisement in 1902" (Wynes 1961, 39).

DISFRANCHISEMENT AND STRUGGLE

Following the 1883 general election and the restoration of white supremacy in state government, the disfranchisement of black Virginians proceeded apace. As Democrats were establishing one-party rule and relegating the Republican party to oblivion, they were simultaneously finalizing plans for the complete political and social subordination of blacks. The Democrats, reinstituted their former Conservative party's use of threats, physical violence, and economic reprisals against blacks as well as strengthened the legal apparatus of oppression. Adding outright intimidation throughout the state, gerrymandering in all congressional districts to assure complete political control, and embracing the Anderson-McCormick election law, enabled the Democrats to accomplish almost total disfranchisement of black Virginians.

The Anderson-McCormick law, once amended, provided that in 1884 and thereafter, three persons would be elected for each city and county who could then appoint local election officials (Buni 1967, 7; Wynes 1961, 39–40). "The Anderson-McCormick bill," notes Robert Martin, "was passed in the interest of the white people of Virginia. . . . It is a white man's law. It operates to perpetuate the rule of the white man in Virginia" (1938, 100). While the law enabled the Democrats to gain political control of state and local officials, it also paved the way for fraud, widespread corruption, and manipulation of every election with the expressed intent of black political exclusion.

Richmond's black industrial workers grew increasingly alarmed after the Democratic sweep to victory in 1883. As the Democrats began to dismantle the Readjusters' policies, black Richmonders' gains began to diminish. Holton states that "when Democrats returned to power in 1883, many of Richmond's black teachers and all three of the city's black school principals were fired" (1987, 8). This rapid erosion of black political gains made black workers anxious to build an independent political and economic base that would grow out of their cultural nationalism, that is, existing black cultural institutions, and attracted them to the Knights of Labor.

The Knights of Labor, a nationally based interracial trade union that included both male and female workers, made its appearance in the city in 1884. Each local assembly was autonomous, although collective workers' action in a given region had the support of the larger national organization. Despite the alarm raised by the Democratic industrialists and their efforts to court white workers to effect racial hegemony in Virginia, the Knights of Labor evinced tremendous growth, from 700,000 to 2 million members in two years nationwide. In one year in Richmond, there were eleven white local assemblies and twelve black assemblies. District assemblies were created so that these local chapters could pool their resources around ethnic, racial, trade, or community ties. The black assemblies were organized into District Assembly 92, and, months later, Local Assemblies 3929 and 4096, two black female local chapters, were founded (Rachleff 1984, 117–38, 143–46).

To capture the moment of popularity and increase membership, the Knights took up the cause of the coopers, calling for a mass consumer boycott against Haxall-Crenshaw Flour Company, which was one of the largest users of convict barrels. Since coopers' productivity depended upon the making of barrels for agricultural and industrial enterprises, they were vulnerable when companies undercut their wages by using convict laborers to make the barrels. From the beginning, the boycott was a family affair and depended on women refusing to purchase Haxall-Crenshaw products. Many blacks who had grown disillusioned with the Republican machine and its silence on disfranchisement found their racial solidarity and popular expression under the Knights revitalized. After nine months, the boycott was a resounding success, increasing the Knights' membership by the thousands.

The Knights' success at mass consumer boycotts, putting pressure on the city to use black and white laborers, and the internal program of mass education, eventually found the organization in opposition to the city's industrialist-planter alliance. Continuing to mobilize the workers and gain a political base, the Workingmen's Reform party, formed by the union leaders, won the city elections in 1886. But their inability to handle the leadership reins of local government was immediately evident. The council slate had been all white and, once elected, they were unresponsive to the needs of black citizens. In fact, the Workingmen's Reform leaders were not prepared to govern a complex urban area. Part of the problem may have stemmed from the fact that the Knights of Labor had grown too large too quickly and was too loosely organized to be an effective tool for political leadership. Finally, some of the Workingmen's Reform party members stated openly that they were Democrats, placing them in opposition to white and black workers' interests in Richmond. By 1888, the Knights had literally disappeared from the political landscape.

Although the horizon appeared bleak for black Virginians in 1888, their long struggle since emancipation always brought brief moments of victory and inspiration. Those brief moments had to be nurtured to empower and fortify them for renewed struggle. In 1888, John Mercer Langston ran for the congressional seat from the Fourth Congressional District in Petersburg. Langston was a graduate of Oberlin College, former dean of Howard University Law School, former minister to Haiti, and president of Virginia State College at Petersburg. Black Richmonders knew him because he was the president of the only black institution of higher learning in the state and because he and Frederick Douglass had been affiliated with the Freedman's Savings Bank in its declining stages.

Langston had attempted to run as a Republican candidate, but having been stonewalled by William Mahone, he ran as an Independent Republican and won against Democratic favorite Edward C. Venable and Republican regular Judge R. W. Arnold. But Langston's victory was mired in the Democratic corruption and fraud that had declared Venable the winner. When Langston demanded a recount, a lengthy investigation by the U.S. House of Representatives declared him the winner. Finally, seated in the last week of the Fifty-first Congress, Langston served as the lame-duck representative until March 1890. The mobilization of black voters from the Fourth Congressional District inspired other districts to continue to challenge the system.

Despite Langston's successful congressional bid in the late 1880s, blacks had few political alternatives in the 1890s. Even the Populist movement, a grass-roots coalition of farmers who were opposed to the Democratic aristocracy, thwarted black involvement for fear of the racial stigmatization that had dogged the Republican party. White Republicans were now distancing themselves from blacks in hopes of regaining some of the party's momentum of prior decades and created a "lily-white" faction that supported black exclusion from Virginia politics. In many senses, the so-called lily-whites were as conservative as the Democrats, especially in regard to black political participation. It may be in light of this political landscape that Booker T. Washington, a native Virginian and recognized spokesman for blacks, emphasized education and economic advancement and de-emphasized political participation.

However, black Richmonders continued to struggle for political inclusion against the rising racial barriers of disfranchisement. They developed a broad-based strategy of black nationalism that emphasized their racial pride, racial solidarity, and economic initiatives that built upon their established cultural infrastructure. While the masses wedded their nationalism to a working-class ideology that included race, gender, and class, the rising black middle class made use of some of that same consciousness in strengthening the facets of economic and cultural nationalism in the community. Most of the black middle class in the 1880s had come of age in the post-emancipation period, when there was a strong black infrastructure in place, educational opportunities, and when they had developed entrepreneurial acumen and ambition that was thwarted with disfranchisement. While their black consciousness did not preclude interracial coalitions, these "new issue" blacks supported economic nationalism, encouraging black institutional development and "buy black campaigns" as a bulwark against rising racism. John T. Mitchell Jr., editor of the *Richmond Planet*, the largest black weekly in Virginia, called for blacks to "continue to save money and property. . . . Any colored man who opposes race enterprises among the colored people is his own worst enemy" (*Richmond Planet*, Mar. 14, 1903).

Black Richmonders' focus on "race enterprises" was evincing strong progress in the 1880s and 1890s. They founded the Savings Bank of the Grand Fountain United Order of True Reformers, the first black bank, in 1888. This was followed in 1893 by the founding of the Southern Aid and Life Insurance Company, one of the first black insurance companies in the United States, as well as the founding of the Saint Luke Penny Savings Bank in the same year by Maggie Lena Walker, the first woman bank president in the United States. Black Richmonders had continued to collectively pool their resources, and this was prominent in three of the major mutual benevolent societies, all of which opened black banks. The Grand Fountain United Order of True Reformers, the Knights of Pythias, and the Independent Order of Saint Luke all had thousands of members by the end of the century and were all prosperous.

Fig. 3. John T. Mitchell Jr., 1921. Courtesy of the Library of Virginia.

Some of these societies were founded and led by black women. Just as their forebears had done, black women were pooling their collective resources to promote economic development and social reform activities. Class distinctions were often blurred when black women engaged in collective endeavors to "uplift the race" and improve the quality of all of their lives. Rosa Dixon Bowser, for example, widely known for being a teacher at Navy Hill School in the 1880s, established a plethora of clubs and associations to benefit young men and women (Lee 1993, 25). Additionally, "she organized the first night school in Richmond for black men and boys" (ibid.). Similarly, Ora Brown Stokes, another social activist in Richmond, had a lifelong commitment to "gender and race work." Stokes and a group of Richmond women organized the Richmond Chapter of the National League for the Protection of Colored Girls to rescue newcomers to the city "from unscrupulous men" (Lee 1993, 39–40; *Richmond Planet,* Mar. 31, 1917).

Modern societies, whose emphasis was on economic, political, and social development, like the Independent Order of Saint Luke, followed the traditions of pooling collective resources and providing benefits, but they also typified a new age of multilevel business development, economic expansion beyond community boundaries, and strong visionary black female leadership. In many senses, although these women pursued acceptable reform activities despite the trepidations of black men about women's clubs, they were also contra conventional in promoting a consciousness of race and gender concerns. This consciousness was born of struggle of generations of black women in Richmond (Brown 1988, 173–78). In some senses, they were urban pioneers.

Representing this "new black woman" was Maggie Lena Walker, who joined the Independent Order of Saint Luke at age fourteen and

Fig. 4. Maggie Lena Walker, 1901. Walker was the founder and president of Richmond's Saint Luke Penny Savings Bank and the first woman bank president in the United States. Courtesy of the National Park Service, Maggie L. Walker National Historic Site.

was immediately immersed in the intergenerational bonding of black women. From this vantage point, Walker grew to maturity, graduated from Colored Normal School in 1883, and fortified a consciousness of "gender and race work" shaped by the dynamic forces of separation and segregation in Richmond. Walker, along with other women, founded the Woman's Union, a female insurance company. Just as her larger social purpose was promoted through her association with the Richmond Council of Colored Women, the National Association for the Advancement of Colored People, the International Council of Women of the Darker Races, and the Richmond Urban League, her business acumen shaped the Independent Order of Saint Luke.

In 1899, Walker became the grand worthy secretary of the fledgling Independent Order of Saint Luke following the resignation of the then-current secretary, William M. T. Forrester. Immediately, Walker notes, "my first work was to draw around me women" (Walker 1928, 57) in her initial efforts to impose upon the traditional society's base an innovative program of economic prosperity. Certainly, her most visionary and pragmatic idea was the creation of the Saint Luke Penny Savings Bank in Richmond in 1903. Walker encourages her followers to ". . . do something towards giving employment to those who have made it what it is. . . . let us have a bank and a factory" (ibid.). Walker's creation of the *St. Luke Herald* disseminated information on the organization as well as community news. In 1905, this predominantly black women's organization opened a department store, the St. Luke Emporium, which employed black women as clerks (Walker 1928, 63; Brown 1988, 187–90). Eventually, Walker's economic activity encouraged a more assertive stance in local politics, and she ran for state office in 1921 on the Virginia Republican ticket, an effort by black leaders to spearhead independent political action by black Richmonders. Walker combined a strong economic determinism with her protest against black disfranchisement.

Like Walker, other black Richmonders found that the increasing erosion of their rights, despite overwhelming odds, promoted participation in local politics. One vehicle that was still open was the election of councilmen from Jackson Ward who would focus on community improvement. "Most significantly," notes Chesson, "between July 1871 and June 1898, thirty-three blacks served on the city council" (1982, 191). In general, black Richmonders chose men that were moderate politically, well established, educated, and possessed strong ties to the Republican party. Although blacks had no influence upon state elections, the gerrymandering of Jackson Ward meant that blacks could elect up to eight city representatives who could serve on the city council. Even though the relationship between blacks and the Republicans was rocky in the 1890s and early 1900s, blacks were still tied to "the party of Lincoln."

Certainly, John Mitchell Jr. was one of the more active councilmen; he served for eight years, starting with his election in 1888. Although such factors as factionalism in Jackson Ward, different ideological perspectives, and others vying for leadership, may have curtailed some of Mitchell's influence, clearly the *Richmond Planet*'s article on what black councilmen had accomplished pointed to his commitment to the ward and was an opportunity for self-promotion. Reporting in 1895, the *Planet* indicated that as a result of blacks on the city council, the community had received funding for a new school building, a night school for day workers, fuel for poor black residents, an armory for black troops, and better streets and lighting for Jackson Ward (Alexander 1972, 203; Chesson 1982, 202–10, 216–17).

Black councilmen were normally assigned to the lowest-ranking committees on the council. They were, at all times in the 1880s and 1890s, a minority group, never more than seven or eight in a forty-eight-member body, and had meager influence on the entire council. Blacks usually served on the Committee on Streets, generally overseeing maintenance; the Police Committee, where they were buffers against police brutality; the First, Second, and Third Market Committees; and the Committee on Elections, to stifle black protest on election fraud and manipulation by the Democrats (Chesson 1982, 208). However, black councilmen also served on the more prestigious School Committee, which deliberated over the public school expenditures for black students, and the Committee on Retrenchment and Reform, deciding on budgetary cuts (208–9). Although blacks would no longer serve on the council after 1898, until the civil rights movement, there were measured successes despite the racial and political obstacles.

The 1890s produced a renewed vigor on black disfranchisement and social segregation. Already blacks were migrating to northern cities to escape the oppression. In some senses, John Mitchell Jr.'s bid for reelection in 1896, which he lost in a fraudulent election by several hundred votes, signaled that blacks were no longer considered a political entity in Richmond. Social segregation was rigidly enforced throughout the city, blacks schools were declining rapidly, low wages for black males and females persisted, and there was a step-up of police brutality to reinforce the oppressive laws and quell black protest. In 1894, the Walton Act, designed to keep pre-literate blacks away from the polls in local elections by using ballots with no party symbols or designation, coupled with the stalling tactics of Democrats of closing polls down while hundreds of blacks were waiting to vote, crippled black participation on Richmond's Common Council. Coinciding with the erosion of blacks' political rights, and undoubtedly catalytic, was the U.S. Supreme Court decision in *Plessy v. Ferguson* in 1896 which legalized social segregation.

Thus, the way was paved, following the Walton Act, to hold the new state constitutional convention to revise the Underwood constitution and legally disfranchise blacks. Arguments supporting the disfranchise- ment came from "friends" of blacks as well as their sworn enemies. Democrats argued that the graft and corruption in the electoral process, which was so pervasive it was a source of embarrassment throughout the state, would not be necessary if blacks were excluded from participation. Some southerners supported the notion that blacks should be disfran- chised because they could be manipulated too easily by politicians (Wynes 1961, 62). Some Republicans, who had established a lily-white faction, "favored a convention and disfranchisement of the Negro on the grounds that only by removal of the colored voter from Republican ranks could that party make itself respectable in the eyes of the masses of white Virginians" (57). Still other southerners thought that the elimination of blacks from politics was a progressive measure until blacks were suffi- ciently educated to handle suffrage (63).

The state constitution established at the 1901–2 convention elimi- nated blacks from the political process. The franchise article, or suffrage provisions, stated that a registered voter must be a Civil War veteran, the son of a veteran, own real property, or be able to read and understand portions of the new constitution. After January 1, 1904, in addition to the age and residency requirements, there was a poll tax of $1.50 for the three preceding years, and persons must give a written personal voting narrative in the presence of a registrar as well as answer all relevant ques- tions. The poll tax, after January 1, 1904, was increased from $1.50 to $4.50. The constitutional delegates sought to plug every possible legal loophole to not only deny blacks their constitutional amendment rights but also to ensure there was no possible course of redress.

Disfranchisement devastated the political and social potential of blacks in Richmond. Richmond could still boast of 6,427 registered black voters in 1900, but inside of two years that number had shrunk to a dis- mal 760 (Buni 1967, 24; *Richmond Times-Dispatch*, Oct. 2, 1902). What was most troubling was that Jackson Ward—where so much of black political and social activism had shaped the city, electing twenty black councilmen and several aldermen since 1865—had 2,983 black voters in 1896, but by 1903 that number had diminished to 33 (Buni 1967, 25; *Richmond Times-Dispatch,* Oct. 2, 1902; *Richmond News Leader,* Sept. 29, 1903). In the same year, Jackson Ward was once more gerrymandered so that any potential viability would be lost.

By the dawning of the new century, blacks in Richmond were mobilizing a legal assault upon the system to challenge the legality of the state constitution of 1902. While some blacks had resigned themselves to the entrenched white power structure, others were marshaling their forces to "test" the laws of disfranchisement. In 1900 the Virginia Education and Industrial Association, and in 1901 the Negro Industrial and Agricultural League, shifted their attentions to politicizing the community, hiring attorneys, and taking a keen interest in politics. The *Negro Advocate,* a Richmond newspaper, was established to protest and lobby against the state constitution of 1902. The public was also kept informed by other black weeklies grouped under the rubric of the Negro Press Association.

James Hayes, a black lawyer, and John S. Wise, a former Conservative-Democrat and now New York Republican, centered their court cases around the unconstitutionality of the new state constitution, since it had never received popular approval and had deprived people of their rights as guaranteed under the Underwood constitution of 1869. Two cases, *Jones et al. v. Montague et al.* and *Selden et al. v. Montague et al.* filed in 1902 tested these issues. In *Jones et al.,* the counsel argued that Governor Montague, members of the board of election, and the constitutional convention members had deprived blacks of their legal rights by not submitting the constitution for popular approval. Given that the new constitution was invalid, so was the election of Virginia members of the U.S. House of Representatives, and the members should be barred from being seated. In *Selden et al.,* the counsel argued that William Selden, an undertaker who could read, write, and owned property, had failed the "understanding clause" because of discrimination of the registrars against blacks (Buni 1967, 44). Both cases were dismissed by the chief justice of the Supreme Court of Virginia on the grounds that it lacked jurisdiction.

While these two cases were on appeal, two other court cases established legal precedent. In *Jackson W. Giles v. Board of Registrars of Montgomery County, Alabama,* Giles was deprived of his right to vote under the new Alabama constitution. In the second case, *Taylor v. Commonwealth of Virginia,* Taylor was found guilty, without a jury trial, of breaking and entering. Since the court's authority stemmed from the constitution, and the constitution was invalid, there was no basis for Taylor's conviction.

The Appeals Court of Virginia upheld the lower court's decision in the *Taylor* case and affirmed the constitutionality of the constitution. The U.S. Supreme Court, a year later, dismissed both *Jones et al.* and *Selden et al.*, saying that it was out of their jurisdiction. Other cases, such as *Brickhouse v. Brooks*, and *Lee v. Montague*, met with the same fate as segregation and disfranchisement became the law of the land (Buni 1967, 47–49).

The practice and sanction of de jure segregation and disfranchisement of blacks reinforced the lily-white direction of the GOP in the early 1900s. Although many moderate Republicans had clearly distanced themselves from blacks in the party in the 1880s, the establishment of Republican "lily-whitism," when Republicans believed that all future campaigns would be more successful without blacks as GOP baggage, followed black disfranchisement in 1902. Tired of the "Negro taint," many Republicans openly endorsed the removal of blacks from politics and "rather enjoy(ed) the condition in which the Negroes (found) themselves" (Buni 1967, 42). "With disfranchisement in 1902, the G.O.P. grasped the opportunity to shake itself loose from the party of the Negro label it had borne since Reconstruction. Virginia Republicans watched with interest the successful establishment of a 'lily-white' party in North Carolina and were quick to follow suit" (41).

Thus, in the efforts of the Republican party to restore its former prominence in the state, the "disfranchisement and shunning" practices of the Republican party against blacks became even more blatant. Blacks, for example, were excluded from Republican meetings and conventions, they were not expected to participate in nominating conventions where full white slates were presented to the body, and they were not welcome in GOP political circles. Should blacks appear at white meetings uninvited, those blacks were segregated into special seating areas. Blacks were also denied patronage jobs and their protest brought no relief (Buni 1967, 41–44). On occasion, lily-whites also supported white Democratic candidates in predominantly black congressional districts in efforts to sanitize the electorate. Outspoken republican Capt. C. H. Caussey stated, "I am opposed to the Republicans making any attempt to contest the franchise clause of the new Constitution. A white man's country for me. A white man's country" (42).

Despite these prodigious attempts to cast blacks out of the Republican party, the Democrats could not afford to eliminate the psychological imagery that "black rule" evoked in the white electorate. The pervasive voter apathy of whites, once the Democratic hegemony was assured, was only reenergized when racial tactics dominated the campaign. Other issues, such as land distribution, the education of poor whites, poor job training, low wages for black and white workers, healthcare, and overall general economic progress, were obfuscated as long as white supremacy dominated political life. Thus, the ruling class of industrialist-planters had their political and economic power at stake in promoting the "black specter" in politics. The regeneration of the Ku Klux Klan in Richmond and other cities where blacks went seeking jobs, consistent voter intimidation of blacks, and election fraud fortified their hegemony. Indubitably, they relied on an electorate who believed that white supremacy was worth any price.

In the new century, blacks continued to counter their political exclusion by fielding their own slate of independent congressional candidates in 1906, sending a clear signal to the Republican party that the disaffection of blacks was imminent. Although this gambit elicited no response, it may have marked the beginning of the shift away from the Republican party. Following World War I, a renewal of job opportunities, and the impending Nineteenth Amendment granting black female suffrage, black Richmonders' political spirits were once again renewed. Black activists believed that the combination of black male and female voters would have a decisive impact upon the electorate.

With the anticipation of the passage of the Nineteenth Amendment, the legislature had already decided that it was "of paramount importance to protect the electorate from the colored female voters" by using the same disfranchisement mechanisms that eliminated black male voters (Flood Papers). Maggie Lena Walker's prediction that five thousand black female voters would register in Richmond fell wide of the mark. Such registration tactics as delaying the processing of the voters, slowing down the long lines with voter questions to determine eligibility, and carefully perusing the applications severely limited black female voter registration.

In the time that it took to register 650 white female voters in Richmond, the registrar could only register 100 black women, and charges of manipulation of the process were apparent. Walker was among those who noted the partiality of the registrars and observed the long line of black women daily waiting to register when the offices closed (*Richmond Times-Dispatch*, Sept. 21, 1921). Despite much anticipation of black women's suffrage, "Richmond, with a female Negro population of 29,365, registered approximately 2,500" (Buni 1967, 79). In total there were approximately twenty thousand black men and women registered voters, and they had little impact on the 1920 presidential elections or the Senate race, where they fielded the black candidate, attorney Joseph Pollard.

Fig. 5. Attorney J. Thomas Newsome, 1921. Courtesy of the Collection of The Newsome House Museum & Cultural Center, Newport News, Virginia.

Empowered, however, by the community's resurgence of political activity, by 1921 blacks had combined statewide forces to field "The Republican" ticket for the gubernatorial race, making a complete break with the Republican party. The ticket was led by John Mitchell Jr. for governor, Theodore Nash of Newport News for lieutenant governor, J. Thomas Newsome for attorney general, Thomas E. Jackson of Staunton for treasurer, J. Z. Baccus of Lynchburg for secretary of the common-wealth, Maggie Lena Walker for superintendent of public instruction, and J. L. Lee of Roanoke for commissioner of agriculture (*Richmond Times-Dispatch*, Sept. 7, 1921). Blacks argued that the reasons for the separation were that they had a voting constituency of twenty thousand strong, which had been poorly treated in the Republican party, and they had a desire to be treated as citizens (*Richmond Planet*, Aug. 20, 1921).

While blacks knew that they had no realistic chance of winning the state elections, the political statement of separation from the Republican party was a profound move indicating a newfound independence. The internal problems were certainly evident because the community was now besieged with political apathy. Furthermore, there was a lack of cohesive strength that had always mobilized black Richmond, as well as disunity among black leaders. For example, P. B. Young, editor of the *Norfolk Journal and Guide*, was in vocal opposition to Mitchell's candidacy, and that dissension rippled throughout the community (*Norfolk Journal and Guide*, Oct. 22, 1921). Although the elections were certainly lost before the campaign had begun, blacks were now empowered with political determination to change the face of Virginia politics. Realistically, however, the practice of de jure segregation in the South, sanctioned by the U.S. Supreme Court in several cases, destabilized black Richmonders' enfranchisement and relegated them to second-class citizenship.

3

Black Political Mobilization

The Byrd Era

Wallace never said anything but "Negro" in public, recalled
Tony Hefferman, a United Press International reporter in the
1960s, but in personal conversation, they were "niggers."
. . . Lyndon Johnson seemed to revel in using the "n" word
in private conversations with white southern politicians.
Decent, reasonably open-minded southerners like Big Jim
Folsom often talked about "niggers," while more fastidious
politicians like Harry Byrd of Virginia masked their racist
feelings and actions behind a facade of verbal politeness.

Dan Carter, *The Politics of Rage,* 1995

BYRD THE POLITICIAN

Dan Carter's definitive study on George Wallace, *The Politics of Rage,* dif-
ferentiates between Wallace's staunch segregationist views on race and
the views of comparable prominent white southern politicians such as
Jim Folsom and Harry Byrd. Wallace's style, Carter suggests, was one of
"in your face racism," whereas politicians like Byrd seem to engage in a
form of "kinder, gentler racism" (Shull 1993). Thus, whichever racist style
one wants to ascribe to Byrd, by most accounts, Byrd was just as much a
racist and segregationist as Wallace, Strom Thurmond of South Carolina,
Lester Maddox of Georgia, and Theodore Bilbo of Mississippi. Moreover,
although Byrd himself did not engage publicly in overt race-baiting campaign tactics like a Wallace or Bilbo, his support of such measures as the
poll tax, along with his steadfast refusal to support even token attempts

to integrate Virginia's public schools, clearly demonstrate his commitment to perpetuating the legacy of white supremacy in Virginia.

Byrd's role in and fidelity to the massive resistance movement illustrate how his views on race reform were just as conservative and unwa-
vering as those of his southern contemporaries. Historian Ronald L.
Heinemann's recent biography on Byrd, *Harry Byrd of Virginia,* and
Robert A. Pratt's *Color of Their Skin,* on Byrd's role in the rise of the MR
movement, clearly demonstrate that Byrd was not a "kinder, gentler"
racist, as some scholars have suggested. According to Heinemann, Byrd

> was active in supporting the Southern Manifesto and contributed to its cre-
> ation. And Senator Fullbright, who reluctantly signed the manifesto, credited
> Byrd with asserting very strong leadership in stirring up the resistance of the
> South. . . . Historian Frances Wilhoit has concluded that Harry Byrd, more
> than any other single individual, determined the shape and style of the
> movement as it evolved in the decade after 1954. Putting it more negatively,
> Robert Whitehead in 1957 said that Byrd was more responsible for the pres-
> ent racial tension than anyone else in the whole South. Instead of channel-
> ing the South's frustration in a positive direction, he pushed it toward
> defiance. (Heinemann 1996, 335)

Pratt notes that "Byrd coined the phrase massive resistance in February
1956, and . . . he encouraged Lindsay Almond to block integration, and
Almond forsook massive resistance only over the adamant objections of
Harry Byrd. Almond, in many ways the real tragic figure of the entire
episode, later commented: I lived in hell" (1992, 9). These two illustrations of Byrd's role in the rise of the MR movement in the South in general and Virginia in particular corroborate certain aspects of Carter's
argument that politicians like Harry Byrd of Virginia masked their racist
feelings and actions behind a facade of verbal politeness (Carter 1995).

In addition to his socially conservative views on race, Byrd was a tra-
ditionalist on matters pertaining to women. For instance, he opposed
women having access to equal education and to the professions of
their choice, and he voted against the suffrage amendment in 1920
(Heinemann 1996). In addition, Byrd revealed in a letter to Mrs. E.
Virginia Smith of Winchester, Virginia, that the primary reason he
opposed the suffrage amendment was because the amendment would
permit black women to vote, and he felt that by allowing black women
to vote, their votes could have grave consequences for the white power
structure in certain areas of the state:

> I agree that it would be impossible for the Negroes to permanently dominate
> Virginia, yet in counties in southern Virginia, where the Negro predominates

in number, it would certainly be a most dangerous thing to permit them to vote without restrictions either the male or the female. . . . I endeavored to make my position clear when I met your committee; viz, that until the same restrictions in voting can be imposed upon the Negro female as now are imposed upon the Negro male, I would be opposed to the ratification of the Federal Suffrage Amendment by the State of Virginia. When that objection has been removed, while I am frank to say that I have strong personal prejudice against women voting, yet if any substantial number of women desire to vote I can see no logical reason to deny to them this privilege. (Heinemann 1996, 27)

Byrd's letter reveals two disturbing and important points that might explain his hidden agenda for opposing the suffrage amendment. First, he was not opposed to white women voting, but he was definitely opposed to black women voting unless they could be prevented from voting like black males. Thus, if Byrd could be convinced that black women would not be granted the vote, he would not oppose the suffrage amendment. Second, Byrd actually opposed women voting because the arrival of women in the political arena would only expand the voting electorate, thus forcing him to become accountable to a larger voting populace. In other words, a larger voting populace could erode some of Byrd's organizational strength. An interesting point about Byrd's position on women voting that was not revealed in his initial letter to Smith was his elitist views. In a follow-up letter to Smith, Byrd wrote, "As you say, I was opposed to woman suffrage yet at the same time, I think that now every women should register and vote and I am inclined to think that the influence of women in politics will tend to greatly improve conditions providing that the better class of women take an activist interest" (Heinemann 1996, 27). Byrd, it appears, welcomed women's political participation as long as white, privileged women were the dominant actors.

Based upon the information presented thus far, it appears that Byrd, like most of his fellow southern racists during his era, was antagonistic toward blacks and women in the political arena.

BYRD AND BLACK POLITICAL LEADERS

The political relationship existing between Byrd and the black community, and between the Byrd organization and the black community can best be explained in this manner. Byrd was a socially conservative southern Democrat and a staunch segregationist. Although labeled a conservative, he was also considered a progressive governor by Virginia's political standards (Wilkinson 1968). He was identified as a progressive governor because he "abolished the state tax on land, and promoted rural electrification, conservation and the tourist trade," and because he eliminated the state's financial deficit and "sponsored strict legislation which made lynching a state offense and all members of a lynch mob subject to murder charges" (6). Byrd's decision to make lynching a state offense was not solely motivated by his altruistic concern for blacks. One plausible explanation of why he sponsored the legislation that made lynching a state crime was his concern for damages that could occur to property when a lynch mob becomes disorderly after a lynching incident (6). Byrd's motives for making lynching a state offense, and the requirement that its participants be charged with murder, thus appear questionable. For instance, when President Truman's Fair Employment Practices Commission (FEPC) recommended to the president the means by which blacks' civil rights could be secured, one of the recommendations strongly urged by the FEPC was the passage of federal anti-lynching laws. Byrd's reaction to the FEPC's list of racial reforms, especially the anti-lynching law, prompts us to question his sincerity. He defended Virginia's anti-lynching law and accused the FEPC of being a "coercive force" in America (Heinemann 1996, 256). If Byrd's motives for establishing anti-lynching laws in Virginia were genuine, why would he oppose the FEPC's recommendations? Furthermore, if Byrd had already successfully sponsored and passed legislation that made lynching a state offense in Virginia, why would he oppose federal protections for those living in such repressive states such as Mississippi, where lynchings were a common occurrence during this period? The only conceivable response to these questions was that Byrd was perhaps blinded by his racism and his steadfast belief in states' rights, not his concern for human rights.

In spite of his support for a strict law against lynching, Byrd was undeniably a social conservative on matters pertaining to race. For instance, according to V. O. Key, Byrd and his machine/organization supported the poll tax because between 1925 to 1945, "the machine owed its existence to a competent management and a restricted electorate" (Key 1949, 20; Buni 1967, 134–35). Key hypothesized that "in Virginia the low number of voters contributed to the manageability of elections" (135).

Byrd's aristocratic opposition to social and political equality for African Americans forces one to ask why the African American community did not politically oppose the Byrd machine. African Americans were unable effectively to oppose Byrd for three important factors. First, blacks had been successfully disfranchised in Virginia after Reconstruction.

Second, although Byrd opposed racial violence, he also opposed black political empowerment, or any other forms of social equality between the races. Moreover, one could assume that even if blacks could have voted in large numbers during this period, they probably would have reluctantly opted for Byrd simply because he might have been perceived as the lesser of two or three evils given the political alternatives during that era. Third, blacks were unable successfully to oppose Byrd because the poll tax prevented a substantial number of African Americans from voting. For instance, in 1931 between two thousand and three thousand blacks in Richmond were qualified to vote (Buni 1967). In addition to these three major factors, fear and political apathy among black voters was commonplace in most local and state elections, even after the white primary had been ruled unconstitutional by the U.S. Supreme Court. Besides, the small number of black registered voters was insignificant. Thus, the small number of registered African American voters could not have mounted any sizable political threat to the Byrd organization. Although Byrd was a Democrat, or as former President Truman preferred to call him, a Demopublican, he constantly changed his political affiliation to suit his political needs. Consequently, since a majority of blacks in Richmond were also Democrats, they consistently opposed the Byrd Democrats at the state level while consistently supporting the Democratic party at the national level (Buni 1967, 171–72; Heinemann 1996, 255). Blacks supported the Democratic party nationally because the Democratic party in Virginia and throughout the South had historically excluded blacks from participating in party functions (Ladd 1969, 35). Furthermore, the federal government's "passive resistance" to protecting African American constitutional rights also impeded any efforts by blacks effectively to mobilize against the Byrd organization. The occurrence or the convergence of some of these factors at one time or another prevented the African American populace from posing a political threat to Byrd or his organization.

The Byrd machine's relationship with the African American community in Virginia, and Richmond in particular, was basically the same. According to Key, "In the cities, where Negroes vote in highest proportions, they have often been allied with local arms of the Byrd organization, which in turn protected their right to suffrage" (Key 1948, 32). Those blacks who aligned themselves with the local arms of the Byrd machine did so because it was politically and economically expedient. Key noted in his study of Virginia that Byrd was the machine and it clearly reflected his political persona. In other words, one could not separate the organization from the individual who created it.

Finally, by the time the Byrd machine had become firmly entrenched in Virginia's political arena, and although black Richmonders still opposed all vestiges of Virginia's Jim Crow society, most blacks in Richmond and throughout this nation had subconsciously accepted certain aspects of this country's dual society while consciously continuing to fight it. In fact, this point can be substantiated for Richmond and the nation as well. In Richmond, for instance, there were two prominent African American citizens in two different time periods who urged fellow blacks to recognize the reality of segregation and strive toward improving the Negro economy. John T. Mitchell, founder and editor of the *Richmond Planet* (later called the *Richmond Afro-American*), echoed these kinds of sentiments as early as 1903, and Professor Gordon Blaine Hancock of Virginia Union University, a staunch supporter of political and social equality for blacks, also expressed similar views concerning blacks acknowledgment of their political reality during the 1930s. Mitchell

> continued the fight against discrimination at the polls, even recommending Negro boycotts of white businesses and products. Thereafter, he became resigned to the hopelessness of the situation and eschewed politics. Typical of his brief weekly Words of Advice, concerned mainly with the Negroes' progress economically and industrially, is the following, Colored men, continue to save money and buy property. . . . Any colored man who opposes race enterprises among the colored people is his own worst enemy. . . . Colored men should make friends with the better elements of white men in the southland. It should not be forgotten that colored men are directly responsible for many of the ills from which they suffer. (Buni 1967, 37–38)

Hancock concurs with Mitchell's views when he reinforces the pragmatism of the older race men: "Racially speaking . . . we oppose segregation, but economically speaking it forms the basis of our professional and business life. There is nothing to indicate . . . the slightest change in this bi-racial attitude" (Gavins 1977, 69).

Hancock constructed his idea of the Negro economy on Du Bois's idea of a segregated economy, which appeared in Du Bois's article "A Negro Nation Within the Nation" (1935, 270). Du Bois urged his fellow African Americans to concede the political reality of segregation because the pleas for justice for blacks had simply been ignored. Therefore, the only recourse for African Americans was to support the Negro economy (265). "There exists today a chance for the Negroes to organize a cooperative State within their own group," he declared. "By letting Negro farmers feed Negro artisans, and Negro technicians guide Negro home industries, and Negro thinkers plan this integration of cooperation, while Negro artists dramatize the beauty of the struggle, economic independence can be achieved" (270). In essence, the relevance of mentioning these specific views is to illustrate the enormous political difficulties African Americans confronted in their attempts to battle not only the Byrd machine but institutionalized racism as well. In fact, the quotations also indicate that the black intelligentsia sent mixed signals to the black masses. One signal communicated to the black masses was to accept segregation, while the other communicated that the struggle for political and social equality was a complex struggle and any solutions to these problems would have to be long term.

Thus, for those who ask why the African American population of Richmond did not adopt more radical solutions to their political dilemma, the answer is that it would have been rejected then by force and later by redistricting measures. For instance, in 1922, Marcus Garvey appeared in Richmond. Garvey's rousing speech to black Richmonders did not persuade those in attendance to join his movement (Gavins 1977). Black leaders in Richmond, such as Mitchell, supported Garvey's self-help programs but opposed his back-to-Africa philosophy. Conservative attitudes were clearly prevalent, even among Richmond's so-called progressive black leaders, and this conservative inclination hindered the political struggle for equality and justice. The relationship between the Byrd organization and the African American community had an impact on the progression of black political development in general and black conservative politics in particular. The Byrd organization did not help or actually hinder the progression of black conservative politics, because Byrd really did not need the assistance of black conservatives to undermine black political unity in Richmond or the state. For instance, the number of black registered voters was insignificant during the peak years of the organization, and black voters were probably perceived by Byrd's organization as more of a political annoyance than a significant political threat to the organization. Although some blacks on several occasions did assist the Byrd organization in undermining black political unity, the costs that a black conservative would have to pay for publicly supporting the Byrd organization simply outweighed the benefits. The kind of public humiliation that a black conservative could accrue if suspected of collaborating with the Byrd organization, or with the local white power structure, is reflected in the following quotation from a civil rights organizational meeting held in the church of Reverend C. C. Scott during the initial planning stages of a major civil rights boycott in 1960: "Most of the speakers pressed for the continuation of the boycott against Thalhimer's and other stores. There was one brave speaker, Reverend C. C. Scott, who suggested to moderate the boycott, stating, 'You've won a great victory up to this point. But it may be that we need to detour just a little bit,' only to be smothered by the audience's displeasure through boos and foot stomping" (Williams 1990, 45).

Finally, the Byrd organization did not need the support of black conservatives to undermine black political unity because black politics in Richmond were already fractionalized, and thus there was no pressing need to divide them. The Republican party at the state and local levels consistently issued public pronouncements to white voters reassuring them that their party was still lily white (Buni 1967). Historically, blacks in Richmond treated those blacks who collaborated with fervent white supremacists politicians at different periods in some form of retaliatory manner. For example,

> about a week before the election, some two hundred and fifty Conservative Negroes of Richmond, at the risk of personal violence from the colored Radicals, arranged a barbecue for their men and invited a number of prominent white conservatives. The speeches on both sides were harmonious and good feeling prevailed. The hosts displayed a banner upon which was a picture of a white man and a colored man shaking hands. Under the picture was written, 'United We Stand Divided We Fall.' By an unhappy coincidence a nearby bridge fell soon after the appearance of this banner, carrying with it a crowd of people. Many were injured and several were killed. (Morton 1973, 75)

While this illustrates an extreme case of how some blacks in the past have responded toward other blacks who were perceived as colluding with white supremacist interests, Richmond blacks generally have responded to political betrayal by politically repudiating the alleged perpetrators. An excellent illustration of this point occurred when black political groups such as the RCV exercised their political clout in local elections by announcing their support for a specific slate of candidates for office the Sunday before each city council election. The implications of the RCV's announcement ploy was twofold. First, the announcement was used to solidify its control over Richmond's black body politic. Second, the announcement was used to punish those black candidates who may have been perceived as being aligned with the Byrd machine or white supremacist interests. This point can be substantiated by the Cephas and Mundle case in which two black conservative incumbents were not endorsed by the RCV for the 1968 council election:

If the Crusade endorsement was to mean anything, it would have to show that blacks could reject black candidates who were well-known incumbents (but not endorsed by the Crusade) and vote for Crusade endorsed white candidates. The election results proved the point. Cephas and Mundle were defeated. . . . What is particularly noteworthy is that in virtually every black precinct, the voters overwhelmingly preferred the Crusade-endorsed white candidates over the two black candidates not endorsed by the Crusade. (Moeser and Dennis 1982, 84)

Thus, blacks who were perceived by black political groups as supporting conservative or white supremacist interests were eventually rejected and defeated in the political arena for their alleged betrayal.

Consequently, impassioned black conservatives rarely did so. Furthermore, the political price for associating with those forces opposed to the struggle for political and social equality for blacks in Richmond was a heavy one. Yet if one associated with the Byrd organization, it was done in a very discrete manner. A. J. Dickinson's research supports this view, based upon information that was provided to him by a former reporter. The reporter revealed during an interview that "he saw a list of Negro ministers and real estate men who could be bought, a list which was kept [by the Byrd people] until at least as late as 1950s" (Dickinson 1967, 14).

One could conclude on one level that the Byrd organization, and the state's white supremacist doctrine, prevented blacks from participating in the state and local political parties. By preventing their participation in the parties, one could argue that the African American population was not allowed to develop into a viable political force. Moreover, for blacks who were opposed to the Byrd organization and Virginia's white supremacist status quo, the Byrd machine actually strengthened their efforts to challenge it. Black Richmonders would not effectively challenge the Byrd organization until the mid-1950s, during the black political mobilization era.

THE BLACK POLITICAL MOBILIZATION ERA, 1942–1956

The political mobilization of Richmond's African American community could historically best be described as a battle waged on two fronts. On one front, the African American community has had to contend with and constantly react to white overt and covert racist political behavior. This racist behavior has frequently forced the African American community to respond from a defensive or reactionary posture. On the second front, African Americans have constantly sought political inclusion through the courts, protest marches, and other forms of political demonstrations. Additionally, to the external constraints and pressures that were being routinely placed upon them by the local political and economic elites, like most African American communities across America, they frequently had to contend with political divisiveness within their own community, primarily over which or what particular strategy should be adopted to alleviate or attack a given problem or sets of problems.

The African American's quest for political, economic, and social equality in Richmond was a major undertaking, primarily because the local political and economic elites were committed to perpetuating their notion of white control over the city at any cost (Moeser and Dennis 1982, 32–33). The attitude of maintaining white control over Richmond stemmed from two distinct factors. The first was the belief that social equality between the races would not work in the South. This point of view, which is held by some whites and persists in Richmond's political and economic circles, contends that African Americans are inferior and ill equipped to govern any city, let alone the state capital (Harris 1991). The second factor was the perception by political elites that Richmond was still the capital of the Confederacy as well as the capital of Virginia. For instance, whenever the African American population increased to 40 percent or more, one of the first rallying calls for expanding Richmond's boundaries, thus taking in more white voters, was that if blacks gained control of the city, they would destroy Monument Way (which is lined with monuments to the dead Confederate generals) (77). In other words, if whites failed to stop the political advancement of blacks, then blacks would eventually destroy Richmond's culture and quality of life. White hysteria in response to black demands for political equality was parallel to a scene out of D. W. Griffith's classic movie *The Klansman*. Whites actually were convinced that Richmond had to be safeguarded against the ever-present dangerous black presence.

In essence, political mobilization of Richmond's African American community has had certain developmental complexities. The quest for political, economic, and social equality for Richmond's African American community can generally be traced to three distinct yet interconnected periods of black political development: (1) 1940s, (2) the period arising shortly after the landmark case of *Brown v. Board of Education* in 1955–56, and (3) the 1970s, which saw the eventual emergence of an African American political majority. In the remaining portion of this chapter, the rise of Richmond's black political mobilization throughout the Byrd era will be explicated by focusing exclusively upon the embryonic stage of mobilization and, finally, upon the rise and decline of a major black political organization in Richmond. The subsequent emergence of a black political majority on city council will be examined in greater detail in chapter 5.

Failed Alliance

One explanation of why Richmond's black community was ineffective against the Byrd organization until the mid-1950s was that key black leaders in Richmond and throughout the southern region adopted a strategy of gradual reform of the Jim Crow system. Byrd and his organization were absent from any meetings that involved the participation of black leaders whose primary objective was to alter Virginia's system of segregation because Byrd and his organization were committed to maintaining white supremacy. Thus, even though Byrd's organization was firmly entrenched politically throughout the state of Virginia, blacks, notwithstanding, never abandoned their struggle against segregation. One illustration of blacks' attempt to combat the system that controlled their daily lives was the gradual reformism strategy adopted by moderate southern blacks during the early 1940s.

During the 1940s, moderate African American leaders attempted to improve race relations in the South by establishing a formal dialogue between black and white leaders. Their objective was to persuade white southern leaders to reform Jim Crow (Moeser and Silver 1995, 64–65; Redding 1943). The leaders of these attempts were Benjamin Mays, former president of Morehouse College in Atlanta; Gordon Blaine Hancock, a professor at Virginia Union University in Richmond and an ordained minister; and George Washington Lee, a black Republican and major black member of the Crump political machine in Memphis, Tennessee (Moeser and Silver 1995). Mays and Hancock represented the two interconnecting institutions that eventually played a pivotal role in CRMs during the national civil rights era, especially in the South, black churches, and black colleges (Morris 1984).

Interracial forums were convened in Durham, North Carolina, in 1942 and Atlanta, Georgia, in 1943. Northern blacks were excluded for several reasons. First, according to Gordon Blaine Hancock, in "Writing a New Charter of Southern Race Relations," an article published by the Southern Regional Council in 1964, their meeting would be doomed if some northern Negro leaders were invited to the meeting (Hancock 1964). Second,

Hancock and a small fraction of southern black leaders were apprehensive of northern black participation and were convinced that acting alone they could be more effective in persuading southern white leaders to reform Jim Crow. In *The Separate City,* Moeser and Silver assert that black leaders

> urged the white South to demonstrate greater fairness to blacks and to provide evidence of greater opportunities for southern blacks, although they stopped short of calling for an end to segregation. They made it clear that without some tangible evidence that white leaders were willing to make some concessions, the black masses would begin to turn increasingly to black "extremists" outside the South who would demand nothing less than complete abolition of all segregation and discrimination. (1995, 65)

The challenge for the southern black leadership was to convince southern white moderates to make concessions in race relations before the black masses were influenced by more extreme elements within the African American community. The black leadership was clearly moderate, conservative, and perhaps even accommodationist. Had black leaders approached moderate southern whites in a belligerent manner or radical posture, they would have been denied access to the political system.

Moeser and Silver maintain that Virginius Dabney, a leading white southern moderate from Richmond, former editor of the *Richmond Times-Dispatch,* and Pulitzer Prize winner, refused to chair the second meeting in Atlanta in 1943 if A. Phillip Randolph of the Brotherhood of the Sleeping Car Porters Union and Roy Wilkins of the NAACP attended (Moeser and Silver 1995). Dabney and other southern white moderates opposed the participation of northern blacks, especially Wilkins and Randolph, because Randolph was viewed as a traitor to the United States for his threatened March on Washington to oppose Jim Crow hiring practices in defense plants in 1941; Wilkins was disapproved of because his organization promoted social equality. Both views contradicted the white supremacist underpinnings of the Jim Crow system. Dabney, in his article "Nearer and Nearer the Precipice," published in the *Atlantic Monthly* in 1943, stated that Wilkins and Randolph were considered undesirable participants at their conferences because of their radical views. Reflecting the attitudes of white southern moderates, Dabney further stated that if radical blacks persisted with their unreasonable demands for racial integration, blacks could expect a negative reaction from most southern whites: "Extremist Negro leaders and Negro newspapers in this country are demanding an overnight revolution in race relations. . . . If an attempt is made forcibly to abolish segregation throughout the South, violence and bloodshed will result" (Dabney 1943). Neither Randolph nor Wilkins attended the Atlanta meeting. The long-range result of southern moderate black leaders excluding their black northern brethren from their meetings to placate the interests of white southern moderates was that their strategy eventually backfired on them and consequently undermined their credibility within the black community.

The southern interracial meetings continued until 1954 but did not persuade southern white moderate leaders or politicians to address major racial matters. Despite their moderate tone, the meetings were severely criticized by southern white conservatives such as Eugene Talmadge, former governor of Georgia, who actually labeled them communist-inspired. Attacks by conservative whites frustrated black leaders, and some southern white moderates, such as Dabney, became disillusioned with southern whites' unwillingness to adopt even token social reforms. Dabney concluded that "the best way to provoke bitter race clashes in this region over an indefinite period is for whites to turn their backs on the legitimate appeals of Negroes for justice. The crisis is upon us, and we shall ignore it at our peril" (Moeser and Silver 1995, 66). The inability of southern African American leaders to broker a political arrangement with moderate southern whites to reform the Jim Crow system produced three significant outcomes. First, black leaders who organized the interracial forums were politically discredited in their respective black communities and labeled "accommodationist." An example of the black liberal criticism that was hurled against the black moderate leaders who participated in these interracial meetings is "A Negro Speaks for His People," an article by J. Saunders Redding (1943). The Redding article appeared in the same *Atlantic Monthly* issue as Dabney's article and was a rebuttal of Dabney's views:

> There are also events of greater magnitude. In the first place, the old Negro leadership in the South was outstripped by its (theoretical) following. The old leadership had been chosen and maintained by the white South because it was too weak to make encroachments upon the basic assumption of Negro inferiority or upon the racial status quo. The old leadership was maintained because it threatened no change and no essential modification of the mores of the South. . . . It was a leadership meant to be effective for progress in a world in which black would remain forever unequal to white. . . . There is no refuge in conservatism. There is no road back from liberalism except to a precipice. The road lies ahead, and we built it. It is our right and our duty to lead the way along it. (Redding 1943, 58)

Black moderates' failure to modify Jim Crow exhausted their leadership and political capital. The new and younger black leaders who emerged to lead CRMs in cities such as Richmond would not settle for incremental reforms in the Jim Crow laws but demanded total abolishment of the system. A second important outcome of the failed alliance was that the failure to reform Jim Crow contributed to modern CRMs in cities such as Richmond. For instance, if the reader will recall, the interracial meetings ended in 1954, the year of the *Brown* decision, and Virginia was one of the states affected by that decision. Moreover, Virginia is further relevant to our discussion because it was in Virginia that the strategy of MR to integrate public schools was first conceived by James Kilpatrick and enthusiastically supported by none other than Harry F. Byrd (Moeser and Silver 1995). The final outcome of the failed alliance was in Richmond: the threat of MR in Virginia would precipitate the decline of groups like the Richmond Civic Council (RCC), a ministerial-dominated organization, and the emergence of yet another black insurgency, the RCV (Randolph 1998; Randolph and Tate 1995). The emergence of the RCV and its successful assault on de jure segregation will be expounded upon later in this chapter.

The Rise and Decline of the RCC

The principal African American political organization that emerged after the war and eventually dominated Richmond's black body politic until the mid-1950s was a group called the RCC (Moeser and Dennis 1982, 32). The RCC was simply a decentralized triumvirate of black conservative middle-class civic associations, fraternal societies, and religious groups whose primary focus was to increase the number of registered African American voters (Moeser and Dennis 1982, 32; Holton 1987, 33). As a decentralized organization, RCC operated with a central governing structure that consisted of representatives from each of the different organizations that comprised its body (33). Thus, due to its decentralized structure, the central body was reluctant to discipline its member groups and their representatives because each member group retained its independence from the governing body. In other words, an organization with a weak governing body illustrated the factionalized nature of Richmond's black politics. Dwight Holton's study, "Power to the People," explains why a decentralized structure was preferred by the RCC leadership: "The decentralized nature of the Civic Council suited the clergymen of the organization, who held a disproportionate amount of power and influence. Other community leaders were active in the Council, but ministers were the one group that could reach and influence a large number of Negroes effectively and consistently, and their leadership was natural" (Holton 1987, 34). The RCC's initial reason for concentrating on voter registration was threefold. First, unlike blacks in the Deep South, blacks in Richmond were rarely intimidated with violence when attempting to register to vote. However, because Virginia imposed a poll tax on individuals who attempted to register to vote, black registration levels were generally low until after the Second World War (ibid.). Virginia's poll tax operated in the following manner: "As established by the 1902 state constitution, registration required the payment of a $1.50 poll tax for the three years preceding an election. If the registrant had not paid the tax in the past years, he or she could pay the cumulative total of $4.50" (ibid.). The poll tax disproportionately affected African Americans because a sizable number of blacks were impoverished and many during this period were often employed in menial positions. Furthermore, those blacks with professional skills comparable to or even greater than their white counterparts did not receive comparable compensation. An excellent illustration of this point is to be found in the pay discrepancy between black and white teachers. According to the late Ethel T. Overby, the first black female principal of a Richmond public school, black teachers

> worked so hard and were paid so little that I decided to begin a movement for higher salaries for Negro teachers. My first visit was to Mrs. Mary Mumford, a member of the Richmond School Board. There were nine members on the Board, eight men and one woman. When I began to talk with her concerning the differential between Negro and white teachers' salaries, she said, It does not cost you coloreds as much to live as it does a white girl. For instance, if you were going to have a birthday party, it would not cost you as much as it does a white girl. (Overby 1975, 5)

The significance of discussing the economic conditions of black Richmonders here is to point out that the poll tax was just as much an impediment to Virginia blacks desiring to register to vote as was the physical violence that blacks endured in Mississippi when they attempted to vote during this time period. In essence, the end result of both methods was to frustrate, and eventually deny, African Americans the right to exercise their constitutional rights. In addition, the poll tax requirement was simply another political ploy by Virginia's political and economic elites to maintain white supremacy.

A second reason the RCC focused on registration was because no African American had served on the city council since 1895. One explanation for this was that Richmond's old district system had been gerrymandered by the white power structure to the point that African Americans could not get elected even under a ward/district system. This point is significant because it negates conventional political science wisdom that electing officials by districts or wards enhances the electability chances of those candidates representing women, the poor, and minority communities of a given area of a city (Judd 1988, 109–14). In other words, candidates did not have to appeal to all of the voters to get elected. Instead, a candidate only had to appeal to a specified, geographically defined area of voters in order to get elected to city council.

The final reason the RCC concentrated their efforts on voter registration was that given the disfranchisement schemes that were being perpetrated by the white power structure against the African American community, the group was convinced that if African Americans voters supported the charter reform movement of 1947, the black community would obtain some form of political concessions from the Richmond Citizens Association, which spearheaded the charter reform movement in Richmond (Moeser and Dennis 1982, 32–33). Furthermore, members of the RCC firmly believed that the concessions obtained from the RCA and reform movement could be translated into a major political victory for the African American community. The RCC further believed that any political concessions obtained as a result of blacks participating in the reform movement could serve as a galvanizing force to rally the community around other future key political and economic issues. The one immediate symbolic spinoff victory that occurred as a result of Richmond's black community supporting the charter reform movement was Oliver Hill's candidacy for the Virginia House of Delegates. Although Hill, a noted black civil rights lawyer, did not win the election in 1947, his narrow defeat generated and eventually sustained enough political enthusiasm within Richmond's black body politic to help elect Hill to city council in 1948 (34). Furthermore, after the new charter was approved by the voters in November 1947, black Richmonders entered 1948 with high expectations of greater inclusion in Richmond's larger body politic. Black expectations of greater inclusion in Richmond's political arena was not unfounded. In fact, some black leaders describe this period as one of good feeling or optimism with respect to improved race relations in the city.

An excellent illustration of this era of optimism occurred with the RCC's leadership. The RCC was so optimistic about the black community's political future that they were anxiously anticipating establishing a working coalition with the RCA on the upcoming city council election

(40). In other words, the RCC leadership surmised that because blacks had supported the RCA's charter reform movement, the two groups would perhaps jointly support a slate of candidates for city council. Thus, from the RCC's perspective, if a black candidate was supported by the two groups, then conceivably a black candidate with the support of a biracial coalition could get elected to city council. Although the RCC's motives for anticipating a working relationship with RCA are not clearly reflected in any of the literature written about the RCC, one could interpret their actions as an attempt on their part to broker a biracial coalition with RCA. The idea of RCC trying to broker a biracial coalition in 1948 was not groundless. For instance, the actions that were taken by the RCC leading up to the 1948 election appears to confirm our argument for three reasons. First, the RCC began to shift its organizational focus from that of voting registration to that of political mobilization. For example, the RCC immediately established voting schools and supported seminars for the purpose of educating blacks on how and for whom they should vote for in the upcoming municipal election. Second, the RCC also began to sponsor voter registration drives and rallies that were designed to get out the vote, a move to demonstrate to the RCA that the black community's vote would be a decisive factor in the upcoming election. Last, the RCC attempted to ensure that a black candidate would be included on the RCA slate by encouraging the black community to support one black candidate and to avoid "slingshot" voting, a strategy often employed by groups to secure the election of a particular candidate in an at-large election by encouraging their voters to vote for that candidate only (Holton 1987, 45). In addition, during the 1948 city council election, the RCC immediately endorsed Hill when he announced his candidacy, and they did not endorse any other black candidates seeking a seat on city council. We believe that the RCC adopted this stratagem to convince the RCA that Hill was a solid candidate with a strong support base in the black community (41).

It appears that the actions taken by the RCC were undeniably a political ploy on their part to establish a biracial coalition with the RCA for the municipal election of 1948. Furthermore, if the RCC's political overtures were not a ploy to attract the RCA's attention, where did the RCC get the idea that a biracial coalition between themselves and RCA was even desired by the RCA? The following quotation substantiates the claim that the RCC believed that a coalition between themselves and the RCA was no happenstance: "The Citizens Association [RCA], which was preparing to field a nine-member slate in the at-large election in June, conducted a vigorous membership drive in all parts of the city. Citizens Association President G. E. Marlow, noting that co-operative action by Richmonders from all walks of life had given Richmond one of the finest charters in America, declared that all Richmonders were welcome in the RCA, regardless of class, race, or political creed" (Holton 1987, 38).

Accordingly, if one accepts the RCA's rhetoric, it is safe to conclude that the RCA meant what it said during the campaign of 1947. However, intent and reality are sometimes incongruous. Moreover, the intent of RCA may have been genuine at the moment but perhaps was more Machiavellian in reality. Consequently, in spite of the RCC's political maneuvering and its catering to white interests, the RCA disappointed black Richmonders when it refused to endorse Hill's candidacy. For most black Richmonders, the RCA's refusal to endorse Hill's candidacy was an act of betrayal from whites. The betrayal argument was not unfounded because the RCA's decision may have been racially motivated. Holton notes that the "*Afro* reported on March 20 that the RCA was engaged in a heated debate as to whether endorsing a black candidate was a wise course of action" (1987, 40). Thus, when the RCA publicly announced its slate of candidates, Hill's name was noticeably absent. Race seems to have been an important factor in RCA's decision to run a "lily-white" slate of candidates for city council in 1948. Although Hill was not endorsed by the RCA, Hill collected 28,343 total votes, of which more than 4,000 came from sympathetic whites (42). The election of Attorney Oliver Hill, Richmond's first African American on the city council since 1895, was an important political victory for Richmond's black populace.

RCC's failed attempt to form a biracial coalition with the RCA is important to this discussion because it revealed a major defect when a minority group attempted to broker a biracial coalition with a white group in a racially polarized political climate. The initial mistake made by the RCC when it attempted to pursue a coalition with the RCA was that the primary basis for forming a political coalition between blacks and whites was never established. Raphael J. Sonenshein, in his classic text on Los Angeles' politics, *Politics in Black and White*, states that "minority mobilization and liberal ideology are the cornerstones of any interracial coalition pursuing minority incorporation" (Sonenshein 1993, 20). In the case involving the RCC and RCA, based upon the information presented thus far, we are convinced that even if the RCA was willing to form a biracial coalition with the RCC, given the state of race relations in Richmond during 1947, liberal politicians were definitely a scarce commodity in a very conservative state. In addition, whites who would have agreed to form a coalition with blacks would not have entered into the coalition with the purpose of incorporating blacks into the governing coalition. Also, even though the middle-class RCC and the white, middle-class, and business-dominated RCA shared similar values, the prospect of establishing a biracial coalition based upon mutual interests was simply impossible at that time because of the racially polarized climate. Finally, although Richmond's black community was highly factionalized in 1947, what appeared to be missing in Richmond that would have made a biracial coalition possible was the absence of interracial leadership ties. The presence of such ties is a critical ingredient to forging a successful biracial coalition. Again according to Sonenshein, "To understand such leadership ties, it is necessary to look within the [b]lack and white communities. Such coalitions are likely to be far stronger than alliances based upon shifting sands of self-interest in the absence of ideological affinity. They are also likely to be much stronger than coalitions based on goodwill alone. Goodwill alone is not enough, but neither is cold self-interest" (1993, 20). Hence, RCC's failed attempt to form a biracial coalition with the RCA simply revealed the difficulties involved when the issue of race is such an historical and divisive factor in a political community.

In spite of what appears to have been a major political coup for RCC during the 1948 municipal elections when Hill was elected to city council, and in 1950 when the RCA included Hill on their slate of candidates for city council, the RCC itself soon faced political legitimacy. The political legitimacy issue that confronted the RCC involved the second form of betrayal, and that was betrayal from within. The idea of the RCC engaging in a form of betrayal from within stemmed from a series of questionable incidents and a major political debacle involving the RCC leadership. An excellent illustration of this betrayal occurred with the political debacle surrounding the 1952 municipal election. In 1950, Oliver Hill lost his bid for reelection to city council, and in 1952, Hill announced that he would not run for office, primarily he was arguing the Prince Edward County desegregation case before the U.S. Supreme Court (Holton 1987, 48). Thus, with the absence of a proven candidate of Hill's stature, the RCC was initially unable to find a candidate who was acceptable to RCA. The one person who would eventually surface as a candidate acceptable to RCA was Dr. W. L. Ransome, who, incidentally, was then president of the RCC and a member of the RCA board. When Ransome's candidacy was discussed during an RCC meeting, Hill immediately opposed it because he believed that Ransome, at seventy-three years of age, was simply too old for the position. Moreover, Hill feared that Ransome, a Baptist minister, could alienate voters who were suspicious about clergymen who ran for elected office. Hill further opposed Ransome's candidacy because of Ransome's association with Mayor Bright. According to Hill,

> Ransome had served on Bright's Advisory Committee on Housing, where he supported construction of a housing project which would have razed scores of homes in Jackson Ward. Bright, who employed only a handful of blacks in city jobs during his sixteen years as mayor, represented the status quo against which blacks had voted during the charter reform movement. Ransome's association with Bright aroused fears that he would be overly conciliatory if elected to City Council. (Holton 1987, 48)

The Ransome issue burgeoned into a debacle when an article appeared in the April 12 issue of the *Afro,* accusing the RCC of trying to prevent another candidate from obtaining the RCA endorsement by supporting Ransome. The controversy surrounding the endorsement began in early April when public speculation surfaced that RCA was going to endorse a black life-insurance executive named David C. Deans. The endorsement became even more muddied when Ransome announced his candidacy for city council. When Ransome announced he would run, one could consider his action a conflict of interest, because he had been selected by the RCA board to serve on a committee that was given the charge of selecting a black candidate who was acceptable to the RCA. Thus when Ransome announced his candidacy, it was at this precise point that the RCC was accused of foul play. The April 12 article further stated that "Ransome supporters immediately approached the RCA and told members of the organization that colored voters will not accept a hand-picked candidate of the RCA. Ransome, who had been defeated in a bid for the House of Delegates in 1949, was apparently determined to force the RCA to endorse him" (49). The Ransome-Deans controversy became even more heated when Ransome attempted to force the RCA into choosing him as the candidate. On April 13, the RCA endorsed only one black candidate and that was Deans. The RCC attempted to mediate the dispute by trying to broker an internal unity deal that would allow the RCC to endorse two candidates. A vote was taken within the RCC, and by a narrow margin of twenty-one to nineteen, the RCC endorsed both Deans and Ransome. In spite of the show of unity, the organization was undeniably divided (Holton 1987, 49). The divisiveness became even more pronounced during the show of unity, and the divisiveness eventually undermined the truce agreement when the Ransome and Deans camps began to accuse each other of wrongdoing. For example, Hill, representing the Deans camp, accused Ransome of being unacceptable to black voters because he was too closely tied to the RCC, and Ransome accused Deans of being aligned with the Byrd organization. Consequently, when the 1952 municipal election was held, no black was elected to city council and the group that was assessed a large part of the blame for public display of black infighting and erosion of black political strength was the RCC.

Events such as the Ransome-Deans debacle, along with the public display of black infighting, would eventually lead to a decline in the RCC's political credibility. Consequently, some in the African American community began privately and publicly to accuse the ministers of aligning themselves with white conservatives and supplementing their incomes by taking money from white conservatives and selling out the African American community for personal gain. The ministers' political alignment with white conservatives created a perception that they had been co-opted by the white power structure (Moeser interview 1991; Dickinson 1967). Thus, the RCC's political departure resulted from rumors circulated in the black community that the leadership of the organization had been bought off by the white power structure. As a result of these allegations, some of which were proven, the African American community strongly rejected the RCC (Dickinson 1967). The RCC was rejected because it was no longer respected in the community, and because of its history of aligning itself with white conservative politicians who basically were ideologically opposed to any meaningful social, political, and economic progress for Richmond's African American community. By 1954 the RCC had become so impotent that for survival purposes it eventually had to merge with the Virginia Voters' League (Holton 1987, 53).

Several factors led to the ultimate demise of the RCC. First, the organization's ill-fated attempt to broker a biracial coalition with the RCA was actually the beginning of the unraveling of its political influence in Richmond's black body politic. Second, the RCC's attempt to thwart the endorsement of Deans by supporting one of their officers to oppose Deans was unquestionably a fatal mistake. This particular episode resulted in a protracted public display of black infighting (Holton 1987, 61). Furthermore, when the RCC willingly accepted a junior partnership/subordinate role with the RCA and other white conservative groups, it simply was no longer a credible player within Richmond's black body politic. Finally, the last factor that would lead to the RCC's downfall was MR. The MR campaign was the collapse of moderate and accommodationist black leaders throughout the South and especially in Virginia. Just as the MR campaign attracted whites who wanted to maintain segregation, the same resistance campaign galvanized blacks to end Jim Crow. Black leaders who had accommodated white interests on segregation were no longer acceptable to the black populace (Holton 1987). Moreover, black moderates and/or conservatives were of little use to the white power structure simply because white leaders could no longer count on them to placate the black masses during a crisis. An excellent illustration of this point occurred when Thomas B. Standley, former governor, convened black leaders during the MR campaign:

> Earlier in May, Governor Stanley called in five black leaders, a group that included attorney Hill and Dr. R. P. Daniel, president of Virginia State College, for a private consultation, urging the leaders to convince blacks to support public school segregation. The leaders rejected his request and, in turn, asked Governor Stanley to support public school integration. Stanley refused, thus casting the die for polarization of the issue among segregationists and integrationists. (Williams 1990)

Stanley, like the rest of Virginia and the South, eventually realized that not all black leaders were willing to accommodate white interests. Furthermore, when Richmond's black community was forced to wage a battle on two fronts, in the courts and in the streets, the battle that was waged in the courts, via *Brown*, would be the death blow to groups like the RCC, which were perceived as accommodating white interest.

The RCC's declining political clout proved to be a catalyst for the emergence of a group of young African American middle-class professional/activists. This group of young political turks felt that a new type of organization had to be created. They envisioned one that was politically and economically independent of white economic elites and thus could articulate the needs of the African American community to a white politically dominated power structure, without the fear of political or economic reprisals. The group that would emerge in 1956 to dominate Richmond's African American community politics would be the Richmond Crusade for Voters (Moeser and Dennis 1982, 34).

Given the demise of the RCC, it became apparent to some African American leaders that if their people wished to progress any further, the formation of an independently led African American grass-roots movement was desperately needed in Richmond. With the emergence of the RCV, a new era and approach to addressing the needs of the community was ushered in. Under the tutelage of the RCV, the African American community's approach to politics would eventually shift from focusing exclusively on voter registration to that of electoral politics and political mobilization. The issue of MR, along with the role of the RCV during the period of MR, will be discussed in greater depth shortly.

The Rise of the RCV

In *Political Process and the Development of Black Insurgency, 1930–1970* (1982), Doug McAdam explains three prerequisites for a generation of insurgency: (1) organizational readiness within the aggrieved population, (2) a level of insurgent consciousness within an exploited population's mass base, and (3) a structure of political opportunities accessible to an insurgent population. In other words, an insurgency is likely when there is an organization within the aggrieved population, along with a collective belief in the success of the venture, and an alignment of groups within the larger political environment (McAdam 1982, 40–41). Richmond's African American community during the early 1900s had achieved some of these preconditions. For instance, Richmond's black community had several ad hoc groups acting on its behalf. However, even before the emergence of the NAACP, different ad hoc groups perceived themselves as acting for the aggrieved population, and the organizations that were formed before 1917 believed that they could change the political system. Notwithstanding, the local ad hoc organizations at that time were not connected to national affiliates and lacked what McAdam termed "structure of political opportunities" (McAdam 1982, 40–77). The primary structure of political opportunities absent in Richmond during this period was the inclusion of African Americans in political and policy decisions. Consequently, blacks lacked the political means to successfully repel Jim Crow.

According to Ann F. Alexander, in her *Black Protest in the New South*, when Jim Crow was imposed, African Americans reacted angrily. John Mitchell expressed the sentiment of the majority of Richmond's blacks: "If you do not desire my company, I can assure you that I have no wish for yours" (Alexander 1972, 326). Outraged over the introduction of Jim Crow into their lives, but powerless to prevent it, blacks protested against de jure segregation. In 1904, they collectively protested the segregation of Virginia's streetcars. Prodded by John Mitchell and the *Richmond Planet*, African Americans boycotted the Virginia Passenger and Power Company, which operated the streetcars (ibid., 327). Richmond's streetcar boycott was probably the first mass-based, organized protest movement by African Americans in the twentieth century. It predates the Baton Rouge boycott by at least forty-nine years and the Montgomery bus boycott by fifty-one years (Morris 1984, 1–50). The boycott was organized principally by Mitchell, Maggie Lena Walker, and other Richmond African American newspaper editors at a meeting in the True Reformers Hall. Mitchell, the primary speaker at the meeting, urged all African Americans to walk rather than ride; he argued that a "people who willingly accept discrimination . . . are not sufficiently advanced to be entitled to the liberties of a free people." He pleaded with African Americans who had to ride the streetcars to obey the law (Alexander 1972, 328). White newspapers such as the *Richmond Times-Dispatch* were convinced that disturbances would occur (329), but by advocating nonviolence, Mitchell employed a strategy that would prove successful some fifty-one years later.

The boycott was endorsed by Richmond's black business and professional classes, and, according to Mitchell, the boycott was initially 90 percent effective (Alexander 1972, 329). It eventually failed, however, because during the strike, Richmond's African American community was attacked on several political fronts. On one front, segregationist members of the Virginia Assembly introduced legislation to eliminate appropriations for black schools (286). The boycotters, and their limited resources, shifted from the strike toward the issue of safeguarding black education (Alexander 1972). Blacks' shifting their focus from a streetcar strike toward a hostile legislator's threatened elimination of funding for black schools is significant because the relationship between blacks asserting their civil rights and a threatened closure of black schools would occur again in 1956 under MR. A second reason the strike failed, and perhaps a more important one, is that in 1906 the Virginia General Assembly mandated segregation on all streetcars in the state. African Americans were forced to accept a new political reality. Although the boycott ended in 1906, Mitchell refused to ride the streetcars again. According to Alexander, once when Mitchell arrived in Richmond's train station, there was no one to escort him home. Rather than violate his promise of refusing to ride the segregated streetcars, Mitchell walked sixteen blocks to his house with his luggage (331).

Although the Richmond boycott failed, it was probably one of the longest boycotts in America, and it may have influenced the Montgomery bus boycott. Francis Foster, a Richmond dentist, civil rights activist, and acknowledged expert on the history of black Richmond, and a cofounder of the RCV, stated that in the mid-1950s, Martin Luther King Jr. asked his father about the Richmond boycott of 1904 when King and the Montgomery leaders were contemplating a similar boycott. The racial pride emanating from the 1904 boycott was discussed more than once with this researcher by different interview informants (Francis Foster interview; Gales interview 1993; El-Amin 1993). The 1904 boycott became ingrained in the historical fabric of Richmond's African American culture. An oral account of the boycott was passed down generationally in Richmond's African American community as a reminder of African Americans' willingness to sacrifice comfort in order to preserve dignity and self respect. In the African American tradition, the 1904 streetcar strike became a symbol of community sacrifice for social justice. Even though the boycott did not integrate the streetcars, it did serve as a rallying cry for future boycotts and political protests that would eventually remove de jure segregation.

From 1906 until the mid-1950s, black Richmonders sought to overturn de jure segregation. For instance, boycotts against residential segregation ordinances in 1917 led the NAACP in Richmond to file suit in federal court. The ordinance was subsequently reversed by the U.S. Supreme Court (Rachleff 1996). In 1921, black women directed an unsuccessful campaign to gain suffrage. And in 1921, John Mitchell and Maggie Lena Walker ran on the "Republican Ticket" for state offices to protest and to oppose the Republican lily-white ticket (ibid.). Although, most historians dubbed Mitchell and Walker's ticket the "lily black ticket," Mitchell and Walker never used the term to define themselves or their slate of candidates. In fact, the term first appeared in an August 7, 1921, article in the *Richmond Times-Dispatch* titled "'Lily Blacks' Will Hold Big Conference Today" ("Lily Blacks" 1921). The significance of this title is twofold. First, it was written by whites and appeared only in the major white newspaper in Richmond and is a clear indication of how whites defined blacks. Second, an examination of the front page of the September 10, 1921, edition of the *Richmond Planet*, the major black newspaper in Richmond, beared no reference to a "lily black" ticket. In fact, a bust photo of Mitchell appeared on that page. The name of the ticket printed along side of Mitchell's bust photo was "The Republican 7," not the "lily black" ticket ("The Republican 7" 1921). Thus we conclude that the term was racist in nature because whites were once again attempting to define African Americans who refused to accept second-class status and refused to be excluded from the political process because of their race.

Later, in the 1940s, the spirit of the 1904 boycott again led moderate Richmond black leaders to make unsuccessful attempts to modulate segregation by appeals to white moderate leaders. The black leaders' inability to dent the armor of Jim Crow inevitably precipitated the decline of black moderates and groups such as the RCC. Thus, the failure of black moderates and the RCC to broker even token reforms in the South's de jure system of segregation would eventually ignite the emergence of another black insurgency, the RCV (Randolph 1998). The RCV would challenge de jure segregation on the Virginia terrain in the courts and the streets.

Massive Resistance and the Rise of the RCV

The factors that contributed directly to Richmond's CRM and the rise of the RCV, were the two *Brown* decisions, the rise of massive resistance in 1955, and the decline of RCC. The manner in which these interconnecting factors energized Richmond's modern-day CRM will be explained shortly.

The *Brown* decision affected the civil rights movement in two different ways. First, the decision struck a major blow to the tripartite system when the U.S. Supreme Court ruled that the doctrine of separate but equal was inherently discriminatory and thus unconstitutional. The Court's unprecedented decision was an important contribution to the CRM because it would create an atmosphere that would foster political alignments of groups within the larger political environment. In essence, the Court's decision would provide both political and legal opportunities for blacks to openly challenge the legitimacy of the tripartite system (Tushnet 1994; Berry 1994). Second, the Court's decision would fuel southern white resistance to any attempts by blacks to integrate the public schools or overturn the tripartite system. For instance, on May 31, 1955, the U.S. Supreme Court in *Brown v. Board of Education (Second Case)* (1955) declared that Virginia's Prince Edward County Schools' policy of maintaining racial discrimination in public education was unconstitutional (Mason and Beany 1968; Picott and Peeples 1964, 394). When the Court's verdict was publicly announced, Virginia's white political elite developed a strategy of interposition that was "predicated on the notion that the United States are no more than a loose confederation of independent political entities and that each of the state governments is, in fact, politically superior to the federal government" (Picott and Peeples 1964, 394). The doctrine of interposition was crafted by James J. Kilpatrick, editor of the now-defunct conservative *Richmond News Leader* (Moeser and Silver 1995). Kilpatrick's use of the doctrine of interposition was simply another ploy by segregationists to justify their racist system and to make white belligerency to the Supreme Court's decision respectable (Williams 1990). The doctrine of interposition eventually became labeled as the southern strategy of MR. According to Moeser and Silver, "The interposition argument provided the constitutional justification for southern defiance, and Kilpatrick exploited it for all it was worth" (Silver and Moeser 1995, 70). Virginia's MR strategy was officially born on May 31, 1955. Essentially, what occurred in Richmond as a result of the U.S. Supreme Court decision was an attempt by the white power structure to thwart the integration of all Virginia's public school systems by placing a referendum on the ballot that allowed local communities to close their schools and thus avoid integration (Picott and Peeples 1964, 394). In essence, the MR campaign was simply another series of political ploys conceived by segregationists to maintain a segregated school system at any cost, even if the cost meant closing Virginia's entire public school system.

The significance of the MR strategy is twofold. First, according to Picott and Peeples in their article "A Study in Infamy: Prince Edward County, Virginia," one of the objectives of MR was to "drive most moderate and liberal whites into seclusion, quietude, and ineffectiveness. Negro opinion, as one would suspect, was entirely disregarded by the decision makers. Prince Edward County was, of course, a microcosm of all these conditions" (1964, 394). The idea of suppressing moderate white voices was also supported by Richard K. Scher in his *Politics in the New South:* "The southern circling of wagons took place quickly and forcefully. Its effect was to eliminate moderate voices and pragmatic political discussion from most areas of the South. The southern political stage seemed to be taken over by extremists who sought to define issues in polarizing terms, the effect of which was to stifle, even quash, discussion and dissent" (1997, 200).

It appears that the MR strategy was intended to ensure that whites would circle the "race wagons" and capitulate to the racist agendas of Virginia's white political elites. Moreover, those who refused to comply with MR, or who even challenged the validity of the MR strategy, would be subjected to intimidation or even face social ostracism from other whites. Thus, Virginia's white leadership intention of coercing whites blindly to comply to the MR strategy was not unfounded. Again, according to Picott and Peeples, "Many persons believing in the principles of segregation, but nevertheless wishing to comply with the court order, suffered much of the same that the integrationist endured" (1964, 394). Consequently, those whites desiring to avoid social ostracism from their white peers, or who wanted to avoid any further intimidation, often found themselves capitulating to the racist demands of politicians such as Byrd of Virginia.

Second, the MR strategy was quickly adopted by most of the southern states (Moeser and Silver 1995). The only states that had episodes of violent resistance to the *Brown* decision were Arkansas and Louisiana (Tushnet 1994). The strategy produced two additional immediate repercussions for the African American community throughout the southern region and some long-term political consequences for not only Virginia but also for other southern states that emulated Virginia's strategy. The first immediate repercussion that emerged from the MR campaign was the adoption of anti-NAACP laws by Virginia and most of the southern states. Once the South realized the implications of the decision, it reacted by enacting anti-NAACP laws. The anti-NAACP laws were designed primarily to outlaw the NAACP from operating within their respective states. The anti-NAACP laws, as they would be referred to by historians and legal scholars, were a series of laws passed by southern state legislatures from 1956 to 1957, aimed primarily at the NAACP (Morris 1984; Tushnet 1994). These laws ranged from an extreme form, outlawing the NAACP in Alabama, to the more sophisticated methods of legal controls exercised against the NAACP by states such as Virginia. For instance, some states like Alabama required the NAACP to provide a list of its members in order to operate within that state. The significance of requiring the NAACP to reveal its membership list was to destroy the organization by exerting political and economic pressures on its members. For example, if someone was a schoolteacher, principal, or even a custodian as well as a member of the NAACP, that person could be fired if he or she was discovered to be a member (Tushnet 1994; Morris 1984). An illustration of this policy occurred in the case of Septima Clark, a former public school teacher and later director of the renowned Highlander Citizenship Education Program. Clark lost her job as a teacher in South Carolina because of her association with the NAACP in 1956. "I refused to disown the NAACP," she recalled, "and lost my job as a public school teacher in South Carolina as a result of my membership and inter-racial activities" (Robnett 1997, 88). Virginia, on the other hand, enacted a more sophisticated version of the anti-NAACP laws in 1956. In *Making Civil Rights Law,* Mark V. Tushnet states that the statues passed by the Virginia legislature "were known throughout the litigation by their designation as chapters in Virginia code" (1994, 272). Virginia's code prevented anyone from soliciting funds and/or spending them on litigation that the individual was not personally involved in. Moreover, Virginia's laws required all organizations involved in activities that might lead to interracial tensions or whose group promoted racial integration to register with the state and disclose the names of their officers along with a list of its members (ibid.). Although Virginia did not ban the NAACP from operating within its border, the idea that Virginia required the disclosure of its membership list was no different from what Alabama demanded of the NAACP. In essence, the objectives of both states were basically the same, to destroy the NAACP.

In addition, Virginia prohibited groups from engaging in barratry or the "persistent incitement of law suits" (Silver and Moeser 1995, 71). Virginia also forbid the "advocacy of suits against Virginia and giving assistance to such suits" (Tushnet 1994, 275). The state's passage of the NAACP laws in 1956 was another example of the political ploys that were constantly employed by the white power structure to impede civil rights activity by attacking the lawyers who represented African Americans in court. The South's strategy simply was to stem the rising tide of black agitation against their tripartite system by attacking its orchestrator. Southern leaders believed the NAACP and its band of lawyers were the chief orchestrators of the attacks on their system. The late Thurgood Marshall, U.S. Supreme Court justice and noted civil rights lawyer, best expressed the intent of the anti-NAACP laws when he publicly described the laws as being "an act to make it difficult . . . to assert the constitutional rights of Negroes" (Tushnet 1994, 272).

The second immediate repercussion of the MR campaign was the collapse of moderate and accommodationist black leaders throughout the South and especially in Virginia. Just as the MR campaign attracted whites who wanted to maintain segregation, the same resistance campaign galvanized blacks to dismantle Jim Crow. Black leaders who had accommodated white interests on segregation were no longer acceptable to the black populace (Holton 1987). Even James J. Kilpatrick, a diehard segregationist, in *The Southern Case for School Segregation*, recognized that southern blacks changed their attitudes toward whites in the South during MR. "The most important immediate force at work to emancipate the Negro of the South . . . is the Southern Negro himself," he observed. "A great change has come over him. He is no longer an Uncle Tom, or even the kind of Negro approved of by Booker T. Washington. He now talks back. He has a new self-respect, a new confidence, a new independence. Increasingly he is depending less on Northern Negro initiative and leadership and is supplying his own" (Kilpatrick 1962, 99). Virginia's MR led to the decline of black conservative and moderate leadership. For instance, as we alluded to earlier, critics of black conservative groups such as the RCC insinuated that its leadership had sold out to the white power structure and lost its political credibility in the black community. Moreover, Dickinson's research reveals that the RCC was perceived by blacks as corrupt because some white elites funded some members of the RCC's leadership (1967, 13–14). Furthermore, we maintain that the rumors surrounding the RCC (whether true or untrue) provided enough corroboration for those skeptics in the African American community who were already committed to reducing the influence of the RCC. The RCC's declining credibility among blacks eventually led to its demise in 1956. The RCC's leadership compromised relations with the white power structure and its failure effectively to challenge white domination eventually led to the creation of a competing group, the RCV.

Thus, when southern leaders adopted a get-tough policy toward any form of black resistance, they unexpectedly triggered a black insurgency. Accordingly, the long-term consequence of MR throughout the South was the ignition of black insurgency groups like the RCV. Precipitated by alleged corruption within the RCC, the RCV evolved around 1956 from an earlier ad hoc organization, the Committee to Save Public Schools or CSPS (Moeser and Dennis 1982, 34; Dickinson 1967, 24–27). The white power structure thwarted the integration of Richmond's public schools by placing a referendum on the ballot that allowed local communities to close their schools. The referendum passed, and the RCV was born (Dickinson 1967, 24–27). The RCV leadership was closely aligned with the NAACP's local leadership of mostly male, highly educated, upper- and middle-class professionals in Richmond's African American community. Ministers were members of the RCV, and although they did not dominate as they had in the RCC, they still had behind-the-scenes access to the white power structure. In Richmond,

> many ministers were older men, jealous of their own prerogatives of leadership in neighborhoods and churches and with little desire to upset a status quo in which they were at least nominal leaders. Many lacked a formal education, a situation which did not increase the respect in which they were held by their white counterparts or by educated Negroes. Thus, the Civic Council often became a platform for class and regional conflict. The marks of dissension appeared too readily to any astute politician who wished to divide the Negro vote. Perhaps the major weakness of the ministers was economic. . . . A willingness to accept perhaps necessary outside financial assistance was at least suspect and certainly contributed to the numerous rumors that the Negro vote, particularly in the thirties and forties, was cynically sold to white politicians. (Dickinson 1967, 14)

Scholars may have been too hasty in assuming that the church was the major leader during the civil rights era. Charles M. Payne's study of Mississippi, *I've Got the Light of Freedom* (1995), argues that ministers did not dominate the leadership of most of the CRM. Payne argued that the

> church has gotten more credit for generating the leadership of the movement than it deserves, probably a matter of people looking at the movement's national leaders, many of whom were ministers, and assuming they were all the leadership that mattered. In fact, the local situation could be very different. In the urban South, where churches were larger and better financed, where ministers were not so subject to reprisal, churches could afford to play a more active role in the early stages of the movement. Even so, SCLC's [Southern Christian Leadership Conference's] Wyatt Walker noted that during the Birmingham campaign no more than ten percent of the Black ministers were actively supportive. (Payne 1995, 165)

Finally, Silver and Moeser note that in Richmond's social and political reform groups, ministers were not the dominant actors. They contend that "in local political organizations and social reforms groups, there was a wide array of local black leaders besides ministers. Two black professionals, Attorney Oliver Hill and Physician Dr. J. M. Tinsley, took center stage in the politicization of the black community in the 1940s" (1995, 57). The fact that ministers in Richmond were not the dominant actors during Richmond's burgeoning CRM, seems to contradict Aldon Morris's thesis about the major role that ministers played in cities throughout the South during the CR era. For example, according to Morris, activist ministers were generally from cities because rural ministers were paid less and were dependent upon external funds (Morris 1984, 1–54). In southern cities, pastors were expected to be full-time ministers, and those who were financed adequately by their congregations were generally very active in the CRM. However, Richmond's RCC emergence in an urban setting seems contradictory to Morris's thesis. The bankrupt politics of groups such as RCC, and the white backlash against civil rights activity in the South, helped the RCV to realize that their political progress required an independently led African American grass-roots movement in Richmond. With the emergence of the RCV, a new era and approach to addressing the needs of the African American community began.

Under the RCV, the African American community's approach to politics shifted from voter registration to electoral politics. In fact, the crusade's greatest impact on Richmond occurred in politics (Randolph and Tate 1995). In addition, when the RCV appeared in Richmond, the conditions McAdam identified as prerequisites for a generation of insurgency to occur were in place. The RCV was the dominant organization within the aggrieved population, and it had what McAdam identified as "organizational readiness." Moreover, because the RCV leaders were closely aligned with the leadership of the local NAACP, they had access to the NAACP's national organization. Additionally, the RCV possessed a level of insurgent consciousness within an exploited population. When the RCV appeared in Richmond, a structure of political opportunities was accessible to an insurgent population and was prevalent during this period. For example, the federal courts in 1954 had already ruled in favor of civil rights groups in several key cases such as *Brown v. Board of Education*. Additionally, a federal district court ruled that Virginia's anti-NAACP laws violated the Fourteenth Amendment, which "protected NAACP members from compulsory disclosure" (Williams 1990, 33). Finally, at the state level, the Virginia Supreme Court delivered two rulings favorable to civil rights groups in *Harrison v. Day* and *James v. Almond* which essentially ended MR. In both cases the Virginia Supreme Court declared that the state's decision to close public schools and cut off state aid to avoid school integration violated the state constitution and the Fourteenth Amendment (Picott and Peeples 1964, 364; Pratt 1992, 11).

Thus, white domination over blacks was established in Richmond during slavery, carried over during Reconstruction, and continued until 1960. Richmond's white political elites' refusal to accommodate the changing social and political milieu resulted in antagonism between themselves and blacks. With the emergence of the RCV, a second black insurgency appeared in Richmond to challenge the white power structure. RCV was the dominant group during this second insurgency because of the failure of black moderates and the decline of groups like RCC. Furthermore, when the state adopted a MR strategy to decelerate civil rights activity, and with the demise of the RCC, along with the occurrence of federal and state action that was favorable to the exploited population, all of these factors converged to precipitate the rise of a second black insurgency. The RCV emerged in Richmond to confront MR by challenging the authority of its primary drum major, Harry F. Byrd.

Original Revolutionaries or Black Political Gentry?

William Thornton, one of the cofounders of the RCV, stated during a personal interview with A. J. Dickinson in 1967 that the RCV were the original revolutionaries. If one interprets Thornton's perception of the RCV through the political lens of 1998, one might easily conclude that his description of the RCV was slightly exaggerated. However, if one reexamines his impression of the RCV through a different pair of political lenses, such as those of 1956, Thornton's perception of the RCV would be an appropriate description of that organization during that time period. Furthermore, Thornton's depiction of the RCV in 1956 as a revolutionary organization is not a groundless perception. Thornton's description of the RCV can be supported if one examines the RCV based upon its mission, organizational structure, and its membership structure.

In terms of its mission, the RCV was clearly different from any previous black organization that had emerged in Richmond, including the RCC during the 1940s. For instance, although the leadership of both the RCV and the RCC was middle class, the similarities between the groups ended there. The RCV's mission was unique because, unlike groups such as the RCC, the RCV was concerned with obtaining black political and economic empowerment. For instance, according to an RCV flyer that was printed in 1956 by the RCV, the organization was committed to "increas[ing] the Negro vote in Richmond, Virginia through year-round voter registration activity, and to increas[ing] political awareness of Negroes. [Also, we are committed] to study[ing] the records of candidates and giv[ing] recommendations. [Finally, we are concerned with] push[ing] for equal job opportunities in city hall" (RCV Archives). Moreover, the RCV was also committed to total black political participation and representation in Richmond's political arena. In addition, the organization underscored its mission by stressing honest and pragmatic politics (Holton 1987, 62–64). Thus, if one examines the RCV by its mission for 1956, it could be perceived as revolutionary in terms of its stated purpose, because prior to the emergence of the RCV, the stated purpose of most black groups was generally unclear. In addition, the RCV could be perceived as a revolutionary group during that time period, because of the fearlessness demonstrated by the founders in establishing a black independently led organization for political change. Thus, the RCV was revolutionary for its time because for any black group to publicly announce during a period of intense political and racial polarization throughout the South that it was going to engage the most termagant southern white supremacist organization in unbridled political battles demonstrated an enormous amount of courage. In addition, the RCV was a radical departure for most black organizations in Richmond, given the history of corrupt and balkanized politics that appeared to have engulfed most black groups in the past. Therefore, the RCV could be perceived as being a revolutionary departure from the past, in terms of the manner in which black political organizations operated in Richmond.

Although the use of the term "revolutionary" has recently been exploited by advertising agencies for commercial purposes to appeal to the American consumer mainstream, one has to be careful when applying this kind of label to describe an organization. "Revolutionary" should not be understood as indicating a radical organization that is leftist in its origins or committed to the overthrow of an established government. Thus, the RCV was not a revolutionary group in the truest sense. In fact, civil rights–era groups were not radical groups at all. As Richard Scher notes in his *Politics in the New South*,

> Southern blacks sought equal opportunity and treatment in American life. These were not new or radical notions. They represented precisely the goals that white Americans sought for themselves prior to the Declaration of Independence and were included both in that document and in the Constitution. . . . Thus southern blacks did not seek a departure from mainstream American life and values. Rather, they sought to enter them. It was the Jim Crow South that was out of step with the rest of America and its political traditions, not black demands for civil rights. (Scher 1997, 243)

Accordingly, if we view the RCV with Scher's quote as our frame of reference, then the RCV was probably perceived by white politicians and their conservative allies as somewhat of a revolutionary departure from previous black groups.

In terms of its organizational structure, the RCV could also be perceived as being a radical departure from the past for the following reasons. First, although the leadership of the RCV was closely aligned with the NAACP, the RCV on paper was a separate organization. Even though the two groups shared similar leaders, they operated independently for legal and political reasons. For instance, groups like the NAACP, which held tax-exempt status, were legally constrained from engaging in certain kinds of political activity, whereas groups like the RCV, which were not legally constrained, could operate more freely in the political arena. In essence, the RCV on one level was an independent organization; however, on another level, the RCV could be perceived as being a political action organizational wing of the NAACP. The NAACP's role was to challenge segregation through the courts, whereas the RCV's role was to organize politically Richmond's black community and attack segregation in the streets and through the ballot box. Therefore, if we view the RCV through a much broader lens, once again the appearance of the RCV in terms of Richmond's black body politic would be perceived as revolutionary. Unlike the RCC, the RCV was not an organization seeking a junior partnership, biracial coalition with an established white group. Instead, the RCV focused its attention on consolidating its power and strengthening its political support base within Richmond's black community (Dickinson 1967, 25–29; Holton 1987, 64–65).

Another reason the RCV could be perceived as revolutionary for its time stems from its organizational structure. The internal structure of the RCV was revolutionary for black organizations in Richmond because the internal structure of the RCV closely resembled the organizational structure of a political machine. The RCV was both similar and yet dissimilar to the old political machines that emerged and dominated the political arenas in some of America's large urban centers. The RCV was similar to the old political machines for four reasons.

First, the old machines were dominated by a party boss and a central committee, whereas the RCV was dominated by a chair, executive board, and officers. Even though the RCV had a chair, unlike its counterpart, the machine, the RCV was not dominated by a powerful party boss figure. Instead, the RCV was dominated by a powerful executive board. The RCV's executive board consisted of a chair of the board, executive board, and officers of the organization (Dickinson 1967, 28). Although the RCV appeared to be a democratic organization on paper, the executive board controlled the business and direction of the organization. Holton's analysis of the RCV reinforces the argument that the executive board was a determining factor in shaping the direction of the organization:

> By organizing on a local level, the Crusade was able to deal with local problems (through precinct club representation), and thus present at least the image of being a fairly democratic organization. Despite the democratic structure, however, the real power of the organization lay with the Executive Board, which determined the Crusade's agenda. The Crusade's powerful Executive Board significantly contrasted the board of the Richmond Civic Council, which was dependent on non-political local groups such as churches and fraternal groups. Working with a structure imposed from above, the Executive Board proved to be much more independent and influential among crusaders than the RCC's board had been among its membership. (Holton 1987, 65)

In spite of this carefully constructed appearance of a democratically run organization, the RCV was vulnerable to potential abuses in the hands of an autocratic chair. The idea that the RCV was vulnerable to such abuses was not unfounded because, according to Dickinson's analysis of the RCV, this could have occurred. Dickinson notes that "though the chairman's power is not necessarily absolute or dictatorial, it is limited primarily by self-restraint, of which Dr. Thornton has a great deal" (1967, 28–29). Although Thornton did not abuse his authority, the opportunity for abuse could have developed if authority were ever placed in the hands of an autocrat. Thus, because the executive board was actively involved in running the organization, an autocratic leader did not emerge for this reason. Consequently, the RCV could not be considered a pure illustration of an urban political machine because it was not dominated by a powerful party boss.

Second, the RCV was similar to the old political machines because, like the machines, the organizational hierarchy was structured in the form of a pyramid. Under the RCV, actual power appeared to have resided at the top within the executive board. A typical urban machine was either controlled by a powerful party boss or power was shared between the boss, who could have been a mayor or the just party boss, and the central committee.

Third, in terms of its remaining structure, the RCV was only slightly similar to an urban machine. For instance, the RCV's internal organizational structure did not formally involve the participation of precinct clubs or captains; however, if one compares the level of involvement of the RCV's precinct clubs with those of the precinct clubs under an urban machine, such as the Chicago machine under the late mayor Richard J. Daley, there is no comparison between the RCV's and Daley's precinct clubs. The precinct clubs and wards under Daley's machine were definitely an essential factor in terms of getting out the vote for machine candidates during an upcoming election (Grimshaw 1992). However, when we compare the RCV's relationship with precinct clubs to the machine's relationship with its precinct clubs, the relationship between the precinct clubs and the two organizations is vastly different. The primary difference in the RCV's relationship with precinct clubs was that the RCV could not punish precinct club leaders if they failed or refused to support a particular candidate that was endorsed by the RCV. Thus, machines can force precinct club and ward leaders to comply with the machine's demands by replacing them, or by reducing their level of patronage, or if necessary, denying them access to patronage positions inside of city hall.

Thus, the RCV cannot compel total allegiance from precinct club leaders because, unlike the machine, the RCV cannot dispense patronage to precinct club leaders. An excellent illustration of how the Daley machine could punish some of its ward leaders who were deemed disloyal is depicted in William J. Grimshaw's classic text, *Bitter Fruit: Black-Politics and the Chicago Machine 1931–1991*: "Mayor Daley also sacked those black ward leaders, all of them civic notables, who displayed the

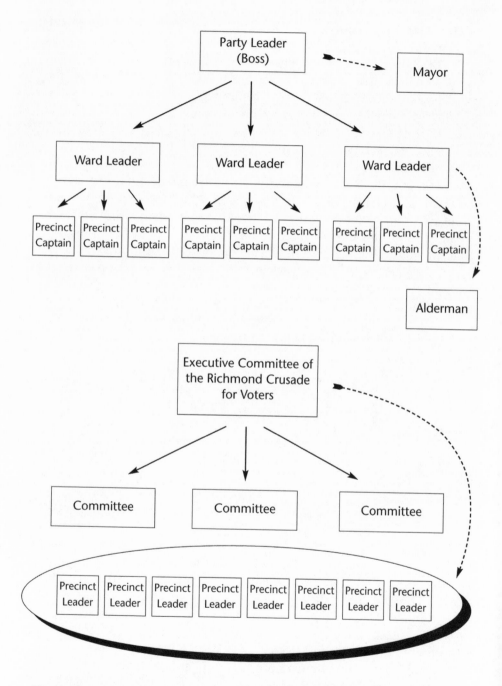

Fig. 6. The organizational structures of an urban political machine compared with the organizational structure of the Richmond Crusade for Voters.

temerity, however, limited in scope, to take a community position in opposition to the machine" (1992, 135).

To further illustrate the organizational differences between an urban political machine and the RCV, see figure 6. One will quickly notice the direct organizational ties between the machine and the precinct captains. However, if one closely examines the RCV at the bottom of the figure, the linkage between the RVC and precinct clubs is more of an indirect relationship because the precinct clubs are not directly part of the RCV's formal structure.

Fourth, the RCV's internal structure is again different from that of a political machine because of the manner in which local representation is elected. During the time in which the RCV emerged in Richmond, public officials were elected at-large in nonpartisan elections. However, in Chicago, during the time in which the RCV emerged, public officials were elected by wards and the elections were partisan. The purpose in pointing out the differences between the two organizations is that under a machine format, the role of wards in sustaining the power of the machine is critical (Judd and Swanstrom 1994, 56). Moreover, under the RCV structure, there is no ward system. During the time the RCV appeared on Richmond's political landscape, blacks were systematically locked out of the local political process. Thus, for this reason alone, the RCV could not be considered a perfect example of a machine because, unlike a typical urban machine, the RCV could not divvy out any forms of political patronage to its precinct representatives because it was locked out of the political system entirely. Also, unlike the machine in Chicago, the RCV was not affiliated with a local political party. The RCV was not an affiliate of either the Republicans or Democrats in Richmond because of institutionalized racism. Blacks had been shunned by both parties since the post-Reconstruction era. Also, the voting restrictions that had been placed upon a large segment of the black populace prevented them from becoming a political threat to the white power structure. Consequently, the absence of large numbers of other kinds of racial and ethnic groups in the city, along with the racially polarized climate that prevailed in Richmond during the civil rights era, prevented the formation of any possible stable coalition between blacks and whites. Accordingly, for these reasons, the RCV could not be considered a prime example of an urban political machine.

Once again, by Virginia's political standards in the mid-1950s, the organizational structure of the RCV could be deemed somewhat revolutionary when compared to other black political groups that had emerged in the past. Although the RCV was not the best example of an urban machine, the RCV unquestionably paralleled similar black organizations that emerged in the Deep South during the 1950s and early 1960s. The organizations that closely resembled the RCV were the Greenville City and County Voters Crusade (GCCVC) in Greenville, South Carolina; the Winston-Salem Democratic Voters Club (WSDVC) of Winston-Salem, North Carolina; and Atlanta's Negro Voters League (ANVL) in Atlanta, Georgia (Ladd 1969, 90–296). These organizations closely paralleled the RCV because, like the RCV, almost all of them either originated from or had close ties to their local NAACP organizations and maintained a close working relationship with the NAACP throughout the CRM era. Another reason why the RCV closely resembled the deep southern voting groups was because their activities centered specifically on projects involving voting education/registration, endorsement of candidates, and electoral politics.

In terms of its membership, the RCV, by 1956 southern political standards, was revolutionary, because it publicly promoted itself as an integrated group, opening its meetings to anyone who wanted to attend, including whites. If whites attended the RCV's meetings, they automatically became members of the organization (Dickinson 1967, 28). The idea that a black group would openly welcome whites to join their organization during the height of MR was somewhat revolutionary, especially given the political climate. Moreover, the RCV did not maintain a membership list, possibly to protect its members from political harassment by the state of Virginia and/or protect its members from political and economic reprisals from employers. Perhaps the RCV learned an important political lesson from the South's assault on groups like the NAACP. If the RCV was taken to state court and required by law to present their membership list before a magistrate in order to operate within the state, then it could not be compelled to produce something that it did not have. Thus, without a membership list, the RCV could protect its members from legal and or political intimidation.

If one cautiously applies the term "revolutionary" to describe the RCV that emerged during the mid-1950s, the RCV was a revolutionary group. For example, when we examined the organizational structure of the RCV, the RCV initially did resemble a urban political machine. However, after examining the RCV's organizational structure more closely, we were convinced that the RCV actually resembled more of a mini machine or a deep southern voter crusade, voter club, and/or voting league rather than a pure urban political machine.

Although the RCV emerged during a period of crisis and for a noble cause in 1956, the question that has to be addressed at this point is whether or not the RCV was a black elitist organization that manipulated the politics of Richmond's African American community during the civil rights era to advance their own class interests. The issue is a valid one, because some of the critics of the RCV in the past have made this allegation. Thus, to address this concern, we intend to examine the assertions of elitist factions within the RCV by explicating the manner in which key class and gender concerns unfolded in the organization and how they were addressed by the RCV leadership during the civil rights era in Richmond.

According to several published accounts on the history of the RCV, the organization was unquestionably dominated by Richmond's black professional and middle classes (Harris 1991). In fact, its founders were physicians William S. Thornton and William Ferguson Reid, and Johnny Brooks (RCV Archives). The black middle and professional classes' domination of the RCV's leadership can be substantiated. The evolution of black professional and middle-class domination of the leadership ranks of Richmond's black political organizations actually occurred in several stages. According to historian Greg Kimble, Richmond's black professional and middle-class domination can actually be traced to the historical development of black political organizations and social groups in Richmond dating back to early Reconstruction. In an unpublished paper, "Race and Class in a Southern City: Richmond, 1865–1920," Kimble describes how black professional and middle classes were able to capture control of early black organizations (Kimble 1992). Black organizations that emerged during the early periods of Reconstruction, he notes, were dominated by working-class blacks:

> The development of race and class ideology in Richmond's African American community falls into two overlapping periods. The first period runs from Emancipation into the 1880s, when black leadership was held not by business and professional men serving the white community, but by a diverse group of artisans, workers, small shopkeepers and a few professionals. Richmond's black leadership was strongly working class, partially because of the city's antebellum industrial heritage. (Kimble 1992, 2)

Chesson, in his study "Richmond's Black Councilmen, 1871–1896," bolsters Kimble's argument when he argues the same point. "The development of Negro political leaders seems to have gone through at least four phases between 1865 and 1896," he states. "The years 1865 through 1870 were dominated by orators and firebrands, some of whom were relatively poor and uneducated, whereas wealthier or more moderate men increasingly shunned politics" (1982, 191). Kimble's and Chesson's views are relevant to this discussion because both of them present compelling documentation that black leadership during the early stages of Reconstruction was indisputably dominated by the black working class. And if working-class blacks dominated Richmond's black leadership ranks initially, the question that has to be addressed at this point is, How did the black professional and middle classes gain control of Richmond's early black political organizations?

Chesson provides one account of how black professional and middle classes were able to gain control over the early black political organizations. He states that between 1882 and 1890, the city of Richmond witnessed the emergence New Negroes, or, as Chesson describes them, "new issue Negroes" (1982, 191):

> In the years 1882 to 1890, the new issue Negroes who were born in the closing days of slavery or after emancipation, came to prominence. Examples of such men on the council included attorneys James H. Hayes, Edwin A. Randolph, and physician Robert E. Jones. These men were often prominent members of the customhouse gang; but they had more influence and independence in their own right, as befitted their backgrounds, and, in these cases, their professional status. The final type of black leader, who was not always a "new issue," overthrew the ruling clique in Jackson Ward, partly by using racial pride against white bosses outside the ward and partly by allying with independent local Republicans in Jackson. Men like John Mitchell worked with whites like James Bahen, a grocer and ward boss, against the city branch of William Mahone's state machine and increasingly against the policies of the national Republican party. John Mitchell, Jr. was among the most prominent Negroes and was perhaps, the most assertive black to sit on the council. (Chesson 1982, 191)

Chesson's new issue Negro closely parallels Alain Locke's "New Negro," a term which, incidentally, was introduced by Locke to the literary community in *The New Negro*, an anthology published by Locke (Hayden 1968, ix). The relevance of bringing Locke's concept into this discussion is to reveal to the reader how the New Negro was different from the Old Negro in America during the early part of the twentieth century. According to Locke, the New Negro

> articulates the crucial ideas of a generation in rebellion against accepted beliefs and engaged in racial self-discovery and cultural re-assessment. It affirms the values of the Negro heritage and expresses hope for the future of the race in this country, stressing the black man's Americanism. . . . The main

thrust of The New Negro is clearly integrationist, not separatist. Dr. Locke and most of his collaborators thought of race consciousness and race pride as positive forces making the Negro aware of the true worth of his contributions to American society and helping him to achieve his rightful place in it. (Hayden 1968, xiii)

Whichever interpretation one subscribes to, either Chesson's new issue Negro or Locke's New Negro, both undoubtedly describe a new type of African American that was full of race pride and willing to assert his rights (Chesson 1982, 191; Hayden 1968, xiii). The significance of Chesson's quotation is to illustrate how black professional and middle-class males managed to gain control of Richmond's internal black political leadership during a span of eight years. It is relevant to this discussion because it reveals further how the mantle of leadership shifted from organizations that had initially been dominated by the black working class to the black professional and middle classes. Thus the shift in leadership from the working class to the professional and middle classes occurred when the black professional and middle classes allied themselves with powerful local white political figures to wrestle leadership away from the black working class. But the fact that the black professional and middle classes gained control over black political organizations does not adequately explain how they were able to maintain their dominance up to the period in which the RCV was formed. One plausible explanation is that after the black professional and middle classes usurped political control over black political organizations during the early stages of Reconstruction, they were able to sustain their control because the black working class was disorganized and Richmond's black body politic was balkanized.

Black professional and middle-class dominance over Richmond's black body politic went unchallenged from the 1880s through the modern-day CRM era because political control remained in the hands of the black professional and middle classes (Moeser and Silver 1995, 57–58). Further, although internal political control of Richmond's black body politic shifted from one group to another group, one important factor remained consistent throughout the shifting of power: the internal control of Richmond's black politics remained in the hands of the black professional and middle classes. This point can be substantiated because during the 1920s and 1930s, black political leadership was dominated by black business leaders such as Maggie Lena Walker and John Mitchell, both of whom were products of middle-class upbringing. Moreover, the time line of black professional and middle-class dominance over black leadership remained intact, even when the RCC was established during the 1940s and continued on with the establishment of the RCV. For instance, the RCC was formed by a group of middle-class black conservative ministers, whereas the RCV was formed during the 1950s and it too was founded by another group of black professional and middle-class leaders. Thus, since the 1880s, the black professional and middle classes have retained their dominance over Richmond's black political leadership.

Consequently, when the black professional and middle classes usurped control of black political leadership, three groups were excluded from the leadership ranks: women, working-class people, and poor people. Although women like Maggie Lena Walker were acknowledged leaders within Richmond's black community and recognized leaders within male-dominated and mixed-gender organizations, we contend that, during the early twentieth century, Walker's ascendancy to leadership was an exception, not the norm, for most black women in Richmond. We maintain this even though black women in Richmond during this period demonstrated a long history of leadership in the black church (Kimble 1992, 25). Walker was an exception and not the rule because of the sexism that prevailed at that time in Richmond's black and white communities. During the period in which she ascended to political prominence in Richmond's black body politic, middle-class and professional black males shared the same views on the roles of women as their white counterparts. Kimble's research supports this point. "At the same time that black businessmen followed the path of so-called civilization," he notes, "they couched it in a language and ideology of race pride. W. W. Browne of the True Reformers claimed that 'The Freedman's Saving and Trust Company was the black man's by name and the white man's by possession and management. The Savings Bank of the Grand Fountain is the black man's by name, possession and management'" (1992, 24–25).

Thus, black professional and middle-class dominance over the leadership ranks produced a leadership that was elitist and sexist. When the modern-day CRM emerged in Richmond during the mid-1950s, the participation of women, working-class people, and poor people in the CRM was limited to the role of foot soldiers and/or subleaders. And just as these groups' roles were marginalized by the black professional and middle-class leadership, so too were their interests. Hence, the earlier question that was raised, as to whether or not the RCV was the original black revolutionary group, or simply black political gentry, can be answered in the affirmative. Yes, the RCV on one level was some-what revolutionary in terms of its organizational structure during the period in which it emerged; on another level, it was also a continuation of the black political gentry line that had dominated Richmond's inter-nal black body politic since the late 1880s. Accordingly, given the elitism and sexism that seems to have evolved within Richmond's black profes-sional and middle-class leadership ranks, the question that now has to be addressed is, How were the issues of gender and class addressed within and by the RCV during the CRM era?

Gender, Class, and the RCV

Based on interviews conducted for this study, and on available published and unpublished materials, gender bias was prevalent inside the RCV during Richmond's civil rights era. The manner in which the gender bias unfolded within the group can be illustrated by information that was obtained from the Richmond Crusade for Voters Archives. The first instance of gender bias that seems to have emerged within the RCV dur-ing the civil rights era actually occurred when the history of the organi-zation was written. According to all published accounts, the original founders of the organization were black males. The identities of the founders is relevant to this discussion because most written accounts have overlooked one important part of the RCV's history: two of its orig-inal founders were women. The two women missing from the list of the original founders were Lola H. Hamilton and Ethel T. Overby. Their role as cofounders was confirmed by their obituaries. According to the *Rich-mond News Leader* of July 11, 1977, Overby, in 1956, "helped found the Crusade for Voters, a predominately black political organization" (5). Another tribute to Overby's life, which appeared in the July 9, 1977, issue of the *Richmond Afro-American,* corroborates the *Richmond News Leader*'s claim. Overby, it stated, was a "founder of the Crusade for Voters, the city's most powerful political organization" (1). These news account of her life are significant because to date neither story has been refuted.

Moreover, Overby's role as one of the cofounders of RCV can be sub-stantiated even further. For instance, in the original draft of her book, *It's Better to Light a Candle than Curse the Darkness,* her role in the creation of the RCV was corroborated even further when Dr. Hertha Riese stated in her testimonial praise of Overby's accomplishments during a ceremonial program honoring Overby and twelve other Richmonders "for their work in developing better job opportunities for Negroes in [the] city" (Overby 1974, 122–23). The program was sponsored by the Richmond Urban League, and Riese's testimonial clearly supports our claim that Overby was a cofounder of the RCV: "The apex of Mrs. Overby's present date activity centers in the esteemed work of the Crusade For Voters. This organization, which she helped to found and with which she has worked diligently far beyond the call of normal duty, epitomizes all of her life's dreams to make her fellow men a dominant factor in the political life of this community" (ibid.). Finally, Overby's role as one of the cofounders of the RCV was validated by Naomi Morse and Virgie Binford, both life-long friends and teachers who worked under Overby when she was a principal in the Richmond Public Schools. Morse, who was actively

Fig. 7. Ethel T. Overby, September 1965. Overby was the first black female principal of a Richmond public school and an original founder of the Richmond Crusade for Voters. Courtesy of Naomi Morse.

involved with voter registration projects in Richmond during the civil rights era, revealed during a personal interview in 2001 that "it was Mrs. Overby's idea to form the RCV when she was involved with the CSPS in 1956. In fact, the RCV was her brain child and she was the one who 'coined' the name for the organization" (Morse interview 2001). Binford stated categorically that Overby was a cofounder of the RCV:

> Mrs. Overby has never been credit for the founding of the RCV because she was not part of Richmond's black political establishment. In fact, I remember her calling Dr. Thornton and Dr. Fergie Reid about her idea to creating the RCV. She and her husband began collecting newspapers to raise money for the RCV. She personally contacted one hundred people to see if they would pledge twelve dollars a year to support the RCV. The RCV was her brain child. Moreover, the headquarters for the RCV was her house. Also, there was no letter head with the address of the RCV written on it, because the RCV was a secret organization (as you well know this was doing MR time). After Overby's death, the RCV leadership sponsored a big gala dinner event which featured a film on the history of the RCV. The film offended me because Mrs. Overby's name was never mentioned either as the person who came up with the name, or even as an individual who supported the organization. They did not even mention her name at all. The omission of Mrs. Overby's name could only be explain because of "gender politics." In other words, the film was made by the men, and it "showcased" the men. (Binford interview 2001)

Lola H. Hamilton's role as a cofounder of the RCV was also confirmed by published accounts of her life when she died in 1985. The source confirming her role in the RCV was an unidentified newspaper account of her life. The published account of her life states authoritatively that Hamilton was "one of the founders of the Crusade for Voters and a former Richmond deputy registrar" (RCV Archives). Thus, until these accounts are refuted, both of these women should be listed as cofounders of the RCV. The explanation of their omission from current histories is that gender bias prevailed among the RCV leadership.

Another illustration of how gender bias operated inside the RCV concerned the participatory role that was assigned to black female members of the RCV. According to the RCV Archives, during the civil rights era no female served as president. The fact that no woman served as president of the RCV throughout this era is significant for two reasons. First, the absence of women in visible leadership roles supports the findings of Belinda Robnett in her article "African American Women in the Civil Rights Movement, 1954–1965": "It was not that women were prevented from participating in important ways, but that their participation options were limited" (1996, 1669). Second, their absence reinforces the findings of other civil rights scholars on the absence of black women in more visible roles of leadership, and it again reveals that the RCV was just as sexist as other civil rights groups in other southern states and northern states during this era (Morris 1984; Giddings 1984; Cone 1992; Robinson 1987; and Standley 1993). Moreover, the absence of women from key leadership roles throughout this era inside the RCV is relevant to this discussion, because it may help explain why the first woman to be elected president of the RCV did not occur until 1973 (RCV Archives).

Examination of the RCV Archives reveals that the roles assigned to women appear to have been consistent with Robnett's notion of gendered roles in the civil rights movement. As we indicated earlier in this section, committees played an integral part in the RCV organization. Thus, if one wants to identify the roles performed by black women inside the RCV, then one has to examine the type of committee assignments that were given to them in the organization. The RCV Archives indicated that the committees assigned to black women during this period usually dealt with voter registration, voter education, welfare, and the newsletter (RCV Archives). The type of committee assignments that were delegated to black women supports findings revealed by Robnett's research. Robnett explains that women's activities inside the Montgomery Improvement Association were restricted to fund raising, membership, recruitment, and community welfare (1996, 1670). Also, even when women were assigned the task of chairing important committees, such as when Overby served as chair and Lille Thomas served as vice chair of the finance committee in 1961, they reported directly to the treasurer of the RCV, who was male. Furthermore, from 1961 until 1975, when Overby served as chair of the finance committee, she continued to report to the treasurer of the organization.

As a result of Overby's service to the RCV, she was consistently praised for her performance as chair of the RCV finance committee. In recognition of her service, she received a letter from a Walter B. Gentry, the city treasurer of Richmond. In the letter, dated April 15, 1975, Gentry praised Overby for the splendid job she had done during her tenure as chair of the RCV's financial committee:

> I read with a great deal of pleasure the wonderful financial report you prepared for the Crusade of Voters. I congratulate you on this fine report and I must say that the Crusade could look far and wide, they would not find such a person of Mrs. Overby's caliber to be their financial chairman. You have

done a wonderful job over the years, and I pray that God will give you the
strength and stability to continue for many years to come. I am with you
always—keep up the good work. (Overby 1975, 49)

Gentry's letter establishes Overby's credibility as a competent comptrol-
ler and an invaluable asset to the RCV. In addition, at the time this letter
was written to Overby, she was eighty-two years old and still functioning
as the chair of the RCV finance committee. If she was capable of functioning so effectively as chair of the finance committee at eighty-two
years of age, why wasn't she the treasurer of the organization? The only
credible response to this question is that gender bias prevented her from
obtaining that position.

Another illustration of how the RCV's gendered roles had an impact
on the participatory roles of black women occurred in the case of Lola
Hamilton, who helped to establish the volunteer voter education and
registration organization in 1966. After she helped to establish these
organizations, she went on to serve them in the capacity as vice president, secretary, and finance chair. In addition, Hamilton served the RCV
in the capacity as its office manager, and she directed the RCV's Get Out
the Vote Campaign (RCV Archives). Thus, one cannot ignore the fact
that Hamilton was highly competent and could have performed admi-
rably in any capacity for the RCV, including the role of an officer of the
organization. In essence, our concern about the lack of formal leadership
opportunities for black women within male-dominated organizations is
a valid concern, because as scholars we can no longer presume that
women such as Hamilton and Overby were content with operating in
the shadows of men. Hence, we must assume that if they were not
afforded the opportunities to perform visible leadership roles, then the
only conceivable explanation of why these two highly skilled women
were not officers in the RCV was because of their gender. Consequently,
and based upon the manner in which Hamilton, Overby, and other black
women were excluded from visible leadership roles within the RCV during the civil rights era, we must concur with Robnett's analysis that their
exclusion was brought about because their participation options were
limited by the male-dominated leadership.

The existence of gender bias and class cleavages within the RCV can
be demonstrated further when one examines the manner in which the
RCV addressed issues of gender and class outside the organization. The
best illustration of this was the manner in which the RCV endorsed candidates for electoral office: via the research committee.

The research committee was the most powerful committee in the RCV. Its primary task was "to dig down through emotionalism, sentiment and other political razzle dazzle to bring to the surface hard political facts and use these facts to recommend the best possible team of candidates for your consideration" (RCV Archives). The committee was organized into two tiers. The first tier consisted of the chairman, president, and two members from the RCV elected at-large, all identified as "the consultants." The consultants were individuals who actually made the decision as to which political candidate would receive the RCV's endorsement in an upcoming election. After examining the RCV Archives and the membership roster of the research committee, we discovered that the consultants were exclusively male throughout the civil rights era (RCV Archives). Although males dominated the RCV's research committee, one black female served on the committee during the civil rights era. According to Ora Lomax, a member of the RCV and a civil rights activist, in an interview with this researcher, she was a member of the RCV research committee during the early 1960s (Lomax interview 1993). Lomax stated that when she was the lone female member on the committee, the male members expected her to endorse blindly the same candidates they supported. When she refused to support the committee's endorsement of a particular candidate, she was scolded by some of her male counterparts for "not being a team player" (ibid.). Furthermore, Lomax's unwillingness to support the research committee's endorsement vote on a particular candidate for elective office revealed to her committee members that she would not endorse any political candidate whose views or policies violated her principles. The significance of mentioning Lomax's tenure on the research committee is to illustrate how when women were placed on this important committee, their input appears to have been disregarded. Thus, from our perspective, if the input from independent thinking black women could be disregarded, then one could surmise that women whose views were compatible with the males, or who were perceived as less intimidating, were probably more acceptable to this male-dominated committee.

The second tier of the RCV's research committee was designated "the members." The members' tier was larger, and it was here that we witnessed the participation of women. With the exclusion of women from the consultant ranks of the research committee throughout the civil rights era, it will become apparent very shortly how the research committee had an impact on the political aspirations of black women during this era. How the research committee's endorsement process negatively affected the political aspirations of black women is seen in the case of Ester Smith of Richmond. In 1962, when the research committee submitted its recommendations for candidates for city council, they failed to endorse Smith, the lone black female candidate. Smith was a housewife, and her husband was an auto mechanic:

> Endorsements were announced in Richmond's predominantly black churches. The endorsement included six white RCA candidates, two white independents, and a black independent, Clarence Newsome. The Crusade did not endorse the only other black candidate, Mrs. Ester Smith. Despite much concern among Crusade leaders that the organization would be sharply criticized if it failed to endorse both black candidates, the Research Committee made its recommendations in accordance with the Crusade's "practical politics." (Holton 1987, 74)

Although the quotation does not specify why Smith was not endorsed by the RCV, gender and class considerations could have played a factor. The front page of the *Richmond Afro-American* for June 9, 1962, offers a conceivable explanation for the exclusion. The article, "It's Spring, Voters Being Wooed by All," features a brief review of each candidate's views and platform position on current local issues for the upcoming city council election. Smith's platform concentrated on gender and class issues (Randolph 1998, 69). The article described Smith as a representative of the "working class and the poor" and gave her position on social welfare issues: "She laments that so few jobs and training opportunities are available to welfare clients. She proposes also a boarding school for mothers of more than one illegitimate child, the mothers to do all the work at the school on a rotating basis, and help support themselves. This project she says would save them money, and assure supervision of the mothers and proper care of their children" (2).

Smith's practical approach to welfare issues in Richmond may have been too liberal to merit endorsement by the RCV. Her opponent, Clarence W. Newsome, the RCV's candidate, emphasized desegregating local hospitals, slum removal, and improvement of city schools. Newsome was the safer candidate from the RCV's perspective. The RCV Archives contained a questionnaire given to all candidates by the research committee in 1960. None of the questions concern class, gender, and social welfare issues. Most were safe questions, such as, "How do you yourself think the city government should go in hiring people without regard to race, religion or color?" (RCV Archives). Still another question was, "How would you yourself seek to get necessary revenue in order to meet the rising cost of operating the city government?" (RCV Archives; Randolph 1998,

69–70). The instrument seems clearly designed to eliminate prospective candidates, such as Smith, who publicly championed gender-related issues and the cause of the poor and working classes. Another reason why Smith may not have been endorsed by the RCV was gender bias. The RCV's research committee, which screened prospective candidates and recommended to the larger body which candidates should and should not be endorsed for state and local elections, was clearly dominated by males during and after the civil rights era (RCV Archives). Women did not become consistent members of the research committee's consultants until 1973, when Edwina Clay Hall was elected as the first female president of the RCV. Thus, the systematic exclusion of women from the ranks of the consultants during the civil rights era can explain why Smith was not endorsed for council in 1962.

Gender bias was definitely prevalent in the RCV. The RCV Archives contain a special report compiled for the RCV and the Richmond Citizens Advisory Committee (RCAC), a local movement center during Richmond's civil rights era, by a member (who signed it "Your Roving and Free Lance Reporter—C") for a September 1962 meeting (RCV Archives). The report reflects the gender bias operating during that period that lead to the exclusion of women in some of the civil rights organizations: "The maid informed me, that Mr. Kramer with his Oregon Hill Heritage-Culture tries to be a regular fellow, but he has missed the point in that he is not at all polished in his speech. He has not learned that a Negro woman might smile at what he might say, but still will not appreciate what he says because she is a woman" (RCV Archives). Although the report's author acknowledges the maid's analytical and rhetorical gifts, he devalues her authority to exercise them because of her socioeconomic status and her gender. These kinds of views can account for the absence of women in RCV leadership roles. Moreover, these same kinds of views reinforced the belief that women should maintain an ancillary role in civil rights organizations during this period. As we mentioned earlier, women did not obtain leadership roles such as president or vice president of the RCV until 1973. Prior to Hall's election in 1973, the highest ranking woman in the RCV during the civil rights era was Ethel T. Overby, chair of the RCV's finance committee. However, the RCV finance committee was controlled by the treasurer, who was a male. That women such as Overby were relegated to nonexecutive positions within the RCV and reported directly to a male member of the organization is consistent with the findings of Bernice McNair Barnett and Robnett in their research on the role of black women in the civil rights movement (Robnett 1996, 1669–77; McNair Barnett 1993, 167–76).

The relegation of black women to nonexecutive positions in the RCV is substantiated further by the personal accounts of Ruby Clayton Walker, a member of both the RCV and the NAACP. According to Clayton Walker, as long as women were willing to serve the organizations as secretaries and did not pursue real leadership positions, there was no problem; however, when women began to contend for leadership during the civil rights era, they faced sexism. Clayton Walker's experiences in the NAACP and the RCV suggest that her role was consistent with what Robnett defines as a bridge leader. According to Robnett, "Rather than focusing upon their limited positions within the movement, women shifted their leadership efforts toward bridging the movement to communities. This gender bias within the movement was, of course, a reflection of the times. It did, however, create a specific effect. Since women, because of gender exclusion could not be formal leaders, they more readily became bridge leaders" (1996, 1676). (The concept of bridge leader will be expounded upon in greater detail in chapter 4.) Although black women were key participants during Richmond's civil rights era, the marginalization of their contributions and their disproportionate representation in nonexecutive positions in the RCV appear to be consistent with Charles Payne's analysis of the role of women in civil rights activities. Payne argues that

> much of the activity in which women are expected to specialize—caring for children and the home, seeing to the fabric of day-to-day relationships—does not qualify as "work" and is thus effectively devalued. In the same way, I think there is a tendency in the popular imagination to reduce the civil rights movement to stirring speeches and dramatic demonstrations. The everyday maintenance of the movement is effectively devalued, sinking beneath the level of our sight. (Payne 1990, 165)

In spite of the marginalization of their contributions during the civil rights era, most African American women activists concentrated their energies toward ending racism. They chose not to contend against the gender bias they encountered. Their goal was to dismantle de jure segregation; African American women deferred gender issues. The movement in Richmond was just as sexist as the movement in other southern states and in northern states during this era (Morris 1984; Giddings 1984; Cone 1992; Robinson 1987; and Standley 1993). Our examination of the RCV's response to the issues of gender and class reveals that the RCV was undeniably sexist and elitist.

The Civil Rights Movement in Richmond and the Structuring of Protest Activity

The cross is something that you bear . . . and ultimately that you die on. . . . There can be no resurrection without the crucifixion, no freedom without suffering. . . . The cross we bear precedes the crown we wear. To be a Christian one must take up his cross, with all of its difficulties and agonizing and tension-packed content and carry it until that very cross leaves its mark upon us and redeems us to that more excellent way which comes only through suffering. . . . Unmerited suffering is redemptive. . . . At the center of the faith of Christians is the fact of the death and resurrection of Jesus Christ—our reminder that though evil may triumph on Good Friday, it must ultimately give way to the triumph of Easter. . . . Evil may so shape events that Caesar will occupy a palace and Christ a cross, but one day that same Christ will rise up and split history into A.D. and B.C., so that even the life of Caesar must be dated by his name.

Martin Luther King

QUIET INTEGRATION PRIOR TO 1960

The convergence of pre–black insurgent activities, marked organizational development in Richmond's African American community, and a belief by this aggrieved population of the vulnerability of the political system set the stage for the civil rights activity that surfaced in Richmond during the late 1940s and early 1950s. According to McAdam (1982), a generation of insurgency will occur if there is an organization within the aggrieved population, along with a collective belief in the success of the venture, and a political alignment of groups or structure of political opportunities within the larger political environment. By the mid-1950s, Richmond's black community unquestionably possessed a collective belief in the success of the venture with the destruction of de jure segregation. Also, by the mid-1950s, Richmond possessed organizations within the aggrieved population, for example, the NAACP and the RCV. However, the third factor that was required by McAdam for insurgency activity to take place actually began in 1947 and during the early 1950s because of changes taking place within Richmond's political system. The basis of this part of McAdam's argument stems from his concept of cognitive liberation. According to McAdam,

> One effect of improved political conditions and existent organizations is to render this process of cognitive liberation more likely. . . . In effect, the altered responses of members to a particular challenger serve to transform evolving political conditions into a set of cognitive cues signifying to insurgents that the political system is becoming increasingly vulnerable to challenge. Thus, by forcing a change in the symbolic content of member/challenger relations, shifting political conditions supply a crucial impetus to the process of cognitive liberation. (McAdam 1982, 48–49)

If one places McAdam's words in the context of Richmond's black community during the period 1947 to 1956, the events that occurred during this period may have been early cognitive cues that Richmond's black community was taking from the political system, cues suggesting that changes were possible, even if the changes were incremental. Moreover, Richmond's black community may have gathered from these changes that the political system was vulnerable. Thus, whichever perspective was used by Richmond's black community to decipher these changes is beside the point, because when these changes occurred, blacks may have subliminally exploited them during their struggle against de jure segregation. With these thoughts as a frame of reference, the period 1947 to 1956 in Richmond created a context for ensuring changes.

The period from 1947 to 1956 was a time of "quiet integration," a term that stems from "Richmond's Quiet Revolution," an article written by Virginius Dabney for the *Saturday Review* in 1964 (Dabney 1964, 26). Dabney's article praised the capital of the confederacy for its voluntary efforts to integrate and reminded the readers that Richmond has always had satisfactory race relations (26). However, after reading Dabney's article and examining the activities that occurred during this period, one can surmise that Dabney's portrait of Richmond may have been misleading.

In 1947, the Richmond Public Library was voluntarily desegregated by a majority of the library board members. The rationale for the shift in policy could not be discerned. Moreover, in 1950, the city hired its first black firemen. Subsequently, when a black fireman attained the rank of captain, he was given command of an all-black fire station. The promotion of a black to the rank of captain, along with the simultaneous establishment of an all-black fire station, illustrates how Dabney's depiction of Richmond as being a progressive southern city is misleading, because as soon as a black was promoted to the rank of captain, the city wasted no time in resorting to its steadfast belief in the "separate but equal" view. In other words, did Richmond establish an all-black fire station because it was unwilling to assign a black captain to a station where he would have command over whites, or was the hiring of blacks to the fire department a deception so that the city could be looked upon favorably by businesses wishing to relocate there? Due to the lack of written documentation on this particular issue, we may never know Richmond's motives.

In 1953, Richmond hired its first black policemen. The significance of this event was that, unlike cities in the Deep South, Richmond gave its black officers the same authority as white officers (Dabney 1964, 27). In other words, black officers' authority was not restricted to the black section of town, nor were they prohibited from arresting white suspects. Also, in 1956, the city buses were voluntarily desegregated (Dabney 1964, 27). Our uneasiness with Dabney's perception of Richmond's integration efforts forces us to question that assumption. Because if one accepts Dabney's article without any critical examination, one could easily be mislead into believing that Richmond's efforts at integration were those of a city trying to do the right thing. However, Richmond's motives may not have been that magnanimous. For instance, one reason the city may have voluntarily integrated its buses in 1956 was because that was the same year the Montgomery strike was settled. City leaders may have realized that Virginia's segregated bus seating arrangement would eventually be challenged in court. Furthermore, Richmond officials must have been aware that a protracted bus strike replete with negative publicity would not be good for long-term business. Jack M. Bloom's research, in *Class, Race, and the Civil Rights Movement* (1987), corroborates this hypothesis:

In case after case, business and middle classes intervened to counter the resistance to civil rights demands and to accommodate blacks. These steps were often taken grudgingly—businessmen were often no less hostile toward blacks than anyone else—but they were taken. The businessmen acted in this way because they were economically and socially vulnerable to black pressure in ways that the agrarian elite had never been and could never be. (Bloom 1987, 215)

Although Richmond unobtrusively integrated its transit system in 1956, the city did not hire its first black bus drivers until 1962 (*Richmond Afro-American*, Apr. 14, 1962, 1). Perhaps the city officials' motives were political and not as humanitarian as Dabney portrayed them in his *Saturday Review* article. Examining an article in the April 14, 1962, issue of the *Richmond Afro-American* applauding the Virginia Transit Company's decision to hire black drivers reveals that the city may have been forced to make this decision because of pressure placed upon it by the Richmond Urban League (RUL) and the Richmond Citizens Advisory Committee: "The men were employed through the interest and efforts of the Richmond Urban League and the Richmond Citizens Advisory Committee . . . with [the] vice-president and manager of the VTC Richmond division" (*Richmond Afro-American*, 1962, 1).

Thus, white political elites may have made these gestures toward integration not for altruistic reasons, but because of the rising importance of the black vote in Richmond. For instance, a *Richmond News Leader* editorial titled "Moves Across a Southern Chess Board" warned Richmond's white community that the size of the city's black population was reaching "decisive strength, the only recourse will lie in annexation of white voters from Henrico and Chesterfield" (Holton 1987). The editorial was reprinted by the *Richmond Afro-American*, whose editor sternly warned black subscribers about white racist plots (ibid.). Additionally, the editorial urged African Americans to register to vote. Thus, the white power structure's gestures at integration were only token.

Quiet integration would continue its course with the assistance of two important pre–black insurgency events involving Thalhimer's department store in Richmond. Both of these activities were led by African American women, and although not highly publicized, their successes were significant. In 1959, Alpha Kappa Alpha (AKA), an African American sorority composed primarily of class-advantaged women, reserved Thalhimer's auditorium for an activity for African American teenaged women. Thalhimer's knew the group was black, yet they allowed the AKAs to use the auditorium in violation of Virginia's segregation policy.

Janet Ballard, former civil rights activist, former social worker, and first woman executive director of the Richmond Urban League (RUL), stated that at the insistence of one of the organization's most conservative members, she was persuaded to call the auditorium manager in advance to remind her that the group was black and to find out if they could still hold the event there. The auditorium manager informed Ballard that the AKA's event was still on. According to Ballard, even though the event was not heavily publicized initially, it received follow-up coverage in the *Richmond Afro-American* (Ballard interview 1993; Randolph 1998, 66).

In the second incident, Ballard, an original member of a private organization called the Richmond Council on Human Relations (RCHR) and an active member of the AKAs during this period, single-handedly integrated Thalhimer's beauty salon when she refused to have her hair dried and set in a separate room specifically for African American women. When Ballard went to the salon, she realized that she was being separated from the white patrons. She proceeded to question the operator's decision to place her in a separate room. The operator responded by informing Ballard that some other women were comfortable with the arrangement of having their hair dried in this room. According to Ballard, all of the women the operator identified were black, were schoolteachers, and were personally known to Ballard. She believed that the women tolerated this particular indignity because they were glad to have their hair done at Thalhimer's. After several heated exchanges with the manager, Ballard prevailed (Ballard interview 1993). When Ballard returned home, she performed two important tasks, the first of which was immediately to telephone those women who had been identified by the operator and who accepted the dual policy. One of the women who was questioned at length by Ballard tried to deny she knew about the policy; however, the woman eventually admitted that she knew of it. At this point, the woman responded to Ballard's queries by simply asking Ballard, "What could we do?" The second task Ballard performed after returning home from the salon was to inform her black female friends of the salon's new policy. According to Ballard, "African American women immediately started patronizing the salon" (Ballard interview 1993). The irony of black women patronizing Thalhimer's is that it would eventually lead to a reduction in patrons for black beauty salon businesses that had a virtual monopoly on the black hair industry because of de jure segregation. Despite Thalhimer's relaxed policy in the salon, the rest of the store adhered to Virginia's de jure segregation policies. The beauty salon, on the other hand, in contradiction of local law and custom, was quietly integrated before the 1960 boycott.

The significance of these two pre-1960 events is that African American women directly and indirectly pressured Thalhimer's to integrate. Although the initial changes by Thalhimer's were incremental, one still wonders why Thalhimer's risked its reputation with the white community by obliging African American women. Perhaps these were chivalrous privileges extended to class-advantaged black women. Edward Peeples, a retired professor at Virginia Commonwealth University (VCU) and a former white civil rights activist in Richmond, postulates that Thalhimer's acquiesced on some matters because the operating principle was that some whites could engage in risky behaviors. In other words, as long as whites held political and social hegemony, exceptions to the rules were tolerated. As long as whites were in control, Thalhimer's could allow African American society women to have their hair washed, dried, and set in the same room with white women.

There are three primary reasons for accentuating Ballard's role during Richmond's period of quiet integration. First, Ballard was not a novice when it came to testing the Jim Crow policies of the South. For instance, she initiated the integration of some white restaurants in Richmond. She was particularly courageous because she consciously and consistently violated segregated policies; for example, she refused to drink out of the coloreds-only water fountain. During her first trip to Atlanta to attend a YWCA meeting in 1947, she entered the train from the front and sat in the section normally reserved for whites. When she reached her destination, however, she was confronted by the conductor and informed that she was in violation of the state law. Reluctantly, she exited the train from the rear. Ballard's position was that if she was with a group, she would follow the Jim Crow policies. If she was alone, she would not adhere to the policies because she had been socialized by her parents and especially her father that she was just as good as anyone else (Ballard interview 1993). Another plausible explanation as to why Janet consistently challenged Jim Crow was because she simply refused to drink out of the coloreds-only fountain because of her principles and her notion that these laws were simply immoral and unjust. Another example of Ballard's principles being tested occurred when she and her young daughter were in a train station waiting to catch a train. According to Ballard, when she asked the station manager for the location of the nearest restroom, the manager acknowledged Ballard's request by informing her that the nearest colored restroom was down two flights of escalators. Ballard responded to the manager's statement by informing the manager that she did not ask him where the nearest colored restroom was, but where the nearest restroom was. She intended, she informed him, to take her daughter to the nearest restroom. The station manager responded to her statement by informing Ballard that it was against the law for her to use the whites-only restroom. When Ballard heard the manager's reply, she informed him that if her daughter was not allowed to use the whites-only restroom, she would have her daughter release herself in the middle of the train station's carpet floor. The manager capitulated and allowed Ballard's daughter to use the whites-only restroom.

Fig. 8. Janet Jones Ballard, September 1986. Ballard was a civil rights activist, a social worker, a founding member of the Richmond Council on Human Relations, and the first woman executive director of the Richmond Urban League. Copyright *Richmond Times-Dispatch*—Used with permission.

Prior to the incident at Thalhimer's, Ballard was not a neophyte in the area of civil rights organizing. She had previously undergone nonviolent direct action training with the Southern Christian Leadership Conference (SCLC), with Martin Luther King and Andrew Young, and she was very instrumental in organizing RCHR. Ballard was not only a major actor during Richmond's CRM, but she indisputably personified Robnett's concept of a bridge leader, especially a professional bridge leader. Belinda Robnett, in her text *How Long? How Long? African-American Women in the Struggle for Civil Rights,* expounds upon the concept of a bridge leader. According to Robnett, bridge leaders were those individuals who

> utilized frame bridging, amplification, extension, and transformation to foster ties between the social movement and the community; and between prefigurative strategies (aimed at individual change, identity, and consciousness) and political strategies (aimed at organizational tactics designed to challenge existing relationships with the state and other societal institutions). Indeed, the activities of bridge leaders in the civil rights movement were the stepping stones necessary for potential constituents and adherents to cross formidable barriers between their personal lives and the political life of civil rights movement organizations. Bridge leaders were able to cross the boundaries between the public life of a movement organization and the private spheres of adherents and potential constituents. . . . One's position as a bridge leader was socially constructed and largely determined by one's race, class, gender, and culture. . . . Bridge leaders were not always women, but it was the most accessible and acceptable form of leadership available to them. (Robnett 1997, 19)

Ballard embodied the attributes of a bridge leader according to the criteria established in Robnett's text. She was not excluded from leadership because she had no previous leadership experience but because of her gender. Moreover, Ballard was able to make contacts with the masses that formal leaders were unable to make because, as Robnett states, she was able to operate in organizational free spaces. She initiated new organizations and often did the groundwork to establish these new organizations (1997, 20). In addition, she helped form new organizations in Richmond, such as Richmond's first human relations organization. And it was Ballard, not male leaders of the RUL, who organized and planned a RUL event to acquaint the Richmond Chamber of Commerce (RCOC) with the RUL and its activities. Ballard's organizing the meeting between the RUL and white RCOC is consistent with the traits of bridge leaders who "tend to advocate more . . . nontraditional tactics and strategies because, unlike formal leaders, they do not need the legitimacy with the state" (ibid.). Thus, when Ballard organized this historic gathering it was definitely perceived by the black conservative members of the RUL leadership as nontraditional. The more conservative members of the RUL would not have initiated this kind of integrated gathering because of their reluctance to risk damaging their political ties to Richmond's white economic elites.

Ballard epitomizes the traits of a bridge leader in the organizational skills she and her mother employed in organizing the Thalhimer's boycott picket line. Her expertise undergirded much of the local movement. Additionally, Ballard held formal positions in other organizations, such as the RUL, and she was involved with several organizations in Richmond (Robnett 1997, 20). Underscoring Ballard's role during Richmond's quiet period of integration were not only two successful attempts at integration but also her success at convincing other African American leaders that a boycott of Thalhimer's was perhaps their best opportunity to successfully challenge Richmond's system of de jure segregation.

UNSUNG HEROINES OF RICHMOND'S CRM ERA

In addition to Janet Ballard, there were three other women who made important contributions to Richmond's CRM. Ethel T. Overby, Ruby Clayton Walker, and Ora Lomax were selected to be the focal point of this discussion because informants frequently identified them as being some of the forgotten female activists and contributors to Richmond's CRM. Overby, Walker, and Lomax made unique and important contributions to black Richmond's struggle for racial equality.

As stated previously, Overby was one of the original founders of the RCV and an active supporter of various social causes throughout her life in Richmond. Like Ballard, Overby was also adamantly opposed to de jure segregation. For example, the following personal account relates her refusal to leave an area reserved for whites only:

> Mrs. Guild, a white friend of mine who had been traveling abroad, wrote asking me to meet her at the Broad Street Station, as she planned to visit me as soon as she arrived. This was during the days of complete segregation. I went to the station and stood at the white entrance. A policeman came up and ordered me to go the back entrance. I explained to him that I could not meet my friend at the back entrance. I refused to move, and told him that he

would have to arrest me. He didn't arrest me, and I met my friend. That was the way you had to live; your whole life was like that. (Overby 1975, 34)

Overby further demonstrated her opposition to de jure segregation when she refused to have the parents of her students sign the pupil placement sheet during the period of massive resistance:

In Richmond, Negroes who did not sign Pupil Placement Sheets could not send their children to school. The pupil placement sheets showed that the parents were not concerned about integration. I was given a batch of the Pupil Placement sheets and did not want my parents to sign them. I also did not want my teachers to become involved with this because it was an order from the administration. I did not know just how I would get around it. One of my patrons, the Reverend Elegant . . . had two of his children in my school. I asked him if he was going to sign, and he said No. When he would come to school with his children in the morning, and parents asked me about the pupil placement sheets, I would say, Go over there and ask Reverend Elegant. And the Reverend Elegant would tell them not to sign. (Overby 1975, 32)

Overby's opposition to the pupil placement statement reveals her defiance of state policy and her determination to undermine Virginia's system of de jure segregation when the opportunity presented itself. If one views Overby's opposition from the perspective of that era, she was actually helping to undermine the very system that was providing her with employment. She was the first black woman to be appointed to the post of principal in the Richmond public school system, and she used her position as a platform to further the cause of civil rights. For example, she played a critical role in securing equal pay for black teachers in Richmond, starting from the late 1920s through the late 1950s (Overby 1975, 5–33). Her decision privately and publicly to advocate the equalization of black teacher salaries with those of whites is important, because for twenty-one years, Overby was denied a principal post by a former white superintendent of the Richmond public school system who told Overby that as long as he lived she would never be appointed to that post. His reason for this firm stand was to punish her for disregarding "his instruction to cease her activity to get a pay increase for Negro teachers" (Overby 1975, 36).

A third reason Overby is significant to Richmond's CRM is that she single-handedly prevented the Ku Klux Klan from doing away with the RUL. In her autobiography, *It's Better to Light a Candle than Curse the Darkness,* Overby explains how the KKK attempted to sabotage the RUL through donations to the Richmond Community Chest (CC). According to Overby, the KKK persuaded some large contributors to the CC to sign a petition that would have required the CC to drop the RUL as one of its members. Moreover, if the CC failed to comply with the KKK's demands, the CC would lose over one hundred thousand potential dollars in donations (1975, 30–31). Overby further revealed that when the total amount of contribution dollars exceeded one hundred thousand the RUL was dropped by the CC. Overby prevented the RUL from total annihilation when she persuaded black teachers and the PTA of her school to contribute five dollars a month to the RUL. Thus, with the contributions from black teachers, well-meaning whites, the PTAs, and the national Urban League, the RUL was able to remain solvent (31). Although the RUL was able to survive in spite of the KKK's racially motivated covert attack on the organization's funding sources, these kinds of schemes were common occurrences throughout the South during this period. The occurrence of these kinds of maneuvers can be corroborated further by Bloom's research. According to Bloom,

> They drew a hard line between white and black. Crossing the line was made very difficult, lest the line itself disappeared; white solidarity had to mean increased hostility to blacks. Black and white associations suddenly became taboo. . . . This change was felt in small ways: black college chorus performances before white audiences were dropped; black groups were excluded from holiday parades and festivities. . . . Carl Rowan was told by a southern moderate in Mississippi that at Christmas time wealthy whites would no longer make contributions to buy presents for poor black children. The Urban League was excluded from Community Chest fund raising efforts in several Southern cities where it had. previously participated, including Little Rock, Richmond, New Orleans, Jacksonville, and Fort Worth. (Bloom 1987, 132–33)

The kind of economic pressure that was placed upon the CC directly by groups like the KKK, along with the ensuing action that was taken by the CC against the RUL, appears to be consistent with the kind of retaliatory action white elites and their KKK allies throughout the South were implementing to subvert black activism during the early period of the CRM. In other words, white elites utilized economic retaliation against blacks in general as a means to reassert their white political hegemony over blacks.

Finally, Overby again used her position as a platform to champion the cause of civil rights by incorporating voter education into the school curriculum. She accomplished this task by educating black children and adults about the role and responsibility of citizenship. Overby implemented her voter education program because she was convinced that the only way of attacking the road block to black political empowerment was to attack the poll tax:

> For twenty-five years as an elementary principal, my faculty and I carried on a program of Citizenship education, emphasis being made upon the duties to be performed if one wished a government of the people, by, and for the people. We had to ease the road blocks in the way of Negro voting. The blank sheet of paper was removed when we taught all pupils beginning with the third grade, how to register. They in turn taught their parents and received a gold star for their efforts. We raised money and set up a citizenship loan fund so that even parents on relief could pay their poll tax. . . . The children felt a sense of achievement as they not only persuaded their parents to become voters, but also their relatives and neighbors. Our precinct had more qualified Negro voters who actually voted than any other Negro precinct in our city.
> (Overby 1975, 11)

Overby carried out her program of citizenship education by staging mock elections and educating blacks about the poll tax, and by stressing the importance of blacks voting in large numbers. She was convinced that if blacks voted in large numbers, they could alter their unbearable conditions (1975, 11). Thus, through her role as an educator, Overby made a quiet but important contribution to Richmond's civil rights struggle. Like Ballard, Overby was a professional bridge leader who possessed significant civil rights experience prior to Richmond's civil rights activity during the 1960s. For instance, Overby was an active member in such groups as the RUL, the NAACP, the RCV, Virginia State Teachers Association (VSTA), and the Delver Woman's Club (30–51). Her contribution to Richmond's CRM is corroborated by an interview with Janet Ballard. According to Ballard, Overby never received the proper recognition that she deserved, in the past or in the present, for her contributions to Richmond's CRM. Overby's many personal sacrifices, along with the many causes she championed in the fight for civil rights, are important because of her steadfast commitment to the struggle for black political empowerment during a repressive era in Richmond's history.

Two additional women who made quiet but important contributions to Richmond's CRM were Ruby Clayton Walker and Ora Lomax. Walker became involved in Richmond's CRM because of the social and racial injustices she witnessed on a daily basis as case worker for the Richmond Welfare Department (Walker interview 1993). She also became involved because her parents stressed racial uplift, and because, like so many blacks of her generation, she felt that they "had the power to realize our goal if we could fight for justice with others who shared the vision of a free society for all" (Walker 1990). Walker, like Ballard and Overby, was a bridge leader. She was not excluded from leadership because she had no previous leadership experience but because of her gender. She was, for example, one of the early presidents of the RCHR, a racially and gender-mixed organization. If Walker could serve as leader of such an organization, surely she could have served in that same capacity with the NAACP and RCV. One plausible explanation of why Walker could preside as president over the RCHR but not the NAACP or RCV was because in the nonhierarchical structure of the RCHR there was more leadership mobility. This point is significant because it is consistent with one of Robnett's arguments that bridge leaders tend to "have greater leadership mobility in nonhierarchical structures and institutions" (Robnett 1997, 20). Clearly, the reason Walker did not hold a more formal position within either of the male-dominated organizations was because of her gender. Moreover, Walker, like Ballard, was able to make contacts with the masses that formal leaders were unable to make because, as Robnett states, she was able to operate in organizational free spaces. Even though Walker encountered gender exclusion from black male–dominated organizations, she still continued to serve organizations such as the NAACP in the capacity of Assistant Youth Advisor to the Youth Council, and later, as a board member of the NAACP. Walker was involved with the Thalhimer's boycott, walking the picket lines on her lunch break. She demonstrated even greater courage when she helped to integrate restaurants in Richmond's downtown section, so that future blacks would not have to suffer the social indignities that were daily inflicted upon Richmond's black populace (Walker interview 1993; Walker 1990). As Walker expanded the scope of her concerns for social justice, she became involved in the antiwar movement through her affiliation with the International Women's League for Peace and Freedom (IWLPF).

In addition to her involvement with groups like the RCV and other social causes she supported during the 1960s, she subsequently expanded the scope of her social concerns even further when she became involved with injustices that occurred inside the criminal justice system. For instance, one of the most celebrated causes with which Walker became involved was the case of Joann Little, who was accused of killing a white guard and escaping from jail (Davis 1983, 175). Walker helped organize support rallies for Joann Little's defense fund. When Little was taken to

Fig. 9. Ruby Clayton Walker. Courtesy of L. Douglas Wilder Library, Virginia Union University.

court, it was later revealed through her testimony that she killed the guard with an ice pick in self-defense because the guard had raped her and threatened to kill her with the same ice pick (ibid.). Walker became involved in this case because she knew innocent black women in the South who had been raped by white men, and against whom no formal charges were ever brought. Thus, like Ballard and Overby, Walker was a silent yet an important contributor to Richmond's CRM.

Although Ora Lomax was not a bridge leader in Richmond, her contribution to Richmond's CRM was important. The daughter of a share-cropper in Franklin County, North Carolina, Lomax became involved in the CRM when she moved from North Carolina to Richmond (Lomax interview 1993). She worked for and was trained by Lorraine James, the black owner of a women's boutique called Jamie's. According to Lomax, it was James who provided her with the skills that she would later employ to challenge Richmond's de jure segregation. And, according to Lomax, it was James who would help to raise her political consciousness about the cause of civil rights by involving her in civil rights meetings and activities. Through her contact with James, Lomax became involved with such groups as SCLC out of Petersburg, Virginia, and she played an instrumental role in bringing Martin Luther King to the First African Baptist Church in Richmond for an important fund-raising event. Based upon the information that Lomax provided us of her relationship with James, it would appear that James was unquestionably mentoring Lomax. James may have taken it upon herself to mentor her because James may have seen something special in her. In essence, with James instilling the idea of racial uplift in Lomax, James may have been preparing Lomax for her ultimate role in Richmond's CRM of tester. The idea that James was performing a racial uplift function in developing Lomax can be corroborated indirectly by Patricia Hill Collins's notion of racial uplift in her *Black Feminist Thought:*

> Educated Black women traditionally were brought up to see their education as something gained not just for their own development but for the purpose of race uplift. This feeling was so strong that the women founding the National Association of Colored Women's Clubs chose as their motto "Lifting As We Climb." Coppin describes this deep commitment on the part of Black women as teachers/activists in this arena of the struggle for group survival: "It was in me to get an education and to teach my people. This idea was deep in my soul. Where it came from I cannot tell, for I had never had any exhortations, nor any lectures which influenced me to take this course." (1991, 150)

Lomax's major contribution to Richmond's civil rights struggle was her role as a tester. According to Lomax, her role was to integrate those white-owned boutiques and clothing stores that had previously refused to hire black sales clerks or buyers. She was able to perform this role because of the enormous and diversified work experience she had attained while working for James. As a result, Lomax became the first black to integrate such fashionable white stores in downtown Richmond as Raybeys, Lerner, L-Pells, La Vouges, and the May Company. Lomax integrated these stores because each had a long history of refusing to hire qualified blacks as sales clerks. Also, Lomax personally felt that these stores had to be integrated because blacks, and especially black women, spent more money on their apparel than any other group in Richmond.

From Lomax's perspective, if blacks were spending a sizable portion of their disposable income at these stores, why shouldn't qualified blacks be hired as sales clerks and buyers? Although Lomax was able to integrate the sales counters of some of Richmond's most fashionable white clothing stores, she was still unable to advance to higher positions within those stores for three important reasons. First, due to the historic racism still prevalent at that time, Lomax was simply unable to make any meaningful advancement. Second, the leftover psychological scars stemming from the daily overt racism affected her ability to move up the company ladder where she was employed. For instance, when black customers came to shop in the stores where she was the only black sales clerk, they would avoid her and go straight to the white sales clerks who often treated them in a disrespectful manner. Also, when white customers would enter the stores where she was the only black sales clerk, they occasionally would spit on her, or even refuse her assistance when she was the only sales person available. Third, she was unable to advance in most of the stores she integrated because her white colleagues would undermine her successes by constantly trying to cheat her out of her sales commissions. Some of the white sales clerks even went so far as to frame her for theft by planting items from the store in her locker. Although whites attempted to frame Lomax, she never left a store for theft or an accusation of theft. Consequently, she often found herself combating white racism on a daily basis, and often was ignored by black patrons due to internalized racism. The idea that black patrons ignored Lomax upon entering boutiques where she worked is consistent with a concept that was introduced by Charles Johnson, a National Book Award–winning novelist, in his most recent novel *Dreamer,* which is set against the backdrop of the CRM during the King years (Johnson 1998, 138). In it, Johnson introduces a concept called "mind-forg'd manacles": "After liberating lunch counters, winning court battles and homes in nice neighborhoods, we must in our next campaign free consciousness itself from fear, from what William Blake called 'mind forg'd manacles.' But to do this we must unlearn many things" (ibid.). Johnson's metaphorical usage of the term "mind-forg'd manacles" and its relevance to this particular discussion is that it painfully reveals how African Americans even in victory, in this case being able to freely patronize white owned establishments, are still not free until they rid themselves of the demons that still afflict them from their nightmarish experiences under de jure segregation.

Lomax had to sue stores such as Thalhimer's and Miller and Rhodes, two of Richmond's fashionable stores, because of racial discrimination.

Her contribution to Richmond's CRM was that she was a first, and in being a first, like a Jackie R. Robinson, she paid a high emotional price for breaking down Richmond's racial barriers. The only support Lomax could depend upon during this period of emotional turmoil was that given to her by her husband and a small group of black women. She made a quiet but important contribution to the struggle for equality in Richmond during the civil rights era.

The significance of discussing Richmond's unsung heroines in the CRM is twofold. First, all of these women at some point during the pursuit of equality in Richmond displayed immense courage when challenging the system of de jure segregation. Additionally, at some critical juncture in Richmond's civil rights struggle, all of these women made important personal sacrifices in standing up for the cause of civil rights. Second, all of these women were interconnected in one way or another. For instance, all of them had direct ties to Janet Ballard, either professionally or through associational affiliations. Ruby Clayton Walker and Janet Ballard were some of the original members of the RCHR. Both had served as president of the organization during its early stages and both at one time or another had worked for the Richmond Welfare Department. Ethel T. Overby and Janet Ballard knew each other because of their association with the RUL, and Ethel T. Overby, Ora Lomax, and Ruby Clayton Walker knew each other through their memberships with the NAACP and the RCV. These interconnecting relationships substantiate a viewpoint put forth by Robnett:

> In spite of women's limited official power within the SCLC, their contributions as bridge leaders were critical. Though women did not generally hold positions as officers, they did bring to the organization all the skills in their possession, leadership included, exercising those abilities whenever they found themselves. And as leaders women can be credited with building the SCLC's mass base of support. Ella Baker provided the organizational foundation for the SCLC. Septima Clark, also a professional bridge leader, imparted her knowledge and skills regarding citizenship education and literary to hundreds of others, who in turn spread the word throughout their communities, dramatically increasing voter registration throughout the South. Miss Carol F. Hoover's initiative in fund raising provided the SCLC with an economic base to sustain its protest efforts. (Robnett 1997, 97)

In essence, just as Baker, Hoover, and Clarke provided valuable resources (that is, their skills and knowledge base) to national civil rights organizations, Overby, Ballard, Walker, and Lomax provided comparable skills and knowledge in assisting local civil rights organizations. Thus, the individual and collective skills of these women were invaluable assets that helped sustain Richmond's CRM during the 1960s, especially during the Thalhimer's boycott of 1960.

The most visible vestige of racial discrimination was segregation at Thalhimer's and the other major department stores. The Thalhimer's boycott of 1960 was Richmond's version of the Montgomery bus boycott. African Americans' boycott of Thalhimer's department store was a defining moment in the history and direction of Richmond's CRM. Yet underneath the surface of African American unity were class and gender divisions which will be examined throughout this discussion (Randolph 1998, 66).

THALHIMER'S DEPARTMENT STORE BOYCOTT

The boycott of 1960 has generally been described by observers and participants as a spontaneous event in which several Virginia Union University (VUU) students, inspired by the Greensboro lunch counter sit-ins in 1960, decided to show their solidarity by staging a similar sit-in at Thalhimer's lunch counter (Holton 1987, 76; Foster interview 1993). However, several staged boycotts actually began on February 20, when a group of Virginia Union students "marched from the campus on Lombardy street, down Chamberlayne Avenue, to Woolworth's department store on Broad Street. Once there, the students staged the first sit-ins in Richmond when they occupied all of the thirty-four seats at the store's lunch counter" (Williams 1990, 41). Woolworth's closed its lunch counters, and the students left. According to some accounts, students repeated this scenario at the lunch counters at G. C. Murphy's, People's Drug Store, Thalhimer's, W. T. Grant, and Sears and Roebuck (ibid.). No violence occurred, and there were no arrests because the store owners closed their operations rather than risk escalating a public confrontation. Charles Sherrod, a seminarian at VUU and co-organizer and student leader of the Thalhimer's boycott, stated on February 20, 1960, "Sherrod gives credit to the *Richmond Afro American* for inspiring him and other fellow students to become interested in the movement. 'Back then, that paper was like hot cakes for me,' stated Sherrod, who began to ponder about the possibilities of starting a sit-in movement in Richmond. 'If they [blacks in Greensboro and other cities] were doing it, why shouldn't we be doing it?'" (Williams 1990, 41). The sit-ins on February 20 were dress rehearsals for the boycott on February 22, 1960.

Fig. 10. Civil rights Demonstration in front of Thalhimer's department store, Richmond, 1960. Courtesy of the Valentine Museum/Richmond History Center.

The boycott was not spontaneous (Foster interview 1993). According to Wendell T. Foster, a Richmond schoolteacher and one of the original thirty-four students arrested for trespassing at Thalhimer's on February 22, Charles Sherrod and Frank Pinkston, another seminarian at VUU and a co-organizer and student leader of the boycott, met with Thomas Henderson, then president of VUU, late in the evening of the twenty-first in his office. Foster revealed overhearing Sherrod and Pinkston telling the other students who would eventually participate in the boycott that he and Pinkston had informed President Henderson that they were going to sit-in at Thalhimer's the next day (Foster interview 1993; Randolph 1998, 66). Foster further revealed that Sherrod and Pinkston stated that the president would not oppose or support the sit-in. President Henderson's decision to remain neutral was the typical public stance of most presidents of historically southern black colleges and universities (HBCUs) during the sit-ins. They could not publicly support the sit-ins because if their institution were private, they were concerned about alienating prominent white donors; and if their institution were public, they would certainly suffer financial repercussions from state legislatures. Most presidents of HBCUs had to straddle the political fence during this period (Newsom interview 1983; Bloom 1987, 127).

On February 22, led by Sherrod and Pinkston, thirty-four VUU students once again requested service in the tea room and lunch counter at Thalhimer's. Asked by the store officials to vacate the premises, the students refused. Consequently, the store officials called the city police, and the students were escorted away from the store. As the students were being escorted by the police, they emerged from Thalhimer's carrying American flags. Before the students were placed into police vans, they received emotional and verbal support from five hundred supporters. The students were arrested for trespassing (Williams 1990, 43). The black public was outraged over the arrest of the students. Then, VUU students demanded a boycott of Thalhimer's, and they implored all black patrons to turn in their credit cards and stop buying from the store. On February 23, picket lines were installed and volunteers were recruited to man the picket lines. The boycotters wore "placards that advocated the boycott of Thalhimer's" (Williams 1990, 43). As the boycott unfolded, both sides dug in their heels and prepared for a protracted strike. As Richmond's boycott began, the white response to the boycott was somewhat different from that of their white brethren in deep southern cities like Jackson, Mississippi, and Birmingham, Alabama. For instance, unlike Jackson, Mississippi's closed society, or the horrible images of Birmingham's police chief, Bull Connor, and his police using fire hoses to spray demonstrators or turning their K-9 attack dogs on and wielding police sticks indiscriminately against civil rights protesters, such events did not occur in Richmond during the Thalhimer's boycott. Richmond's boycott of Thalhimer's was so subdued that it prompted Franklin Gayles, a VUU professor and a member of the RCV, to state that "the police did such a good job, I even let my wife demonstrate" (Holton 1987, 77).

The only major controversy that occurred during the boycott was an incident involving Ruth Tinsley. The Tinsley incident is significant because of its impact on Richmond's black community. The arrest of Ruth Tinsley, an elderly African American, senior advisor to the Richmond NAACP's Youth Group, and wife of J. M. Tinsley, former president of the NAACP, would galvanize Richmond's black community into united action. Tinsley was not involved in the sit-in; she was arrested when she did not move as instructed by an officer with the K-9 patrol. Tinsley refused to move because, as she informed the officer, she was waiting to be picked up by a friend who was going to take her home. Tinsley's arrest is important because of her age and class advantage; she was a respected elder in Richmond's black community. Had she been twenty-five years old and working class, her arrest would not have elicited the same outpouring of sympathy (Robinson 1987; Randolph 1998, 67).

Although the Montgomery case was unique, age, class, and gender were issues there, too. Moreover, the inaction of Montgomery's black community when younger black women were arrested prior to the arrest of Rosa Parks parallels the attitude of Richmond's black community. Jo Ann Gibson Robinson's memoir, *The Montgomery Bus Boycott and the Women Who Started It,* reveals the lack of reaction of Montgomery's black community to the arrests of three black women. In the first arrest, Robinson describes the black community's reaction:

> Then [on March 2, 1955] the day came when Claudette Colvin was arrested. She was a fifteen-year-old student at Booker Washington High School—an "A" student, quiet, well-mannered, neat, clean, intelligent, pretty, and deeply religious. . . . The question of boycotting came up again and loomed in the minds of thousands of black people. . . . But some members were doubtful; some wanted to wait. The women wanted to be certain the entire city was behind them, and opinions differed where Claudette was concerned. Some felt she was too young to be the trigger that precipitated the movement. She might get hurt! The time for action was not now. (Robinson 1987, 37–39)

In Robinson's account of the second arrest, the black community again failed to respond: "In October 1955, Mary Louise Smith, an eighteen-year-old black girl, was arrested and fined for refusing to move to the rear of the bus. Her case was unpublicized and no one knew about it until after her arrest and conviction. She too was found guilty; she paid her fine and kept on riding the bus" (1987, 43). Robinson's accounts of Colvin's and Smith's arrests illustrates the uncertainty among Montgomery's black community whether to support the two young women. However, in the third incident involving Rosa Parks, Robinson presents a different reaction from the same black community:

> The straw that broke the camel's back came on Thursday, December 1, 1955, when an incident occurred which was almost a repeat performance of the Claudette Colvin case. . . . A prominent black woman named Mrs. Rosa Parks was arrested for refusing to vacate her seat for a white man. Mrs. Parks was a medium sized, cultured mulatto woman; a civic and religious worker; quiet, unassuming, and pleasant in manner and appearance; dignified and reserved; of high morals and a strong character. She was—and still is, for she lives to tell the story—respected in all black circles. By trade she was a seamstress, adept and competent in her work. . . . I made some notes on the back of an envelope: "The Women's Political council will not wait for Mrs. Parks consent

to call for a boycott of city buses. On Friday, December 2, 1955, the women of Montgomery will call for a boycott to take place on Monday December 5." (Robinson 1987, 43–45)

The community response in Montgomery was favorable to Parks because of her age, class, gender, and standing within the black community. In the case of the younger women, age and social standing were not in their favor, and they did not gain community support. Thus, the black communities of Richmond and Montgomery responded affirmatively to Tinsley and Parks because of their gender, class, age, and standing in the community.

Tinsley's arrest was photographed by local and national newspapers. The photograph, which was published locally and nationally, showed two white officers accompanied by an attack dog dragging an elderly African American woman across the street to the police van (44). Tinsley's arrest galvanized blacks finally, and collectively, to confront white domination. The photograph stirred an emotional understanding of Martin Luther King Jr.'s words: "There can be no resurrection without the crucifixion . . . no freedom without suffering" (Cone 1992, 128). Tinsley's arrest signaled to the black community that they had suffered enough.

The boycott of Thalhimer's unified the African American community against de jure segregation. After the students were arrested and released on bond, a mass meeting was called, and a fifteen-member committee was established to plan strategy for the Richmond movement. The committee consisted of such representatives as Charles Sherrod, Frank Pinkston, Oliver Hill, famed NAACP civil rights lawyer, and Reverend Wyatt Tee Walker, who would later become the first executive director of the SCLC. When the meeting was adjourned, African Americans had created their own local movement center, the Richmond Citizens Advisory Council (Williams 1990, 45; Morris 1984). According to Morris, a local movement center is a

> social organization within the community of a subordinate group, which mobilizes, organizes, and coordinates collective action aimed at attaining the common ends of that subordinate group. A movement center exists in a subordinate community when that community has developed an interrelated set of protest leaders, organizations, and followers who collectively define the common ends of the group, devise necessary tactics and strategies along with training for their implementation, and engage in actions designed to attain the goals of the group. (Morris 1984, 40)

The RCAC's leadership was dominated by middle- and upper-income black males who served as spokespersons for the group and the movement. The leadership was represented by individuals from both the NAACP and the RCV. Black male leadership dominating the ranks of the RCAC is reflective of how the black middle class dominated the important social and political organizations within Richmond's black body politic.

The boycott against Thalhimer's ended on August 30, 1961 (Williams 1990, 48), when an agreement was reached between the RCAC and the Retail Merchants Association in Richmond. Although the boycott focused primarily on Thalhimer's, it included six other stores that had refused to serve African Americans: Miller and Rhodes, People's Drug Store, W. T. Grant, G. C. Murphy, Sears and Roebuck, and Woolworth's. Although Thalhimer's, Miller and Rhodes, and People's signed the agreement, these three stores did not completely desegregate until a year later (ibid.).

The question that has to addressed at this point is, why was Thalhimer's selected by the boycotters? According to Peeples; John Moeser, VCU professor in the Department of Urban Studies; Willie Dell, former Richmond city councilperson; and Ballard, Thalhimer's was selected as the store to boycott because it represented old Richmond and the old power of racial domination (Dell 1995). According to Moeser, middle-class African Americans who frequently shopped at Thalhimer's were angry that although they were of a higher economic status than most of the white patrons, they still were humiliated by white sales clerks. Most stores in downtown Richmond, especially Miller and Rhodes, forced African Americans to buy blind, meaning they must either know their exact sizes or guess them because they were not allowed to try on the clothing inside of the store. Even if the clothes didn't fit, the stores would not allow returns or exchanges. Thalhimer's, however, was the only Richmond store that did not impose a buy-blind rule on African Americans. In spite of Thalhimer's comparatively liberal policy, Ballard contends that the store was selected because the spending of middle-class African Americans accounted for a sizable amount of its revenue and made the store vulnerable to a protracted boycott (Ballard interview 1993).

Unity was also an issue in the 1960 boycott. An ad in the *Richmond Afro-American* alludes to a breach of unity within the African American community. The ad pleaded with African Americans suspected of secretly buying clothes from Thalhimer's and having purchases delivered to their homes in unmarked trucks to stop the practice because they were undermining the boycott. The newspaper notice emphasized that "purchases made by telephone also was crossing the picket line" (Williams 1990, 46). The allegation about upper-income blacks ordering clothes over the phone does have merit for two reasons. First, according to Ora Lomax, who participated in the Thalhimer's boycott, the allegations about some middle-class blacks who ordered their clothes over the phone during the boycott has merit:

> It was common knowledge that some black upper middle class persons were crossing the picket lines by ordering merchandise over the phone. For instance, these individuals would order their merchandise over the phone, and their merchandise would be delivered to their homes in unmarked vans. As I stated earlier it was common knowledge because the only blacks who could afford to have merchandise delivered to their homes were those who could afford a credit card with stores like Thalhimer's. I am talking about black doctors and lawyers. (Lomax interview 1993)

Harmon Buskey, former chair of the NAACP's Direct Action Committee, confirmed during an extended phone interview that some middle-class teachers and doctors crossed the Thalhimer's picket lines (Buskey interview 1996). Although Buskey's and Lomax's accounts provide some interesting insight into the state of unity among the ranks of black middle-class people, without any additional hard evidence we may never know exactly who betrayed one of Richmond's most important social protest boycotts. The issue of race unity is important because it raises some interesting additional questions. For example, would the boycott have lasted more than six months, or have succeeded, if the African American community had targeted a store whose patrons were mostly white? Furthermore, would the African American community have been able to maintain its solidarity if the boycott had occurred in a store patronized by lower-class, rather than middle-class, African Americans? Given the historical factors surrounding the Thalhimer's boycott, answers to both of these questions will most likely remain unanswered.

Under the leadership of Harmon Buskey, a working-class-led boycott group called the East End Neighborhood Association (EENA) successfully directed a strike against a major local drug chain store, the Springer Drug Company, in 1960 (*Richmond Afro-American*, Apr. 30, 1960). During the boycott, the black middle class did not cross the picket lines. According to Buskey, the primary reasons the black middle class supported their picket lines were that their lines were manned twenty-four hours a day and the Buskey forces publicly announced that all violators would be "severely dealt with if they were caught crossing their lines" (Buskey interview 1996). The working-class-led boycott is significant because it occurred during the Thalhimer's strike and was settled seven months earlier than the Thalhimer's boycott. The primary reason the EENA strike was successfully resolved before the Thalhimer's strike was the all-or-nothing policy of negotiation with white store owners. The all-or-nothing policy meant that the EENA would not accept any proposal that included the idea of partial integration of store facilities for blacks as a solution. In other words, they demanded complete desegregation or nothing (Buskey interview 1996). For instance, if a drug store owner refused to accept their demand of all or nothing, the boycott would continue. Moreover, the all-or-nothing approach was strengthened when the boycotters were able to convince white stores owners that their clientele was predominantly black. When groups such as EENA would boycott a store, they would convince the white store owners to capitulate to their demands by having 100 percent black participation supporting the strike. Thus, if a strike lasted at least two weeks, and no blacks crossed the picket lines, and if the store owner was vulnerable to black economic pressure, then that particular store owner would have no choice but to grant the boycotters' demands (Buskey interview 1996).

The boycott of stores by groups such as EENA reveals that class issues existed in Richmond's African American community. For instance, although this boycott was settled before the Thalhimer's strike, the amount of coverage devoted by the *Richmond Afro-American* was noticeably smaller in terms of space allocation and absence of a follow-up story in comparison to the Thalhimer's strike (*Richmond Afro-American*, Apr. 30, 1960). In essence, the lack of coverage allotted to this story suggests a middle-class bias on the part of the *Afro-American* in covering the two civil rights stories. Furthermore, the bias against the working-class-led boycott persists today, because when the *Richmond Free Press* ran a thirtieth-anniversary story on the Thalhimer's boycott in 1990, the EENA boycott was never mentioned in the series of stories devoted to Richmond's civil rights past (*Richmond Free Press*, Mar. 18–20, 1993). The only plausible response to all of the aforementioned questions is that the Richmond boycott was unique because of the apparent class overtones that seemed to have clouded the boycotts; and the boycotters guessed correctly when they elected to boycott Thalhimer's. Finally, Thalhimer's was selected because African Americans in Richmond thought that if they could successfully boycott Thalhimer's, the other stores would follow suit. In other words, blacks perceived a defeat of Thalhimer's as being a prelude to a domino effect for the other stores that mistreated their black patrons (McAdam 1982, 48–51).

The idea that Richmond's middle-class African American population was convinced that it could defeat Thalhimer's segregation policy in a protracted boycott is a valid assumption because some of the African American leaders were responding to the subtle cognitive cues that Richmond's tripartite system was perhaps vulnerable to a challenge from Richmond's African American population. Consequently, when the African American middle-class leadership responded to these cues, a collective protest was triggered. The protest occurred because the African American protesters had achieved their cognitive liberation (McAdam 1982). The twin concepts of cognitive cues and cognitive liberation can best be illustrated by a quotation from McAdam:

> To summarize, movement emergence implies a transformation of consciousness within a significant segment of the aggrieved population. Before collective protest can get under way, people must collectively define their situations as unjust and subject to change through group action. The likelihood of this necessary transformation occurring is conditioned, in large measure by the two facilitating conditions discussed previously. Shifting political conditions supply the necessary cognitive cues capable of triggering the process of liberation while existent organizations afford insurgents the stable group-settings within which that process is most likely to occur. (McAdam 1982, 51)

The momentum of the boycott carried over into other segregated areas of Richmond. For instance, on September 6, 1960, the Richmond public school system began its incremental and stonewalling tactic of desegregating the city's schools. Richmond's white elites' reaction to blacks exerting their constitutional rights was to stonewall and/or stymie the process. Robert A. Pratt, educational historian and survivor of Richmond's desegregation plan during the early 1970s, described Richmond's early attempts at desegregating its schools in the 1960s as being a half-hearted effort:

> Under the new law, the state Pupil Placement Board would continue to have statewide authority in the matter of pupil assignment, but a locality could now opt to remove itself from under the placement board's jurisdiction. This could be done, however, if both the local school board and the local governing body agreed. In their closing report, the placement board members said that their policy had been to fight, with every legal and honorable means,

any attempted mixing of the races in the public schools. They added: The board does not feel that it was, nor should its successors feel that they should be, obligated to take one positive step toward the mixing of races in the public schools. (Pratt 1992, 25)

Richmond's white elites had no intention of integrating the city's schools with "all deliberate speed," as was stated by the Warren Court in its landmark *Brown v. Board of Education II* decision in 1955. Instead, it would appear that Richmond intended to engage in a form of passive resistance to desegregation (Orfield 1996, 7). According to Bloom's research, Virginia's elites, along with the assistance from the local white media, were committed to undermining any attempts to integrate the public schools. According to Bloom, "While calling for resistance and rejecting the authority of the Supreme Court, the *Richmond News Leader* also rejected outright physical resistance as unworkable: 'We tried that once before.' Instead they proposed 'to enter upon a long course of lawful resistance. . . . Litigate? Let us pledge ourselves to litigate this thing for fifty years. If one remedial law is ruled invalid then let us try another; and if the second one is ruled invalid, then let us enact a third'" (1987, 107). Pratt also illustrates how the elites were clearly committed to undermining any attempts to integrate when he revealed the kind of tactics that were employed by the Pupil Placement Board (PPB) when assigning black students to previously all white institutions. Pratt states that when the PPB finally admitted two black female students to Chandler Junior High School, on September 6, 1960, Richmond's armor of segregation proved to be extremely durable. Richmond's segregation armor was so impregnable that it was able to ward off its attackers for several years (1992, 25). In essence, with the law on their side, blacks during the civil rights era would continue their battle for equal education in Richmond.

The city's parks were desegregated in 1960, and in 1962, Richmond's city council passed a resolution that stated employees of the city would be employed and promoted based upon merit, and not race (Moeser and Silver 1995; Dabney 1964; Pratt 1992, 32–41). Even though the city council passed the resolution supporting fair employment practices, the city bureaucracy continued to engage in bureaucratic resistance to the city's resolution. Fair employment practices would not take place until the black majority on city council was elected in 1977. In spite of these changes in Richmond, African Americans continued their fight against other vestiges of de jure segregation.

The final concerns discussed in this section are the role of gender and class in Richmond's CRM. Based upon interviews conducted for this study, and available published and unpublished materials, sexism did exist in Richmond's CRM. Lomax, Ballard, and Walker agreed that the picket line was organized and manned for the most part by African American women six days a week. Lomax insisted that older women and female and male college students walked the picket lines most of the time. The idea that women were manning the picket line during the Thalhimer's boycott is consistent with current civil rights literature. According to Belinda Robnett, "It was not that women were prevented from participating in important ways, but that their participation options were limited" (1996, 1676). Payne supports Robnett's argument when he asserts in his research on Mississippi that "the tendency in popular imagination and in much scholarship has been to reduce the movement to stirring speeches—given by men—and dramatic demonstrations —led by men. The everyday maintenance of the movement, women's work, overwhelmingly, is effectively devalued, sinking beneath the level of our sight" (1990, 165). Payne and Robnett's points are further corroborated by John Dittmer in *Local People: The Struggle for Civil Rights in Mississippi*, in which he contends that "the cadre of young male organizers had assimilated much of the notion of women's proper place, then dominant in the larger American society. For example, men often assigned to themselves the most dangerous work, such as canvassing on white-owned plantations. Male chauvinism also manifested itself in other forms, and numerous examples of discrimination against women in the movement can be (and have been) recited" (Dittmer 1994, 126). If you apply the spirit of all these quotations to the Richmond boycott, clearly women's work consisted mainly of manning the picket lines, a contribution which was devalued. In essence, women manning the picket lines during a boycott was comparable to union picket lines being manned by the foot soldiers or the rank and file union members. Moreover, in both the civil rights and labor movements, the formal leadership rarely walked the picket lines, except during photo ops, because, as Payne suggested in his research on Mississippi, men were the spokespersons who negotiated with management, whereas women kept the organization going (Payne 1995). In other words, the rank-and-file union members and the women in a local civil rights movement were relegated to grunt work, whereas the leaders did the important work (that is, negotiate and settle disputes). Therefore, women walking the picket lines in Richmond seems to be consistent with the notion of gendered roles in the civil rights movement. Older men were frequently absent from the picket lines because they had to work. However, those women who were professionals also had to work. For example, Walker and Lomax admitted that they would leave work during their lunch hour and take their turn on the picket lines. If those African American women who walked the picket lines were fired by their employers for participating in civil rights activity, their loss of income could have been economically disastrous for African American middle-class households. According to Paula Giddings in *When and Where I Enter*, African American women have been significant contributors to the development of most African American middle-class households (Giddings 1984, 247–48). The African American household was equally threatened by the loss of either the male or female income if either one of them was fired for civil rights activity. Since the men and women were equally threatened, it seems the older men's absence from the picket lines appears to be an admission that manning the picket line was somehow devalued. However, Richmond's black men behaved no differently than other African American males who were involved in similar boycotts throughout the South during this era (Giddings 1984; Robnett 1996; Robinson 1987, Standley 1993).

Sexism in Richmond's CRM during the civil rights era can be illustrated further through personal accounts offered by Ballard and Walker. Ballard encountered sexism more frequently when she became the first woman to serve as executive director of the RUL in 1964. When she joined the RUL, she said "sexism hit her like a ton of bricks" (Ballard interview 1993). When she planned an RUL event to acquaint the RCC with the RUL and its activities, she was the only female in the room. Furthermore, when the president of the RUL Board asked everyone to introduce themselves, he did not acknowledge Ballard, nor did he bother to introduce her. According to Ballard, the excuse that Henderson provided for not introducing her was that Ballard was "staff and not a board member" (Ballard interview 1993). The only problem with Henderson's excuse was that he did not pass over the lone white female who also was in attendance. Ballard felt that if she were a man this incident would never have occurred.

Ballard encountered even more sexism when she first went to work for the RUL. According to Ballard, she started as a volunteer with the RUL. As a volunteer, she was actually performing the task of the executive director. The significance of Ballard's performing the job of the executive director is that the RUL already had an executive director who was a minister and who was being paid. Ballard's arrival at the RUL bears some close resemblance to Ella Baker's situation in the early days of SCLC. For instance, Ballard, like Baker, was doing the same job for the executive director, who, incidentally, happened to be a minister, and she too was not being paid. In both cases the ministers were not performing adequately on the job, and in both cases the ministers would eventually resign. In Ballard's and Baker's situations the male-dominated organizations hesitated before appointing both women to the post of executive director. The only difference in the two cases is that Baker was made acting executive director, whereas Ballard actually was appointed to the post of executive director (Morris 1984; Ballard interview 1993). Ballard got the position because she was a native Richmonder and because the board finally arrived at the realization that the male executive director was not performing effectively in the position. The question that begs to be asked at this point is, would the RUL have appointed Ballard executive director if another male had been available for the job, after the previous male executive director resigned? One could only surmise that given the level of sexism prevalent in Richmond during the civil rights era, Ballard may not have been appointed to the post if another black male had been available for the job. Thus, the problems that Ballard had to endure as executive director of the RUL during the civil rights era appear to mirror the treatment of black women leaders that was reported by Denise McNair Barnett's research findings in her classic article, "Invisible Southern Black Women Leaders in the Civil Rights Movement: The Triple Constraints of Gender, Race, and Class" (McNair Barnett 1993, 162). The following excerpt taken from McNair Barnett's research supports the treatment that women like Ballard, and even Overby, under the RCV had to endure in Richmond during the civil rights era. McNair Barnett asserts that

> even while suffering the daily indignities heaped on them by their location in the structure of society, many southern Black women were much more than followers in the modern civil rights movement; many were also leaders who performed a variety of roles comparable to Black male leaders. Although seldom recognized as leaders, these women were often the ones who initiated protest, formulated strategies and tactics, and mobilized other resources (especially money, personnel, and communication networks) necessary for successful collective action. (McNair Barnett 1993, 162)

Walker also provided a personal account of the sexism she encountered as a member of the NAACP and the RCV. Her claims documenting gender exclusion within the RCV cannot be dismissed. According to Walker, as long as women were willing to serve the organizations as secretaries and not pursue real leadership positions, there was no problem;

however, when women began to run for leadership positions during the civil rights era, they began to encounter sexism. Ballard and Walker's assertions support the notion that gender exclusion from the leadership ranks existed during the civil rights era in Richmond, and they are consistent with Robnett's research findings. Yet sexism in the Richmond NAACP still exists, and during the time of this interview, Walker was seriously contemplating forming a subgroup within the NAACP called WIN, or Women in the NAACP.

During the civil rights era, most African American women activists concentrated their energies toward ending racism. Subsequently, they chose not to tackle the gender bias they encountered. Their overall goal was to dismantle de jure segregation. Thus, for African American women, gender issues were deferred. These accounts and the omission by African American male leaders about the contribution of African American women in Richmond's CRM substantiate that the movement in Richmond was just as gender biased as the national CRM during this era (Morris 1984; Giddings 1984; Cone 1992; Robinson 1987; and Standley 1993). Although the issue of gender was not as salient an issue as was race during Richmond's CRM, gender concerns were prevalent during this period. Additionally, the issue of class was an emerging issue in Richmond during the civil rights era. Curtis J. Holt Sr., an important grass-roots community leader during the CRM and a major political actor during the post–civil rights era in Richmond, was a bridge leader. Like Janet Ballard and Ruby Clayton Walker, Holt was also a bridge leader during the CRM because of his socioeconomic status as well as his acknowledged leadership in Richmond's working-class communities. Becoming a bridge leader was not restricted to women, because males of low socioeconomic status could also become bridge leaders. According to Robnett,

> Gendered hierarchy and racial and class constraints, in addition to Black cultural norms, shaped the structures of the civil rights movement and defined the nature of activist participation. Moreover, these created a particular substructure of leadership that became a critical recruitment and mobilizing force for the movement. In other words, race, class, gender, and culture were significant determinants of who became a formal leader and in what context others participated in the movement. (Robnett 1997, 7)

Curtis Holt was born in Rocky Mount, North Carolina, in 1920, one of eight children in an impoverished family. Holt's father was a farmer who died when Curtis was thirteen years old. Holt's mother, along with her children, migrated to Richmond, Virginia in 1934. When the Holt family finally settled in Richmond, Curtis had to quit school at age fourteen and obtain employment to help support his family. Holt supported his family by securing jobs as a construction worker, a forklift operator, and as a factory worker in a tobacco plant (Worrell 1983, 2–3). Quitting school at an early age to help support the family was not uncommon for young blacks, especially males, during that era (Anderson 1988). Holt's entry into the work force would be interrupted on two occasions because of injuries that he sustained while working. The first interruption occurred in 1941, on a construction job at VUU. This injury left him unconscious, hospitalized, and unemployed for three years. Holt recuperated and returned to the work force, but he was injured again in 1963 when he fell down an elevator shaft. This injury would finally force Holt completely out of the work force. As a result of both of these injuries, Holt would spend the remaining years of his life on Social Security disability. Furthermore, Holt's reduction in income would also force Holt, his wife, and children to live in public housing (Worrell 1983, Moeser and Dennis 1982).

Holt's impoverished background, along with his work disability, converged to shape and inspire his activism. His activism was initially shaped by his disability and his increased political awareness. His disability shaped his activism because although he was unable to work anymore, he was determined to make a difference in the world. He started actualizing his dream by becoming an ordained minister in 1970 (Worrell 1983). Utilizing a religious prism, following in the footsteps of so many black civil rights leaders, Holt hoped to transform his faith into a vehicle of liberation. According to Alto Mae Holt, his widow, Curtis became increasingly involved with political issues, especially after he returned from the March on Washington and after meeting Martin Luther King Jr. (Holt interview 1997). Soon thereafter, Holt began to express to his wife and friends his distaste for the all-white city council's political and social neglect of blacks, especially poor blacks. Holt's political consciousness about the conditions of blacks was enhanced further when he became an active member with such black groups as the NAACP and RCV (Carwile Papers). His political and social realization of the conditions of blacks appears to have coincided with his involvement with those two organizations. The surge in his political awareness, along with the simultaneous occurrence of his involvement with the RCV and NAACP, was no happenstance; social movement scholars such as Aldon Morris argue rather convincingly that the point of entry for most blacks into the CRM was the black church or the NAACP (1984). The primary reasons the black church and the NAACP were so interconnected during this period was because the NAACP was the dominant protest group throughout the South before the arrival of the Southern Christian Leadership Conference, and because most southern local NAACP chapters were actively supported by black churches. Thus, Holt's simultaneous involvement with the black church, the NAACP, and the RCV is consistent with Morris's analysis. Furthermore, his simultaneous involvement with these groups during that era served as "rite of passage" for Holt, who was politically and spiritually committed to making a difference in the daily lives of black Richmonders

Although Holt's involvement with these groups may have elevated his political and racial consciousness about the black struggle, his participation did not address his emerging class consciousness. Holt's class concerns would find a more receptive audience with groups such as the RCHR and the Creighton Court Civic Association (CCCA), a group that he formed while living in public housing. Holt would also expand his class consciousness through his involvement with working-class whites in predominantly white public housing, and with local populist white politicians such as Howard Carwile, an attorney, radio talk show host, and progressive member of Richmond's city council. Holt's frequent contacts with these kinds of groups and individuals, and his views on black class and gender concerns, would become even more radicalized when he moved into public housing under the Richmond Redevelopment and Housing Authority (RRHA).

During the mid-1950s, when Curtis Holt moved into Creighton Court, a public housing project, he quickly discovered that living conditions were poor and repressive for the tenants. For instance, the RRHA prohibited tenant organizations, and tenants could not meet on Creighton Court property. Moreover, when Holt attempted to form a Boy Scout troop for young boys who resided in Creighton Court, he was told by RRHA officials that this type of activity was forbidden. The policies of the RRHA appeared to restrict the constitutional rights of free speech and assembly of public housing tenants. Thus, under this repressive climate, Holt decided, in the mid-1960s, to organize tenants into the CCCA (Worrell 1983). The CCCA was formed to provide tenants with an organization that could serve as a liaison between them and RRHA officials. Holt's formation of this group would eventually lead to his receiving an eviction notice from the RRHA for organizing a group in violation of housing rules.

Holt's eviction notice was controversial because the RRHA was actually evicting Holt for failing to report unreported income. According to newspaper accounts, the RRHA argued that Holt had an unreported income of $99. But when Holt challenged the RRHA's allegations in court, with assistance from the Justice Department and the NAACP, it was discovered that the income Holt was alleged to have earned from cutting hair in his apartment and painting a tenant's apartment did not exist. The RRHA's accusation about Holt's unreported income of $99.00 could not be substantiated in court, because Holt did not charge the children for cutting their hair, nor did he charge the elderly tenant for painting her apartment. Furthermore, as revealed in court, Holt's income consisted of a monthly Social Security disability pension of $150, and his wife received a weekly salary of $18 as a hotel maid. The Holt family's total reported monthly income was $222. If one deducted the $42 monthly rent the Holt family paid to the RRHA, their actual reported monthly family income was $180.

When Holt revealed this information in federal district court, the federal judge rejected RRHA's argument that it was evicting Holt for failing to report unreported income. Consequently, the judge permanently enjoined the RRHA's eviction of Holt from public housing because the judge surmised RRHA's actions were taken because of Holt's activities with the CCCA and not because of unreported income. In addition, the judge further stated that RRHA's actions against Holt were questionable because no other tenant had ever been evicted for failing to report income ("Court Bars Eviction" 1966).

Holt's legal battle with the RRHA in 1966 was important because it lead to a series of ongoing battles between Holt and the RRHA over the rights of public housing tenants. The following quotation from a newspaper interview with Holt reveals his personal commitment to championing the cause of the black poor:

Why did Holt do it? "Very simple," he says. "I'm a child of God. The majority of residents of the projects still live under fear," he said[,] "afraid that if they raise complaints, or make trouble, they will run afoul of the authority and may find themselves without a place to live." Holt is still trying to help the downtrodden, the under-represented. "It's very important that we have representation of the grass roots (people) as well as the middle and upper class," he said. "They are the foundation of the country." (Worrell 1983)

In addition to championing the cause of poor blacks, Holt also championed the cause of women, especially black women. For example, he supported the cause of several women who were evicted from public housing in 1967 by the RRHA for violating the "illegitimacy policy" ("Authority's Policy" 1967). In essence, women who had children out of wedlock were to be evicted for moral degeneration. Holt became involved with this issue because, according to Holt, "women were killing babies and flushing them down the [toilet] . . . so they could remain in the apartment" (Worrell 1983). From Holt's perspective, women having abortions to avoid being evicted from their public housing apartment was wrong, and the housing policy that forced them to take these extreme measures was wrong. The case of the eviction of the women from public housing was taken to court; however, the ruling judge upheld the right of public housing officials to control the morality of its tenants because, according to the judge, "there is no constitutional right to low income housing" ("Authority's Policy" 1967).

Although the women lost their court case, Holt established a precedent when he supported the rights of women, especially black women who were single parents. He was clearly ahead of his time in championing the right of a single parent female to control her reproductive rights and her sexuality without fear of losing her domicile. In other words, for a black leader like Curtis Holt to champion this particular cause in an era when it was unpopular for most men, especially black men, to do so, reinforces Holt's progressive politics.

Holt's activism was not restricted to his public housing. He was also concerned about the safety of poor black children who attended Armstrong School and were forced to cross a busy intersection that did not have a traffic light or a safety patrol. The reason black children had to attend school under these kinds of conditions during the early 1960s in Richmond was because city government and school board officials did not value the safety of black children the way they valued the safety of white children. An excellent illustration of school board officials' neglect of the needs of black children is in an account taken from Overby's autobiographical notes. "We who lived in Richmond for many years recall how concerned the parents had become because of the increase of traffic," she wrote. "They asked the white principal of the school to place safety patrols on the corner. He refused because he said that the pupils might get the idea that one day they might become traffic policemen" (1975). This clearly demonstrates white school officials' insensitivity regarding the safety of black children. In spite of the white principal's resistance, a traffic light was later obtained and paid for by William "Bojangles" Robinson, a renowned black entertainer, to protect the children of Armstrong High school where Chamberlayne Parkway, Leigh Street, and Adams Street intersected. Although Robinson's action was admirable, a private citizen purchasing a traffic light to protect the citizens of a city revealed not only the city's lack of political accountability to its black citizens but also its racial indifference.

Overby's biographical notes reveal yet another incident involving a dangerous intersection that black children were forced to cross on their way to and from school:

> A terrible situation also prevailed at the Booker T. Washington School and the parents also asked their white principal for safety patrol. He refused by saying that the white people coming in from Ginter Park would be so upset being stopped by Negroes! I was still teaching there at that time and since there was no PTA, I decided to organize the parents of my class. We had meetings away from the school and Mrs. June P. Guild worked with an advisor. We soon accomplished our efforts and organized a safety patrol, and the PTA became a permanent organization of Booker T. Washington School. (Overby 1975, 7–8)

The significance of this illustration, along with the previous one, is that once again, it reveals white indifference toward the safety of black children.

According to Mrs. Holt and Willie Dell, Curtis Holt's concern about the safety of school-aged children crossing a dangerous intersection stemmed from his concern as a parent and his concern for the safety of all children (Holt interview 1997; Dell interview 1997). Mrs. Holt stated that her husband took it upon himself to perform the role of a safety patrol, to escort the children to and from school across the dangerous intersection. Holt carried out his task by designing his own stop sign for oncoming drivers. Because Holt's action was not sanctioned by the city police, he risked his personal safety twice a day, five days a week, for three years to ensure the safety of these poor black children. Mrs. Holt further stated that when Holt assumed the role of safety patrol guard, white and black motorists consistently stopped when he escorted the children across the intersection.

Holt's and Dell's versions of Curtis Holt's involvement with the school crossing near Armstrong School was corroborated by other sources. Benjamin R. Murray Jr. of Richmond, Virginia, remembered Holt escorting children across the street because he was one of the youngsters Holt escorted (Murray 1997). The second corroborating source of Holt's involvement in this incident was the city of Richmond. A letter sent to Holt from a John T. Hanna, the city traffic engineer at that time, dated October 10, 1963, confirmed receipt of a petition submitted to his office by Holt requesting a traffic signal at the intersection of Creighton Road and Nine Mile Road. Hanna's letter closed by informing Holt that his request would be studied and Holt would be notified of their findings and recommendations. Holt received another letter from the city, this one from W. F. Thomas, the assistant traffic engineer. Thomas's letter informed Holt that "the Bureau has recommended and the Director of Public Safety has approved the installation of a traffic signal at the intersection" (see Appendix). The two letters clearly reveal that Holt was involved and that he assumed leadership on this issue because all correspondence was sent to him.

Holt's involvement with the installation of a traffic light at a dangerous intersection exposes city officials' racial insensitivity toward blacks and may also reflect the indifference of middle-class blacks toward the black working poor. The only visible black leader involved in the traffic light controversy, which involved poor black youngster from the "projects," was Holt. The indifference on the part of middle-class black leaders toward this local issue may be attributed to the invisibility of the traffic light controversy in the *Richmond Afro-American* newspaper from 1960 to 1966. While the newspaper provided adequate coverage of the issue, more extensive news coverage of Richmond's middle class was daily fare (*Richmond Afro-American*, 1960–66). On balance, the *Afro-American* focused more on the black middle class, excluding most of the critical issues having an impact on the urban poor. One may surmise that if middle-class black children had to cross a dangerous intersection in order to get to school, black leaders would definitely have taken some kind of action. Perhaps another explanation for why middle-class blacks may have remained silent on this issue was that they may have perceived that a fight with an entrenched and racially insensitive white bureaucracy over the installation of a traffic light at a dangerous intersection for "project kids" was simply an "unwinnable" battle. The traffic light issue, along with black middle-class indifference to this problem, will be discussed further in chapter 5.

Curtis Holt emerged as a community bridge leader because when he attempted to organize poor whites in Richmond's public housing, he was actually operating in what Robnett describes as "free spaces" (1997, 21). According to Robnett, a free space is "a niche that is not directly controlled by formal leaders or those in their inner circle. It is an unclaimed space that is nevertheless central to the development of the movement, since linkages are developed within it" (ibid.). In essence, when Holt attempted to establish biracial class linkages among public housing residents in Richmond, not only was he operating in a free space, but he was also attempting to forge ties between poor blacks and whites in Richmond. The significance of his attempt to organize poor whites and blacks on a much smaller scale during the early 1960s is that it predates a similar project that would eventually become King's last campaign in 1968, the Poor People's Campaign, and a similar campaign that was forged by Jesse Jackson during the 1980s called the Rainbow Coalition (Pohlmann 1999, 279–80; McKnight 1998).

Holt typified Robnett's characteristics of a community bridge leader because of his involvement with groups like the RCHR and his increasing involvement with urban populist politicians like Carwile. According to Robnett, community bridge leaders generally worked closely with white mainstream leaders in trying to "forge ties between mainstream White institutions and organizations and the movement" (1997, 21). Robnett also notes that community bridge leaders "often acted as formal leaders during a time of crisis when formal and secondary leaders were unwilling or unable to do so" (ibid.). An example of this occurred when Holt provided safety for poor black children who were forced to cross a dangerous intersection on a daily basis in order to attend school. Yet another illustration of Holt acting in the capacity as a community bridge leader was when he championed the rights of single parent females to control their reproductive rights and sexuality without fear of losing their domicile. In essence, in both cases, Holt assumed a formal leadership role during a time of crisis when the formal leadership, refused to become involved.

Although Holt's activism was clearly driven by his personal commitment to the plight of poor people, his grass-roots leadership, along with the kinds of issues that he championed, were not known outside the poor black and some poor white communities because of the lack of newspaper coverage. Thus, without some form of consistent written public account of activism such as Curtis Holt's, these black leaders' contributions to Richmond's black liberation struggle generally go unnoticed. Hence, if these individuals' contributions are overlooked by the mainstream black and white media, their role and contributions become lost or will remain invisible to both the white community and the larger minority community. Not withstanding this invisibility, the late Curtis Holt Sr. played a significant role in black Richmonders' drive for political empowerment. Holt proclaimed himself a "grass-roots coordinator" because he was "a man who dedicated his life to helping the poor people, here, there, and everywhere" (Holt interview 1997; Carwile Papers). A working-class African American resident of Richmond's public housing, and the organizer of the CCCA in the poor black section of Church Hill, Holt was perceived by Richmond's poor blacks as their champion (Holton interview 1987).

While issues of class and gender were salient during the modern-day CRM in Richmond, class inadvertently surfaced briefly during the Thalhimer's boycott. Although all African Americans in Richmond, regardless of class standing, shared group humiliation and indignities, poor African Americans suffered even more because they had no economic viability. For instance, middle-class African Americans rarely rode public transportation; thus, they could avoid all the indignities associated with a segregated public transit system. Most poor and working-class African Americans had no alternative; they had to use public transportation because their economic livelihood dictated it (Kelley 1993, 109). Richmond desegregated its buses in 1956, but two questions still remain. Where was the African American leadership? And why did the African American middle class behave passively on the issue of segregated buses?

Richmond's African American community, especially its middle-class community, acted passively in regard to segregated buses, particularly during the mid-1950s and especially in 1956, when the black community was distracted by MR and the greater threat it posed to public schools. Therefore, if one had canvassed Richmond's African American populace during the first two years of MR and asked what was the top issue facing them, they may have responded that the closing of public schools was the gravest threat to their children's future and to their happiness. Middle-class indifference to Richmond's segregated bus system prior to 1956 could also be explained by the fact that unlike working-class African Americans, they did not depend upon public transportation to go to and from work or to shop. Consequently, if the African American middle class did not see segregated public transportation as a matter of overwhelming concern, then it might explain why they were indifferent on the bus issue but were more aggressive on the department store incident. Thus, the Thalhimer's boycott could be perceived as a class boycott because the only blacks who could afford to shop there were those with the disposable income to buy things from that store. Furthermore, Moeser contends that the working-class African American population might sympathize with the boycotters out of shared group oppression, but in reality, Thalhimer's was not the kind of store they patronized.

If we compare the Richmond CRM with that in other southern cities, we will notice both similarities with and differences between Richmond and other southern cities during the civil rights era. With reference to similarities between Richmond and other CRMs of the South, the issues of class and gender were largely invisible, though more salient in Richmond. Moreover, in terms of boycotts, the Thalhimer's department store boycott began in the same manner as most other boycotts that had occurred throughout the South during the early stages of the sit-in protests. For example, just as the students of Greensboro, Nashville, and Memphis, were an integral part of their respective boycotts, so were the VUU students in Richmond (Moeser and Silver 1995, 108). Furthermore, this research revealed that African American women in Richmond played a significant role in organizing their community for social change. The role of Richmond's African American women in the CRM was also similar to other CRMs in the South during that era (Woods 1993, 106–16). Finally, serving as a defining moment in the history of Richmond's CRM, the boycott of Thalhimer's department store and the manner in which it was resolved were similar to most of the major boycotts that were successful during that era. Also, the primary reason the Thalhimer's boycott was documented was because the national media covered the story and, more important, national photo journalists photographed Tinsley being dragged across Richmond's streets by city police.

Richmond's CRM was different from most of the lower southern comunities because most of the bus boycotts in the South did not occur until the mid- to late 1950s, whereas Richmond's major boycott did not occur until 1960. Moreover, in the area of desegregation of the public transit system, Richmond's experience was also different from that of other deep southern cities because its city buses were voluntarily desegregated, and personnel and public policies were altered. In addition, unlike Jackson, Mississippi or Birmingham, Alabama, or Montgomery, Alabama, Richmond's movement was not marred by frequent occurrences of violent episodes, (for example, lynchings of black males, church bombings, and fatal shootings of local civil rights leaders) that were often associated with the CRM in the lower South. In addition, the CRM in Richmond was different because its local movement center leadership was not completely dominated by ministers. This was probably due to the ministers losing their political clout when the RCC was discredited during the mid-1950s. Finally, the major factor that ignited Richmond's primary nonviolent boycott was a department store discriminatory policy, whereas in Montgomery it was public transportation discriminatory policy directed against blacks.

This chapter has emphasized that black women like Janet Ballard made important contributions to Richmond's CRM prior to the 1960s, contributions that would eventually prove significant to key civil rights demonstrations such as the Thalhimer's boycott. Also, this chapter demonstrated that women like Ballard, Overby, and Walker were not excluded from leadership because they had no previous leadership experience, but because of their gender. These women—Overby, Ballard, Walker, and Lomax—were unsung heroines who provided a high level of skill and knowledge in assisting local civil rights organizations. Their individual and collective skills were valuable assets that helped sustain Richmond's CRM during the civil rights era.

The dominant event during Richmond's civil rights era was the boycott of Thalhimer's in 1960, which galvanized the African American middle class for a year. Thalhimer's and all the other stores in downtown Richmond were desegregated through the efforts of middle- and lower-class blacks. Although working-class and poor African Americans supported the boycott because of shared group oppression, the boycott was clearly a middle-class event because Thalhimer's was not frequented by poor and working-class African Americans. Another successful boycott that occurred during the same time period was the EENA boycott, which ended in six months with complete integration of all the stores boycotted. Richmond's CRM dismantled de jure segregation and changed Richmond's political arena. For instance, the leaders who advised the student protestors during the Thalhimer's boycott were active with the NAACP and the RCV, and some of them became Richmond's first African American elected officials since Reconstruction.

The issues of class and gender within the CRM, while important, were subordinate to the overriding issue of race. However, when the Richmond CRM shifted from protest politics to electoral politics, issues of class and gender reemerged because they had not been effectively addressed in the past by civil rights leaders or by the emerging African American elected officials. Thus, when the issues of class and gender were ignored by civil rights leaders the emerging black elected officials, it created an impression among poor blacks that the CRM did not really change their political or economic material realities. To some degree the plight of Richmond's urban poor after the CRM is depicted by Leon Dash's Pulitzer Prize winning book *Rosa Lee*, which provides a graphic illustration of how one poor black woman struggled to get out of poverty in the District of Columbia when blacks had already received the "benefits" of the movement:

Rosa Lee's illiteracy shuts her out of almost every entry-level position in the American job market. When Rosa Lee was a young woman, pathways to achievement were opening up in Washington, D.C., just as they were in other cities, but she did not know it. Her exposure to middle-class African Americans was fragmentary, at best, and made no lasting impression. She had a limited understanding of the civil rights movement and its goals, and still does not see what was achieved except that blacks no longer have to ride in the back of the bus. Rosa Lee, like many of the urban black poor, was unprepared to take advantage of those new opportunities. Rosa Lee was a victim of both sexism and racism. She was deliberately raised in and trained to adhere to the rural South's rigid gender and racial roles, which guaranteed her domestic work only. (Dash 1997, 253)

Poor blacks' frustration with Richmond's political arena and the so-called gains of the CRM were exacerbated during the post–civil rights era and will be treated in greater detail in chapter 5, as community activists like Holt influenced not only the transformation from protest to electoral politics, but also the rise of the first black majority on the city council. Additionally, class and gender issues will be explored further in chapters 5 and 6.

Black Political Restructuring and Reconstruction

1965–1983

> The time has come for the people of this city to know the truth. For many years we have believed in good leadership and in those who have led us in politics. This leadership, to me, has come to an end.
>
> Curtis J. Holt Sr.

BLACK POLITICAL RESTRUCTURING

In 1965, the late Bayard Rustin, a close associate of Martin Luther King Jr. and chief organizer of the 1963 March on Washington, published an article in *Commentary* titled "From Protest to Politics: The Future of the Civil Rights Movement" (Rustin 1965). According to Rustin, when Congress passed the Civil Rights Act of 1964,

> the legal foundation of racism in America [was] destroyed. To be sure, pockets of resistance remain; but it would be hard to quarrel with the assertion that the elaborate legal structure of segregation and discrimination, particularly in relation to public accommodation, has virtually collapsed. . . . Thus, the movement in the South began to attack areas of discrimination which were not so remote from the Northern experience as were Jim Crow lunch counters. At the same time, the interrelationship of these apparently distinct areas became increasingly evident. What is the value of winning access to

public accommodation for those who lack money to use them? . . . And what
also became clear is that all these interrelated problems, by their very nature,
are not soluble by private voluntary efforts but require government action—
or politics. (Rustin 1965, 25)

Rustin's argument was an attempt to forewarn civil rights activists that
they needed to shift their focus from boycotts to political action if the
movement expected to make any meaningful changes in the quality of life
for most blacks. Rustin's argument is even more compelling because he
appears to be inadvertently foreshadowing the next phase of the CRM,
which involved voting rights. First, Rustin's article was published in February 1965, and within six months, SCLC and SNCC would be fighting for
voting rights in Selma, Alabama. Second, James Bevel, a civil rights activist
and minister, was making a similar argument during the same time period.
According to Taylor Branch, in the second installment of his trilogy of
books on King, *Pillar of Fire,* "Bevel proposed Selma as an effective testing
ground for a mass movement building from civil rights to voting rights,
and Amelia Boynton, who still kept the honor roll of voter applicants on
the wall of her Selma office, seconded him with a personal appeal for
help" (Branch 1998, 324). Thus, it would appear that the national CRM
was shifting its focus from protest to electoral politics. The national CRM's
decision to shift its focus would have a profound impact on the black body
politic not only throughout the South but especially in cities like Richmond. In this section, we intend to illustrate how key federal actions such
as the Civil Rights Act of 1964, Voting Rights Act of 1965, aided the transformation in Richmond's black community from protest to politics. In
addition, we will elaborate on how specific activities that occurred within
Richmond's black community during the same period may have precipitated, indirectly, the resurgence of black schisms, and how the revival of
these schisms helped shape the direction of Richmond's black body politic
throughout the civil rights era.

From Protest to Politics

The RCV during the civil rights era concentrated initially on voting registration and, later, on electoral politics. The RCV gradually began to
challenge not only the Richmond power structure but also, eventually,
the Byrd machine. Wilkinson, in his *Harry Byrd and the Changing Face of
Virginia Politics, 1945–1965,* states that blacks had a greater impact on the
city's politics, but their impact on state elections was still insignificant.
Wilkinson concluded that although their impact on state politics was
minor, the RCV continued to plague the Byrd organization (Wilkinson

1968). Black voters made their greatest political strides both in the city and state after the death of Harry F. Byrd Sr. Byrd's death was an important political watershed because it essentially marked the end of an era for his style of politics in Virginia, and it eventually led to the defeat of the Byrd organization in the state. An excellent example of the black political advancements achieved after the death of Byrd were the political victories of the RCV at the local level. Along with the death of Byrd, several key federal actions would also contribute significantly to black political empowerment in Richmond. For instance, adoption of the Twenty- fourth Amendment in 1964, passage of the Civil Rights Act of 1964 (CVRA), and the Voting Rights Act of 1965 (VRA) collectively made it possible for African Americans to challenge Richmond's white power structure through the political process.

The adoption of the Twenty-fourth Amendment in 1964 aided blacks in the South and Virginia in particular when it outlawed the use of poll taxes in federal elections (Mason and Beaney 1968, 388). Although amendment protected southern blacks' voting rights in federal elections, the one remaining obstacle that prevented blacks from exercising their full franchise rights within their respective states was the dreaded poll tax. In essence, the Twenty-fourth Amendment did not prevent states like Virginia from using the poll tax to exclude blacks from voting in state elections. However, this particular state measure would eventually be alleviated by federal court action and passage of the VRA.

Second, the exclusion of blacks and poor people from voting in state elections was alleviated through the combined efforts of the VRA and the U.S. Supreme Court. The VRA enabled blacks and poor people to participate in Virginia's political arena because it prohibited the use of literacy and other forms of tests as a precondition for voting. Additionally, the one specific section of the VRA that was crucial in Virginia was the provision that allowed the U.S. Justice Department (JD) to initiate suits testing the constitutionality of the use of poll taxes in state elections (Mason and Beaney 1968, 388–89). Virginia's black populace would be aided in their struggle for political equality when the JD decided to test Virginia's poll tax in the case of *Harper v. Virginia State Board of Elections* (1966). In that case, the Court declared that Virginia's use of poll taxes as a precondition for voting in state elections was unconstitutional. "To introduce wealth or payment of a fee, as a measure of a voter's qualifications is to introduce a capricious or irrelevant factor," the Court stated. "The degree of discrimination is irrelevant" (Mason and Beaney 1968, 388). In essence, in *Harper v. Virginia State Board of Elections,* the Court was emphasizing the economic discrimination that poll taxes imposed on citizens at the state level rather than racial discrimination. The VRA's impact on Virginia's black populace was enormous. Table 1 compares black and white voter registration rates in Richmond from 1960 to 1966, and table 2 illustrates the percentage increases in black voter registration from 1958 to 1966. Both tables clearly reflect the increases in new black voter registrations that occurred in Richmond between 1964 and 1966.

TABLE 1

Black and White Voter Registration Rates in Richmond 1960–1966

	RACE			
	Blacks		Whites	
Year	Total No. Black Reg. Voters	% Increase Reg. Voters	Total No. White Reg. Voters	% Decrease Reg. Voters
1960	15,739	23	51,172	77
1962	17,335	25	52,240	75
1964	18,355	26	52,179	74
1966	29,388	34	57,047	66

In examining the data in table 1, the reader will quickly discover the initial impact of the VRA on black voter registration. In comparing the 1964 figures with the 1966 figures, we notice that the initial impact of the VRA resulted in 18,355 new black registered voters in Richmond. Moreover, when we compare the 1964 figures with those of 1966, we detect that 29,388 blacks were registered to vote. When the 1964 figures are subtracted from the 1966 figures, the difference between the two years translates into an increase of 11,053 new black registered voters. The idea that 11,053 more blacks were able to register cannot be trivialized even by today's standards. For instance, in looking at table 2, this point can be corroborated, because in 1958 only 22 percent of the black population in Richmond was registered to vote. That figure is even more alarming when one realizes that blacks comprised 40 percent of the city's

TABLE 2

New Black Voter Registration in Richmond
1958–1966

Year	% of New Voter Registrations	% Increase New Voter Registrations
1958	22	
1960	23	1
1962	25	2
1964	26	1
1966	34	8

Source: Data used to compile the percentages in this table were obtained from Dwight Carter Holton, "Power to the People: The Struggle for Black Political Power in Richmond, Virginia," (Unpublished Thesis, Brown Univ., 1987).

population during the late 1950s and early 1960s. Also, when one compares the 1966 figure with the 1958 figure, the black voting registration levels in Richmond reflected an increase of 12 percent in eight years. The increase in the number of black registered voters is significant because prior to 1966 the increase in black voting registration occurred on average at a rate of 1 percent annually. The factors that contributed to the increase in black voter registration prior to 1966 were the poll tax and the absence of governmental intervention at the state level in the South on behalf of black citizens.

Thus, without passage of the VRA, passage of the Twenty-fourth Amendment, and the favorable decision that was handed down by the Supreme Court in 1966, the black populace's struggle for political equality would have been impeded.

Finally, the last federal governmental action that favorably affected the black struggle for social and political equality was the passage of the CVRA. The CVRA was important not only to Richmond's black struggle, but to the southern black struggle in general because it contributed to that struggle in two important ways. First, the act itself was an instrumental force in attracting the nation's attention to the South's denial of voting rights to its black citizens. For instance, according to Armstead

Robinson, in *New Directions in Civil Rights,* his edited text on the CRM, "Enactment of the 1964 Civil Rights Act focused attention on the demand for federal protection of voting rights. In November the Republican nominee, Barry Goldwater, managed to carry only five Deep South states, along with Arizona. A smashing electoral victory ensued which enabled President Johnson to rely upon the growing national consensus for a federal role in voting rights" (Robinson 1991, 5).

Second, the act broke down some racial barriers for southern blacks. For instance, in the area of education and employment, Title VII of the CVRA gave government the authority to enforce laws that forbid discrimination in federal assistance programs and to prohibit discrimination in employment. For those blacks in the South during the civil rights era who were educated and had certain kinds of technical skills, the CVRA made a difference. Moreover, the passage of CVRA contributed to the black struggle in two additional ways. According to Gavin Wright in his article "Economic Consequences of the Southern Protest Movement,"

> Most of the writings on the history of the civil rights movement have dealt with political dimensions: leadership, ideology, constituencies, tactics, and strategies. These works often seem to take the achievement of black political organizations and voice as the central objective, for its own sake. Yet the changing economic context in the South was critical to the timing and impact of the movement, and of course, improved economic opportunities for blacks was an important part of the motivation for many movement participants. Despite a flurry of recent studies, for the most part interactions between the economics and politics of the movement remains to be analyzed with the attention they deserve. (Wright 1991, 175)

The CVRA had an impact on the black struggle for political equality by reaffirming belief in the idea that important social reforms could be achieved through nonviolent demonstrations and protest action.

The discussion of which groups or individuals benefited or didn't benefit from CR activity is significant in revealing some of the underlying flaws and pertinent to the research on Richmond. For analysis, Charles V. Hamilton employed two terms to differentiate the various types of benefits that can accrue to individuals and groups through the political process. Hamilton used the term "substantial mass benefits" first in his text *The Black Experience in American Politics* (1973, 249–52). Later, in his article "Public Policy and Some Political Consequences," he employed the same concept, but used a different term—"indivisible benefits"—to describe the same phenomenon. Hamilton further asserts that both terms illustrate how certain benefits that are amassed through the political process can benefit an entire populace (1976, 244–51). The term introduced by Hamilton to explain his second concept of benefits was "individual/divisible." According to Hamilton, individual/divisible benefits are those derived from the political process which generally can accrue to an individual or small groups of individuals. Although the CVRA was an important contribution to the CRM in general, it produced indivisible benefits for most blacks, especially those residing in the South and in the border states who were forced to endure the public degradation imposed upon them under the system of de jure segregation. However, when the CVRA is viewed from the perspective of those African Americans who were poorly educated and lacked the necessary skills to compete in the emerging southern economy of thirty-four years ago, the act only yielded divisible benefits to the middle class because they did not perceive the CVRA as significantly altering their daily reality (Dash 1997, 253).

According to Robin D. G. Kelley, in his "Birmingham's Untouchables: The Black Poor in the Age of Civil Rights," the major victories of the CRM did not alter the economic reality of most poor blacks in the South:

> Although the civil rights movement succeeded in desegregating public space, winning the franchise, securing federal job anti-discrimination legislation, and eventually paving the way for black empowerment, neither the vote nor legislation initiatives were effective weapons against poverty, joblessness, and plant shutdown. Today, as more Birmingham steel and iron mills are turned into museums and fewer high-wage industrial jobs are made available, increasing numbers of unskilled African Americans are forced to turn to public assistance, low-wage service sector positions, or in some cases, crime. (Kelley 1996, 100)

Kelley corroborates one perception of the impact of the CRM that is held by some blacks, that legislation such as the CVRA may have produced divisible benefits only to the black middle class. However, in spite of the flaws that may have beset such legislation, we contend that those blacks who were forced to endure social debasement on a daily basis, under the system of de jure segregation, if given another choice today, would not, under any circumstances, elect to return to the humiliating system of segregation that was dismantled as a result of the CRM. Moreover, the relevance of divisible and indivisible benefits to our study is that both of them did appear in Richmond. The appearance of indivisible benefits in Richmond is supported by Avon Drake and Robert Holsworth's text,

Affirmative Action and the Stalled Quest for Black Progress: "In Richmond, the opposition to massive resistance, the effort to establish a human relations commission, proposals to end discrimination in city employment, the movement to ensure that annexation did not entirely dilute emerging black political power, and the campaign to elect a black majority to the city council were all actions that could result in indivisible benefits" (1996, 110). Although the above quotation only illustrates the indivisible benefits that accrued to black Richmonders, divisible benefits also appeared in Richmond and contributed to the black political schisms along class lines.

Thus, with the assistance of the national government and the courts, Richmond's black community began its transformation from protest to politics. The most visible images of the transformation actually occurred in the political arena itself when black political organizations began to compete with one another for political dominance over Richmond's black body politic. The competition between the RCV and several emerging black political groups was driven by differences in ideology, class, and disagreements over which strategies should be employed to overcome the problem of black powerlessness in the political arena. The competition, along with the ideological differences between the RCV and other black groups, would eventually precipitate the return of black political schisms in Richmond's black body politics shaping the direction of the transition from protest to politics.

RECURRENCE OF BLACK POLITICAL SCHISMS

Once the RCV became the dominant force in Richmond's African American community, it gradually shifted its focus from voter registration to performing the role of black power broker on behalf of the black community in Richmond's political arena. Moreover, as the RCV became a major player in Richmond's political arena, it would eventually find itself endorsing political candidates for local and state elections. The origins of the RCV's role as political endorser in local and state elections actually began in 1960:

> Since its inception in 1956, the Crusade had concentrated on voter registration and helping create interest in politics among Richmond blacks. . . . In 1960, however, Crusade leaders decided that they had laid the proper groundwork necessary to make endorsements in the municipal elections. The

Crusade had registered thousands of voters and thus gained prominence as the city's foremost black political organization. . . . The Crusade decided instead to follow what Dr. Thornton would later call a program of practical politics. . . . If the black community could be the deciding factor for a candidate or a group of candidates, the victors would owe their election to the black community, and thus, it was hoped, could be influenced to support the community on council. If the candidate proved unsympathetic to the black community while serving on City Council, the Crusade would withhold its support in the next election. (Holton 1987, 69–70)

Holton's description of the RCV indisputably establishes the RCV as an organization whose focus was shifting from voter registration/education to endorsing candidates for local office for the express purpose of benefiting Richmond's black community. The RCV was a black political broker. In essence, the organization was transforming itself into a political middleman between the white political elite and Richmond's black community:

Through their manipulations, Crusade leaders have created a unique role for themselves. As go-between for the black and white communities, they co-operated with various white leaders and politicians without acquiring the stain of accommodation. . . . In this capacity they served as a buffer between the two communities, a buffer which kept white political influence at a minimum in the Negro community. Thus they gave the newly enfranchised black voter a chance to mature politically without excessive guidance from whites or from Uncle Toms. (Dickinson 1967, 126)

The RCV may have adopted this strategy because it was evolving from a crisis-oriented organization to a franchise-oriented one. The idea that the RCV may have been shifting from one identity to another can be corroborated by Hamilton, in his article "Public Policy and Some Political Consequences" (1976, 252–53). Although Hamilton's application of these terms was employed to explain the phenomenon of northern urban groups undergoing internal transformation, the same concepts could be applied to the RCV. Hamilton's description of a crisis-oriented organization appears to describe the RCV prior to its organizational transformation in 1960:

A crisis-oriented strategy relies on starts and stops, jerks in the political system, and it does not mobilize enough people for the protracted political struggle. It is most vulnerable to a waxing and waning of political interest. And by this I mean that at a particular low point of political interest, the crisis-oriented organization is quite apt to die or go into a critical stage of limbo from which it might not recover. Martin Luther King Jr. noted some of the weaknesses of his own episodic mass mobilization strategies when he made the following observation: Many civil rights organizations were born as specialists in agitation and dramatic projects; they attracted massive sympathy and support; but they did not assemble and unify the support for new stages of struggle. The effect on their allies reflected their basic practices. Support waxed and waned, and people became conditioned to action in crises but inaction from day to day. (Hamilton 1976, 252–53)

However, when we examine the RCV that was evolving in 1965, it was certainly moving in the direction of a franchise-oriented organization. The focus of such an organization

is on power, not solely programs. It contains an organized constituency that is not required to maintain a constantly high level of civic enthusiasm. It is more readily able to effect transference of political styles (from electoral to protest politics), precisely because it has a sustained base. It has an intact leadership cadre that does not have to be required and reactivated anew with each developing new issue. It does not rely on the requirement of a particularly high level of civic enthusiasms; it can, in other words, withstand inevitable periods of subdued political energy and activism. (Hamilton 1976, 253)

Based upon Hamilton's description of crisis-oriented and franchise-oriented organizations, we are convinced that the RCV evolved from a crisis-oriented to a franchise-oriented group by 1965, and by 1966 the RCV was an organization that was competing with other blacks for political dominance over Richmond's black body politic—and competing against Richmond's white political establishment for power.

The ideas expressed by Rustin in his article indirectly indicate that the RCV, like most blacks groups of that era, may have made an organizationally conscious decision that protest and demonstrations were simply not enough to address those problems that required political solutions. Rustin's ideas are relevant because the intrinsic message conveyed within the article appears to provide a rationale for why the RCV had to shift from protest to politics to garner political power for the black community. According to Rustin,

The urban Negro vote will grow in importance in the coming years. If there is anything positive in the spread of the ghetto, it is the potential political power base thus created, and to realize this potential is one of the most challenging and urgent tasks before the civil rights movement. . . . But we must also remember that the effectiveness of a swing vote depends solely on other votes. In that sense, it can never be independent, but must opt for one candidate or the other, even if by default. (Rustin 1965, 29)

Consequently, when the RCV shifted its focus, it frequently challenged the policies of the Byrd organization and, subsequently, Richmond's white political elite. According to Wilkinson's text, *Harry Byrd and the Changing Face of Virginia Politics: 1945–1965,* blacks had a greater impact on the city's politics, but their impact on state elections was still insignificant. Wilkinson concluded that although their impact on state politics was minor, the RCV continued to plague the Byrd organization (Wilkinson 1968). Even though the RCV was a major player in Richmond politics, the biggest initial challenges to the RCV throughout the CR era appeared to have come from opposing black groups. The black opposition to the RCV seems to have materialized from within the black body politic when the group began endorsing candidates for elective office. Although the RCV initiated its first in a series of annual political endorsements in 1960, black opposition to the endorsements did not occur until 1964 following black politicians' growing recognition of the growing importance of Richmond's black votes in local elections. For instance, when black organizations surfaced to challenge the RCV for hegemony over Richmond's black body politic, the first group to appear and challenge the RCV was Voters Voice (VV). According to the *Richmond Afro-American,* dated March 14, 1964, a new group had formed (*Afro-American,* 1964, 1).

The VV was founded by three Richmond black Democrats, L. Douglas Wilder, Ronald K. Charity, and Neverett A. Eggleston. Douglas Wilder, the principal spokesperson for the group, stated that the VV was not established to compete with the RCV but "was organized principally to inject black community issues into municipal elections" (RCVA). Although Wilder and his associates insisted that they were not forming the VV to compete with the RCV, their intentions may not have been straightforward, because on April 9, 1964, another story appeared on the VV in the *Afro-American.* The headline for this story was "Two Businessmen Endorsed for Council by Negro Group" (2). The two businessmen were Eggleston and Charity, who were both members of the VV, and they were endorsed by none other than the VV, the group they had helped to establish. Thus, the founders of the VV had moved in three weeks from their primary purpose of enlightening the black community on political issues in local elections to endorsing two candidates from within their organizational ranks to run for city council, which undeniably was a challenge to the RCV (ibid.). The motives of VV became even more questionable in the *Richmond News Leader*. The headline for its story on the VV was "Voters Voice Endorses Dr. Haddock" (Oct. 20, 1964, p. 4). According to the story, William A. Taylor, chair of the VV, announced that the VV was endorsing an independent Democrat for Congress and a Republican for the Senate. The article further revealed the real motive of the VV when its chair, Taylor, stated that the group's endorsements were consistent "with the original idea of endorsing candidates in local, state and federal elections" (ibid.). Yet another reason the RCV believed that the VV was an opponent and not an ally was that the VV accused the RCV of accommodating the interests of the white power structure (Silver 1984, 282). In addition, when two of its candidates lost their bid for a seat on city council in the 1964 election, both VV candidates accused the RCV of "working hand-in-glove with Richmond Forward" (Moeser and Dennis 1982, 48).

The VV's advent on Richmond's political landscape is important because the VV was a middle-class-led organization that was perceived by some members of the RCV during this period as a conservative opponent who wanted control of Richmond's black politics (Holton 1987, 85). Moreover, the two candidates who were endorsed by the VV were businessmen with conservative views (*Richmond Afro-American,* Apr. 30, 1964, 2). The conservative VV would continue to compete against the RCV by aligning itself with another emerging black conservative group, the People's Political and Civic League (PPCL), which was accused of being an elitist black conservative organization that had aligned itself with the Byrd organization (Holton 1987, 85). An excellent illustration of how the VV and other black conservative groups would occasionally form coalitions to undermine the RCV's political endorsements occurred in 1964 when the VV and the PPCL endorsed the same candidates, but different from the ones endorsed by the RCV (Holton 1987, 86). Although the RCV's candidates outperformed the VV and PPCL candidates in the 1964 city elections, their involvement in Richmond's political arena forced the RCV to accept a new political reality that as the number of black voters increased, political and ideological divisions between blacks surfaced and subsequently threatened the fragile black solidarity that existed in Richmond's black community.

The arrival of black conservative groups such as the PPCL and VV, and their participation in the local political arena, reveals the ideological and political differences that existed between these groups and the RCV. The black political schisms that had plagued Richmond's black body politic in the past were beginning to reappear. Moreover, the resurgence of black conservative groups on Richmond's political landscape corroborates our notion of a double agenda that is driven by two conflicting agendas. The agendas are the progressive and conservative political agendas, the progressive agenda as the highly visible one and the conservative agenda as muted. The periodic occurrence of schisms within Richmond's black body politic precipitated the rise of the conflicting political agendas that will be examined in the next section.

Although the RCV would continue to experience periodic episodes of challenges from other black organizations, the political skirmishes would continue throughout the civil rights era and into the post–civil rights era. However, the two primary hurdles the RCV would have to overcome during the civil rights era were the endorsement debacle of 1965 involving William Ferguson Reid and the repeated allegations from rival black groups that the RCV had become an accommodationist organization to Richmond's white power structure.

The endorsement debacle of 1965 involving the RCV unfolded in the following manner. Reid was running as a candidate for the Virginia House of Delegates on a Democratic slate; if elected, he would have represented Richmond and a portion of Henrico County. According to Holton's account of the event, the Byrd machine attempted to court black voters by unofficially backing Reid's candidacy. In return, the RCV was to endorse the candidacy of Fitzgerald Bemiss for a state senate seat (Holton 1987, 90). The controversy occurred when the RCV was unable to endorse Bemiss because he was alleged to have had close political ties to the Byrd organization. When the RCV refused to endorse Bemiss, Reid paid a heavy political price; he was excluded from the slate of candidates who were endorsed by the local Democratic party (91). Subsequently, when the endorsements were made public, the political fallout that occurred affected the RCV both internally and externally. The internal impact of the Bemiss debacle on the RCV was immediate. For instance, George Pannel, the president of the RCV in 1965, resigned under protest when Reid's name did not appear with the lists of other candidates who had been endorsed by the local Democratic party. Pannel based his decision on the grounds that he had warned the RCV's research committee that if they failed to endorse Bemiss, their actions could have a detrimental impact on Reid's candidacy and thus jeopardize his chances for getting elected. Accordingly, when Reid's name was omitted, Pannel resigned under protest from the organization (92). The external impact of the Bemiss debacle on the RCV occurred when the white newspapers launched scathing attacks on the RCV by blaming the RCV for Reid's loss.

The political implications of the RCV's action during the Bemiss affair was threefold. First, the RCV could not endorse Bemiss because of his close political ties to the Byrd organization. Moreover, even if the RCV had ignored Bemiss's ties to the Byrd organization, the RCV surely would have been attacked by rival black political groups and accused of "selling out" to the white power structure. The significance of the selling out accusation had they endorsed Bemiss cannot be ignored because similar kinds of allegations had already been hurled against the RCC, which eventually led to its downfall. Consequently, the RCV must have remembered that painful political lesson of the past when they decided not to endorse Bemiss. Furthermore, the chronic episodes of the black political schisms that afflicted Richmond's black community were somewhat similar to the balkanized politics that Richard E. DeLeon discussed in his study on San Francisco, *Left Coast City* (DeLeon 1992, 13). According to DeLeon, "Dennis Coyle probably has it right: Baghdad by the Bay is now the Balkans by the Bay. Everything is pluribus, nothing is unum. Hyperpluralism reigns. The city has no majority; its majorities are made, not found. That is a key to understanding the city's political culture: Everyone is a minority. That means mutual tolerance is essential, social learning is inevitable, innovation is likely, and democracy is hard work" (1992, 13). In Richmond the conflict occurred predominately among blacks, whereas in San Francisco the political skirmishes that typically erupted in that city generally transpired between different racial and ethnic groups. Obviously, differences exist between the two cities' political cultures; however, in spite of their apparent differences, we believe that DeLeon's concept of "balkanized politics" can be applied to Richmond's black body politic, especially during periods of intense political infighting.

The second implication of the Bemiss affair was that it placed the RCV in a no-win situation in which neither blacks nor whites would have been satisfied with any course of action taken by the RCV. The final and long-term implication of the Bemiss debacle was its effect on the possible formation of any viable biracial political coalition. The political fallout that occurred, which subsequently may have prevented the formation of a viable biracial coalition during the civil rights era and early post–civil rights era, can be explained in a number of ways. First, the prevention of a possible biracial coalition in Richmond actually occurred prior to the Bemiss debacle, when the RCV had been accused by the VV and PPCL of placating the interests of Richmond Forward (RF), a moderate biracial group that evolved from a more conservative white group called Richmond Citizens Association (RCA) in 1964 (Silver 1984,

280). Rival black organizations' repeated assertions that the RCV was an accommodationist organization forced the RCV to operate from a defensive posture when responding to the allegations of betraying the black community. Thus, the idea that the RCV had to defend its actions against these kinds of charges in the black body politic cannot be disregarded in terms of its importance in preventing the formation of a viable biracial coalition. The RCV was reluctant to forge a biracial coalition with RF. According to Holton, "In 1964, the challenge by the Voter's Voice forced the Crusade to begin distancing itself from the white power structure. The Richmond newspapers' attack on the Crusade in 1966 moved the organization even further from the community's dominant political organization, Richmond Forward" (1987, 113).

The accommodationist label, which was a specter from Richmond's recent political past, had held major ramifications for the RCC. The organization was accused by several rival black groups of doing the same thing the RCV was accused of in 1964. Moreover, the accusation that the RCC was an accommodationist group ironically occurred when the RCC began contemplating brokering a deal to establish a biracial coalition with the RCA during the late 1940s. Although a biracial coalition was never established, the accusations against the RCC ultimately contributed to the group's downfall. The RCC's downfall of recent memory indicated that the RCV was not an anomaly in the art of organizational survival but sought to avoid the same pitfalls that had plagued the RCC by consciously resisting any formation of a biracial coalition (Downs 1967, 9–10). Furthermore, the RCV in 1964 had to choose between forming a biracial coalition or maintaining black solidarity. Accordingly, the group elected to abandon the idea of forming a biracial political coalition and instead decided to maintain black solidarity in Richmond. The first and most obvious reason the RCV pursued black solidarity was Goldwater's presidential candidacy. According to Holton, "At least one other factor contributed to black Richmond's increased interest in voting in 1964: Barry Goldwater helped a great deal. Black Richmonders wanted to do all they could to prevent the Republican nominee, who unsuccessfully sought an agreement with Lyndon Johnson to remain silent on Civil Rights, from becoming the thirty-seventh President of the United States" (1987, 87).

The necessity of black unity for political power was the second reason the RCV pursued black solidarity: "Solidarity is more important than any one election or candidate. We can always vote out a bad candidate, but we can't do that if we don't keep our solidarity, the Crusade told the

Afro American for its pre-election issue" (Holton 1987, 85). The RCV, then, was unable to enter a biracial coalition in 1964 because of internal political constraints emanating from Richmond's black body politic, which were being applied by rival black groups against the RCV. In essence, the black internal politics prevented the formation of a viable biracial coalition. The other internal factor that prevented the formation of a viable biracial coalition was the RCV's utmost concern about maintaining black solidarity, seemingly at any cost, because of the 1964 presidential election and the negative consequences that could have occurred if Goldwater, and not Johnson, had been elected. Given Goldwater's opposition to the CVRA, we can assume that as president, he would not have supported the act. Therefore, from the perspective of southern black leaders, concern about the possible outcome of the 1964 election was not an exaggeration on the part of the RCV.

In addition, the Bemiss debacle may have prevented the formation of a viable biracial coalition in Richmond during the civil rights era because the RCA, RF, and its successor, Team for Progress (TOP), over-reacted negatively to Richmond's growing black population, perceiving the increase in blacks as a potential threat to white political hegemony. The political polemic over the expanding black population only exacerbated a political climate that was already polarized. Moreover, with the success of the RCV, along with Richmond's polarized political climate, all of these factors converged to prevent the formation of any kind of biracial coalition from emerging in Richmond during the civil rights era and the early part of the post–civil rights era. When the RCA became defunct, it was replaced by the RF. That the RF started out as a biracial, moderate organization is somewhat misleading. For instance, when the organization first emerged, the type of blacks who were attracted to it were typically conservative. This did not go unnoticed in the black community. For example, when the two black incumbent city council members, B. A. Cephas and Winfred Mundle, both publicly announced that they intended to run for reelection on the RF slate of candidates, a story immediately appeared in the February 19, 1966, edition of the *Afro-American:* "Mundle Sides with White Power Structure." In addition to Cephas and Mundle running for office on the RF banner, RF also appointed Dr. Alix B. James, then vice president of VUU, as chair of the executive board of RF. When James's appointment became public, some in the black community immediately became suspicious of RF's ulterior motives. Ray Boone, editor of the *Afro-American,* in an interview with Holton, stated that these men were

> representative of the black community's silk stocking elite. These men were
> by no means leaders in the Crusade, nor were they even closely identified

with the Crusade, the leaders of which were much more militant than Cephas, Mundle, and James. Ray Boone considered these men nice, gentlemanly, orderly. . . . The Negro leaders made by the white power structure. . . . Richmond Forward clearly hoped that it could placate black voters by appointing silk stocking blacks to positions of authority, while overlooking the Crusade's leaders. (Holton 1987, 101)

Boone's view corroborates our earlier assertion about the appearance of a double agenda operating within Richmond's black body politic. On the one hand, the progressive agenda of the RCV was undeniably revealed by the RCV's compulsion for sustaining black solidarity at all costs and thus steering the black vote in the most constructive manner possible. In other words, the RCV was orchestrating political strategies that they thought were in the best interests of blacks, especially in an important upcoming political election. But on the other hand, black elected officials' conservative agendas were hidden. The black conservative agendas of Cephas and Mundle support our earlier claim about the double agenda for the following reasons. First, Cephas was a loyal follower of RF's policy as a member of the city council, even though he had voted initially against RF's staggered term provision (Holton 1987, 100). Mundle, on the other hand, was also closely affiliated with the white power structure. Moreover, Mundle, like his black conservative colleague Cephas, supported RF's staggered terms provision and, again like Cephas, had also voted against staggered terms when he was a member of the City Planning Commission (Holton 1987, 100). In essence, the black conservative's contradictory public policy positions are an excellent illustration of the concept of a double agenda. Cephas's and Mundle's political and policy loyalties seem to have been based upon a quid pro quo relationship, in which the prime beneficiaries of policy and political decisions were the interests of Mundle and Cephas, not the interests of the black community. The idea that their loyalties were not congruous with those of Richmond's black community is reflected in Holton's research: "The Crusade had learned, however, that Cephas and Mundle could only be counted on for the most meaningless of votes" (1987, 112).

Second, Cephas's and Mundle's conservative agenda appears to have been an obvious case of political opportunism, which in turn was carefully concealed under the guise of black political solidarity. It also appears that Cephas and Mundle actually exploited the black community's political immaturity by pretending to support black solidarity. For example, in 1966, Cephas and Mundle were popular among black voters; however, neither voted in the affirmative on those issues that had a major impact on Richmond's black community. It is possible that black

voters were so overwhelmed with electing one of their own to city council during the mid-1960s that they may have inadvertently demonstrated
a higher threshold level of tolerance for certain kinds of contradictory
political behavior. Furthermore, Cephas's and Mundle's secret conservative
agenda enabled them to receive black votes because of their race and to
receive votes from whites because of their ultra conservative views. Roland
Turpin, a native Richmonder, former official with the Richmond Redevelopment and Housing Authority, executive director of the Dayton Housing
Authority, and nephew of Cephas, remarked that his uncle was extremely
conservative and was deemed by the white business community as being
a safe Negro (Turpin 1991). In addition, Turpin stated that Cephas's rationale for voting with the business community was that "it was good for business." In essence, Cephas did not vote on issues that were in the best
interest of blacks, but supported those issues that were congruous with the
interests of Cephas and Richmond's white business elites (Turpin 1991).
The subtleties of this double agenda occurred more frequently when the
political squabbles pitted black progressives against black conservatives
and will reemerge with the increasingly more powerful role of black conservatives during the decline of the black majority on city council.

Boone's viewpoint suggests not only that did Cephas and Mundle
forge an alliance with the white power structure but also that RF was
committed to maintaining white conservative political hegemony over
city hall. This possibility cannot be dismissed because by 1965 the issue
of white fears of black takeover of city hall, along with whites' pressing
need for annexation, were clearly established as an important political
agenda issue for the RF in the 1966 city council election. This point is
supported by Holton's research when he suggests that RF was already
developing race as the dominant issue for the upcoming 1966 election:

> One city official, who was asked to prepare a projection on when the city
> would become fifty percent black, told Dennis and Moeser you could feel a
> political change in City Hall. In 1958, the Richmond News Leader had pre-
> dicted that eventually annexation would be necessary to keep control of city
> politics in white hands. By 1965, race had indeed become the central issue of
> annexation; the city was going black. . . . Richmond Forward began defining
> the issue of the 1966 councilmanic elections as early as December 1965,
> when the RF members of Council secured approval of an ordinance asking
> the General Assembly to establish staggered four year terms for City Council.
> (Holton 1987, 97)

Possibly, the RF sought approval from the Virginia General Assembly
to adopt staggered terms could be that there was a desire to reduce

the size of Richmond's city council. Under this scheme, the RF's goal was to reduce the size of city council from nine to five members. Moreover, under the RF's scheme, the four highest vote getters would serve for four years, while the fifth place winner would serve for two. The RF's initial rationale for reducing the size of council was to create a sense of continuity. However, there was another possible motive behind the RF's plan: to ensure that very few blacks, if any, would be elected to city council (Holton 1987, 97–100). Also, if any blacks were to be elected to city council, the blacks who would be elected would be those individuals who were deemed safe, or those blacks who held ultra conservative views and who were supported by RF. Hence, under this scheme, the RCV would find it increasingly difficult to get its candidates elected to city council. The reason the RF wanted fewer members on city council was to safeguard their plan of annexing more whites into the city and thus preventing a black takeover of city council by the RCV. RF was convinced that if more blacks were on city council when the issue of annexation arose, an increase in black members on city council would lead to additional opposition against annexation because blacks would perceive annexation as an attempt by whites to attenuate their political power (97). In engaging RCV in this game of political chess, the RF were exacerbating tensions between black and white leaders. Thus, the concern over annexation from the perspective of the RF in 1965, their prognostication on the possible outcome to annexation that would occur with an increase in black membership on city council was probably correct.

The state's initial approval allowing Richmond to expand its legal boundary was eventually altered by the late Sergeant Reynolds, delegate to the Virginia General Assembly, when he introduced a bill "that required voter approval of staggered terms in a city-wide referendum, which would coincide with the June 1966 councilmanic elections" (Holton 1987, 99–100). Reynolds's measure was narrowly approved in the assembly. His role in the annexation controversy is significant, because he was an RCV endorsee (Holton 1987). Moreover, when the measure was defeated in the assembly, RF knew that the proposal for electing city council members by staggered terms was an unpopular issue among Richmond's black population. Furthermore, even with two black conservatives, Mundle and Cephas, running on the RF ticket, the staggered terms provision in the election of city council members was soundly defeated in the 1966 city council election. The 1966 election, along with its impact, will be discussed later in this section.

The RF's action in 1965 made the formation of a viable biracial coalition unattainable during the civil rights era because Richmond, like some of its white urban counterparts, had attained what Marcus Pohlmann and Michael Kirby described in their study on Memphis as "their threshold of racial divisiveness or point of racial reflexivity" (1996, 200–201). Pohlmann and Kirby defined racial reflexivity as a point in which the "political reality severely limited the chances of deracialized city politics, at least at the mayoral level" (200). Although the application of the authors' terminology to Richmond does not apply directly to mayoral politics, nevertheless, its usage here provides an accurate interpretation of why a biracial coalition was untenable during this period. In addition, even if a biracial coalition had emerged in Richmond during this period, the most likely form that it would have taken was that of a conservative coalition. A conservative biracial coalition was more likely to appear in Richmond because the emergence of a liberal coalition in Richmond throughout the civil rights era was simply impossible. First, Byrd's MR strategy initiated during the 1950s decimated any chance of liberals and/or moderates emerging as an alternative political force to Richmond's political conservatives. Second, because Richmond did not have a substantial white liberal presence in the political arena during this period, the absence of more liberal whites simply exacerbated Richmond's political climate, precipitating the level of racial reflexivity that was evolving in the city. "Had Memphis history developed differently, allowing the city to retain a larger number of more liberal whites, this degree of racial reflexivity might not have evolved," state Pohlmann and Kirby. "White candidates would have had to have been more racially neutral in order to win, while black candidates could have withstood the defection of the most race-conscious blacks by regularly supplementing their vote totals with a reasonable number of white votes" (1996, 201).

The idea that a conservative biracial coalition was the most plausible coalition that could have emerged during that period is inconceivable, as most conservatives would not join a biracial coalition. Sonenshein reinforces this idea: "Racial attitudes structure political choices. . . . A racial conservative is highly unlikely to join a biracial coalition, especially if one of the coalition's explicit goals is African American political incorporation. Shifting interests are unlikely to shake that basic view of the world" (1993, 10).

The final reason a viable biracial coalition could not have emerged in Richmond throughout the civil rights era is the Richmond newspapers' coverage of blacks and their reactionary attacks on groups like the RCV. The *Times-Dispatch* and the *News Leader* supported MR, and both consistently exploited white fears about a black takeover of city hall. "White organizations also conducted voter registration drives. The *Richmond Times-Dispatch* and *News Leader,* concerned about the high rate of black registration, urged residents to register if they had not already done so," notes Holton (1987, 88). Of the two newspapers, it was the more conservative *Dispatch,* throughout the civil rights era, that consistently attacked King, the NAACP, and other national and local civil rights activists. The idea that the *Dispatch* was a socially conservative newspaper can be corroborated by an excerpt from a letter that was submitted by the RCV to the *Dispatch* and subsequently printed in that paper:

> Who are the Richmond newspapers? . . . They are the champions of segregation. They cried: No, No, Never to the U.S. Supreme Court Decision in 1954. They banned a Pogo comic strip that ridiculed segregation. . . . These are the papers that have repeatedly attacked the NAACP . . . Martin Luther King . . . James Meredith; [and] now they are attacking the Richmond Crusade for Voters. . . . [The papers] have repeatedly used statistics on illegitimate births and crime in an attempt to show that Negroes are inferior. . . . [They] will not publish engagement announcements or publish wedding notices for Negroes on an equal basis with whites. (Holton 1987, 105)

The allegations that were made against the *Dispatch* by the leadership of the RCV demonstrates the conservative practices of the paper in its treatment and coverage of Richmond's black citizens. The *Dispatch's* attacks on the RCV would escalate during the late 1970s, when the black majority on city council was installed. Additionally, the *Dispatch* would continue its attack on individual members of the black majority whose views differed from those of Richmond's business and corporate elites. The socially conservative views of the *Dispatch,* along with its negative reporting on blacks in general, its attacks on the RCV and the black majority on city council, contributed to the evolving level of racial reflexivity that was prevalent in Richmond's political climate, hindering the formation of a viable biracial coalition in Richmond.

In 1966, five important political events occurred in the city of Richmond which would usher in a transitory stage, and which would have long-term political implications for the African American community. The first was the increase in black registered voters in 1966. Blacks were finally able to exercise some of their political puissance because the poll tax had been outlawed in federal elections in 1965 (subsequently, the federal courts would ban the use of poll taxes in state and local elections). Thus, 1966 actually became the test year for blacks and whites in which the city would witness a partial impact of the VRA on Richmond's black population. The next event, which occurred in the same year, was the change in racial demographics of the city. According to Holton, white politicians became alarmed over the 1960 census projected population loss for the city's white population. The report projected that by 1965, the city would undergo massive white flight. A projected decrease in whites would eventually force the white power structure to devise an annexation scheme to offset the expected loss. The RF's hidden agenda behind the annexation movement would eventually lead to a legal challenge of Richmond's annexation scheme. The third event, which is closely connected to the previous, was the transformation of the major white political organization in the city, the Richmond Citizens Association (RCA), to a new group called RF. In essence, the emergence of RF on Richmond's political landscape as a moderate organization would eventually become increasingly conservative and the primary white adversary of the RCV at the local level.

The fourth event occurred in the black body politic of Richmond, when the RCV pulled off a major political coup. Two of the candidates it endorsed, Henry Marsh, a member of the RCV and a civil rights lawyer, and Howard Carwile, a southern white urban populist, were elected to city council (Holton 1987). The election of Marsh and Carwile elevated the level of black enthusiasm in local elections, an enthusiasm that would spill over into future elections. An excellent illustration of how black voter enthusiasm would have an impact on future local elections occurred in 1968, when the African American community elected another RCV-endorsed candidate to city council. James Carpenter, a white minister of a predominately black Presbyterian congregation, was elected to city council along with the two RCV incumbents, Marsh and Carwile. Holton noted that in both the 1966 and 1968 elections, as the RCV became increasingly successful in getting its endorsed candidates elected to office, it was actually precipitating the emergence of a new white political opponent, RF: "By 1968, continuing animosities resulting from the 1966 election, and RF's fear of a black take-over, led the Crusade to present Richmond Forward with a direct challenge for control of City Council" (1987, 113).

The final event that occurred during 1966 was the unexpected death of former U.S. senator Harry F. Byrd Sr. (Baker 1989). Byrd's death was a major milestone in the history of the black struggle for political equality because Byrd reminded most blacks in Virginia of the massive resistance era and of the state's segregationist past. Moreover, when Byrd died, the organization that was dubbed by V. O. Key as the Byrd machine was basically weakened; after all, Byrd was the organization. With Byrd gone from the Virginia political landscape, the RCV would now focus its attention on challenging groups like RF for political control of the city.

Thus, 1966 would witness the arrival of five interconnecting transitions that would have major long-term political ramifications for blacks and whites in Richmond. Accordingly, the five transitions eventually would force Richmond's white power structure to adopt a reactionary posture to a growing black populace, and a defiant black leadership that was being challenged by rival black groups to further distance itself from forging any alliances with any white groups, especially the RF. Furthermore, the battle over hegemony of Richmond's city council would occur when city officials attempted to annex adjacent lands for the purpose of diluting the Richmond black vote. The manner in which the political battle over annexation unfolded in Richmond will be explained initially by examining the motives behind annexation.

As stated above, Richmond's city officials desired to expand the city's legal boundaries for the purpose of trying to maintain white domination over a growing black populace. City officials also wanted to annex twenty-three miles of adjacent lands near Richmond because they believed that without the annexation of those lands, Richmond would suffer substantial economic losses in the future (Holton 1987). City officials' economic justification for annexation was not the exclusive concern of white officials. For instance, the RCV also shared comparable concerns about the city's economic future without annexation. The following quote from Holton's analysis reveals that the RCV

> had formed a committee during the sixties to research the advantages and disadvantages of boundary expansion. The committee concluded that expansion was important to the economic livelihood of the city, but should not be advocated at the expense of diluting the black vote. Apparently, the Crusade hoped, even after the adoption of the Horner-Bagley line, that the economic benefits which were important for everyone in the city, would outweigh the dilution of black voting strength resulting from the influx of white voters. (Holton 1987, 121)

This suggests that the RCV was indisputably willing to accept a dilution of black voter strength for what they perceived as the greater good of the city. The RCV's strategy on annexation revealed a major flaw in their approach, which was that the group that they were in agreement with on the issue of annexation was the same group that had attempted to undermine black political unity by endorsing two black conservative candidates, and whose ulterior motive was to maintain white political dominance over the capital of the Confederacy at any cost. Thus, the flaw in the RCV's strategy would also be criticized and subsequently challenged by Curtis Holt, the grass-roots activist, through the courts. Holt's legal challenge on the annexation issue subsequently revealed the emergence of another black political schism in 1970, that of class.

The class schism initially appeared in 1966 when Holt formed the CCCA. He subsequently registered three thousand new black voters, and the CCCA would endorse Marsh's candidacy for city council in 1966 (Holton 1987). However, the class schism would not become a visible and important political issue in Richmond's black body politic until 1970, when Holt began his assault on Richmond's annexation scheme.

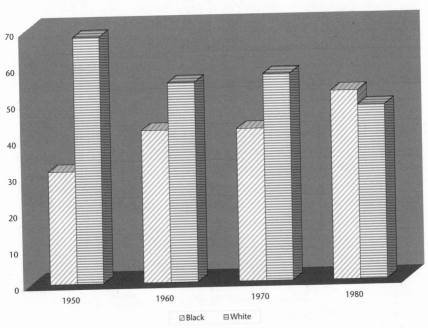

Fig. 11. Percentage of blacks in the total population of Richmond, 1950–1980.

BLACK POLITICAL RECONSTRUCTION: THE DOUBLE AGENDA

We contend that because the first reconstruction for Virginia was not only very brief but politically undermined from the start, African Americans did not exercise their actual political rights as citizens of the state and city until 1977. Moreover, due to the constant political battles that they were forced to endure to obtain their rights, black Richmonders did not achieve their full political strength until they were able to elect a black majority city council in 1977. In effect, black Richmonders have only experienced a real reconstruction since 1977. The double-agenda aspect of this section involves the illumination of the two conflicting political agendas, that of black progressives and black conservatives, that were prevalent during this period, the former being the highly visible agenda and the latter the less obvious. Additionally, the black political reconstruction and the double agenda converged with the rise and subsequent demise of the first African American majority on city council. The collective interplay and impact of race, class, and gender on the city's political arena and especially on Richmond's black body politic became pronounced in the subsequent political schisms over the progressive direction of the black majority city council and the Project One controversy.

The Rise of the African American Majority on City Council

The contributing factors that led to the rise of the first black majority on city council were the changing demographics in Richmond's population, RF/TOP and city officials' racially motivated annexation political agenda, the 1970 and 1972 city council election, Curtis Holt's lawsuit, and an invigorated black voting electorate.

Changing Demographic

The increase in Richmond's black population since 1960 can basically be traced to the steady migration of southern rural blacks to the city in search of jobs and upward mobility (Randolph 1990; Moeser and Dennis 1982), and to the outmigration of the white middle class, which left the city in large numbers between 1950 and 1980. For instance, since 1950, the city has been consistently losing an average of 5 to 10 percent of its white population (Randolph 1990, 144). The loss in Richmond's white population is shown in figure 12.

The city lost 20 percent of its white middle-class population from 1950 to 1980, while the black population increased by the same amount. Richmond's declining white population appears to have been absorbed by the nearby counties of Henrico and Chesterfield (Randolph 1990; Moeser and Dennis 1982). Another explanation as to why Richmond's African American population has increased since 1970 is that, according to a special study conducted by the U.S. Census Bureau monitoring black migration patterns from 1970 to 1980, there has been a steady migration of African Americans returning to the South, especially during the 1980s

(Green interview 1989). The study further revealed that African Americans were not migrating to the rural South; instead, they were migrating to southern metropolitan centers because of employment opportunities. Thus, given the fact that Richmond is a southern metropolitan center, one would expect it to attract its share of African Americans in search of employment opportunities. In essence, the new wave of African American migration to the south can account for the steady increase in the number of African Americans living in Richmond.

The demographic and social changes that occurred in Richmond created several political ramifications for the city. First, the changes in the racial composition of Richmond would eventually propel Richmond's white city officials to craft annexation around the issue of race having convinced themselves that Richmond would eventually become a predominantly black city. Consequently, the city's reaction to the demographic changes was to pursue and implement an annexation policy that was racially motivated. That is, the city was determined to annex areas that were predominantly white with the primary objective of diluting any potential voting strength of the African American community in local elections. The history of race relations and the idea of sharing power with a population that had been racially subordinate to the white elite was simply regarded as politically unacceptable. Second, a direct consequence of the demographic changes that occurred in Richmond would be the eventual election of a slim African American political majority on city council, creating the worst possible "nightmare on Elm Street" case scenario for Richmond's power structure.

Although the demographic changes that occurred in Richmond from 1970 to 1980 produced a numerical black majority in the city, blacks, and especially the black middle class, were not politically incorporated, even as a junior partner, in governing the city. Richmond's white political elites could be deemed politically unenlightened when it came to accommodating an emerging black majority city. That is, white political elites were so blinded by their own racism that any notion of sharing power equally with the black population was simply unacceptable to them. Also, the white political elites' steadfast refusal to abandon their social and economic conservative style of governance prevented them and city officials from approaching the incorporation of blacks even for pragmatic reasons. For instance, Clarence Stone, in his text *Regime Politics: Governing Atlanta, 1946–1988* and in a recent coauthored article, "Atlanta and the Limited Reach of Electoral Control," indirectly reinforces our position that Richmond's white political elites were simply unenlightened and intransigent. According to Stone's research, Hartsfield, the mayor of Atlanta prior to

Atlanta's becoming a black majority city, was credited with the successful incorporation of Atlanta's black middle class into the city's governing coalition. He was effective in persuading Atlanta's white elites to incorporate the black middle class into the governing establishment as a junior partner (Stone 1989; Stone and Pierannunzi 1997). Thus, Hartsfield was effective as a politician and elected official because he was able to convince both groups that economic growth and racial moderation were in the long run in the economic best interest of Atlanta (Stone and Pierannunzi 1997, 165). However, Hartsfield's pragmatic political approach to resolving racial conflict to Richmond was impossible because the city did not have a Hartsfield-style politician on hand, nor did it have a white political elite that was willing to listen, compromise, or share political power, even on a junior partnership level, with African Americans. Finally, one major economic ramification that occurred as a result of the demographic changes that occurred in Richmond over a twenty year period was the continued out-migration of the city's white middle-class population. The implication of this particular loss of population was that it reduced the city's income. The political significance of the annexation controversy, along with political reaction from the African American community to that controversy, was that it produced a black majority on city council.

Racially Motivated Annexation Political Agenda

With respect to annexation, the following 1968 quote from Bagley, the former mayor of Richmond, reflects the views of Richmond's white political establishment: "As long as I am the Mayor of the City of Richmond the niggers won't take over this town." On still another occasion, Councilman James G. Carpenter noted that on September 12, 1971, while he and Bagley were attending a meeting of the Virginia Municipal League at Virginia Beach, the mayor drew him aside and at one point in their conversation indicated that "niggers were not qualified to run the city" (Moeser and Dennis 1982, 93). Moreover, Bagley's opinions were shared by other white city officials. One public official was quoted in the *Richmond Times-Dispatch* as stating, "As the Negro population grows, so does the Negro voting strength. City officials, accustomed to a relatively light Negro vote, admit that they are concerned over the possibility that years from now Negro voters in Richmond will outnumber whites" (Silver 1984, 223). Moeser and Dennis's research on Richmond annexation politics indicates that other white city officials' views on annexation were congruous with those of Bagley. For example, James C. Wheat Jr., a city council member in 1968, publicly echoed Bagley's sentiments: "Throughout the Council campaign, Mr. Wheat perhaps has hit hardest at the issue of annexation. If the city cannot merge or annex, he says, Richmond will become a permanent black ghetto, a happy hunting ground for ambitious political opportunists" (Moeser and Dennis 1982, 82).

Given these kinds of publicly expressed statements by city officials, it is obvious why the proposed annexation was morally and politically rejected and eventually challenged by some in the African American community, such as Curtis Holt, who felt he had no acceptable alternative but to pursue legal redress in the courts. Given Richmond's longstanding history of racially polarized politics, and the proposed annexation scheme, one cannot readily dismiss Richmond's black community's concern as being rooted in political paranoia.

Consequently, the racist scare tactics repeatedly employed by city officials and by RF/TOP officials to discourage blacks from mobilizing instead only served to galvanize them on the path toward black political empowerment. Thus, when the city was forced to adopt a single-member district system, blacks were able to elect a black majority to council. In spite of what appears to have been a major political victory for the African American community, the path to a successful black political mobilization effort was not an easy one. In fact, the path often times was undermined from within and from without.

City Elections of 1970 and 1972: Holt's Lawsuit

In 1966, Holt was beginning to establish himself as a political force in Richmond's black community and could no longer be ignored by the black political establishment. Holton notes the increasing influence of Holt in the political arena:

> His English was by no means flawless, and he was not an outstanding orator, but he did boast an extensive grassroots following. In 1966, he helped to register three thousand blacks to vote, and subsequently endorsed Crusader Henry Marsh in his 1966 bid for city council. Upon announcing his candidacy for city council in 1970, Holt explained his feeling that we've got to have some representation for the poor. We need someone to tell it like it is. Although Holt's statement did not criticize the Crusade directly, he clearly recognized the middle-class nature of the organization. (Holton 1987)

Holt acknowledged the class contradictions prevalent in Richmond's black body politic. In spite of the apparent class schisms within Richmond's black community, he remained committed to the cause of black political unity in Richmond. Although Holt was committed to preserving black political unity, Richmond's black middle class did not reciprocate the same kind of commitment to the working-class black community, or to Holt. For instance, after Holt announced his candidacy, the black middle class not only opposed his candidacy but also attempted to persuade him to withdraw from the city council race in 1970. That Holt's candidacy was opposed by many middle-class blacks is supported by Holton's research. During the campaign, "Holt received several phone calls from middle class blacks urging him to withdraw from the race. 'They tell me I'm not qualified,' Holt explained, 'If my speech offends those better educated, I'm sorry. But believe me, brother, I know what's happening.' Some middle class blacks no doubt feared that Holt might challenge their control of the crusade, but in 1970, at least, the organization was willing to support him" (Holton 1987, 125). By 1970 the RCV had endorsed Holt, realizing that he was an emerging political force. They may have endorsed him to avoid alienating his supporters or to show Richmond's black community that the RCV supported candidates who represented the entire class spectrum of the city. In spite of the RCV's endorsement, Holt was defeated in the election. Table 3 presents the percentage of votes

TABLE 3

Percentage of Votes Cast in Black Precincts for Black Candidates for RCV-Endorsed Candidates, 1970 City Council Election

	Candidate		
Precinct	Holt	Kenney	Marsh
Black Working Class (21 Precincts)	59	72	85
Black Middle Class (7 Precincts)	51	73.1	87

Source: Office of the General Registrar, Richmond,Va., Feb. 24, 1998.

Note: During the 1970 election, city council candidates were at-large and voters could vote for multiple candidates.

cast for the three black candidates who were endorsed by the RCV in seven black middle-class and twenty-one working-class precincts for the 1970 city council elections.

Table 3 reveals the following information. First, it shows that Kenney and Marsh received more votes individually and collectively than Curtis Holt. For instance, when one compares only the black candidates' performance in the working-class precincts, Kenney and Marsh received over 70 percent compared to Holt's 59 percent. Holt may not have received more black working-class votes because Marsh and Kenney may have had a better name recognition than Holt. Another plausible explanation of why Holt finished third even in the black working-class precincts, may have been due to the fact that when Holt decided to run for office in 1970, it was his first time ever running for elected office. Thus, those candidates who are neophytes in a citywide general election will undoubtedly make mistakes, unless they have a professional campaign staff to help them avoid the trappings that beset so many new candidates. However, in Holt's case, his socioeconomic status and his lack of political savior-faire may have contributed to his poor showing even in black working-class precincts. Holt's dismal showing in these precincts could have occurred because some of the voters from the black working-class precincts may not have taken Holt's campaign seriously; they may have perceived Holt as having no real chance to win. Thus, the voters from the black working-class precincts may have elected to vote for those black candidates whom they perceived as being more electable than Holt. Moreover, the fact that black working-class voters supported the middle-class candidates rather than supporting a black candidate who openly championed their cause is not contradictory. According to Piven and Cloward in their classic text *Poor People's Movements*, the working class and the poor are the most difficult groups to organize and convince to vote their political self-interest (Piven and Cloward 1979).

Table 3 also illustrates how Marsh and Kenney individually and collectively received more votes than Curtis Holt. For example, when one compares the performance of the three black candidates only, in the black middle-class precincts, Kenney and Marsh received over 76 percent compared to Holt's 51 percent. Possibly, Holt did not do as well as Marsh and Kenney in black middle-class precincts because (1) according to Holton's account, when Holt was endorsed by the middle-class-dominated RCV, a sizable portion of the RCV's members who were in attendance at the nomination committee's meeting openly booed the group's decision to support Holt's candidacy; the middle-class members' vocal disapproval may have accounted for Holt's poor showing in all of the black middle-class precincts; (2) Holt's opponents had better name recognition in the black middle-class precincts, and Marsh was an incumbent; (3) the voters in the black middle-class precincts may have been opposed to Holt because of his decision to publicly chide the black middle-class for their lack of empathy toward poor blacks; and (4) Holt's public championing of the cause of working-class and poor people in Richmond may have turned away middle-class voters. A final explanation of why Holt lost the 1970 citywide election may have been that Carpenter and Carwile, the two white incumbents endorsed by the RCV, ran effectively in both black working- and middle-class precincts. Table 4 illustrates Carpenter's and Carwile's effective showing in black middle- and working-class precincts and in white middle- and working-class precincts.

Table 4 is relevant to Holt's performance in the 1970 election and to this discussion for the following reasons. First, it reveals almost the identical trends indicated in table 3. For example, just like their black counterparts who were endorsed by the RCV, Carpenter and Carwile received more support from black voters in the black middle- and working-class

TABLE 4

Percentage of Votes Cast in Black and White Precincts for Holt and RCV-Endorsed Incumbents, 1970 City Council Elections

	Precinct			
	Black Working Class (21 precincts)	White Working Class (16 precincts)	Black Middle Class (7 precincts)	White Middle Class (26 precincts)
Holt	59	11	51.7	4.1
Carpenter	69	37	78	34
Carwile	86	44	82	31

Source: Office of the General Registrar, Richmond, Va., Feb. 24, 1998.

Note: During the 1970 election, city council candidates were at-large and voters could vote for multiple candidates.

precincts than did Holt. In other words, when one compares Holt's performance with that of Carpenter's and Carwile's performance combined, Holt's percentage points are slightly reduced in the black middle- and working-class communities when compared to those of Kenney and Marsh. So Holt also did not get elected to city council in 1970 because of the presence of Carpenter and Carwile. The presence of Carpenter and Carwile in the 1970 election cannot be discarded because both of the white candidates had a large support base in black middle- and working-class precincts. Carpenter was pastor of a predominantly black Presbyterian congregation in Richmond and was perceived by blacks as being progressive and supportive of issues that were of interest to most blacks at that time. Carwile also had a sizable support base in black middle- and working-class communities because of his populist politics, his support of civil rights, and his consistent opposition to white racism. Furthermore, both Carpenter and Carwile were incumbents who were popular in most of Richmond's black middle- and working-class communities. Also, Holt's city council election performance may have been diminished further because, with Carwile and Holt in the same race, both candidates were politically courting the same class of voters. In other words, given the fact that Carwile and Holt engaged in populist politics, the two candidates were both appealing to the same voting base, thus canceling each other out. In essence, in a political race without the presence of Carwile, Holt may have been elected.

Table 4 also reveals the impact of race on Holt's election bid. In spite of his attempts to cooperate with white working-class communities, and because the RCV endorsed Holt and the two white candidates, Holt could not duplicate the same success in white middle- and working-class precincts that Carpenter and Carwile were able to achieve in black middle- and working-class precincts. Thus, when one examines Holt's performance in white middle- and working-class communities, race and class were clearly determining factors in the outcome of the 1970 city council election. The impact of race on the outcome of the election can be substantiated further by table 5.

When one examines table 5 more closely, one sees that all of the black candidates, with the exception of Marsh, were not effective in gaining a sizable portion of white support in white middle- and working-class precincts. For instance, even Henry Marsh, an incumbent with plenty of name recognition and from Richmond's black upper middle class, could not overcome the issue of race because he was able to obtain only 27 percent of the white middle-class votes in the white middle-class precincts.

Thus, if Marsh had not maintained a strong showing in black middle- and working-class precincts, he may not have been reelected to city council in 1970.

Although the reasons for Holt's losing convincingly in the black middle- and working-class precincts were numerous, we believe that the primary reason Holt lost was because of his race and class. For instance, class accounts for Holt's lack of political support in black middle-class precincts, but the combination of race and class also accounts for his lack of political support in white middle- and working-class precincts. Thus,

TABLE 5

Percentage and Number of Votes Cast for by Selected RCV-Endorsed White Precincts, 1970 City Council Election

RCV-Endorsed Candidates	% of Votes Cast All White Working-Class Precincts	No. Votes Cast All White Working-Class Precincts	% of Votes Cast, All White Middle-Class Precincts	No. of Votes Cast, All White Middle-Class Precincts
Black Candidates				
Holt 11	686	4	758	
Kenney	18	1,159	8	1,672
Marsh	31	2,045	27	5,541
Black Totals	60	3,890	39	7,971
White Candidates				
Carpenter	38	2,439	34	6,917
Carwile	44	2,860	31	6,191
White Totals	81	5299	65	13,108

Source: Data for Table 5 was obtained from the Office Of the General Registrar, City of Richmond, February 24, 1998.

the RCV's endorsement of Holt did not translate into a political victory for the champion of the poor. Furthermore, the influence of class within the black precincts and their contribution to Holt's defeat cannot be ignored because neither Holt nor any other member of the poor and/or working classes were endorsed by the RCV in the 1972 city council election. The RCV may have elected not to endorse Holt because of the internal constraints that were being placed upon the RCV's leadership by its black middle-class members. According to the *Richmond Afro-American,* "The suggestion that the Crusade endorse Holt drew boos from the Crusade executive committee" (Holton 1987). Furthermore, in the 1972 election, rather than endorse Holt, the RCV elected to endorse two teenagers and two TOP white candidates. Holt was eventually endorsed by a group he helped to form, called the Grassroots Political Organization (GPO) (Holton 1987). Without the RCV's endorsement, Holt subsequently lost his second bid for election to city council. Class resentment was clear among Richmond's black poor. Holt echoed their sentiments in a letter to the *Richmond Afro-American* in 1972: "The time has come for the people of this city to know the truth. For many years we have believed in good leadership and in those who have led us in politics. This leadership, to me, has come to an end. . . . You will have to be very careful not to be influenced by the Crusade any more" (Holton 1987, 125–26). The class cleavages that were emerging between poor and middle-class blacks in Richmond during this period can be substantiated even further by the following excerpt from a letter written to the *Richmond Times-Dispatch* editor by Jeroline E. Russell on June 2, 1970:

> It makes me seething mad to see middle-class blacks rake in votes of the poor black people whom they have done nothing for. Some of them, a poor black person cannot even present a problem to, because if they have ever had their problem they don't have it now and they just don't care or understand it. I think it is time we poor blacks elected someone who really can represent us because he is one of us. Such a man has finally come on the horizon in the person of Mr. Curtis Holt, Sr. I am going to vote for Mr. Holt because as a poor black man he would know from both past and present experience what I am going through in Richmond today as a poor citizen. Mr. Holt has always championed his people and there are many who can testify that in their darkest hours of distress they sent for Curtis Holt and he was right there. (Russell 1970, 2)

Although class may have accounted for Holt's poor showing within the black community, the issue of race also explains why Holt was defeated in the citywide council race.

Holt's political defeat in 1970 and 1972 would prove costly to the white power structure and beneficial to the entire black community, especially the black middle class, in the long run. Yet Holt's role in altering the balance of political power in Richmond would not occur because of a electoral victory but because of a lawsuit he would file against Richmond for its annexation of forty-seven thousand whites to the city's population (Holton 1987).

Holt was the only person who challenged Richmond's annexation of whites in Chesterfield County in 1970 (Moeser and Dennis 1982, 143–44). He sued the city on the grounds that the annexation was a racially motivated attempt to dilute the voting strength of Richmond's African American voters (Randolph and Tate 1995). However, his decision to file suit may also have been prompted by his fear that the black middle- and upper-class leadership might betray Richmond's black populace. For instance, prior to Holt's suit, the RCV leadership had publicly adopted a political strategy of courting white voters from the annexed area. Moreover, the RCV "had also endorsed three white candidates from an organization in the annexed area called Richmond United (RU)" (Holton 1987, 124). Furthermore, the RCV leadership's "grand strategy" was to unite with the whites who opposed the annexation. The RCV surmised that once these whites were brought into the city boundaries, the two united groups could defeat their common foe, the Richmond power structure (Holton 1987). However, the RCV leadership miscalculated the resentment level among whites in the annexation area toward Richmond's power structure as well as their racism toward black Richmonders.

Thus, when the additional forty-seven thousand white voters cast their ballots in the 1970 election, they voted along racial lines. The RCV's grand strategy had backfired on them, and as a result, "an eight percent reduction in the black proportion of the city's electorate which resulted from annexation had a major impact on black voter strength in Richmond" (Holton 1987, 126). Likewise, when established black political leaders failed to act on this issue, Holt perceived that Richmond's black community may have been betrayed by its leadership. Hence, he did not file his lawsuit because he was a sore loser but because he sought political justice for the black populace in the electoral arena, on the one hand, and political inclusion for poor blacks on the other hand. Holt's legal challenge was an attempt on his part to confront the issue of race, which had historically paralyzed blacks in Richmond, and also the issue of class, which had historically divided them.

Holt initially was denied legal assistance by the Virginia NAACP (Moeser and Dennis 1982). He then sought the services of Cabell Venable, a young, unknown, white attorney who took the case pro bono publico (Moeser and Dennis 1982). In 1971, in *City of Richmond v. United States* (95 S. Ct. 2296, 1975), the Supreme Court ruled that Richmond's annexation of land in Chesterfield County, coupled with an at-large council system, was evidence of the city's attempt to dilute the voting strength of African Americans (Moeser interview 1991). The annexation, along with an at-large council electoral system, made it extremely difficult for blacks to be elected to city council (Moeser and Dennis 1982). The Court resolved the matter by accepting a compromise that changed the city's at-large system to a single-member ward or district system (Moeser and Dennis 1982; Murphy 1978). When Richmond was forced to adopt a single-member district system, blacks were able to increase their representation on the council. The adoption of a nine-seat, single-member district system in 1977 increased African American representation on city council. With Holt's lawsuit of 1970 and 1972 decided, the special election enabled the RCV to become the majority party on city council and for the first time in the city's history produced (by a slim margin) an African American majority on city council. Furthermore, when Richmond's African American community elected an African American majority to city council in 1977, all of the African American members were also members of the RCV. The RCV's ability to elect an African American majority to council in 1977 clearly illustrates the political strength of the organization. The 1977 election produced the city's first African American mayor, Henry Marsh (Moeser and Dennis 1982).

One irony regarding the election is that Marsh was one of the NAACP lawyers who had turned Holt away (Moeser interview 1991). The NAACP's decision was painful for Holt, whose widow, Alto Mae Holt, proudly displayed for us the decorative lifetime membership plaque that her husband received from the NAACP. A lifetime membership in the NAACP cost five hundred dollars. An organization that was enthusiastically supported by poor people like Holt, on fixed incomes, indisputably contradicts the spirit of the NAACP's historical organizational efforts in the South. For instance, it was individuals like Holt who helped to raise funds that kept the NAACP alive throughout the South during the period of massive resistance when most southern states were outlawing the organization. When the NAACP refused to provide legal assistance to Holt, who was engaging in protracted lawsuits to achieve such basic rights as increased black representation, this did not speak well for the group's image as a historical fighter for social justice. Holt sought out the NAACP first, because, after all, he, like most southern blacks, truly believed that the only organization he could depend on during a legal crisis was the NAACP.

Another irony regarding the special election in 1977, and regarding the first regular election, which was held on May 2, 1978, was that Holt, and no other candidate representing the interests of poor people and poor blacks, would be endorsed by the RCV for city council. Although Holt, the poor people's champion, had not been endorsed by the RCV, William S. Thornton, one of the group's founders, exhilaratingly proclaimed after the election that the "city's political leadership will be more receptive to the needs of the city's poor residents, and will support more social issues and social programs including the public schools" (Moeser and Dennis 1982, 180–81). The inconsistency of Thornton's elated reaction to the 1978 election returns was that neither of these promises would be kept, especially the promise of the leadership being more responsive to the needs of the poor. An excellent example of how the newly elected black majority on council would not be responsive to the needs of the poor, especially the black poor, was the incident involving the traffic light that had not been installed near Creighton Court public housing.

The primary reason the traffic controversy was not resolved was class indifference on the part of the newly elected black majority on council. When the black majority was elected in 1977, the traffic light had not yet been installed. The light would not be installed until 1986, after Holt's death. Why was a traffic light approved in 1963 not installed until 1986? First, racial insensitivity by the white-controlled city council and its bureaucratic allies from 1963 to 1977 was definitely a contributing factor. Also, even after the black majority on city council was installed, the entrenched white bureaucracy may have been engaging in its own version of bureaucratic inertia in order to resist any changes that were put forth by the black majority on city council. Another explanation for the late installation of the traffic light could be the power struggle that occurred between the Marsh-led black voting bloc on city council and Richmond's white economic elite between 1977 and 1986. Even though a power struggle between the black majority voting bloc on council and the white economic elite may have occurred during this period, the idea that a traffic light had not been installed is still unacceptable, because when West, a black conservative, was elected mayor in 1983, the traffic light issue remained unresolved. Moreover, city council's failure to address the traffic light after 1983 is even more ironic because West, who would succeed Marsh as mayor, had formerly been a principal at a middle school in Richmond. Thus, it appears that neither the previous liberal black majority nor the black-led white conservative majority were interested in addressing this issue. A final explanation for the late installation of the traffic light could be Curtis Holt's untimely death in 1986 (according to Mrs. Holt, her husband suffered from a prolonged illness before dying). It is possible that Holt's removal from the political arena may account for the lack of responsiveness by the black majority on city council toward a poor and powerless black population.

Although a traffic light was installed at one section of the dangerous intersection on Nine Mile Road when we visited the area in August 1997, we discovered, with the assistance of some of the current Creighton Court residents, that there are two remaining stretches of Nine Mile Road that run by Creighton public housing that do not have a traffic light. The two

Fig. 12. Grave of Curtis J. Holt Sr. Photograph taken by Lewis Randolph.

remaining sections involve a side and corner section of the road that are still dangerous crossing areas for those children from Creighton Court who must cross those sections of the road in order to attend school.

The traffic light installation issue closely parallels a case study in Michael Parenti's classic article "Power and Pluralism: A View from the Bottom" (Parenti 1970). Parenti's case study involved a community's struggle in Newark, Jersey, for political accountability from its city's bureaucracy. His study, ironically, also focuses on a city bureaucracy's failure to install a traffic light near a dangerous intersection in a poor neighborhood. In both cases, the powerless were combating an entrenched bureaucracy that was unresponsive to their needs. Although the Richmond and Newark traffic light incidents involved some similar circumstances, the two were also different. For instance, in Newark a poor multiracial community unsuccessfully attempted to combat an entrenched white bureaucracy, whereas in Richmond a poor black community first had to combat an insensitive white-controlled city government and its entrenched bureaucracy and, later, had to face an unresponsive black majority on city council. In other words, the two cases differ significantly because, in Richmond, the poor black population did not get the kind of responsiveness one would expect from a city that had elected a black majority on city council. Whereas in Richmond race was a major factor first and class later became a major road block, in Newark race was the overriding issue.

Overall, class issues influenced the direction of Richmond's African American political empowerment in two ways. First, Holt, a representative of blacks and their interests, started the process by successfully engaging the tripartite system of oppression in the courts. After Holt's legal victory, middle-class African Americans capitalized on the Supreme Court's decision when middle-class black leaders ran for political office and won. Thus, class becomes relevant to this discussion because when Holt ran for office and was defeated in the general election, one could ask how the level of political discourse and the urban public policy agenda debates between blacks on city council might have been altered by an assertive, poor African American sitting on Richmond's city council. Although this issue may never be resolved, one could deduce that Holt might have forced the inclusion of the concerns of poor blacks in the city council policy discussions. Curtis Holt was a person who was called to conscience, refusing to accommodate the interests of Richmond's white elite in withdrawing his challenge to Richmond's annexation policy, and he did so on principle, deciding that withdrawing his claim of

Fig. 13. Swearing in of Richmond City Council members, July 1, 1978. Left to right: William I. Golding Sr., Walter T. Kenney, Willie J. Dell, Wayland W. Rennie, Claudette Black McDaniel, Henry W. Richardson, Mayor Henry L. Marsh III, Aubrey H. Thompson, and Vice-Mayor George Stevenson Kemp Jr. Courtesy of Richmond Public Library, Richmond, Virginia.

de-annexation was not a matter of political expediency. In retrospect, the African American majority on council was the direct result of the black community's political and legal challenges, Curtis Holt's demand for legal redress in particular, to Richmond's white political establishment.

Richmond City Council's First African American Majority

A special election was held on March 1, 1977, because the city had been prevented by the courts from holding any elections until the legal challenges to the city's annexation proposal was resolved in court. Moreover, the Holt lawsuit against the city had been resolved. Consequently, the seven-year-old court injunctions against elections was lifted (Moeser and Dennis 1982). When the election was over, Richmond had elected a black majority on city council, consisting of the following individuals: Henry Marsh and Willie Dell (incumbents) and newcomers Walter Kenney, a postal worker and postal union official; Claudette McDaniel, chief of special activities in the Occupational Therapy Department of the Medical College of Virginia; and Henry W. "Chuck" Richardson, a former planner with the Richmond Regional Planning District Commission and a graduate student in Urban Planning at VCU during the time of the city council election (Mason 1977). All five were members of the RCV. Also, even though the special election was marred by one of the lowest voter turnouts for a city council election, the outcome enabled the RCV to become the majority party on city council (Moeser and Dennis 1982). The election also produced the city's first African American elected mayor, Henry Marsh.

The reaction of Richmond's black community was generally one of euphoria and pride. In the March 19, 1977, issue of the *Richmond Afro-*

American, ten Richmond blacks selected for interview by the newspaper spoke out regarding the election of a black majority. The ten were ecstatic and expressed optimistic visions about Richmond's future. Below are the responses of four of the ten individuals—Reuben Greene, graphics specialist at Fort Lee; Geraldine Hill, a student at J. Sergeant Reynolds Community College; John D. Evans, retiree; and L. Delores Greene, curriculum specialist at Carver Elementary School—to the newspaper's question, "How do you feel about having a black majority on City Council?"

> *Reuben Greene:* They will help the city. They know the problems the people are talking about. I think we will see much more progress than in the last seven years.
>
> *Geraldine Hill:* It can't get worse. You've got to give blacks a chance to govern.
>
> *John D. Evans:* It's wonderful to have black people in those positions. Any issue that black citizens bring up will be looked into a lot more thoroughly.
>
> *L. Delores Greene:* We have a good group now who will work as a team. There are people on council now who can relate to all segments of Richmond.
>
> (*Richmond Afro-American,* Mar. 19, 1977)

The four individuals' responses are indicative of how most black Richmonders reacted after electing a black majority on city council for the first time in the city's history. In spite of the optimism regarding the city's future, however, by 1983, that optimism would be replaced by cynicism. The shift in black attitudes, along with the reasons for the shift, occurred in tandem with the demise of the black majority on city council.

Although the black community responded positively to the RCV's historic political victory, the RCV and other black leaders reminded the black community that the black majority on city council would only serve for one year and would face reelection on March 2, 1978, when the first regularly scheduled city council election would be held. On March 2 the first black majority on city council was reelected, and this time they would serve a two-year rather than one-year term. The election of the first black majority on city council would also occur during a period in Richmond's political history in which two critical changes were simultaneously taking place. The first change was the occurrence of low voter turnouts, especially in poor black precincts when the black majority on council was being elected. For instance, when Dell ran for reelection in 1977, she ran uncontested. However, when she ran for reelection in 1982, she would lose in part because of low voter turnout in poor black precincts. In discussing the demise of the black majority on council, the low voter turnout could be attributed to the black majority's inability to resolve some important social and economic issues that were of concern to Richmond's black poor.

The second change that occurred when the black majority on council was initially elected was the quiet resurgence of black conservatives in 1977. According to Larry Sabato's research on *Virginia Votes, 1975–1978,* black voters in selected predominantly black precincts in Richmond cast 58.1 percent of their votes for Marshall Coleman, the Republican candidate for attorney general. Sabato credits Coleman's strong showing in part to his Democratic opponent's support of MR (Sabato 1977, 66). Moreover, Sabato further stated that Coleman received "almost a third of the black vote, a far better performance than that recorded by most Republicans (but less than Linwood Holton's 37.2 percent in his winning 1969 gubernatorial bid). . . . Nevertheless, Coleman's voting strength is proof enough that the black vote is not irrevocably Democratic" (ibid.). The reemergence of a black conservative vote in Richmond during 1977, precisely at the time when blacks were electing a black majority on city council, is significant because of the role that black conservatives would play in the destabilization of the first black majority on council. But the election of the black majority on city council would also raise another important question in Richmond's political arena: Who governs Richmond?

WHO GOVERNS RICHMOND?

Origins of Political Confrontation

On March 1, 1977, the black community was savoring its greatest accomplishment; however, Richmond's white political establishment deplored the moment because their historic fear of a black takeover of city government had finally been realized. That the white establishment feared a black majority on council can be substantiated by information provided to us by one former white official during a personal interview. R. Allen Hays, former project manager with the Richmond Redevelopment Housing Authority and political science professor at the University of Northern Iowa, stated that the fear of a black majority council not only permeated the white elites but also filtered down to Bill Leidinger, the former white city manager who eventually was fired by Marsh. Hays further stated, "I cannot remember being in meetings where the potential impact was nervously discussed, particularly since Bill Leidinger, the city manager who had really pushed Project One, knew his job was suddenly in jeopardy" (Hays interview 1993).

There were several reasons why the white political establishment's fear of the newly elected black majority on council had merit. First, the white political establishment was convinced that a black majority on council would usher in a radical shift in public policy. For instance, Richmond's elites feared that the black majority on council was not going to give them carte blanche control over the city's resources and the direction of development policy. The local elites may have harbored these fears because, historically, Richmond's elites had dominated the city's development policy, a fact corroborated by Chris Silver's *Twentieth-Century Richmond: Planning, Politics, and Race* (Silver 1984). Silver states that the

> absence of public leadership in city development policy owed most to the way planners perceived their role. As outgoing city planning director James Park remarked in 1979, Richmond had always been guided by a fairly stable planning philosophy that emphasized a light touch on controlling development decisions. In his words, we have not been avant garde planners in Richmond but rather have adhered closely to the dictates of City Council and its strong allies in the downtown business communities. (Silver 1984, 315)

Another reason Richmond's white political establishment feared the new black majority on council was because they were all former members of the RCV. Moreover, because the RCV had a longstanding opposition toward the white political establishment's ultraconservative policies on race relations, along with the city's historical exclusion of blacks in the past from the political process, the elites feared how they might be treated by blacks now that their political roles were reversed. In spite of the white elite's fears of what they perceived would happen to Richmond under a black majority council's control, their worst fear, that the black majority on council would implement radical development policy, simply did not occur (Silver 1984).

The radical policy implementation did not occur when the black majority on council took office because the council actually tried to democratize the city's policy process by being more responsive to the needs of neighborhoods. The black majority's attempt to shift the focus of planning from downtown business dominance to neighborhood planning had already begun in the city prior to 1977, and the council was simply implementing policies that were already on the policy agenda. Second, when a private/public partnership organization called Richmond Renaissance was created, the city still managed, even with shrinking federal funds, to provide "$1.25 million in seed money for Richmond Renaissance [which] was extracted from the city's slender pool of federal funds intended for community development. To do this required diversion of funds from previously slated for use in rebuilding city neighborhoods" (Silver 1984, 319). The black majority's support of a project such as Richmond Renaissance lends support to our earlier assertion that the alleged radical policy that was to have occurred under a black majority on council was simply unfounded. In addition, the black majority's financial support of Richmond Renaissance was their attempt to ameliorate the racially polarized climate and, at the same time, to placate white fears by supporting economic development projects that were sponsored by the same group of whites who were critical of the black majority's performance.

Third, the black majority on council's support of projects like Richmond Renaissance may have eroded some of their long-term political capital with the very groups that supported them at the political polls on March 1, 1977. When the black majority on council was diverting funds from neighborhoods to support downtown business-inspired projects such as Richmond Renaissance, they may have inadvertently revealed to poor blacks especially the major political dilemma facing blacks: an increase in the number of blacks in political positions did not immediately lead to restructuring of the social and economic imbalances that still plagued many black communities. Although protest politics created a climate that put able-bodied black leaders into office, the political system rendered them impotent and unable to fulfill the expectations of the black community.

In spite of repeated attempts by the black majority on council to placate white fears by supporting different economic projects, and their consistent public and private pledges assuring white leaders that they had no intentions of allowing Richmond to end up like Newark, the white political establishment refused to abandon its stated objective of undermining or, if possible, unseating the black majority on council (Silver 1984). One incident illustrating this occurred when four white members of council, along with some of the city's most prominent business and corporate executives, traveled to Washington, D.C., to meet with U.S. JD officials to present their case to have the JD reject the black majority on council's proposal for redistricting (Moeser and Dennis 1982). The rationale provided by the white members of council, along with Richmond's white elites, was that the black majority on council's proposal for

redistricting discriminated against white citizens. The group contended that the present city council does not adequately or fairly represent the city's white population, and that if the plan proposed by the majority is adopted, blacks would be able to maintain their edge in municipal elections for the next ten years, or at least until the next redistricting. William L. Leidinger, former city manager who was fired by the black majority on council in 1978, and won a council seat in 1980, was the general spokesman for the group. (Moeser and Dennis 1982, 184)

Richmond's white political elites were not only determined to impose a politically subordinate relationship on the Marsh-led black majority on council, but they also attempted to undermine the black majority on council in two other ways. The first was to hold secret meetings with white members of city council. According to Dell, the African American members of council were not informed of these meetings or what was discussed at the meetings. Dell maintained that when she learned of these meetings, she was not surprised, given the reaction of the establishment to the election of the first black majority on council (Dell interview 1993). Dell further stated that even if the white members of council were conducting secret meetings with Richmond elites, the black majority on council would not, because she believed that if the black majority had conducted city business in private consultations with black political elites, the press would have attacked them severely. Dell supported her argument by revealing that the black majority on council was astutely aware that every decision they made was being closely scrutinized by the white political establishment and, especially, the press (Dell interview 1991; Baker 1989). Thus, because the black majority on council were cognizant of the press's close scrutiny of their actions, they decided as a group never to conduct council business without the presence of the full council. Obviously, the black majority on council held themselves to a higher standard than their white counterparts.

Dell's explanation of why the black majority on council did not retaliate against white members of council by engaging in similar meetings with black political elites can be better understood in the historic context of the kinds of repressive measures that were sometimes employed by Richmond's white elites to undermine black political mobilization in the past. A. Peter Bailey, an independent Richmond journalist, indicates in his article on the RCV, "Challenging Richmond's Crusade for Voters," that during his research, former RCV officials informed him during personal interviews that a "sign of our effectiveness in maintaining secrecy was a warning from the black Richmond police lieutenant Frank Randolph (now deceased) to be very careful about what we said on our phones because they had been tapped" (1988, 42). The significance of this is that it illustrates the most extreme kinds of repressive measures used by some of Richmond's previous white political elites to maintain white political hegemony over the city and social control over blacks. Furthermore, we could infer that the only way in which the phones of RCV officials could have been tapped was with the assistance of white city officials. Therefore, if in the past white elites, along with the cooperation of city officials, were willing to violate the constitutional rights of black political organizations by instituting questionable wire taps, one could assume that similar arrangements were in place in 1977. Thus, given the previous kinds of repressive measures that were employed to control blacks by Richmond's elites, we could once again assume that since the black majority on council were all former members of the RCV, they were aware of the measures that could be employed to monitor their activity.

The second ploy used by the white political establishment to undermine the black majority on council was to consistently attack the black majority's political credibility in public with the assistance of their ally, the white press. The groups that engaged in these attacks were white members of council, the white business and corporate elites, and both of Richmond's major white newspapers. All of these groups in one way or another placed a negative spin on all major policy decisions made by the black majority. These kinds of repeated attacks on any government official, and especially the first black majority on council, would eventually affect that governing body's ability to perform effectively. According to Donald P. Baker in his biographical text on former governor L. Douglas Wilder,

> The first five years of the black majority rule on the council were often tumultuous, with Marsh and his black colleagues generally shaking up the long-ruling white establishment. . . . When the council fired the white city manager—who subsequently was elected to council—the Times-Dispatch accused it of raw racism, comparing its majority to a band of black Bilbos, a white supremacist. The more strident afternoon *News Leader* compared the council's black majority as monkey-see, monkey-do leaders of a banana Republic. (Baker 1989, 131)

It was clear that based upon the white political establishment's political and social perceptions of African Americans in general, the white power structure had no intentions of accepting the new political reality of their city being governed by a black majority on council.

Why? Because Richmond's white power structure was unwilling to accept a black leadership that was rejecting a black subordinate political relationship with whites. According to former city councilwoman Claudette B. McDaniel, "The white civic and business leaders treated us like window washers. . . . Well, I don't wash their windows" (Baker 1989, 131). The relationship between the two groups was being redefined for the first time by the Marsh-led black majority's refusal to perform a political subordinate role that was being assigned to them by Richmond's white political establishment. It was just a matter of time before the Marsh-led black majority on council's interpretation of their newly found political power would result into a major political confrontation with the local white power structure. The firing of Leidinger and the Project One controversy exacerbated the brewing racial tensions already in evidence.

Leidinger Incident

Contrary to the fears of most whites, the only major shift in public policy that occurred initially under the black political majority was the inclusion of the needs and concerns of the African American community in the overall development of the city. With the exception of including African Americans' needs into development policy, the new majority did not institute any radical changes in public policy. Some development policies that had been initiated in the past were continued under the black majority's leadership. Perhaps the only political element in Richmond that might have interpreted the council actions as moving in a radical direction would have been ultraconservative whites who believed that any direction toward social, political, and economic equality for African Americans was radical. Thus, the differences between the black majority on council and their white adversaries would finally be played out in the Richmond political arena when the black majority fired Leidinger.

William J. Leidinger was the sitting city manager when the black majority were elected to city council. Although Leidinger was a holdover appointment from the outgoing city council, his association with that council did not become problematic until 1978 (Moeser and Dennis 1982). By August 2, 1978, the Marsh-led majority on council had become increasingly disenchanted with Leindinger's performance as city manager. Consequently, Mayor Marsh met with Leidinger and informed him that the majority members of council were not pleased with his performance and wanted him to resign his post. Leidinger was eventually fired by the black majority council on the grounds of "philosophical and policy differences, and replaced by an African American city manager" (Edds 1987, 126; Moeser and Dennis 1982, 181). According to Moeser's research on Leidinger's firing, when Leidinger left his meeting with Marsh, he informed his business and corporate allies of his firing. The white elites immediately requested and were granted a meeting with Marsh and the black members of council. During the meeting, the elites expressed their outrage over Leidinger's firing and even accused the black majority on council of being racially motivated. The elites also tried to intimidate the black majority by threatening to suspend construction in the downtown area, and some even went so far as to say that they would move their firms out of the city. Also, some of the business community leaders were so outraged over Leidinger's firing that they threatened the black majority with violent reprisals. Margaret Edds, in her text *Free at Last*, corroborates the threats of violence that were made against the Marsh-led black majority when she reports that Marsh was told by some of the dominant business leaders in Richmond that "if Leidinger was not retained, . . . blood will flow in the streets of Richmond" (1987, 126).

The black majority's firing of Leidinger and the subsequent meeting with the city's white elites revealed three important points. The first was that the political wars between the black majority on council and their white adversaries was only beginning. The second was that Leidinger's firing was not racially motivated. In fact, Moeser's research into the entire incident supports this contention. For instance, although three of the four white council members supported the general perception that Leidinger's firing was racially motivated, one of the white members, Muriel H. Smith, disagreed because she felt that the firing occurred because of his ideological differences with the council. Ironically, Smith was defeated by Leidinger when he ran against her for city council in 1980 (Moeser and Dennis 1982). The perception that Leidinger's firing was not racially motivated can be corroborated by statements that were made by some of the same white business leaders who earlier supported him. For instance, several business leaders were quoted by Moeser and Dennis in their research of the incident as saying that "it was normal for people in Leidinger's position to be asked to resign before being fired. A few businessmen noted that Leidinger was arrogant and should have gone to council for support rather than seeking help from white business leaders" (182). It would appear from the above quote that Leidinger's firing was part of the longstanding practices of most local governments, and that appointed officials serve at the whim of elected officials and can be replaced even by a new administration. Furthermore, if Leidinger's firing had been racially motivated, he could have taken his case to court, especially given the fact that he had been fired in 1978, because throughout the mid- to late 1970s several landmark court cases, for example, *Bakke v. U.C. Davis* (1978), involving the concept of reverse discrimination had already been successfully adjudicated in the courts (Pinkney 1984, 150–66).

The final important point revealed by the Leidinger firing and the black majority's meeting with white elites was that the question of who governed on political matters had been settled. The question was answered by the black majority council when they refused to rescind Leidinger's firing. According to Moeser and Dennis, "Said one writer of the split between the black council members and white business leaders, Economic power had run into political power and it had lost. One businessman-politician saw the diversion as evidence that there were now two centers of power in Richmond" (Moeser and Dennis 1982, 181). We contend that the firing of Leidinger, blacks' and white elites' longstanding distrust of one another, Richmond's historic racial polarization, along with the white political establishment and its media allies' relentless attacks on the black majority on council all converged to precipitate a political grudge rematch between economic power and political power that would be played out through the Project One incident.

Project One Controversy

The white elites' downtown development strategy had two objectives. The first was to retain its retail industry by inducing Miller and Rhodes and Thalhimer's, the two largest remaining department stores in the CBD, to stay downtown (Silver 1984). Richmond's elites were trying to prevent further loss of retail dollars to the surrounding suburbs and adjacent counties. The second objective was to revitalize downtown (Hays interview 1993). Another important factor that was connected to retaining retail industry and downtown revitalization was annexation. The issue of annexation was relevant to the twin components of the elites' downtown development strategy because they perceived annexation as a means to increase the city's white population while diluting the black population. Thus, the elites' agenda was simple: if they could prevent blacks from gaining political control of the city, then the elites' development agenda could proceed unimpeded. However, the elites' inability to reduce the size and political strength of the African American populace enabled Richmond's blacks to elect a black political majority on council. Consequently, the election of a black majority on council would precipitate a challenge to the white elites for inclusion in the formation of the city's development policy.

The white intransigence to black emphasis on political inclusion in the development policy arena will be studied in the case analysis of a controversial downtown revitalization project. The intent of the case analysis is to illustrate how the issue of race was used by the white elites to divide the black community and subsequently destabilize the black majority on council.

Project One was a planned revitalization of downtown Richmond. Initially unveiled in 1956, over time, portions of the plan were dropped and new items added. The plan was the dream of Harland Bartholomew, former consultant to the City Planning Commission, and basically called for the construction of a civic center, a major expressway, and a municipal complex building. In spite of Project One's historical image (especially among African Americans), the newly elected black majority on council reluctantly supported portions of it. For instance, the council supported "the construction of a hotel-convention-center-office complex to be located adjacent to the coliseum north of Broad street"; however, it refused to support the construction of a downtown expressway (Silver 1984, 316–17). Turpin stated that both government and business agreed initially that Project One needed a major hotel chain located within its perimeters to support the coliseum and convention center that had not been completed. Both groups further agreed that if a major hotel were not part of the development scheme, the project would probably collapse.

The philosophical and policy differences between blacks on city council and Richmond's white elites escalated over the 1978 deliberation over the selection of a hotel for the proposed Project One convention center and office complex. The black majority on council recommended selection of the Marriott Hotel corporation, whereas the white elites backed the selection of the Hilton Hotel chain. Moreover, there was white resistance to the planned site of the hotel because of two related factors. Whites opposed the selection, according to George Little, political activist, prominent white attorney, and former school board attorney, because this area was identified by whites as being in the "black part" of Broad Street. They also opposed the site selection because they felt that no "respectable" white person would dare sleep north of Broad street (Lee interview 1993). To the black majority on council, this area was significant because it was once considered the financial hub of the African American community. Furthermore, by locating the hotel chain in that particular area, the council was also attempting to use the site to stimulate the revitalization of the Jackson Ward area, the historic economic and commercial artery of Richmond's African American community. The council believed that this location would alter the direction of downtown economic development and evenly spread economic development dollars throughout the city instead of concentrating the dollars in one area or direction.

The conflict escalated when the city council passed an ordinance requiring that all private development, including hotels in the Project One area, be assessed a development fee based on their potential impact on Project One. Moeser asserts that the council passed the ordinance to protect the Marriott chain, believing that other hotels would saturate the area and Marriott would then pull out. Thus, the project would start to unravel, and the city would lose money. Moeser's premise on the intention of the ordinance was confirmed by Edds:

> When the Hilton Hotel plans were announced, the black majority was stunned at the thought that the hotel, located in a more affluent setting, might make the Broad Street project even less desirable to investors. A consultant's report supported that view. Marsh and the black majority decided to torpedo the Hilton Hotel. On a five to four vote, black-white split that November, the council denied city permission for the transfer of two parcels of surplus land to the Hilton Developers. (Edds 1987, 141)

When the black majority on council refused to reverse its position, Richmond's white elites found themselves engaged in a battle of wills, feeling that they had been pushed too far by the black political majority. Moreover, the white elites flexed their political and economic muscles by threatening to halt construction on projects in the downtown, and, even worse, they threatened to move their businesses out of the city if the council's decision was not reversed. By engaging in a face-saving campaign of economic blackmail, the white elites were convinced that they had to show the black majority on council who actually ran the city (Turpin interview 1991). In spite of the verbal threats, the council did not reverse its decision. To resolve the political stalemate, the Marsh-led black majority on council supported the establishment of Richmond Renaissance (RR) as a goodwill gesture to the white elites (Turpin interview 1991; Towns 1991). According to Clarence Towns, RR evolved out of his personal efforts to persuade Marsh to reestablish lines of communication with the city's corporate and business community by supporting the establishment of a quasi-public economic development corporation called RR (Towns interview 1991). Richmond's business and corporate elites agreed to unite with Marsh on the establishment of RR, because the organizers felt that they could persuade business and corporate leaders to support those kinds of activities that were economically viable to the entire city. The rationale given by the organizers of RR for entering into a political and economic relationship with Marsh can be corroborated by Towns, who, incidentally, was one of the original organizers of RR. According to Towns's interpretation of the events surrounding the creation of RR, "The organizers of RR felt that if they became involved with Marsh to promote social engineering type programs, they were convinced that white business and corporate leaders would not support these kinds of activities. However, the organizers of RR did state that they could prevail upon Richmond's white business and corporate community to support those kinds of economic activities that were viable to both blacks and whites in the entire city" (Towns interview 1991). Consequently, Marsh, with the cooperation of Towns, T. Justin Moore, and the city manager, agreed to support the establishment of RR. Towns stated that Marsh's participation in the creation of RR was critical because without the city's financial support, RR would have had a difficult time getting started (Towns interview 1991). Marsh's role in helping to establish RR was also corroborated by Little. According to Little, the project was conceived by Henry Marsh to heal the city's political wounds from the Project One controversy (Lee interview 1991). Furthermore, after the city agreed to participate formally in the establishment of RR, Towns stated that Richmond's corporate community quickly embraced the concept of the organization. Towns felt very strongly that Marsh never received, nor would he ever receive, any public recognition for his contribution in helping to establish RR (Towns interview 1991).

The local representatives of the Hilton chain eventually sued the city, and the business community claimed that the city council's actions were racist. The city lost the lawsuit, and damages of $5 million were awarded to Hilton. The city council got a vote of "no confidence" in the local white newspapers, rekindling the myth that African Americans were incapable of governing. Some black leaders felt that Mayor Marsh lost stature, particularly in the business community. This inevitably diminished the credibility of the black majority on council and of liberal African American politicians in general.

The loss of the city council's credibility over the Project One controversy triggered the resurgence of black conservative politics and gender and class bias in the black community that would eventually contribute to the 1982 defeat of Willie Dell, a black female liberal member of city council. We contend that Dell became the sacrificial lamb of the controversy that would eventually lead to the election of Roy A. West, a conservative African American, as councilperson and, subsequently, the second black mayor of Richmond. Although Marsh bore the brunt of white criticism hurled against the black majority on council as a result of the Project One controversy, the ordinance that was passed by the Marsh-led black majority on council preventing the saturating of the area near the Marriott Hotel has proven over time to have been the correct choice and in the best interest of the city. For instance, the only hotel that has survived in the Project One area to this day has been the Marriott.

The question of who governed Richmond after the Project One controversy can best be answered by one businessman-politician who observed the conflict and concluded from that conflict that "political power rests with the Crusade for Voters while economic power remains vested along main street" (Moeser and Dennis 1982, 181).

The demise of the black majority on council will be examined in greater detail in chapter 6. The questions we will use to guide our analysis are, How did the political fallout from Project One impact the outcome of the 1982 city council election? What role did the black conservatives of Richmond play in the city council election of 1982? How were gender politics used in the 1982 election? What factors precipitated the demise of the black majority on city council? Also, what were the political and policy implications of the 1982 election?

Demise of the Black Majority on the City Council

My personal affirmation of my Afro-American history and
cultural heritage places me on the side of those who have
worked and suffered for our overdue gains. To do less would
be unethical, unthinkable, and a personal sin against my
commitment to the struggle for human rights.

Willie Dell

We contend that the factors of race, gender, class, and black conservatism contributed to the demise of the black majority on council. We
further assert that all of these factors were significant contributors in the
defeat of Willie Dell's reelection campaign for city council in 1982. We
will explicate how the four interconnecting variables worked together to
destabilize Richmond's first black majority on council and defeat Dell
when we examine the return of gender politics in Richmond during the
1982 election.

WILLIE DELL AND THE RETURN OF GENDER POLITICS TO RICHMOND

Gender politics were prevalent in both the black body politic and the
larger Richmond political arena. As the 1982 election gained momentum, the interplay of gender politics in both the black community and
the city's political arena made Willie Dell a political casualty. Individuals like Martin Jewell and Saad El-Amin (both former officials of
the RCV), along with Moeser, believe that the loss of Dell was a major
contributing factor to the demise of the black majority on council.
Although Dell's defeat was the fatal blow that prevented the Marsh-led

black majority from returning intact on the council, the question that has to be addressed is, How and why did she lose as an incumbent member of council to a black political novice? This chapter examines all of the pertinent factors that contributed to Dell's defeat: racism; gender bias; upper-middle-class opposition to Dell's reelection, along with their character assassination attacks on Dell; low voter turnout; and the redrawing of Dell's district boundaries.

Racism

In 1982, Willie Dell was expected to win her reelection. Her horizons were bright and many surmised that she probably would have been elected vice mayor and, perhaps in two years, elected the first black female mayor of Richmond. However, after the 1982 election, Dell was no longer a member of council. The first factor that contributed to Dell's defeat was racism. According to Dell, Dr. Welling Rennie, a white conservative, a former member of city council who was on the council when Dell was defeated, and a member of TOP, informed Dell after the election that TOP considered her to be "too black" in terms of her political beliefs, and as a result of her outspoken views, they had decided to target her for defeat (Dell interview 1993). Dell maintains that Rennie revealed to her that TOP had initially decided to support Melvin Law, a Richmond black conservative and, to Dell's knowledge, the only visible black member of TOP. Rennie's rationale for supporting Law was that "Law was the whitetist black person" that they could find to oppose Dell in 1980. Rennie's depiction of Law as being the whitetist black person that TOP could find supports William E. Nelson's notion of a "racial nomenclature," which was obviously prevalent in Richmond's society. The term, according to political scientist William E. Nelson, describes the kind of caste system that has historically existed in the U.S. political and social culture. Nelson defines "racial nomenclature" as reflecting

> racial lines of demarcation [to] maintain a system of privilege; social rules maintain the separation of blacks and whites; group membership in each category is lifelong; the basic philosophical boundaries of society have been defined by whites and for their benefit; the social system is only peripherally concerned with how blacks seek to define themselves in society; and very importantly, the system is renewed with the racial socialization of each new generation in the United States. (Jennings 1994, 147)

Applying Nelson's concept of racial nomenclature to Rennie's description of Law as a prospective candidate reveals the presumptuousness of some whites when it comes to how they actually perceive blacks in this society. Rennie's depiction of Law also appears to be consistent with another term, "honorary and temporary whiteness":

> [David E. Hayes-Bustista] explains how the categorization or implication of whiteness conferred privileges for even a "nonwhite" group, like Mexicans: To be Mexican was a disadvantage, while "to be labeled a Spaniard carried no social stigma. . . . There is a reason for this: Mexicans were Indians, dark, nonwhite, and considered uncivilized; Spanish were white, civilized, and European." In fact, until the last decade, the highest compliment an Anglo could pay a Mexican or Chicano was to call him or her "Spanish" thereby conferring an honorary and temporary whiteness. (Jennings 1994, 148)

Although Hayes-Bustista's concept is generally used by urbanists and sociologists to offer explanations of racial and ethnic conflict among African Americans, Latinos, and Asians in American cities, in a political culture like that of Richmond, where there is no sizable presence of other racial and ethnic minority groups, adoption of the term "temporary whiteness" can be applied. Thus, when Rennie described Law as being the "whitetist black person" that TOP could find to run against Dell, he was actually bestowing temporary whiteness on Law.

However, if we view Rennie's depiction of Law from a more gendered perspective, one could surmise that TOP's real motivation behind supporting a Law candidacy was to use a black male to unseat Dell in the upcoming election. If a white male were to have run against Dell, blacks might have perceived a white challenger as being part of a racially motivated ploy on the part of whites to unseat the first black majority on council. A black conservative candidate running against Dell prevented her from exploiting the issue of race to her advantage.

Dell overwhelmingly defeated Law in 1980. Dell's conversation with Rennie revealed that TOP was desperate to find a black conservative to not only challenge her but win. Dell stated that Rennie closed their discussion by informing her that "they did not know about West at the time" (Dell interview 1993). Rennie's statement can be corroborated because, when we examined the Commonwealth of Virginia's State Board of Elections (CVSBOE Records) report and campaign contributions and expenditures for the period covering March 2 to May 25, 1982, we could not trace any of the campaign contributions to TOP or any of its known members at that time. The only campaign contribution that appeared to be of a suspicious nature was the contribution made by a local civic organization called the Washington Park Civic League (WPCL). The significance of WPCL's contribution is the amount of money that was donated to West's campaign: $850 (CVSBOE Records 1982). This particular campaign contribution was viewed with suspicion because during our research we spoke with some Richmond politicians and political observers who thought that $850 from a local civic league to a novice city council candidate was a large sum of money. Dell, during a phone interview in 1998, informed us that the area of her district where the WPCL was located was not a middle- to upper-class community but a lower- to lower-middle-class community (Dell interview 1998). We deduced from this information that under these kinds of circumstances, a community with that socioeconomic profile would have a difficult time raising that kind of money for an established black candidate, let alone a political novice such as West. With the exception of that particular campaign contribution, none of West's campaign contributions could be traced to TOP or any of Richmond's white elites.

Thus, based upon the CVSBOE reports, it appears that Rennie may have been telling the truth when he said that TOP and their elite backers were not aware of West's candidacy. In West's campaign contributions report for 1982, it appears that there was no direct connection to Richmond's white elites and West's candidacy during the 1982 election. However, in an examination of West's campaign contributions for the 1984 campaign against Dell, West's campaign and contributions report showed an enormous increase from business pacs, black conservative pacs, private businesses/individuals and corporations.

Assuming Rennie's version of TOP's motive for targeting Dell for defeat, there may be several reasons why this was a viable political strategy. The first scenario involves a situation where TOP may have acted out of fear because they may have perceived Dell as a legitimate future candidate for mayor. In examining Dell's voting record, along with the kinds of programs and policies that she proposed and/or supported during her tenure on council, while TOP may have overreacted in perceiving Dell as a political threat, her pervasive influence had already been widely acknowledged.

Dell was perceived as a maverick politician within Richmond's political circles because she frequently championed causes that placed her at odds with the white and black political establishments. The one area where she consistently clashed with the white political establishment was her concern for issues involving the poor: "Willie's concern for the poor, blacks, elders, and women has caused her to come under attack from those who don't care if families have food, shelter and clothing. They often accuse her of pro-black attitude and anti-white. To this charge Willie says, That has been said by some folks, and I refuse to deal with it because I would be wasting energy on other folks' agenda. I'm not anti-anything. I'm just pro-black and don't apologize for it" (Marsh 1984, 38–39).

If Dell's political views were deemed too radical for Richmond's white political establishment, then her views on women's issues may also have been deemed radical, especially by southern standards. For instance, when Dell was first appointed to city council, there was no bathroom for women in the old city hall. Dell, in her typical independent fashion, took prompt action to rectify this inequity. According to Dell, when she first learned of the problem, she immediately expressed her displeasure over it in a candid manner with her male council colleagues. The bathroom incident was resolved when council authorized the maintenance department to convert one of the men's rooms into a restroom for women. Dell further stated that after the incident was resolved, she received a congratulatory telephone call from Mary Ellen Sheppard, the first woman mayor of Richmond, who agreed with her action but who disagreed with some of the language she was purported to have used in her discussion with her male counterparts. Dell further revealed that Sheppard admitted to her during their telephone conversation that when she served on city council, she had to use the men's room with a police officer standing guard outside the restroom (Dell interview 1997). It would appear from this incident that Dell was not willing to be a second-class city council person and was unabashed in expressing her views to her male counterparts.

Because Dell refused to compromise her beliefs, most pragmatic politicians and individuals who opposed her agenda tried to discredit her by labeling her a maverick. Whichever label one attaches to Dell, however, it was clear that she was a progressive and compassionate leader. The Dell Papers, along with the Office of the City Clerk (OCC Records) documents on her voting record on city council revealed that Dell supported progressive legislation. For example, she supported tax relief for the elderly and handicapped. She also supported reduced transit fares for all citizens, especially the elderly and handicapped, and she fought for the creation of a neighborhood housing service program that provided low interests loans for housing rehabilitation (Dell Papers; OCC Records). Dell's image as a compassionate leader also was confirmed by an examination of the type of legislation she introduced while serving on city council. Table 6 presents the kinds of issues that Dell supported and sponsored while serving on city council from 1975 to 1982. During her tenure, the type of issues that she supported were those related to redistributive policies. For instance, she consistently introduced legislation or supported legislation that was related to social welfare, the elderly, the handicapped, race, gender, youth, and human rights.

TABLE 6

Number and Kind of Issues Supported and Sponsored by Dell on City Council, 1975–1982

	No. of Times Issue Supported or Sponsored				
	1975–76	1976–78	1978–80	1980–82	Total
Social welfare	10	9	9	8	36
Human rights	0	0	1	1	2
Elderly	5	9	5	5	24
Gender	1	2	2	2	7
Youth	2	7	3	2	11
Handicapped	0	3	0	1	4
Race relations	0	0	3	2	5

Source: Office of the City Clerk, Richmond, Va., 1975–82.

Table 6 clearly illustrates that Dell supported or sponsored issues related to four key issues: social welfare, the elderly, gender, and youth. Dell's support of these four key issues accounted for over 80 percent of the issues that she either supported or cosponsored with proposed legislation while serving on city council. Dell may have focused on these key issues because they were important to her personally, professionally, and politically. In other words, the issues pertaining to the elderly, poor people, youth, and women were important because as a voting constituency, they comprised a significant portion of her political base. Also, an increasing number of the individuals who comprised her political base were African Americans. Finally, although table 6 reveals that Dell did not focus a lot of her attention on issues such as human rights and the handicapped, one can not assume that she was not concerned with these areas. Based upon the information obtained from the Richmond OCC on Dell's voting record, when Dell was presented with problems about the handicapped and concerning human rights, she supported them without hesitation. For example, on the issue of human rights, it was Dell who introduced and later was successful in getting the city to establish a human rights ordinance and later a commission. Also, in the area of race relations, it was Dell, not her successor West, who introduced legislation for minority set-aside programs for business enterprises.

TOP's decision, then, to target her for defeat was a plausible course of action for them to pursue because they may have perceived Dell's consistent support of redistributive policies as posing a potential threat to their access to city resources. Dell's influence was also spreading, and she was initially selected as a candidate by the black majority on city council for the position of vice mayor in 1977. Although she did not garner enough votes for the position, possibly because of the inherent racism and sexism within the city council, it was unquestionable that she was an emerging force in the city's political structure. What may have been the bone of contention with TOP and their allies was the growing recognition that after the 1982 election, Dell would be impossible to beat. Had Dell been selected as vice mayor in 1977, and Mayor Henry Marsh resigned to accept the federal judgeship offered him by the Carter administration, Dell would have been elevated to the post of mayor. By her reelection in 1982, she would have been a sitting mayor with a strong progressive agenda. As Dell informed us, as mayor of Richmond she would not have taken monies from neighborhoods and reallocated them for use in helping to establish RR (Dell interview 1998).

The Role of Class

The Dell-West contest had class overtones because most of West's support came from black upper-middle-class and professional groups such as the Virginia Teachers Association (VTA), and he was overwhelmingly supported by the small, older, white conservative population that had been added to Dell's district. Edds's research on the 1982 election indicates that "West's margin of victory came decisively in three white precincts in the 69 percent black district. West carried the white precincts by about two to one" (1987, 143). The white population was strongly anti-Marsh. If the whites could not defeat Marsh directly, they would defeat him indirectly by voting against Dell, one of his strongest supporters, and supporting West (Williams interview 1991).

Dell may have lost because she was an outspoken woman and because of the strong anti-Marsh sentiment among the voters that was used against her, especially by West. However, one can not attribute her defeat solely to the anti-Marsh sentiment because other gender factors may also have been involved. For instance, Dell believes that she lost her reelection bid because upper- and middle-class black women voted against her. The lack of political support from black middle-class women can be illustrated by the views of one prominent upper-middle-class black woman who expressed her strong dislike for Dell in an interview and revealed that Dell lost because she was an outsider and because the black women that she knew in Richmond did not think that Dell was a "lady." This individual further revealed that Dell was rejected because she did not talk or dress like a "lady" should. In other words, Dell was not perceived by middle- and upper-class black women in Richmond as being the proper preacher's wife.

The criticism and perception of Dell not being a proper minister's wife actually stems from some earlier attacks on her character made during the early 1970s. For instance, Dell's views on the role of women were disclosed again when Dell, along with other ministers' wives, were featured in the *Richmond Times-Dispatch* as part of an in-depth examination of the typical minister's wife. Six ministers' wives were interviewed; four were white and two were black. Throughout the story, Dell consistently stated that she was not your typical minister's wife. For example, she stated at one point in the interview that she "could never be one of those non-persons. . . . I'm authentic and direct. I don't play games. I'm not going to be what other people want me to be. I like to smoke and drink a glass of wine. I'm me. [She also acknowledge that] she was the first woman in her church to come out with an Afro hairstyle" (Griffin 1972, 1–2). Although Dell was being candid about the kind of person she was, her statements were perceived by some members of Richmond's black community as too liberal and damaging to the image of blacks. Her comments caused one individual, J. M. Wright, to write a personal letter to Dell's husband. In the letter, Wright expressed his displeasure with Dell's statements in the newspaper feature story, by stating that "Rev. Nichols' wife spoke with dignity and intelligence, which made the black community feel proud. Mrs. Dell said that she smokes, and drinks her wine, which was a disgrace to the black people to have been put in the paper and also a disgrace to you as a minister. The white people have always had a low opinion of black people; she played right into their hands. To me, as a black person, it was very unpleasant" (Dell Papers). Wright's letter revealed further biases. First, Wright addressed his letter to

Mrs. Dell; however, the actual salutation of the note inside his letter was addressed to Reverend Dell, her husband. Wright begins his letter by comparing another black minister's wife with Dell. He shortly reveals that he favors Minister Nichols's wife's comments because, unlike Dell, she stays at home with her children and does not have a career outside of the home. Moreover, the story further revealed that with the exception of Mrs. Nichols, all of the ministers' wives worked. The purpose of Wright's comparison of the two ministers' wives was to inform Reverend Dell that his wife was not a proper wife because she smoked and consumed alcoholic beverages. Second, Wright's letter reinforces an old stereotype about black women that was discussed in Paula Giddings's book, *When and Where I Enter:* Mrs. Dell does not possess "class" (Giddings 1984). Giddings states,

> Black women were caught between the two functions they were expected to fulfill: enhancing the material quality of life for their families, and at the same time behaving like housewives. With E. Franklin Fraizer setting the tone in *The Negro Family* and *The Black Bourgeoisie,* black women were scolded for being too domineering and too insecure; too ambitious and too decadently idle, all in the same breath. Thus, despite the special socioeconomic circumstances faced by blacks, black men saw black women in the same context that white men saw white women. (Giddings 1984, 252)

Thus, on one level, Wright's criticism of Dell was based upon his viewing black women as he viewed white women. However, on another level, Wright criticized Dell for not having any class because she embarrassed black people (Griffin 1972). Wright's attack on Dell is important because the implication that Dell was not a proper minister's wife was raised again during her reelection campaign in 1982, when several prominent black men and women attacked Dell's character on this very same issue. Consequently, these kinds of attacks on Dell's character may have reinforced black upper- and middle-class voters' negative opinion of her, which in turn might have accounted for the close losses she suffered in two predominantly black upper- and middle-class precincts. How Dell was defeated in the election is depicted in table 7, which shows the 1982 election results for District 3.

Another illustration of how the class issue was manifested in the election against Dell was an incident that occurred during a "meet the candidate" forum held in a church on North Chamberlayne Avenue in Richmond. The members of the audience for this forum were primarily from the black middle and upper classes. Dell stated that she sensed a very hostile audience. In fact, she said that she felt like the enemy.

TABLE 7

Richmond City Council District 3 Election Results by Precinct

	Precinct									Total
	301	302	303	304	305	306	307	308	309	
Dell	316	336	527	656	751	544	78	86	39	3,362
West	344	372	245	190	247	218	571	841	790	3,859
No. of reg. voters	1,328	1,387	1,294	1,525	1,752	1,857	1,450	1,628	1,512	13,773
No. of reg. voters who voted	660	708	772	846	998	762	649	927	830	7,222

Source: Office the General Registrar, Richmond, Va., Aug. 6, 1993.

Before she could be introduced by her campaign manager, her worst fears had become a reality. She was hissed, booed, and even shouted at. Some of the women in attendance even criticized her physical features and her southern dialect. Dell stated that the only person who saved her at this meeting was Saad El-Amin, who was her campaign manager and advised her to leave because he felt that if she remained in the room, the meeting would eventually get worse (Dell interview 1993, El-Amin interview 1993). It would appear from the Chamberlayne Avenue forum that Dell would not receive much political support from this group of black Richmonders.

The Impact of Dell's New District Boundaries

Another factor that may have contributed to Dell's defeat was the Marsh-led black majority on council. In Richmond, most observers of the city's black politics have generally accused West and conservative whites of undermining the black majority council when Dell was defeated. However, the Marsh-led council may also have contributed to her defeat by not closely monitoring the redrawing of the district boundary lines. The lines had to be redrawn because Richmond was under court order to submit city council district boundary plans every ten years to the U.S. Justice Department for their approval (Lynch interview 1993). In other words, before the elections could be held, the Justice Department had to approve the plans. Under the old district boundaries in 1975, Dell's district was 80 percent black and predominantly lower working class. However, when her district boundaries were redrawn by Mary Alice Lynch, the city registrar, Dell's new district in 1982 was 69 percent black and 31 percent white (ibid.). Her new district also included more middle-class blacks and some conservative whites. The changing of Dell's district composition was significant for two reasons. First, we were informed by a former city official that the lines for Dell's district were redrawn to protect Chuck Richardson, a controversial black city councilman, because Marsh believed that he was politically vulnerable and could be defeated if his district boundary was not changed. However, if the population that had been added to Dell's district had been added to Richardson's district, then Richardson may have lost instead of Dell. Second, when the district lines were redrawn, the city and the African American community were deprived of having its first African American female vice mayor. Individuals such as Moeser and El-Amin speculate that by 1984, Dell might have been elected the first black female mayor of Richmond.

Due to Marsh's ongoing political spats with white elites, he may not have monitored carefully the redrawing of the city council district maps.

Thus, Marsh's preoccupation with other matters may have indirectly contributed to Dell's defeat and hence precipitated the destabilization of the African American political majority on council. For further illustration of the city council District 3's changes over a period of time, see maps 1 and 2.

If one carefully examines map 1, one will notice several things. First, prior to the 1982 election, Dell's boundary lines did not cross Chamberlayne Avenue. Chamberlayne Avenue is the dark line on map 1 that separates District 3 from District 2. Chamberlayne Avenue is relevant to this discussion because when the new boundary lines were changed, conservative white voters were added to District 3. These voters were vehemently opposed to the Marsh-led black majority on council and thus opposed to Dell. Second, if one inspects the shaded area on map 1, one will see Precincts 305 and 307. The significance of the old Precincts 305 and 307 is that both were predominantly poor and black, and the voter turnout in the two was generally high (Lynch interview 1993). Moreover, Precincts 305 and 307 were a large part of Dell's political base. Thus, if 305 and 307 had remained the same when the district boundary lines were changed, Dell would have been reelected easily.

Dell's boundary lines were extended beyond Chamberlayne Avenue. And if one inspects the shaded area in map 2, one will notice that Precinct 309 was added to her district, and that Precincts 307 and 308 had been completely redrawn; both were now in the northeastern section of the district. The significance of the new 307 and 308 precincts, along with the addition of 309, is that they were comprised primarily of conservative white voters (Lynch interview 1993). In comparison with map 1, these voters were not part of Dell's district in 1980. These white conservative voters voted overwhelmingly against Dell in the election and were noted to be strongly anti-Marsh as well. We hypothesize that if the whites could not defeat Marsh directly, they would defeat him indirectly by voting against Dell and supporting West. Consequently, the addition of these new voters to the District in 1982, along with the strong upper-income and middle-class anti-Dell vote in Precincts 301 and 302 and the low voter turnouts in almost all of the other precincts, contributed to Dell's defeat and thus shifted the balance of power on council.

The discussion of the white conservative voters in Dell's redrawn district seems to support one of the five possible scenarios that were introduced by Marcus Pohlmann and Michael P. Kirby in their text on Memphis, *Racial Politics at the Crossroads*, when they prescribed alternative futures for interracial politics in that city. According to the authors, one of the alternative scenarios involved a new phenomenon known as the "whites as moderators":

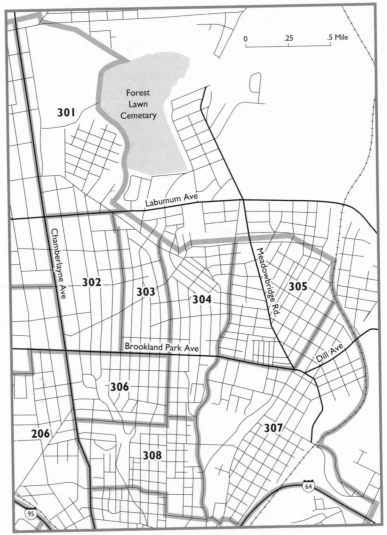

Map 1. District 3's boundary lines prior to 1982.

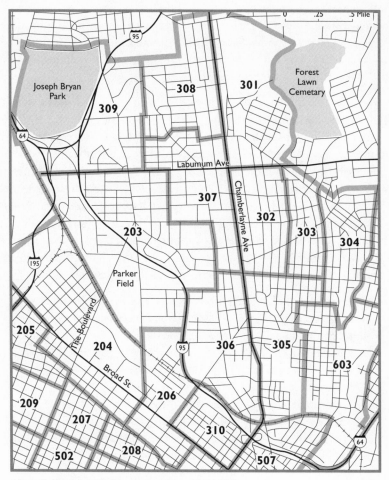

Map 2. District 3's boundary lines in 1982.

> If the black population remains large enough to preclude much of a chance
> for white elected officials to regain governmental control in the foreseeable
> future, a factionalized black community could still allow white voters to play
> a moderating role. In New Orleans in 1986, for instance, Sidney Barthelemy,
> the more conservative of the two black candidates, garnered 86 percent of the
> white vote and only 28 percent of the black vote on his way to defeating the
> more racially conscious William Jefferson. Similarly, in 1989, moderate black
> candidate Michael White won the mayor's office with only 30 percent of
> Cleveland's black vote. (Pohlmann and Kirby 1996, 203)

As with the case in New Orleans in the 1982 election, Dell was cast as the
more racially conscious candidate, while West was cast as the more conservative of the two black candidates. Thus, the new white conservative
voters that were added to Dell's redrawn district became the "whites as
moderators" phenomenon described by Pohlmann and Kirby's research
on Memphis. Moreover, the white conservative voters actually became
the swing vote in the predominantly black District 3. This phenomenon
of whites as the swing vote in predominantly black cities is not new. Corroboration for this occurrence was supported by an article that appeared
in the November 2, 1983, issue of the *Wall Street Journal,* which, incidentally, involved Richmond. According to the article,

> Black municipal officials who historically have gained office on a tidal wave
> of black ballots capped by a smattering of white liberal votes are increasingly
> counting on the support of moderate whites as well. Thus, as black urban
> communities grow more diverse, the whites are emerging as a swing vote.
> And in cities that already have a black mayor, the novelty of a black face in
> city hall is wearing off, and more voters are judging black mayors on per-
> formance instead of color. . . . Moreover, the economic resources are still in
> the hands of whites, says Merl Black, a University of North Carolina political
> science professor. To work effectively, black mayors have to work out some
> sort of accommodation, he said. (Englemayer 1983, 60)

The article seems to imply that the future of black politics in urban set-
tings, and especially in the South, depends on black majorities accommodating the interests of white business. The irony of this statement is
that it suggests that the style of leadership that best suits this type of
political arrangement is that of accommodationist black leaders, an
arrangement rejected by black voters in cities like Richmond during the
MR era. Thus, if blacks are being counseled to support black conservative
and accommodationist candidates, then the white minority swing vote
could conceivably prevent liberal and/or progressive candidates from

emerging from predominantly black districts. In essence, we assert that the conservative white voters in District 3, during a hotly contested election between two strong black candidates, could prevent a liberal or progressive candidate from being elected to city council from that district as it is presently constructed.

Thus, Dell was unable to rally a constituency divided along racial and class lines. Moreover, although we asserted earlier that racism may not have been a dominant factor in TOP's role in the defeat of Dell, it may have been an important factor in the election when the conservative white electorate in District 3 voted overwhelmingly against her. The primary reason that racism may have played a role among the white conservative voters is that the anti-Marsh attitudes exhibited by them against Dell during the 1982 election were probably the same racist perceptions of the Marsh-led black majority that were shared by similar white conservative groups in Richmond, such as TOP.

Role of Low Voter Turnout

Another factor that contributed to Dell's defeat, which may not have had anything to do with race or gender or even with class, was the low voter turnout among her poor constituency. Under Dell's old district boundary lines, she had cultivated a longstanding personal relationship with her poor black voters, who generally demonstrated high voter turnouts during an election. When Dell's district boundary lines were redrawn, she inherited a new group of poor black constituents who typically demonstrated low voter turnout (Randolph and Tate 1995). How the low voter turnout in Dell's district made an impact on the 1982 election is illustrated in table 7.

The election returns clearly show that Dell lost by 497 votes. Moreover, the data also reveal that low voter turnouts in Precincts 301, 303, 304, 305, and 306 prevented her from being reelected. In fact, if five hundred more voters had voted in either 305 or 306, Dell would have retained her seat on council. Thus, some of the blame for defeat can be attributed to a lack of support from her political base. Dell's political judgment may have contributed to the low turnout because she simply did not court these new voters as much as she had done in the past with her old poor voters under the old District 3 boundaries (Randolph and Tate 1995; Edds 1987).

These poor black constituents in Dell's districts became increasingly vocal and dissatisfied with their representation. Consequently, Dell's political opponents thought that if the constituents in her district were politically divided, they could defeat her by exploiting the disenchantment voiced by these constituents about her performance as a council member. The individuals, then, who stood to gain the most from a Dell victory did not support their chief advocate on city council, or vote their political self-interest, when she needed them the most. Her inability to energize and mobilize these new voters made this constituency particularly vulnerable to the resurgence of black conservatives.

The Role of Gender

The character assassinations along with the gender attacks that were launched against Dell were interrelated. For instance, some men had privately accused Dell of serving on council because she "had an unhappy home life or was looking for a man." The first remark clearly reveals an attack on her character by implying that she was unfaithful to her husband, and the second attack reveals the gender hostility. In other words, would these same men have accused West or Marsh of "looking for a woman" as their reason for serving on council? Moreover, the sexist overtones of the Dell-West campaign were evident because both white and black observers of black politics in Richmond could not recall an election with these kinds of personal attacks and slander being used against a man.

The personal attacks launched against Dell by her opposition unquestionably stemmed from the gender bias that was prevalent in Richmond's black body politic. In addition to the gender bias, the personal attacks on Dell's character could also have arisen from her maverick political style. For instance, Dell's maverick style politics occasionally conflicted with the black political establishment. Her conflicts with the black political establishment generally stemmed from her outspokenness, and sometimes from her criticisms of black leaders themselves. This letter excerpt written by Dell to a news editor illustrates how her outspokenness could have created some conflict with the male members of the black political establishment:

> Today's black leaders, who opt for so called peace, quiet and harmony at any price, clearly do not understand the price paid by our ancestral giants. Black families who lost jobs, financial support and even having bank loans suddenly come due when they dared to finally locate the "shifting" voter registration site—and register [to vote]. These would-be-leaders do not understand how Sojourner Truth, while attending a suffrage convention—listening to endless speeches on the need for voting privileges for white women—banged her breast and proclaimed, but ain't I a woman too. I can remember my own

family members being denied voting privileges for want of a $3.00 poll tax. I would submit that others, lacking access to the process of political sophistication, also recollect the pre-voting rights atrocities. My personal affirmation of my Afro-American history and cultural heritage places me on the side of those who have worked and suffered for our overdue gains. To do less would be unethical, unthinkable, and a personal sin against my commitment to the struggle for human rights. (Dell Papers)

Dell's victimization in her reelection bid may also have stemmed from her point of entry into Richmond's electoral politics. She was inspired to run for political office because the local welfare department attempted to abolish its general relief program, and she knew that would adversely impact poor African Americans. Dell responded to this crisis by first trying to lobby city council members on behalf of welfare recipients. City council responded to Dell's efforts by simply ignoring her pleas, because a majority of the members of city council in 1972 accepted the negative stereotypes about welfare recipients as "just want[ing] to drink beer, make babies, shoot crap and drive fine cars" (Marsh 1984, 38–39). Dell's unsuccessful attempt to persuade council to help the welfare recipients forced her to return home that evening and ponder whether or not she should run for elective office. When Dell returned home, her husband and James Carpenter, a white member of city council, tried to convince her to run for office. Although Carpenter and her husband tried desperately to persuade her to run, Dell was not fully convinced that she should seek office (Marsh 1984). However, white and black elected officials, and black established leaders, refused to address the impending welfare crisis, and after having a long discussion with her husband, Dell decided to run for political office. Dell's decision to run is related to her concern for gender related matters because it reveals the sexism within the black community toward those black women who sought political office without either obtaining endorsement or encouragement from the black political establishment of Richmond.

Sexism also became a factor in Dell obtaining a seat on city council (Dell interview 1997). According to Dell, when city councilman James Carpenter resigned in 1973 to pursue missionary work in Ecuador, his seat on council remained vacant for almost a month. Dell was contemplating whether to seek appointment, but she initially waited for someone from the RCV or the black political establishment to endorse her. When no endorsement occurred, she decided to pursue the vacant seat on her own. According to Dell's personal papers, she had announced her candidacy for city council the previous year. But Dell had to wait a year because "the courts had enjoined local elections, the city council was still authorized to fill any vacancies by appointing replacement" (Moeser and Dennis 1982, 170). The city could not hold elections because of Curtis Holt's initial lawsuit against Richmond's annexation scheme. Dell's papers clearly reflect her concern over waiting a year to seek a council seat: "When the councilmanic election was stayed one year ago—I was a candidate for city council. I have remained a candidate for city council since I initially filed! In view of the vacancy that will be created by Mr. Carpenter's resignation—I am again announcing my interest in securing a seat on council. I know council in filing this vacancy will act equally responsible. As a previously announced candidate, I would like to be among the number of individuals they consider for this seat" (Dell Papers).

Dell's comments reveal her trepidation. She knew that as a woman, she had to campaign twice as hard as a man just to be considered a prospective candidate for appointment to council. The only support for Dell's candidacy was made public on April 17, 1972, when WANT, a black radio station in Richmond, first aired its endorsement of Dell. The radio editorial expressed the following about the importance of a Dell appointment to city council in 1973:

> Women have demonstrated time and time again that they are equal to the task of government, whether it be on a local, state or federal level. We feel this way about Willie Dell. . . . A black political newcomer. . . . Who has the background that more than qualifies her for a council seat. Mrs. Dell is an assistant professor in social work at VCU and she has participated in a host of community organizations, including the Urban League. Mrs. Dell believes in the little city hall concept and she is further convinced that by working together. . . . Richmond citizens can help overcome the drug problem, crime, the problems of the aged and the plight of women in our society. Give this woman your vote on May 2nd. (WANT 1972, 1–2)

The pleas from the radio announcement reinforce indirectly the possibility that her gender was preventing Dell from receiving the endorsement of the RCV. Moreover, Dell stated that Ray Boone, then the editor of the *Richmond Free Press*, had told her that then–state senator L. Douglas Wilder had asked Boone, "Who gave her [Dell] permission to submit her name to fill the vacant seat on council?" Dell responded to Boone's statement by informing him that "no one gave Willie Dell permission to seek a seat on council, except God and Willie Dell" (Dell interview 1997). The irony of Wilder's questioning Dell's right to run for political office is that both Boone and Wilder are black, and one would expect them to be supportive of a black candidate for elective office. Their questioning of Dell's right to run for political office is even more contradictory because the only person who not only supported Dell's candidacy without reservation but nominated her to fill his vacant seat on city council was Carpenter, a white former member of city council ("Carpenter Sends Funds to Donor," *Richmond News Leader,* June 2, 1973). In addition, the other person who endorsed Dell's candidacy without any reservation was Holt. Thus, the only plausible explanation of why Boone and Wilder would question Dell's candidacy would be because of her gender and differing political ideology. Dell was subsequently endorsed by the RCV and eventually appointed to the Richmond city council in 1973. Thus, in 1973, she became the first African American woman appointed and/or elected to serve on council. This appointment may have already arouse the ire of Dell' opponents.

By the 1982 election, Dell's opponents had once again targeted her for defeat, and the impact of the election on Dell personally was tremendous. The campaign increased her blood pressure and stress level and produced threats against her life, as well as sexual accusations against her and attacks on her husband's masculinity because she was accused of "wearing the pants" in her household. She was being falsely accused of being the stereotypical "black matriarch" or "sapphire." The use of that stereotype by black men against Dell is consistent with the findings of Paula Giddings, Gayle T. Tate, and Rosalyn Terborg-Penn (Giddings 1984; Tate 1991; Terborg-Penn 1978). As Giddings explains, the negative stereotype of the black sapphire or matriarch has often been a political ploy by black men to prevent independent black women from entering the political arena. It was also frequently a gender red herring to discredit African American women who wanted to be involved in politics. Another factor that impacted the outcome of the 1982 election was the role of black conservatives in the defeat of Dell. ·

The Resurgence of Black Conservative Politics

Throughout the Byrd era, black conservative politics was never dead, but simply dormant, especially during the period of MR, because both parties excluded the participation of blacks at the state and local levels of their respective organizations. Consequently, neither party actively recruited blacks to their respective parties. Furthermore, given the blatant white hostility directed at African Americans in general, black conservatives had no incentives to publicly support the causes of the Byrd machine or Richmond's white elites. Also, since MR coincided with the civil rights movement, the simultaneous occurrence of these two events prevented those black conservatives who might have been inclined to oppose this kind of social movement under normal circumstances from publicly opposing the civil rights movement. Black conservatives were hesitant to openly challenge the civil rights movement because of its religious undertones and moral appeal to white America to correct the social injustices afflicted upon all southern blacks. Even though some black ministers and prominent lay people opposed the civil rights movement, most black ministers in the South were supportive of the movement because of the influence of King and their respective congregations. Black conservatives and/or black Republicans, especially during the 1950s, supported the national Republican party but opposed the state and local Republican party in Virginia because Byrd was supported by the Virginia Republicans and Democrats who supported his MR strategy. Moreover, most black conservatives during this period presumably found it politically undesirable to support the MR strategy adopted by white conservatives. Furthermore, throughout the 1950s, and after the Byrd era, the national Republican Party was basically controlled by the moderate white conservatives, whereas in states like Virginia, and the city of Richmond, the Republican Party was controlled by white political, social, and economic conservatives. Since the white moderate conservatives controlled the national party, and the white social conservatives controlled the state and local organizations, then presumably the moderates during this period were more likely to support such sensitive issues as civil rights. However, at the state level, the social conservatives, who were more conservative than the moderates, opposed civil rights issues and legislation.

Black conservatives found themselves forced to support national Democratic candidates because of the hostility they encountered within their state and local parties. Clarence Towns, an African American and a native Richmonder, was forced to support Lyndon B. Johnson, a Democrat for president, because he felt that he could not consciously support Goldwater, the party's nominee:

> For Virginia Negroes, the Republican National Convention in San Francisco held little hope. Senator Barry Goldwater, who had voted against the 1964 Civil Rights Bill, was nominated on the first ballot. Though his past civil rights record was creditable and he promised to uphold the law, Negroes looked upon him as against civil rights. Clarence Towns, Jr., a Richmond Negro representing the Virginia G.O.P. as an alternate delegate (a history-making precedent, as it is believed he was the first of his race to do so in either party since the turn of the

century), openly stated that he could not follow his fellow delegates as they
voted for Goldwater, 20 to 1. (Buni 1967, 219)

The resurgence of black political conservatives during the 1982 election
was in tandem with the declining influence of the post–civil rights leadership on city council in Richmond.

Meet Candidate West

The loss of the city council's credibility over the Project One issue triggered the resurgence of class bias and black conservative politics in Richmond's African American community (Randolph and Tate 1995). These
two factors triggered the advent of a political novice in Richmond's
black body politic. West was a principal at a middle school in Richmond, a native Richmonder who lived in a quiet middle-class neighborhood in the north part of Richmond (Edds 1987). When West first
ran for public office in Richmond, he was considered a political neophyte, a political unknown to both the white and black political old
guard. He had never been involved in CR, nor had he been identified
with CR groups in the past.

West informed Edds during an interview that he was motivated to
run against Dell because of the infighting that constantly occurred on
city council (143). He entered the political arena in the spring of 1982 to
challenge Dell for the city's District 3 seat. West was described in the
Richmond-Times Dispatch as "an independent thinker and . . . without the
backing of either the predominantly black or predominantly white political organizations" (*Richmond Times-Dispatch,* editorial, 1982). The idea
that West was an unknown political quantity running against city hall
may have been true. However, West's suggestion that he did not have the
political blessing of Richmond's black political establishment was somewhat misleading because he did have the backing of a new black political group called the John Mercer Langston Fund (JMLF), named after
John Mercer Langston, a black Republican who was the first black elected
to Congress during Richmond's reconstruction era. According to Peter
Bailey, a Richmond-based free-lance journalist, the JMLF was established
primarily as "a replacement or contender for political leadership of the
metro area's black community" (1988, 41). The JMLF was established as
a black conservative alternative to the RCV.

West was not an unknown political quantity to Richmond's black
political establishment because he was supported by one of the most
powerful black politicians at the state level, L. Douglas Wilder, then the
only black state senator in the Virginia General Assembly. Thus, we reject

the image of West as a politician who simply came out of nowhere with no political backing to defeat an incumbent member of city council. The significance of discussing whether or not West had political support when he ran against Dell is that we intend to support our claim by demonstrating how West, along with one of his most important supporters, was able to defeat and thus destabilize the first black majority on city council in Richmond. It has consistently been alleged that Wilder undermined Dell's reelection and contributed to the destabilization of the black majority council.

The Wilder Factor

The individual who has frequently been accused by some black and white Richmonders of engineering the defeat of Dell is L. Douglas Wilder, former governor of Virginia and, in 1982, a state senator. Wilder continues to be implicated in Dell's defeat because of the following factors. First, he resided in District 3, which Dell represented, and he publicly disapproved of her leadership style. Wilder also perceived Dell's politics as being too radical, and he did not approve of her wearing African attire to council meetings or her incorrect usage of the English language. Wilder's conservatism is expressed in a *Playboy* interview in 1991 (Range 1991, 70):

> *Playboy:* How do you feel about the nomenclature of race? Is the expression African American important to you?
> *Wilder:* No: when I describe myself it is only as an American. If I got up in the morning thinking I was a particular kind of American—a different American—I couldn't make it. As a matter of fact, it took me some time to get accustomed to black.
> *Playboy:* As opposed to what?
> *Wilder:* Negro.

These views clearly reflect Wilder's conservatism, especially on cultural issues. Thus, he may have treated Dell unfairly during the debate because of his ideological differences with her.

A second reason Wilder continues to be associated with Dell's defeat is because Dell believes Wilder interfered with the election by showing partiality toward her opponent, West, in one of the three candidate debates between Dell and West (Dell interview 1993). The specific debate that Dell refers to was the Ginter Park debate, which was held in the Ginter Park development area of Richmond. According to Dell, she felt that she had been "set-up" for this particular debate because the crowd was predominantly white, and she felt that the audience was drilling her with difficult questions. Moreover, she informed us that she felt that the tone of the crowd was one of anger and hostility toward her. In other words, she did not feel she was in a friendly environment (even inside of her own district). Dell may have thought this particular debate was staged because when the audience was through questioning her, she stated that Wilder, the moderator, started to question her. The problem (from Dell's perspective) with Wilder's involvement in the debate was that he raised issues that she had not heard before, even from her own constituents. For instance, Wilder stated that one of the concerns that had been raised about her was that she was not accountable, nor did she return telephone calls to her constituents. Dell informed us that the allegation was incorrect, because she had resigned her faculty position to become a full-time elected official, a part-time job that paid her three thousand dollars less than her former full time position (Dell interview 1993). She further stated that she had a volunteer staff who manned her office when she wasn't available. In addition, she stated that she frequently attended community meetings, she carried business cards with her home phone number and her previous work number, and she installed an answering machine. Dell said that she quit her full-time job because she wanted to be accessible to her constituents. She became increasingly suspicious as the night progressed because she felt that Wilder consistently asked West more general questions, such as "Roy, as a city council member, how would you deal with the business community in Richmond?" Dell stated that because Wilder began to ask these kinds of questions more frequently, she became suspicious and eventually was convinced that Wilder was not being fair to her during the debate. It appears from this account that Dell believes that Wilder may have been moderating the debate with ulterior motives.

Information from the RCVA files suggests that Wilder was involved in Dell's defeat. The information included minutes from the RCV Executive Committee meeting, dated July 24, 1982, which was held at the Southern Aid Life Insurance Company building in Richmond. According to the minutes of that meeting, state senator Wilder was allowed time to offer his personal reflection on the RCV. During Wilder's talk, his involvement in the 1982 election was asked about by an unidentified person from the audience. Below is the exchange that occurred between Wilder and the unidentified questioner, then between Wilder and Dell:

Unidentified Questioner: [Was] there a defection from the Crusade for Voters on the part of Senator L. Douglas Wilder?

Wilder: This is not so. I was not satisfied with representation in the district. Willie Dell is not my choice was my statement to the former Mayor. . . . If endorsed by the Crusade I would not support her but would not make a statement against her. There has been no defection.

Dell: Why [didn't] you support me?

Wilder: I will get with you later. (RCV Archives)

The exchanges between Wilder and the anonymous questioner and Dell are relevant to our discussion because they reveal that Wilder obviously was not supportive of Dell. Consequently, if he was not supportive of her, one has to question his objectivity in the West-Dell debates. Furthermore, Wilder's response to Dell's question about why he didn't support her was vague at best, and to this day, Dell has yet to have that "I will get with you later" meeting with Wilder.

A final factor that may have contributed to Dell's defeat and to the destabilization of the black majority council was the unofficial political rivalry between Wilder and Marsh. Although Marsh and Wilder were both Democrats, they were still political rivals. One could assert that as the first African American mayor of Richmond, Marsh surpassed Wilder in political stature (El-Amin interview 1991; Moeser interview 1991; Silver interview 1991). Marsh's political stock increased during the time he was first elected mayor of Richmond because he was being politically courted very heavily by the Carter administration and, as a result, was beginning to receive more media attention (Moeser interview 1991). Dell and Moeser, both revealed to us that Marsh was offered a federal judgeship by the Carter administration during the late 1970s. He eventually turned it down because he believed that he could have the greatest impact on people's lives at the local level. Thus Wilder may have envied the attention being given to Marsh during the late 1970s and early 1980s.

Dell explains that the rift between Marsh and Wilder may also have been precipitated by Marsh's failure to attend a summit meeting between the black majority on council and Wilder, then a state senator. According to Dell, Wilder summoned the black majority council members to meet with him behind closed doors in his senate office. Three of the majority agreed to meet him, but not Marsh and Dell. According to Dell, the events of that meeting transpired in the following manner. Dell refused to meet with Wilder, the reason being that the black majority on council had a rule that members of council could not discuss council business with nonmembers. Consequently, Dell surmised that when she informed Wilder of the council rule, she may have angered him, and, in doing so, may have gotten herself into political "hot water" with Wilder. Dell asserts that Wilder's personal indignation toward her and Marsh for refusing to meet with him, along with his inability to persuade the black majority on council to accept his advice in dealing with the political stalemate caused by the Project One controversy, may have prompted him to surreptitiously support West for council, thus indirectly contributing to the destabilization of the black majority council (Dell interview 1992). Although Wilder denies this allegation, some leaders in both the black and white communities believe that he did this. In fact, a similar scenario was described by some unidentified black leaders in an interview with Juan Williams, a writer with the *Washington Post:*

> After he was first elected to the state Senate he kept his hand in Richmond city politics by campaigning against the Crusade for Voters, a group that increased black voter registration and turn-out and had also worked to get Wilder elected. He refused to support the crusade's candidate in the City Council elections, and his candidate, Roy West, won. Thus, according to Richmond sources, Wilder told West, a black newcomer on the council, that he need not support incumbent Henry Marsh, the city's first black mayor, when the council selected a mayor. (Wilder denies this). The loss of West's vote meant defeat for Marsh, a law school classmate of Wilder and a dominant black political figure who, perhaps not coincidentally, overshadowed Wilder. After Marsh's loss, Wilder was left as the top black official in the city and state. (Williams 1991, 16)

Wilder's alleged intervention in the 1982 city council election was also corroborated by Oliver Hill, a prominent black attorney, famed civil rights lawyer, and the first black city council member in Richmond since Reconstruction. In "Did He Sell Out to the Whites?" an article which appeared in the *Washington Post,* Hill questioned Wilder's motives: "Regardless of what advice he did or did not give to West, a lot of black Richmonders want to know why Wilder did not support Marsh, particularly considering the respective qualifications of the two men" (1982, 60).

If one accepts the previously mentioned scenario as a plausible motivation for Wilder's alleged support of West, one must still explain why Dell, not Marsh, was targeted for defeat, especially if Marsh was the one with whom Wilder was upset. One explanation is that Dell was perceived by her adversaries as being politically vulnerable. For instance, her district had been redrawn to include more middle-class blacks, who did not support her, and more whites, who in the past had strongly opposed the

Marsh administration. It is possible that Dell may ultimately have been targeted by black conservatives for gender reasons because they may have realized that Dell was easier to defeat than Marsh.

Thus, based upon Wilder's behavior in the Dell/West debate, along with the material from the RCVA, one could interpret his actions as being biased against Dell. If Dell's allegation is true, then these kinds of charges simply reinforce the suspicions about Wilder's role and substantiate claims that he encouraged Roy West to challenge Dell. For instance, Dell stated that she was accused by her challenger of being everything from racist toward whites to being unresponsive to the needs of her own district.

TABLE 8

Number of Dell's Appointments to Richmond Boards and Commissions, by Race and Gender, 1975–1982

Whites		Blacks	
Men	Women	Men	Women
21	17	44	40

Source: Office of the City Clerk, Richmond, Va., 1975–82.

The accusation of Dell being antiwhite simply was groundless, as table 8 indicates. She appointed almost forty whites to posts during her tenure on city council, and she appointed a sizable number of women to boards and commissions. She supported just as many men as women. Thus, her opponent's allegation that Dell was racist was misleading and unfair.

We maintain that given the unpopularity of the Marsh administration with which Dell had become associated, and with the attacks by West, along with various black professional groups' and the media's endorsements of West, it was impossible for her to mount a successful counterattack against West or to launch a successful reelection campaign. Additionally, Dell was defeated because of low voter turnout among her own supporters and because of the strong anti-Marsh sentiment, especially among white voters who were exploited by her opponent. All of these factors enabled West and his black conservative allies to defeat Dell during the 1982 city council election.

DESTABILIZATION OF THE BLACK MAJORITY

Roy West, a conservative candidate, was elected mayor of Richmond in 1982 (Moeser interview 1989). According to Moeser, some African American leaders strongly suggested that West was elected mayor by politically aligning himself with the white council members, thus weakening the political leverage of the black majority on council (Moeser interview 1989). Moeser's statement is corroborated even further by El-Amin, Williams, Jewell, and Lee, who informed us that West's action did in fact precipitate the downfall of the first black majority on council (El-Amin interview 1991; Williams interview 1991; Moeser interview 1991; Lee interview 1991; Jewell interview 1991). These observers believed that West was manipulated by the white elites.

Although West may have been manipulated by the efforts of some conservative whites in Richmond's political arena, there is a possible alternative explanation for what happened: West may have been a willing participant in a brokered political deal between himself and the white conservatives who wished to regain control of city council. He may have been motivated to align himself with the white conservatives because he might have perceived himself as possibly being isolated on council by the remaining black members. This point can be partially corroborated by Franklin Gales, former city treasurer and supporter of Marsh, who offered his explanation of why West may have entered into this political deal. Gales states that he and some other African American leaders tried to arrange a private meeting between Marsh and West, after West had defeated Dell in the election. According to Gales, the black leaders tried to persuade Marsh to meet with West for the purpose of resolving their political and personal differences behind closed doors. In other words, Gales thought that if Marsh had extended open arms to West, then West might have aligned himself with the Marsh camp instead of with the conservative white members of council. Gales concluded that because Marsh failed to meet with West shortly after the election, then West may have interpreted Marsh's inaction as a political snubbing.

Thus, it appears that West may have felt that he had no alternative but to vote with the whites, thus accepting their alleged political deal. Consequently, when West voted with the white members of council, the white members may have nominated him for mayor, perhaps because of his conservative views and because the white members saw the defeat of Dell and the election of West as their window of opportunity to unseat Marsh (Moeser interview 1991; Lee interview 1991; Gales interview 1993). West broke the tie by voting to make himself mayor, casting the fifth and deciding vote (Edds 1987). Consequently, when West became mayor, a clear political signal had been sent to Richmond's white elites that King Henry Marsh was dethroned and that they could conduct business as usual.

It appears that West's reasons for aligning himself with the white minority members of council may never be fully known; nevertheless, we believe that white manipulation of West, along with West's personal political agenda, were probably the motivating forces behind his decision to align himself with the white minority council members. Although race may not have been the most visible factor in West's decision to enter the campaign or in Dell's defeat, the polarizing climate that was prevalent in Richmond at that time, along with some white business leaders' unrelenting decision to support conservative black candidates against an incumbent like Dell, illustrates their determination to undermine the black majority on council and restore white control.

Eventually, black political class schisms led to the demise of the black majority on city council. Other sources corroborated our argument when they suggested that Dell lost because upper- and middle-class African American women rejected her heavy emphasis on issues of race, class, and gender. She lost by three hundred votes as an incumbent (Randolph and Tate 1995). African American community activists believe that Dell's election loss was a major contributing factor to the demise of the African American majority on city council. According to Saad El-Amin, "The Crusade at one time was probably the best example of the use of African American bloc voting in the United States, says Saad El-Amin. Dell, whose defeat by West is considered by some to have signaled the beginning of the Crusade's decline" (Bailey 1988, 42). El-Amin's sentiments concerning the political cost of Dell's defeat to the RCV in 1982 were echoed by William S. Thornton, one of the group's founding members: "Our major mistake was being so confident of a Willie Dell victory over Roy West in the 1982 City Council race that we didn't put forth our best effort" (ibid.). Dell was a strong supporter of racial solidarity as well as social reform for poor Richmonders. With the exception of Marsh, Dell was the most outspoken leader on city council (Randolph and Tate 1995). With Dell's removal from city council, the conservative white members of the council entered into a political alliance with Roy West and created a new conservative majority (ibid.).

The new conservative majority on council tried to restore the council's credibility with Richmond's white economic elites by publicly declaring that the Marsh era was officially over and they would work more closely with the private sector, especially on development matters (Williams 1990). Under the West administration, council was far less confrontational with economic elites than the previous city administration. The economic elites regained political control of the city by forming alliances with African American conservatives and financially supporting conservative African American politicians. Dell's defeat and the subsequent election of West as council member and mayor of Richmond produced additional problems for Richmond's African Americans. First, Dell's defeat contributed to a resurgence of conservative African American politics in Richmond, most noticeably with the election of West and with the emergence of conservative African American political groups such as JMLF (Bailey 1988). In essence, Richmond's African American conservative elites defeated Dell. Their participation in her defeat was a confirmation that they agreed with the white economic elites that her political views were simply too radical. Second, the conflicting political agendas of the black conservatives and black progressives during the 1982 election precipitated the reappearance of the double agenda. Moreover, the double agenda that appeared supported our earlier claim that the progressive agenda was highly visible in Richmond's black body politic, whereas the black conservative agenda that emerged in 1982 was unmistakably shrouded. Although the black conservative agenda was hidden, the outcome of that agenda was the destabilization of the first black majority on city council. Third, the African American elite's rejection of the progressive politics of individuals such as Dell also led to the disintegration of the first black majority on city council. Therefore, with the defeat of Dell and the election of West, the black majority on city council was destabilized and no longer effective. Furthermore, with the resurgence of black conservative politics and African American elite participation in the 1982 election, Richmond's black body politic was undergoing restructuring. This shift in the political and policy direction of council as a result of the election had short- and long-term implications for the city.

POLITICAL AND POLICY IMPLICATIONS OF THE 1982 AND 1984 ELECTIONS

Short-Term Ramifications of the 1982 Election

One of the immediate ramifications of the 1982 election was the reappearance of the black political schisms that have historically emerged to divide Richmond's black community. The black political schism that divided Richmond's black body politic in 1982 was the double agenda. As we have suggested throughout our research, the double agenda has often involved the illumination of two conflicting political agendas, the black progressive and conservative political. We maintain that the progressive agenda of the Marsh-led black majority on council was a highly visible one involving black political empowerment, which initially appeared during MR under the auspices of the RCV. The agenda was nurtured and aided by positive governmental intervention throughout the civil rights era. Furthermore, it culminated in 1977 with the election of Richmond's first black majority on city council. The progressive agenda that was in place during the 1982 election was the RCV's agenda for black political empowerment. This agenda was controversial at times because throughout its existence, it and the RCV's agenda were often perceived by blacks as being one in the same. This meshing of the two agendas can be traced to Virginia's repressive era, when the RCV was the point organization that often spearheaded the fight for black political empowerment. As the RCV evolved throughout the civil rights era and into the post–civil rights era, so did the progressive agenda. By 1982, the progressive agenda would be externally rejected by Richmond's white elites and subsequently politically challenged from within Richmond's black body politic by the conservative agenda.

We have demonstrated throughout our research that the black conservative agenda has generally been shrouded because of the political and ideological differences that have always existed in Richmond's black body politic. Moreover, the interests of the black conservative agenda are generally incongruous with those of Richmond's black community. When the black conservative agenda has been implemented, it has generally produced negative consequences for Richmond's black community because it essentially has been an agenda of accommodation. Thus, given Richmond's black political history, when the black community has been presented with an accommodationist political agenda, they have generally rejected it. Therefore, we contend that the black conservative agenda that was prevalent in 1982 was shrouded to conceal its accommodation-ist objective. The battle that occurred in the election was precipitated by the two conflicting agendas. Subsequently, the agenda that won out in the short run in Richmond in 1982 was the conservative agenda. The short-term ramification of that agenda was the election of West and the eventual destabilization of the first black majority on city council. The election of West would also reveal the existence of a political coalition between black conservatives and white conservatives, which we believe accomplished the ultimate objectives of those white elites who were determined to regain political control of city government. Our position regarding the ultimate objectives of black and white conservatives can be corroborated by Oliver Hill's comments in the newspaper magazine *Close to Home*. According to Hill, "That is one of the things that makes West's acceptance of the power play by his white carry-me-back-to-the-pre-ward-days supporters so tragic. It serves to strengthen their resolve to keep blacks in their place. Before July 1, Richmond stood as a splendid example of how blacks, through unity, could use the political process to improve the atmosphere of a city. In a single day, Roy West destroyed what took many years to build" (Hill 1982, B8).

The next political ramification that emerged from the 1982 election, which is related to the first, was the impact of Dell's defeat on Richmond's black body politic. The political ramifications of Dell's defeat can be explained thusly. In the short run, her defeat contributed to the resurgence of black conservative politics. The resurgence of black conservative politics became most noticeable through the emergence of such groups as JMLF. Consequently, black conservatives have reasserted their presence in Richmond's black body politic. Dell's defeat also led to the return of black elite control over Richmond's black body politic and enabled Richmond's white elites to exploit politically a divided black community and regain political control of the city. The black conservatives' defeat of Dell ultimately contributed to the demise of the first black majority on city council, which was replaced by a West-led white conservative majority when West was elected mayor.

Finally, the one political and policy ramification of the 1982 election was the city of Richmond losing the lawsuit in the Project One controversy. Moreover, through an agreement signed by West but opposed by Marsh and the remaining black members of city council, the city had to pay $5 million dollars to the Hilton chain. Thus, the immediate ramification of the city settling the lawsuit was that it revealed a political split between West and the remaining members of the original black majority, foreshadowing the division that was maintained throughout West's first term in office. The West-led white conservative majority on council restored the council's credibility with the white business and corporate elites, and were less confrontational with the elites, publicly declaring that the Marsh era was officially over and that they would work more closely with the private sector, especially on development matters (Moeser interview 1990; Williams interview 1991). Reestablishing much of a prior political relationship in which, according to Turpin and Towns, city hall and Richmond's white business and corporate elites were seen as one, the conservative majority on council declared that the Marsh era was over, and so was the season for black political empowerment.

Long-Term Ramifications of the 1982 Election

The first long-term political ramification of the 1982 election was the establishment of a political alliance between black and white conservatives. This alliance created a political climate in which it was increasingly difficult for future progressive black candidates to emerge and get elected to city council, especially in districts such as District 3. Moreover, as long as white conservative voters remain as the swing vote in districts like District 3, liberal black candidates will find it difficult to get elected to council. This particular long-term political ramification has stymied progressive leadership in key districts. In 1984 Dell challenged West in the District 3 city council election seeking to regain her seat. Although the 1984 election had a low voter turnout, Dell's defeat was convincing. For instance, Dell won 36 percent of the total votes cast, while West won 56 percent of the 8,791 total votes cast (RCV Archives). Moreover, Dell was unable to regain her old seat on council because she suffered lopsided losses again in the same upper-middle-class black and conservative white precincts that contributed to her defeat in 1982. Second, two months before the election Dell had raised only $8,700 dollars to run her campaign, whereas West raised approximately $32,000 dollars to run his reelection campaign (CVSBOE Records). It is possible that West was able to amass such a large campaign war chest because in 1982 he was a political novice; however, by 1984, West was a known political quantity and, consequently, he received more campaign contributions than Dell from private businesses inside and outside of Richmond (CVSBOE Records). In addition, West received large contributions from black conservative groups such as the JMLF, which donated $1,000 to his reelection campaign (Campbell 1984; CVSBOE Records 1984). West's alliance with white conservatives even netted him $500 from J. Smith Ferebee, a white conservative businessman who was a staunch supporter of the Byrd organization and had strong ties to Richmond's main-street elites (Campbell 1984). If this trend continues, liberal candidates will find it increasingly difficult to get elected to city council and black conservatives will remain a political force in Richmond's black body politic.

Another long-term political ramification of the 1982 election was the subsequent near-absence of roles for African American women in city politics. When Dell ran against West in the next election, she was soundly defeated. Since her second defeat, Dell has been reluctant to reenter the local political arena (Dell interview 1991). In essence, what appears to be missing from Richmond's political scene is a strong black female presence advocating for the rights of the poor, women, and children. With Dell's defeats in 1982 and 1984, the chief advocate for the poor, women, and children was gone from the political landscape.

A third long-term political ramification of the 1982 election was the coalition that seems to have emerged between conservative black Republicans and conservative black Democrats to the detriment of the black community. Liberal candidates now faced the uphill battle of campaigns against their opponent and their own party as well. The fourth ramification suggests a possible restructuring, yet again, of politics in Richmond. Following the 1982 election, West experienced a negative reaction from some black leaders as well as community residents with regards to his decision to align himself with the white conservatives on council and install himself as mayor. He was publicly attacked in the media by the chair of the RCV and by the president of the Baptist Ministers Conference. Norvell Robinson, board chairman of the RCV, publicly criticized West when he stated that "West is an extension of the people that chastised and lambasted blacks over the years" (Edds 1987, 145). Miles Jones, president of the black Baptist Minister's Conference, criticized West's alignment with whites on council, stating, "Our political strength has been decimated under West's leadership" (145).

The final long-term political ramification of the 1982 election was the emergence of four distinct political camps in the RCV: liberals, conservatives, moderates, and cultural nationalists. We assert that the emergence of these four camps is a reflection of the factionalism prevalent in Richmond's African American community in general (Moeser and Dennis 1982). Furthermore, we believe that a combination of two of the four political camps might eventually compete against one another for dominance over the RCV and may compete against each other for city council elections. If the criticism of West persists, it may force younger black and white liberals of the post–civil rights era to form biracial alliances to run for council seats and reinstate progressive developmental policy for the city.

Our research revealed that race is not universally dominant in most of the illustrations that were presented in this chapter. If racial tension spills over into politics when the class interests of the white and African American elites are congruent, then the event is no longer confined to race solely, but instead involves class and race. Furthermore, if the political stakes involved are high enough, then class and gender factors could occasionally supplant race as the more salient issues. In addition, our study found that race is generally a dominant factor in the political process. When African Americans in Richmond were no longer willing to accept political subordination to the white elites, race was a highly salient issue. When the black majority on city council passed an ordinance to prevent the area surrounding Project One from being oversaturated, racism was used by whites as a divisive strategy to counter the decision. As one observer of Richmond politics astutely stated, "Economic power had run into political power and had lost" (Moeser and Dennis 1982, 181). Race had been used to elect a black majority on city council just as it was used by reactionary conservative whites to exploit a divided African American community and, with the assistance of African American conservatives, to destabilize the black majority on city council.

Our study of Richmond reveals a city still divided by race. It also exposes the problems of class and gender, which we maintain are deeply rooted in the African American community, especially as they pertain to women, traditional "southern etiquette," and, most certainly, electoral politics. Finally, the impact of race, class, and gender on the rise and decline of the black political majority on council was paramount in this study. The political dilemma facing blacks is that an increase in the number of blacks in political positions did not immediately lead to restructuring of the social and economic imbalances that still plague many black communities.

When black political elites helped destabilize the black majority on council, what political messages did this convey to rank-and-file black voters? In other words, did this action convey a signal to the black public that premier black political leadership cannot be counted on? If this kind of message is being conveyed, what are the implications for black leaders in general? Our study suggests that the political reliability of the leadership remains a critical issue in the African American community. Finally, the demise of the black majority on council led to the resurgence of black conservatism. The revival of the black and white conservative political alliance could create a political climate that will make it increasingly difficult for future progressive black leaders to emerge and challenge Richmond's white and black political establishments. If liberal and progressive candidates are to mount such electoral challenges, biracial support may be critical.

Conclusion

This book has explored periods of black mobilization—resistance, social mobilization, and political mobilization—that overarched the political and economic struggle between the white established elite and African Americans in the course of several centuries. In every sense, these are overlapping periods of struggle and development, thereby giving each stage its dialectical character, as African Americans continually defined and redefined freedom in a hostile environment. Undoubtedly, a prevailing theme that shaped racial relations in Richmond and elsewhere in Virginia is the racism that is diffused throughout the society. Thus, as African Americans struggled, initially for freedom, then social change, and finally for access to power and political and social resources, they continually altered the city's political landscape. This struggle was never defined in a vacuum but drew on the larger international and regional struggles that are significant in understanding the development of Virginia's culture and politics and its pervasive influence on the city of Richmond.

The enslavement of Africans in the Virginia Colony in 1619 presaged a turbulent history of black struggle, white oppression, and the assumption of power being played out against the vagaries of cash crop commodity production. As Virginia engaged in the construction of a slave society, with its laws, statutes, and customs that determined the nature and context of the economic exploitation of African peoples, these strangers were eventually stripped of all of their human dignity and rights. In their transformation from African peoples identifiable by their ancestral homeland markings, they became chattel property in the American colonies, to be bought and sold on the auction block, and singular in their economic importance in the marketplace. African slaves labored primarily as agriculturalists on Virginia plantations, planting, cultivating the soil, harvesting the crops, and processing the cash crop of tobacco, and sometimes wheat and corn, for domestic and international markets.

In effect, their labor created not only a sustainable economy but also a white planter aristocracy.

By the end of the seventeenth century, Virginia had solidified its slave system of racial and sexual subordination of African peoples. This formative period of development already evinced the complexities of race, sex, and class as black men and women laborers were embedded into the slave system and southern culture. For the white planter elite, southern culture was merely a manifestation of the emerging ideology of white supremacy, which not only gave whites a notion of entitlement but also served to legitimize and validate the institutionalization of slavery and the racial inferiority of blacks. By extension, all nonwhites, those who constituted the "other," also were racially inferior under this cultural hegemony. It typified what Antonio Gramsci denoted as "an order in which a certain way of life and thought is dominant, in which one concept of reality is diffused throughout society in all its institutional and private manifestations, informing with its spirit all taste, morality, customs, religious and political principles, and all social relations, particularly in their intellectual and moral connotation" (Williams 1960, 587).

The incipient form of mobilization was the resistance of the slaves. As slaves forged their transatlantic community of survival and resistance (an act of sheer defiance that was reinforced, unwittingly, by slave owners), they were simultaneously empowered to overtly and covertly struggle against the slave institution. The melding, then, of disparate African cultures, religions, and traditions fortified the slave community for continuous development and resistance. Although slave resistance was facilitated by "autonomous spaces" in the slave quarters, it was circumscribed by the labor arrangements and terrain. Daily resistance primarily turned on an individual person or a small group of trusted family members and friends and employed several different forms—feigning illness, sabotaging farm equipment, arson, poisoning the master, and running away. Dramatic resistance, in contrast, depended on the collective mobilization of a group of slaves, with an indigenous leader who initiated and led in the planning, organizing, and implementation of the rebellion.

The next phase of resistance was urban resistance, forged by slaves and free blacks, in the city of Richmond. This resistance evinced a broad range of initiatives, including large-scale, organized rebellions, runaways on the Underground Railroad, and building the institutional infrastructure of the antebellum black community. Despite the difference between urban resistance and plantation resistance, urban resistance was an organic continuum of slave struggle being waged on Richmond's terrain.

Urban resistance, a conscious effort of both slaves and free blacks to liberate the slaves, was facilitated by Richmond's industrialization and the city's use of both groups as laborers in their factories. The overtime monies, the independent living arrangements, and the autonomous lifestyle, typical of most urban workers, enhanced their desire for freedom. Paralleling their plantation slave counterparts, they created a community in a hostile urban environment that provided its members with a common source of inspiration and resistance. "The urban environment moreover permitted many runaways to find a sanctuary within municipal boundaries, either by hiding out in some obscure place or with the connivance of other blacks," notes Wade (1964, 214). From that community and nearby plantations, rebel leaders drew their participants for rebellions and other acts of resistance.

Comparable resistance efforts waged by slaves, as well as by free blacks, in other southern cities and in the Western Hemisphere inspired black Richmonders in their struggle to weaken the slave system. The Haitian Revolution, for example, inspired the attempted uprisings of the Secret Keepers and Gabriel Prosser's conspiracy, as the participants perceiving a diaspora connection between the two struggles. Despite diligent legal restraints, slave rebellions were connected with most southern cities. "Among the first was the largest—an uprising in 1811 of close to four hundred slaves in St. Charles and St. John the Baptist parishes in Louisiana," notes Deborah White. "Led by a slave named Charles Deslondes, the slaves sent whites fleeing their plantations for safety in New Orleans" (2000, 197). In 1822, the Denmark Vesey rebellion in Charleston, South Carolina, which included thousands of slaves and free blacks, was simultaneously a source of fear in southern slaveholders and inspiration to black resisters.

Within the larger pattern of resistance, black Richmonders are a part of the more comprehensive struggle by African Americans for human dignity and freedom. The dialectical relations between black resistance and white hegemonic rule created the conditions for a protracted struggle. If black resistance is a struggle for freedom that has endured for centuries on these shores against formidable odds, and we hold that it is, then it plays the critically defining role in the substantive changes in the material conditions and political status of African Americans. The evolutionary development of black resistance creates much of the impetus for black political development and social change in the body politic.

Social mobilization, then, is part of the organic continuum of resistance and was contoured by the antebellum collective activation efforts of black Richmonders. The new status of blacks subsequent to emancipation on April 3, 1965, was viewed as a gift from God, who had heard their prayers and had not abandoned them, as well as a result of their own prodigious resistance. The results of social mobilization efforts of black Richmonders immediately after they obtained their freedom, whether focused on the abolishment of the "pass system" or the desegregation of the city's streetcars, were not only their rights as citizens but, just as important, social justice for an enduring struggle. Social mobilization was critical in creating a cohesive community, in reestablishing black churches as "communication centers," and in creating a forum for strategies of social protest. By extension, the four hundred secret societies that emerged in Richmond's black community within a decade of emancipation were conduits for the collective mobilization of community residents.

Political mobilization resulted in a trajectory that led from black Richmonders' participation in the Republican party directly after emancipation to their participation in the CRM in 1960. This development came in stages, most often truncated by white radical resistance to social equality, and this "aggrieved population" attempted to make use of several political venues to engender social and political equality. One venue was the Republican party, which, though desperate to garner power in the South, activated black participation only when necessary and thereafter marginalized black political participation. Another venue was black participation in the labor union movement and sporadic attempts at biracial coalitions, which expanded the political consciousness and development of blacks but left them with few political and social resources. Thus, the rise in economic nationalism in the 1880s and 1890s, touted by the "new issue" blacks as well as recognized leaders such as Booker T. Washington, was as much an attempt at self-determination as it was the realization that disenfranchisement, and, concomitantly, social segregation were facts of life. It was the protracted legal struggle, however, by black Richmonders in concert with the NAACP in the early 1900s to dismantle segregation, step by tedious legal step, that planted the seeds of the later protest movement.

Although the Baton Rouge bus boycott that began in June 1953, initiating the mass consumer boycotts against segregated city transportation systems, was eclipsed by the *Brown* decision, it ushered in a new phase of political mobilization. Aldon D. Morris noted that "it was the Baton Rouge movement, largely without assistance from outside elites, that opened the direct action phase of the modern civil rights movement" (1984, 25). These events, coupled with the lynching of

Emmett Till in Money, Mississippi, and the courageous resistance of Rosa Parks, sparked the Montgomery bus boycott in 1955. This organized, non-violent, direct-action strategy, which captured international media attention, pitted a courageous but embattled people against southern white intransigence. As the movement spread throughout the South, the coalescing of the media attention, the dignity of Rosa Parks, and the indefatigable leadership of Reverend Martin Luther King Jr. forced the question of the civil rights of blacks on the national political agenda.

Richmond's CRM was sparked by the longstanding grievances against the "tripartite system of domination," the increasing vulnerability of the system, and by the sit-ins of the Virginia Union University students to desegregate the downtown lunch counters. Morris argued that the segregation system, in circumscribing blacks "economically, politically, and personally," created "an arrangement that set blacks off from the rest of humanity and labeled them as an inferior race" (1984, 1–3). Earlier individual resistance by black women, then, proved critical to the movement in locating the system's vulnerability, in effect fortifying the community for struggle and serving as "bridge leaders" to sustain the mass boycott against the downtown department stores. Although the "front" leadership was male, women and students were the center of the movement. The simultaneous launching of a boycott against the Springer Drug Store chain by working-class activists indicated a complementary political mobilization strategy toward collective goals while crystallizing class and gender cleavages in the community.

Richmond's CRM evinced a pattern of political activity similar to that of other southern cities in that it had indigenous black male leadership at the helm, whereas the organizing, mobilizing of the community, and marching placed women and students in the forefront; it was dissimilar in that it started five years after the larger movement had gathered its momentum from the Montgomery bus boycott movement. Critical, too, was the fact that the larger civil rights movement was entering its second phase—"the movement within the movement," that is, the sit-ins spearheaded by college students—when the Richmond local movement was initiated. This suggests further exploration. For example, was the period of "quiet integration" so effective in Richmond that it destabilized the collective activation in the black community? Or was the massive resistance by the Byrd machine so egregious as to truncate earlier black political development? Was the organizing direction of the Richmond Crusade for Voters, whose early emphasis was on voter registration, due to disparate classes of the community? And, finally, were

the existing class and gender cleavages a major deterrent to unified protest strategies?

The legal dismantling of segregation by the U.S. Supreme Court
facilitated the combined efforts of the RCV and grass-roots organizer
Curtis Holt to enfranchise black voters. The two-pronged approach (the
RCV politically mobilizing the community around electoral participation and Holt's initiating a legal challenge to the annexation of Chesterfield County) was successful. The change in the city's representation
from an at-large system with marginal black participation to a nine-seat
single-member system increased black representation on the city council. The 1977 special council election on March 8, 1977, resulted in a
black majority council and the election of the first African American
mayor, Henry Marsh.

The takeover of city government by a black political majority, representing a journey of several centuries, was short-lived, lasting only five
years. Embroiled in a political struggle with the white establishment that
had always possessed hegemonic rule over the city, the Project One controversy symbolized the warring factions for control of city government.
Despite the more progressive proposal by the black majority city council,
a neighborhood revitalization program that would ultimately stimulate
business and social-welfare initiatives, the signs foreshadowing the demise
of the council were already in place. In the wake of controversy (particularly the $5 million lawsuit by Hilton Hotel against the city, ultimately
paid by the next mayor, Roy West), the negative portrayal of the council
in the media, which fed the public's lost confidence in the body, contributed to its demise.

When black Richmonders were battling a common enemy, class and
gender cleavages were somewhat muted; however, these antagonistic
tensions resurfaced in the community, stifling political development
when the storm had passed. As the strength of the black majority council began to wane and the white media attacks became more frequent,
the defeat of Willie Dell in her 1982 reelection bid for her council seat
became paramount in the white establishment's strategy to recapture
the city council and destabilize the black majority coalition. In Judith A.
Garber's terms, Dell had gained a reputation through "a gendered division of political labor in local communities" in which "female local
activism, although true leadership in every sense, had tended to mirror
women's domestic concerns" (Garber 1995, 29).

Dell's defeat had all of the earmarks of the interlocking variables
of race, class, and gender and was engineered from several quarters.

Undoubtedly, the redrawing of her district lines to include a more conservative black and white voting bloc increased her political vulnerability. However, Doug Wilder's support of her opponent, black conservative
Roy West, and the lack of support from middle-class and upper-class
black women were major contributing factors. Although Dell's failure to
reach this constituency was problematic, their view of her as an "outsider," born outside of Richmond and not possessing lineage by their
standards, may have already sealed her fate (Randolph and Tate 1995,
148–50). These decidedly class and gender biases were exacerbated by the
low voter turnout from her generally supportive working-class constituency and together were powerful factors in her defeat.

The election of Roy West to the city council led to a biracial conservative coalition of council members, the unseating of Mayor Henry
Marsh, the destabilization of the black majority council, and the resurgence of black conservatism in Richmond. With conservatism once again
the thrust of city government, progressive initiatives, such as minority
set-aside programs for minority contractors, initiated by Henry Marsh
and implemented during the West administration, were challenged and
ruled unconstitutional by the Supreme Court in *Croson v. Richmond*
(Drake and Holsworth 1991). The *Croson* decision further hampered the
redistributive programs for Richmond. Although some black professionals received city contracts after the decision, their professed political loyalties dovetail the mayor's.

Largely, the African American struggle for political and social reform
in Richmond has been circumscribed by white political and economic
domination. This domination has led to antagonistic struggles between
emerging black leadership and established white elites or to collusions
between conservative blacks and whites—blacks to garner some of the
political power and whites to maintain political and economic power
over the city. In either case, the black woman's political voice has been
muted. A question that needs to be explored further is, Does the city
council's more-inclusive reform efforts automatically pit the white elite
against the council's members? Or maybe the larger question is, When
the white elite cannot exercise total economic control over the city's
redistributive policies, does it feel threatened and seek to destroy those
initiatives?

The gender bias in the black community is a manifestation of existing class cleavages. It is exposed in the struggle of the community to
maintain its pseudo trappings of gentility that assuaged the void created
when black Richmonders were denied liberal reforms in the political

arena. In a sense, Willie Dell's defeat was a liberal reform that was denied to the black community. And her case points to the suppression of the black woman's political voice. Although the issues of race, class, and gender were paramount in this study, the use of gender in the political arena as a means to divert attention from the concomitant issues of race and class should be explored further.

The city's future very much depends on the type of biracial political coalitions that will emerge to enable or thwart black political and economic advancement. In a real sense, the allocation of political and economic resources for all of Richmond's citizens is at issue. The larger questions of black economic development, black and white progressive political coalitions, new ideas and initiatives for the city's growth, creative revenue sources to supplant the out-migration of middle-class residents, and social welfare programs for the poor, women, and the elderly are all deeply intertwined in the city's future. If the white business elite continue to promote their singular interests and blacks continue to counter with internal and external discord resulting in political ineffectiveness, then this weak political relationship will ultimately takes its toll on the city's progress.

The May 3, 1994, election of members to the city council not only reflected the voters' frustrations with the current council leadership but also sounded a clarion call for new hope and vision for the city. In the wake of this major election upset, which possibly shifted the balance of power and foreshadows new directions for the council, four incumbents were defeated, including former mayor Roy A. West and Mayor Walter T. Kenney; they were replaced with five newcomers to the political arena. In a letter to the editor of the *Richmond Free Press*, A. D. Smith writes, "Mr. Kenney will go down in history as one who did very little. History will show Roy West to be the black person who was greatly used by whites to divide blacks and destroy black progress in Richmond. That he did very well" (*Richmond Free Press*, May 19–21, 1994, 9).

What may be equally compelling in this critical election was the presence of loosely formed biracial political coalitions of candidates, organizations, and some black and white businessmen, all forming a broad base of support for these new candidates. For example, black businessman Neverett A. Eggleston Jr. from Jackson Ward and white businessman James E. Ukrop, president and CEO of Ukrop's Super Markets, were instrumental in generating voter turnout and funds for those candidates who were promoting social and economic change for the city's growth (*Richmond Times-Dispatch*, May 8, 1994, p. A1). Team for Progress, a white organization and Richmond Crusade for Voters, worked in concert to support viable black and white candidates who were promoting progressive initiatives to address the city's needs (ibid.).

Most noticeably, these political newcomers to the arena were products of desegregation and held the advantages and gains from the national and local civil rights struggle. The new councilman, Timothy M. Kaine, elected to serve in District 2, is reportedly the first progressive white liberal since former councilman James Carpenter, who served in the late 1960s and early 1970s. The new African American councilperson, Viola O. Baskerville, who ousted Roy A. West for leadership of District 3, embodies the new biracial perspective with this comment: "We realize we were all children of the '60s and the '70s, that we were products of desegregation, affirmative action, and that we had a common need to move Richmond in a direction that was positive; that we could do this as a team, black and white" (*Richmond Times-Dispatch,* May 8, 1994, p. A13). While progressive political coalitions are in the nascent phase of development in Richmond's political arena, and it is too early to tell whether they will have staying power or can be used for future comparative analysis with Clarence Stones's *Regime Politics: Governing Atlanta, 1948–1988* (1989) or Marcus Pohlmann and Michael P. Kirby's *Racial Politics at the Crossroads: Memphis Elects Dr. W. W. Herenton* (1996), their philosophical and pragmatic ideas will be needed for resource acquisitions for the city.

Despite the internal schisms in Richmond's black community, the resurgence, in the wake of the 2000 presidential election, of voting rights for African Americans in the South as an issue may render partial dissolution of class and gender tensions and revitalize community political mobilization around voter registration. Allegations of voting intimidation, manipulation, and other irregularities have surfaced in some southern states. Once again, the NAACP and other organizations are exploring the full extent of the issue of black suffrage and suffrage protection for all citizens. The Richmond NAACP Area GOT-V coordinator and other groups requested a public hearing to be conducted by Congressman Bobby Scott on December 18, 2000, to deal with voting irregularities in Richmond on election day. In a profound sense, the black struggle for civil rights and redistributive policies is a never-ending struggle.

Appendix

CITY OF RICHMOND
RICHMOND, VIRGINIA

DEPARTMENT OF PUBLIC SAFETY
BUREAU OF TRAFFIC ENGINEERING
FOURTH FLOOR UTILITIES BLDG.
900 EAST BROAD STREET

October 10, 1963

Mr. Curtis J. Holt
2004 Creighton Road
Richmond, Virginia

Dear Mr. Holt:

This will confirm receipt of the petition submitted to this Office which requests a traffic signal at Creighton Road and Nine Mile Road, and more school signs around Woodville School on Fairfield Avenue and on 28th Street.

All of these requests will be studied and you will be notified of findings and recommendations.

Thank you for your interest in traffic safety.

Sincerely,

John T. Hanna
City Traffic Engineer

GDS:vfo

cc: Traffic Planning Division

Letter of October 10, 1963, sent to Curtis Holt from John T. Hanna, Richmond traffic engineer.

CITY OF RICHMOND
RICHMOND, VIRGINIA

DEPARTMENT OF PUBLIC SAFETY
BUREAU OF TRAFFIC ENGINEERING
FOURTH FLOOR UTILITIES BLDG.
900 EAST BROAD STREET

November 13, 1963

Mr. Curtis J. Holt
2004 Creighton Road
Richmond, Virginia

Dear Mr. Holt:

As you probably know, the Bureau of Traffic Engineering has conducted several traffic surveys at the intersection of Nine Mile Road and Creighton Road relative to the justification for a traffic signal. Our studies indicate that the location meets the minimum warrants for the erection of a signal. In view of this, the Bureau has recommended and the Director of Public Safety has approved the installation of a traffic signal at the intersection. You should be cognizant of the fact that it will require several months for the planning, the purchasing and the erecting of the equipment.

We appreciate your, as well as the other citizens', interest in Public Safety.

Yours truly,

W. F. Thomas
Assistant Traffic Engineer

WFT:es

Letter of November 13, 1963, sent to Curtis Holt from W. F. Thomas, Richmond assistant traffic engineer.

CITY OF RICHMOND
RICHMOND, VIRGINIA

August 10, 1964

Mr. Curtis Holt, Sr.
Civic Leader
2004 Creighton Road
Richmond, Virginia 23223

Dear Mr. Holt:

This will acknowledge your request for the installation of a traffic signal at 29th Street and Nine Mile Road.

This intersection will be added to the list of intersections to be studied relative to the preparation of a new traffic signal priority list.

The studies will begin this fall after the opening of schools. Over fifty intersections will be studied relative to vehicular and pedestrian volumes, speeds, accidents and other factors. The top eight intersections in greatest need will be signalized for approximately $44,000.

You will be advised when the survey is completed.

Very truly yours,

John T. Hanna
City Traffic Engineer

JTH:fc

cc: Traffic Planning Division

Letter of August 10, 1964, sent to Curtis Holt from John T. Hanna, Richmond traffic engineer.

Bibliography

PRIMARY SOURCES

Manuscripts and Record Books

Commonwealth of Virginia State Board of Elections. Report of Campaign Contributions and Expenditures, 1982 (CVSBOE Records). Richmond, Va.

Carwile, Howard H. Papers (Carwile Papers). James Branch Cabell Library, Cabell Black Collection, Virginia Commonwealth Univ., Richmond.

County and City Data Book. 1988. Richmond, Va.

Court Records of Henrico County, 1677–1692. Manuscript. Virginia State Library, Richmond.

"Debates and Proceedings of the Constitutional Convention of the State of Virginia, Assembled at the City of Richmond." 1868. Richmond: Office of the New Nation. Virginia Historical Society.

Dell, Willie. Personal papers and files (Dell Papers). James Branch Cabell Library, Cabell Black Collection, Virginia Commonwealth Univ., Richmond.

Election Data for Richmond City Council Elections. June 9, 1970. Office of the General Registrar, Richmond, Va.

Everett, Waddy. 1919. Maggie Lena Walker National Historic Site, Richmond, Va.

"Federal Industrial Manuscript Census for Richmond City, 1860." Virginia State Library, Richmond.

Flood, Congressman Henry, to R. H. Willis, Feb. 25, 1920 (Flood Papers). Congressman Henry Flood Papers, Manuscript Division, Library of Congress.

Historical Statistics of the United States, Colonial Times to 1970. 1976. Washington, D.C.: U.S. Bureau of the Census.

Office of the City Clerk Records (OCC Records). Office of the City Clerk, City of Richmond, Richmond, Va.

Overby, Ethel Thompson. 1974a. "It's Better to Light a Candle than Curse the Darkness." Original draft of manuscript. Richmond, Va.

Overby, Ethel Thompson. 1974b. "It's Better to Light a Candle: Autobiographical Notes." Original manuscript. Richmond, Va.

Records of the First African Baptist Church of Richmond, Virginia, 1840–1890. Microfilm. The Library of Virginia, Richmond, Va.

Records of the Freedman's Savings Bank, Richmond Branch, 1867–1874. National Archives Records. Microfilm. The Library of Virginia, Richmond, Va.

Richmond Crusade for Voters Archives (RCV Archives). James Branch Cabell Library, Cabell Black Collection, Virginia Commonwealth Univ., Richmond.

Walker, Maggie Lena. 1928. Diary. Maggie Lena Walker Papers, Maggie Lena Walker National Historic Site, Richmond, Va.

WANT. 1972. "W-A-N-T Endorses Richmond City Council Candidates: The Soul Giant Names Council Choices." WANT, Richmond, Va., Apr. 17.

Interviews

Ballard, Janet. (Deceased.) Former executive director of the Richmond Urban League and civil rights activist in Richmond. Richmond, Va., Aug. 3, 1993.

Barlow, Alma. (Deceased.) Mail supervisor, supply clerk, and former public housing activist in Virginia. Richmond, Va., Dec. 4, 1991.

Binford, Vergie. Former schoolteacher in the Richmond public school system and lifelong friend of Ethel T. Overby. Richmond, Va., June 11, 2001.

Buskey, Harmon. Former civil rights activist in Richmond. By telephone, Oct. 20, 1996.

Clayton Walker, Ruby. Former member of the RCV and current member of the Richmond NAACP. Richmond, Va., Aug. 2, 1993.

Dell, Willie. Executive director of the Richmond Community Senior Center, former member of the Richmond City Council, and former professor, VCU. Richmond, Va., Aug. 23, Dec. 4, 1991; July 28, 1993; Mar. 25, 1997; and by telephone, Jan. 13, 1992; Nov. 15, 1998.

El-Amin, Saad. Attorney and former member of the RCV. Richmond, Va., Dec. 5, 1991; and by telephone, Jan. 14, 1992.

Foster, Dr. Francis. One of the original founders of the RCV. Richmond, Va., July 20, 1993.

Foster, Wendell T. Former VUU sit-in demonstrator arrested at Thalhimer's boycott and schoolteacher in the Richmond public school system. Richmond, Va., July 20, 1993.

Gales, Dr. Franklin. Member of the RCV and treasurer for the city of Richmond. Richmond, Va., July 30, 1993.

Green, Maureen. Bureau of Labor Statistics, U.S. Department of Labor, Washington, D.C. Dec. 21, 1989.

Harris, William. Professor in the City and Regional Planning Department, Univ. of Virginia at Charlottesville. By telephone, July 2, 1991.

Hashgawa, Marie. Former of the Women's International League for Peace and Freedom, Richmond Human Relations Council. Richmond, Va., Aug. 2, 1993.

Hays, Dr. R. Allen. Former project manager with the Richmond Redevelopment Housing Authority and professor in the Department of Political Science, Univ. of Northern Iowa. Boulder, Colo., July 8, 1993.

Hill, Oliver. Former attorney for the NAACP Legal Defense Fund, member of the Richmond City Council, 1948–50, and former attorney in Richmond. By telephone, July 27, 1992.

Holt, Alto Mae. Widow of Curtis Holt Sr. Richmond, Va., Mar. 24, 1997.

Jewell, Martin. Vice president of RCV. Richmond, Va., Aug. 24, 1991.

Lee, George. Attorney. Richmond, Va., Aug. 21, 1991.

Lomax, Ora. Former member of the RCV and civil rights activist in Richmond. Richmond, Va., Aug. 6, 1993.

Lynch, Alice Clarke. General registrar for the city of Richmond. Richmond, Va., July 29, 1993.

Moeser, Dr. John. Associate professor in the Department of Urban Studies and Planning, VCU. Richmond, Va., Sept. 11, 1989; and by telephone, Feb. 16, 1990; July 7, 1991.

Morse, Naomi. Former schoolteacher in the Richmond public school system and lifelong friend of Ethel T. Overby. Richmond, Va., June 11, 2001.

Murray, Benjamin R., Jr. Richmond, Va., Mar. 25, 1997.

Newsom, Dr. Lionel. (Deceased.) Former sociologist, president of Central State Univ., and civil rights activist in North Carolina. Newark, Del., Jan. 15, 1983.

Peeples, Dr. Edward. Former professor at VCU and former civil rights activist in Richmond. Richmond, Va., July 29, 1993.

Silver, Dr. Christopher. Assistant professor in the Department of Urban Studies and Planning, VCU. By telephone, July 7, 1991; Richmond, Va., Aug. 23, 1991.

Thornton, Dr. William. An original founder of the RCV. By telephone, July 27, 1992.

Towns, Clarence. Deputy director of Richmond Renaissance. Richmond, Va., Aug. 21, 1991.

Turpin, Roland. Former executive director for Richmond Housing Authority, currently executive director of Dayton Housing Authority. Dayton, Ohio, Aug. 6, 1991.

Williams, Michael P. Staff writer for the Richmond Times-Dispatch. By telephone, Mar. 2, 1990; Richmond, Va., Aug. 24, 1991.

SECONDARY SOURCES

Books

Anderson, James D. 1988. The Education of Blacks in the South, 1860–1935. Chapel Hill: Univ. of North Carolina Press.

Aptheker, Herbert. 1983. *The American Negro Slave Revolts*. 1943. Reprint, New York: International Publishers.

Bachrach, Peter, and Morton S. Baratz. 1979. *Power and Poverty: Theory and Practice*. New York: Oxford Univ. Press.

Baker, Donald P. 1989. *Wilder: Hold Fast to Dreams*. Cabin John, Md.: Seven Locks Press.

Berry, Mary Francis. 1994. *Black Resistance White Law*. New York: Penguin.

Billingsley, Andrew. 1968. *Black Families in White America*. Englewood Cliffs, N.J.: Prentice-Hall.

Bloom, Jack M. 1987. *Class, Race, and the Civil Rights Movement*. Bloomington: Indiana Univ. Press.

Boles, John B. 1984. *Black Southerners, 1619–1869*. Lexington: Univ. Press of Kentucky.

Bolster, W. Jeffrey. 1997. *Black Jacks: African American Seamen in the Age of Sail*. Cambridge: Harvard Univ. Press.

Branch, Taylor. 1998. *Pillar of Fire: America in the King Years, 1963–65*. New York: Simon and Schuster.

Breen, T. H., and Stephen Innes. 1980. *"Myne Owne Ground": Race and Freedom on Virginia's Eastern Shore, 1640–1676*. New York: Oxford Univ. Press.

Browning, Rufus P., Dale Rogers Marshall, and David H. Tabb. 1986. *Protest Is Not Enough: The Struggle of Blacks and Hispanics for Equality in Urban Politics*. Berkeley and Los Angeles: Univ. of California Press.

Buni, Andrew. 1967. *The Negro in Virginia Politics: 1902–1965*. Charlottesville: Univ. of Virginia Press.

Button, James W. 1989. *Blacks and Social Change*. Princeton, N.J.: Principal Univ. Press.

Carson, David G. 1977. *Power and Politics in the United States*. Lexington, Mass.: D. C. Heath.

Carter, Dan T. 1995. *The Politics of Rage: George Wallace, the Origins of New Conservatism, and the Transformation of American Politics*. Baton Rouge: Louisiana State Univ. Press.

Chesson, Michael B. 1981. *Richmond after the War, 1865–1890*. Richmond: Virginia State Library.

Collins, Patricia Hill. 1991. *Black Feminist Thought: Knowledge, Consciousness, and the Politics of Empowerment*. New York: Routledge.

Cone, James H. 1992. *Martin and Malcolm and America: A Dream or Nightmare*. New York: Orbis.

Dahl, Robert A. 1961. *Who Governs?* New Haven, Conn.: Yale Univ. Press.

Dash, Leon. 1997. *Rosa Lee: A Mother and Her Family in Urban America*. New York: A Plume Book.

Davis, Angela. 1983. *Women, Race, and Class*. New York: Vintage Books.

Dawson, Michael C. 1994. *Behind the Mule: Race and Class in African-American Politics*. Princeton, N.J.: Princeton Univ. Press.

DeLeon, Richard Edward. 1992. *Left Coast City: Progressive Politics in San Francisco, 1975–1991*. Lawrence: Univ. of Kansas Press.

Dey, Charles. 1966. *Ironmaker to the Confederacy: Joseph R. Anderson and the Tredegar Iron Works*. New Haven: Yale Univ. Press.

Dittmer, John. 1994. *Local People: The Struggle for Civil Rights in Mississippi*. Urbana: Univ. of Illinois Press.

Donnan, Elizabeth, ed. 1935. *Documents Illustrative of the Slave Trade to America*, vol. 1. Washington, D.C.: Carnegie Institution.

Downs, Anthony. 1967. *Inside Bureaucracy*. Boston: Little, Brown.

Drake, W. Avon, and Richard D. Holsworth. 1996. *Affirmative Action and the Stalled Quest for Black Progress.* Urbana: Univ. of Illinois Press.

Edds, Margaret. 1987. *Free at Last: What Really Happened When Civil Rights Came to Southern Politics.* Bethesda, Md.: Alder and Alder.

Escott, Paul D. 1979. *Slavery Remembered: A Record of Twentieth-Century Slave Narratives.* Chapel Hill: Univ. of North Carolina Press.

Foner, Philip S. 1941. *Business and Slavery.* Chapel Hill: Univ. of North Carolina Press.

Frankel, Noralee. 1999. *Freedom's Women: Black Women and Families in Civil War Era Mississippi.* Bloomington: Indiana Univ. Press.

Franklin, John Hope, and Alfred A. Moss Jr. 1988. *From Slavery to Freedom: A History of Negro Americans.* 6th ed. New York: Alfred A. Knopf.

Frey, Sylvia R. 1991. *Water from the Rock: Black Resistance in a Revolutionary Age.* Princeton, N.J.: Princeton Univ. Press.

Gamson, William. 1975. *The Strategy of Social Protest.* Homewood, Ill.: Dorsey.

Gavins, Raymond. 1977. *The Perils and Prospects of Southern Black Leadership: Gordon Blaine Hancock, 1884–1970.* Durham, N.C.: Duke Univ. Press.

Genovese, Eugene. 1974. *Roll, Jordan, Roll: The World the Slaves Made.* New York: Random House.

Giddings, Paula. 1984. *When and Where I Enter: The Impact of Black Women on Race and Sex in America.* New York: Bantam Books.

Gilmore, Glenda Elizabeth. 1996. *Gender and Jim Crow: Women and the Politics of White Supremacy in North Carolina, 1896–1920.* Chapel Hill: Univ. of North Carolina Press.

Gosnell, Harold F. [1935] 1969. *Negro Politicians: The Rise of Negro Politics in Chicago.* Chicago: Univ. of Chicago Press.

Grimshaw, William J. 1992. *Bitter Fruit: Black Politics and the Chicago Machine, 1931–1991.* Chicago: Univ. of Chicago Press.

Guild, June Purcell. 1969. *Black Laws of Virginia: A Summary of the Legislative Acts of Virginia Concerning Negroes from Earliest Times to the Present.* 1936. Reprint, New York: Negro Universities Press.

Gutman, Herbert. 1976. *The Black Family in Slavery and Freedom.* New York: Pantheon Books.

Hamilton, Charles. 1973. *The Black Experience in American Politics.* New York: Putnam.

Harding, Vincent. 1981. *There Is a River: The Black Struggle for Freedom in America.* New York: Harcourt Brace Jovanovich.

Haviland, Laura. *A Woman's Life-Work.* Chicago: C. V. Waite.

Heinemann, Ronald L. 1996. *Harry F. Byrd of Virginia.* Charlottesville: Univ. Press of Virginia.

Higginbotham, A. Leon, Jr. 1978. *In the Matter of Color: Race and the American Legal Process: The Colonial Period.* New York: Oxford Univ. Press.

Higginbotham, Evelyn Brooks. 1993. *Righteous Discontent: The Women's Movement in the Black Baptist Church, 1880–1920.* Cambridge: Harvard Univ. Press.

Hill, Robert T. 1972. *The Strengths of Black Families.* New York: Emerson Hall.

Hine, Darlene Clark. 1989. *Black Women in White: Racial Conflict and Cooperation in the Nursing Profession, 1890–1950.* Bloomington: Indiana Univ. Press.

hooks, bell. 1984. *Feminist Theory: From Margin to Center.* Boston: South End Press.

Hunt, Alfred N. 1988. *Haiti's Influence on Antebellum America: Slumbering Volcano in the Caribbean.* Baton Rouge: Louisiana State Univ. Press.

Hunter, Floyd. 1953. *Community Power Structure.* Chapel Hill: Univ. of North Carolina Press.

Jackson, Luther P. 1942. *Free Negro Labor and Property Holding in Virginia, 1830–1860.* New York: Russell & Russell.

———. 1945. *Negro Office-Holders in Virginia, 1865–1895.* New York: Russell & Russell.

Jennings, James, and Mel King. 1986. *From Access to Power: Black Politics in Boston.* Cambridge, Mass.: Schenckman Books.

Johnson, Charles. 1998. *Dreamer: A Novel.* New York: Scribner.

Jones, Jacqueline. 1986. *Labor of Love, Love of Sorrow: Black Women, Work and the Family from Slavery to the Present.* New York: Vintage.

Judd, Dennis. 1988. *The Politics of American Cities.* Glenview, Ill.: Scott Foresman.

Judd, Dennis R., and Todd Swanstrom. 1994. *City Politics: Private Power and Public Politics.* New York: Harper Collins.

Kelley, Robin D. G., and Earl Lewis. 2000. *To Make Our World Anew: A History of African Americans.* New York: Oxford Univ. Press.

Kerr-Ritchie, Jeffrey R. 1999. *Freed People in the Tobacco South: Virginia, 1860–1900.* Chapel Hill: Univ. of North Carolina Press.

Key, V. O., Jr. 1949. *Southern Politics in State and Nation.* New York: Alfred A. Knopf.

Kilpatrick, James Jackson. 1962. *The Southern Case for School Segregation.* New York: Cromwell-Collier Press.

King, Wilma. 1995. *Stolen Childhood: Slave Youth in Nineteenth Century America.* Bloomington: Indiana Univ. Press.

Ladner, Joyce. 1971. *Tomorrow's Tomorrow: The Black Woman.* Garden City, N.Y.: Doubleday.

Lerner, Gerda, ed. 1973. *Black Women in White America.* New York: Vintage Press.

Litwack, Leon F. 1961. *North of Slavery: The Negro in the Free States, 1790–1860.* Chicago: Univ. of Chicago Press.

Marable, Manning. 1983. *How Capitalism Underdeveloped Black America.* Boston: South End Press.

Mason, A. Thomas, and William M. Beaney. 1968. *American Constitutional Law.* 4th ed. Englewood Cliffs, N.J.: Prentice-Hall.

McAdam, Doug. 1985. *Political Process and the Development of Black Insurgency, 1930–1970.* Chicago: Univ. of Chicago Press.

McKnight, Gerald D. 1998. *The Last Crusade: Martin Luther King, Jr., the FBI and the Poor People's Campaign.* Boulder, Colo.: Westview.

Moeser, John V., and Rutledge M. Dennis. 1982. *The Politics of Annexation: Oligarchic Power in a Southern City.* Cambridge, Mass.: Schenckman.

Moger, Allen W. 1968. *Virginia: Bourbonism to Byrd, 1870–1925.* Charlottesville: Univ. Press of Virginia.

Morgan, Philip D. 1998. *Slave Counterpoint: Black Culture in the Eighteenth-Century Chesapeake and Lowcountry.* Chapel Hill: Univ. of North Carolina Press.

Morris, Aldon D. 1984. *The Origins of the Civil Rights Movement: Black Communities Organizing for Change.* New York: Free Press.

Morrison, Minion K. C. 1987. *Black Political Mobilization: Leadership, Power and Mass Behavior.* New York: State Univ. of New York Press.

Morton, Richard L. 1973. *The Negro in Virginia Politics: 1865–1902.* Spartanburg, S.C.: Reprint Company.

Noble, Jeanne L. 1978. *Beautiful, Also, Are the Souls of My Black Sisters: A History of the Black Woman in America.* Englewood Cliffs, N.J.: Prentice-Hall.

Oakes, James. 1982. *The Ruling Race: A History of American Slaveholders.* New York: Vintage Books.

Oberschall, Anthony. 1973. *Social Conflict and Social Movements.* Englewood Cliffs, N.J.: Prentice-Hall.

Okihiro, Gary Y., ed. 1986. *In Resistance: Studies in African, Caribbean, and Afro-American History.* Amherst: Univ. of Massachusetts Press.

Overby, Ethel Thompson. 1975. *It's Better to Light a Candle than to Curse the Darkness: The Autobiographical Notes of Ethel Thompson Overby.* Richmond: Ethel Thompson Overby.

Payne, Charles M. 1995. *I've Got the Light of Freedom.* Berkeley and Los Angeles: Univ. of California Press.

Perdue, Charles L., Jr., Thomas E. Barden, and Robert K. Phillips. 1976. *Weevils in the Wheat: Interviews with Virginia Ex-Slaves.* Charlottesville: Univ. Press of Virginia.

Pinderhughes, Dianne M. 1987. *Race and Ethnicity in Chicago Politics: A Reexamination of Pluralist Theory.* Urbana: Univ. of Illinois Press.

Pinkney, Alphonso. 1984. *The Myth of Black Progress.* New York: Cambridge Univ. Press.

Piven, Frances Fox, and Richard Cloward. 1979. *Poor People's Movements: Why They Succeed, Why They Fail.* New York: Vintage Books.

Pohlmann, Marcus D. 1999. *Black Politics in Conservative America.* 2d ed. New York: Longman.

Pohlmann, Marcus D., and Michael P. Kirby. 1996. *Racial Politics at the Crossroads: Memphis Elects Dr. W. W. Herenton.* Knoxville: Univ. of Tennessee Press.

Pratt, Robert A. 1992. *The Color of Their Skin: Education and Race in Richmond, Virginia, 1954–89.* Charlottesville: Univ. Press of Virginia.

Raboteau, Albert J. 1978. *Slave Religion: The "Invisible Institution" in the Antebellum South.* New York: Oxford Univ. Press.

Rachleff, Peter J. 1984. *Black Labor in the South: Richmond, Virginia, 1865–1890.* Philadelphia: Temple Univ. Press.

Randolph, Peter. 1893. *From Slave Cabin to the Pulpit.* Boston: Earle.

Robinson, Jo Ann Gibson. 1987. *The Montgomery Bus Boycott and the Women Who Started It.* Knoxville: Univ. of Tennessee Press.

Robnett, Belinda. 1997. *How Long? How Long?: African American Women in the Struggle for Civil Rights.* New York: Oxford Univ. Press.

Russell, John D. 1969. *The Free Negro in Virginia, 1619–1865.* New York: Dover Publications.

Sabato, Larry. 1979. *Virginia Votes, 1975–1978.* Charlottesville: Institute of Government, Univ. of Virginia.

Scher, Richard K. 1997. *Politics in the New South: Republicanism, Race and Leadership in the Twentieth Century.* 2d ed. New York: M. E. Sharpe.

Shaw, Stephanie J. 1996. *What a Woman Ought to Be and Do: Black Professional Women Workers During the Jim Crow Era.* Chicago: Univ. of Chicago Press.

Shull, Steven. 1993. *A Kinder, Gentler Racism? The Reagan-Bush Civil Rights Legacy.* Armonk, N.Y.: M. E. Sharpe.

Silver, Christopher. 1984. *Twentieth-Century Richmond: Planning, Politics, and Race.* Knoxville: Univ. of Tennessee Press.

Silver, Christopher, and John V. Moeser. 1995. *The Separate City.* Lexington: Univ. Press of Kentucky.

Sonenshein, Raphael J. 1993. *Politics in Black and White: Race and Power in Los Angeles.* Princeton, N.J.: Princeton Univ. Press.

Staples, Robert. 1971. *The Black Family: Essays and Studies.* Belmont, Calif.: Wadsworth.

Still, William. 1970. *The Underground Railroad.* 1871. Reprint, Chicago: Johnson.

Stone, Clarence N. 1989. *Regime Politics: Governing Atlanta, 1948–1988.* Lawrence: Univ. of Kansas Press.

Stuckey, Sterling. 1987. *Slave Culture: Nationalist Theory and the Foundations of Black America.* New York: Oxford Univ. Press.

Swint, Henry L., ed. 1966. *Dear Ones at Home.* Nashville: Vanderbilt Univ. Press.

Tate, Katherine. 1993. *From Protest to Politics: The New Black Voters in American Elections.* Cambridge: Harvard Univ. Press.

Terborg-Penn, Rosalyn. 1998. *African American Women in the Struggle for the Vote, 1850–1920.* Bloomington: Indiana Univ. Press.

Tilly, Charles. 1978. *From Mobilization to Revolution.* Reading, Mass: Addison-Wesley.

Tushnet, Mark V. 1994. *Making Civil Rights Law.* New York: Oxford Univ. Press.

Verba, Sidney, and Norman N. Nie. 1972. *Participation in America.* Chicago: Univ. of Chicago Press.

Wade, Richard C. 1964. *Slavery in the Cities: The South, 1820–1860.* New York: Oxford Univ. Press.

Walton, Hanes, Jr. 1975. *Black Republicans: The Politics of the Black and Tans.* Metuchen, N.Y.: Scarecrow Press.

White, Deborah Gray. 1985. *Ar'n't I a Woman? Female Slaves in the Plantation South.* New York: Norton.

———. 1999. *Too Heavy a Load: Black Women in Defense of Themselves, 1894–1994.* New York: Norton.

Wilkinson, J. Harvie. 1968. *Harry Byrd and the Changing Face of Virginia Politics, 1945–1966*. Charlottesville: Univ. of Virginia Press.

Wilmore, Gayraud S. 1983. *Black Religion and Black Radicalism: An Interpretation of the Religious History of Afro-American People*. 2d ed., rev. and enlarged. Maryknoll, N.Y.: Orbis.

Wilson, William J. 1980. *The Declining Significance of Race*. 2d ed. Chicago: Univ. of Chicago Press.

Winch, Julie. 1988. *Philadelphia's Black Elite: Activism, Accommodation, and the Struggle for Autonomy, 1787–1848*. Philadelphia: Temple Univ. Press.

Woodward, C. Van. 1974. *The Strange Career of Jim Crow*. 3d ed. New York: Oxford Univ. Press.

Wynes, Charles E. 1961. *Race Relations in Virginia: 1870–1902*. Charlottesville: Univ. of Virginia Press.

Articles, Chapters, and Studies

"Authority's Policy Here Is Upheld: Eviction of Unwed Mothers Ruled Justified by Judge." 1967. *Richmond Times-Dispatch*, July 28.

Bailey, Peter A. 1988. "Challenging Richmond's Crusade for Voters." *Richmond Surroundings* 3, no. 6 (Nov./Dec.): 41–43.

Becker, William H. 1997. "The Black Church: Manhood and Mission." In *African-American Religion: Interpretive Essays in History and Culture*, edited by Timothy E. Fulop and Albert J. Raboteau, 177–99. New York: Routledge.

Braxton, Gloria J. 1994. "African-American Women and Politics: Research Trends and Directions." *National Political Science Review* 4: 281–96.

Brown, Elsa Barkley. 1988. "Womanist Consciousness: Maggie Lena Walker and the Independent Order of Saint Luke." In *Black Women in America: Social Science Perspectives*, edited by Michelins R. Malson, Elisabeth Mudimbe-Boyi, Jean F. O'Barr, and Mary Wyer, 173–96. Chicago: Univ. of Chicago Press. Originally in *Signs* 14, no. 3 (Spring 1989).

———. 1994. "Negotiating and Transforming the Public Sphere: African American Political Life in the Transition from Slavery to Freedom." *Public Culture* 7: 107–46.

Campbell, Tom. 1984. "West First in Campaign Donations." *Richmond Times-Dispatch*, Apr. 25, B3.

"Carpenter Sends Funds to Donors." 1973. *Richmond News Leader*, June 2.

Chesson, Michael B. 1982. "Richmond's Black Councilmen, 1871–1896." In *Southern Black Leaders of the Reconstruction Era: Blacks in the New World*, edited by H. N. Rabinowitz, 191–222. Urbana: Univ. of Illinois Press.

Coleman, Willi. 1997. "Architects of a Vision: Black Women and Their Antebellum Quest for Political and Social Equality." In *African-American Women and the Vote, 1837–1965*, edited by Ann D. Gordon, Bettye Collier-Thomas, John H. Bracey, Arlene Voski Avakian, and Joyce Avrech Berkman, 24–40. Amherst: Univ. of Massachusetts Press.

"Court Bars Eviction of Negro." 1966. *Fairfax Merchant,* Sept. 16.

Crenshaw, K. W. 1993. "Beyond Racism and Misogyny: Black Feminism and 2 Live Crew." In *Words that Wound: Critical Race Theory, Assaultive Speech, and the First Amendment,* edited by M. J. Matsuda, C. R. Lawrence III, R. Delgado, and K. W. Crenshaw, 111–32. Boulder, Colo.: Westview.

Dabney, Virginius. 1943. "Nearer and Nearer the Precipice." *Atlantic Monthly* 171 (Jan.–June): 94–100.

———. 1964. "Richmond's Quiet Revolution." *Saturday Review,* Feb. 29, 18–28.

Deutsch, Karl. 1961. "Social Mobilization and Political Development." *American Political Science Review* 55, no. 3 (Sept.): 493–514.

Dill, Bonnie Thornton. 1979. "The Dialectics of Black Womanhood." *Signs* 4: 543–55.

Drake, A., and R. D. Holsworth. 1991. "Electoral Politics, Affirmative Actions, and the Supreme Court: The Case of Richmond v. Croson." *National Political Science Review* 2: 65–91.

Du Bois, W. E. B. 1935. "A Negro Nation Within the Nation." *Current History* 42 (Apr.–Sept.): 265–70.

Eaton, Clement. 1960. "Slave-Hiring in the Upper South: A Step toward Freedom." *Mississippi Valley Historical Review* 46, no. 4 (Mar.): 663–78.

Edney, Hazel T. 1993. "The Battle to End Segregation in Richmond." Special Report. *Richmond Free Press,* Mar. 18–20, 3.

Egerton, Douglas R. 1990. "Gabriel's Conspiracy and the Election of 1800." *Journal of Southern History* 56, no. 2 (May): 191–215.

Englemayer, Paul A. 1983. "Roy A. West, Richmond's Black Mayor, Is Facing Major Problems Because Most Blacks Dislike Him." *Wall Street Journal,* Nov. 2, 60.

Garber, Judith A. 1995. "Defining Feminist Community: Place, Choice, and the Urban Politics of Difference." In *Gender in Urban Research: Urban Affairs Annual Review 42,* edited by Judith A. Garber and Robyne S. Turner, 24–43. Thousand Oaks, Calif.: Sage.

Gravely, Will B. 1997. "The Rise of African Churches in America (1786–1822): Re-examining the Contexts." In *African-American Religion: Interpretive Essays in History and Culture,* edited by Timothy E. Fulop and Albert J. Raboteau, 133–51. New York: Routledge.

Griffin, Alison. 1972. "The Minister's Wife: Color Her Anything but Gray." *Richmond Times-Dispatch,* Apr. 30, 1–2.

Hamilton, Charles. 1976. "Public Policy and Some Political Consequences." In *Public Policy for the Black Community: Strategies and Perspectives,* edited by Marguerite Ross Barnett and James A. Hefner, 237–55. New York: Alfred.

Hancock, Gordon Blaine. 1964. "The Origins of the Southern Regional Council: Writing a New Charter of Southern Race Relations." *Southern Regional Council* 19, no. 1: 18–21.

Hayden, Robert. 1968. "Preface to the Atheneum Edition, *The New Negro,*" edited by Alain Locke. In *Studies in American Negro Life,* general editor August Meier.

Hill, Oliver W. 1982. "Did He Sell Out to the Whites?" *Close to Home, Washington Post*, July 25, p. B8.

Hill, Ricky. 1994. "The Study of Black Politics: Notes on Rethinking the Paradigm." In *Black Politics and Black Political Behavior: A Linkage Analysis*, edited by Hanes Walton Jr., 11–17. Westport, Conn.: Praeger.

Jennings, James. 1994. "Conclusion: Racial Hierarchy and Ethnic Conflict in the United States." In *Blacks, Latinos, and Asians in Urban America: Status and Prospects for Politics and Activism*, edited by James Jennings, 143–57. Westport, Conn.: Praeger.

Johnston, James Hugo. 1929. "The Participation of Negroes in the Government of Virginia from 1877 to 1888." *Journal of Negro History* 9: 250–69.

Jones, Mack. 1978. "Black Political Empowerment in Atlanta: Myth and Reality." *Urban Politics: The Annals of the American Academy of Political and Social Science*, vol. 439: 90–117.

———. 1992. "The Black Underclass as Systemic Underclass as Systemic Phenomenon." In *Race, Politics, and Economic Development: Community Perspectives*, edited by James Jennings, 53–65. New York: Verso Press.

Joyner, Charles. 1994. "Believer I Know: The Emergence of African-American Christianity." In *African-American Christianity: Essays in History*, edited by Paul E. Johnson, 18–46. Berkeley and Los Angeles: Univ. of California Press.

Keiser, Richard A. 1997. "After the First Black Mayor: Fault Lines in Philadelphia's Biracial Coalition." In *Racial Politics In American Cities*, edited by Rufus P. Browning, Dale Rogers Marshall, and David H. Tabb, 65–93. New York: Longman.

Kelley, Robin D. G. 1993. "We Are Not What We Seem: Rethinking Black Working Class Opposition in the Jim Crow South." *Journal of American History* 80 (June): 75–113.

———. 1996. "Birmingham's Untouchables: The Black Poor in the Age of Civil Rights." In *Race Rebels: Culture, Politics, and the Black Working Class*, edited by Robin D. G. Kelley, 77–100. New York: Free Press.

Kilson, Martin. 1996. "An Anatomy of the Black Political Class." In *The Politics of Minority Coalitions: Race, Ethnicity, and Shared Uncertainties*, edited by Wilbur C. Rich, 13–33. Westport, Conn.: Praeger.

King, Deborah K. 1988. "Multiple Jeopardy, Multiple Consciousness: The Context of a Black Feminist Ideology." *Signs* 14, no. 1 (Autumn). Reprinted in *Black Women in America: Social Science Perspectives*, edited by Michelins R. Malson, Elisabeth Mudimbe-Boyi, Jean F. O'Barr, and Mary Wyer, 265–95. Chicago: Univ. of Chicago Press, 1988.

King, Mae C. 1975. "Oppression and Power: The Unique Status of the Black Woman in the American Political System." *Social Science Quarterly* 56: 116–28.

Kulikoff, Allan. 1978. "The Origins of Afro-American Society in Tidewater Maryland and Virginia, 1700 to 1790." *William and Mary Quarterly* 35, no. 2 (Apr.): 226–59.

Ladd, Everett C. 1969. "Negro Political Leadership in the South." In *Studies in American Negro Life,* general editor August Meier.

Lewis, Shelby. 1988. "A Liberation Ideology: The Intersection of Race, Sex, and Class." In *Women's Rights Feminism and Politics in the United States,* edited by Mary Lyndon Shanley, 38–44. Washington, D.C.: American Political Science Association.

"'Lily Blacks' Will Hold Big Conference Today." 1921. *Richmond Times-Dispatch,* Aug. 7, 2.

Link, William A. 1998. "The Jordan Hatcher Case: Politics and 'A Spirit of Insubordination' in Antebellum Virginia." *Journal of Southern History* 64, no. 4 (Nov.): 615–35.

Marsh, Clifton E. 1984. "Willie Dell: Class Without Pretense." *Los Angeles: Mainstream America* (June/July): 37–39.

Martin, Robert E. 1938. *Negro Disfranchisement in Virginia.* Howard Univ. Studies in the Social Sciences 1. Washington, D.C.

McAdam, Doug. 1992. "Gender as a Mediator of the Activist Experience: The Case of Freedom Summer." *American Journal of Sociology* 97: 1111–40.

McNair Barnett, Bernice. 1993. "Invisible Southern Black Women Leaders in the Civil Rights Movement: The Triple Constraints of Gender, Race, and Class." *Gender and Society* 7, no. 2 (June): 162–82.

Meier, August, and Elliott Rudwick. 1969. "The Boycott Movement Against Jim Crow Streetcars in the South, 1900–1906." *Journal of American History* 55 (Mar.): 756-75.

Mintz, Sidney W., and Richard Price. 1976. *An Anthropological Approach to the Afro-American Past: A Caribbean Perspective.* ISHI Occasional Papers in Social Change, No. 2. Philadelphia.

Moore, James T. 1975. "Black Militancy in Readjuster Virginia, 1879–1883." *Journal of Southern History* 41, no. 2 (May): 167–86.

Murphy, Thomas P. 1978. "Race-Base Accounting: Assigning the Costs and Benefits of a Racially Motivated Annexation." *Urban Affairs Quarterly* 14, no. 2 (Dec.): 169–94.

Nelson, William E. 1987. "Cleveland: The Evolution of Black Political Power." In *The New Black Politics: The Search for Political Power,* edited by Michael B. Preston, Leoneal J. Henderson Jr., and Paul Puryear, 172–99. New York: Longman.

Nicklin, Walter. 1970. "They're Still Haulin' in the Vote(rs) in Virginny." *Washington Post/Potomac,* Nov. 15, 42–44.

Obituary. 1986. "Curtis Holt Dies at 66; Champion of Civil Rights." *Richmond Afro-American,* Nov. 29, 6, 14.

O'Brien, John T. 1978. "Factory, Church, and Community: Blacks in Antebellum Richmond." *Journal of Southern History* 44, no. 4 (Nov.): 509–36.

Orfield, Gary. 1996. "Turning Back to Segregation." In *Dismantling Desegregation: The Quiet Reversal of Brown v. Board of Education*, edited by Gary Orfield and Susan E. Eaton, and the Harvard Project on School Desegregation, 1–22. New York: New Press.

Parenti, Michael. 1970. "Power and Pluralism: A View from the Bottom." *Journal of Politics* 32, no. 3 (Aug.): 501–30.

Payne, Charles M. 1990. "Men Led, but Women Organized: Movement Participation of Women in the Mississippi Delta." In *Women and Social Protest*, edited by Guida West and Rhoda L. Blumberg, 156–63. New York: Oxford Univ. Press.

Picott, J. Rupert, and Edward H. Peeples. 1964. "A Study in Infamy: Prince Edward County, Virginia." *Phi Delta Kappan* 45, no. 8.

Prestage, Jewel L. 1991. "In Quest of African-American Political Woman." *Annals of the American Academy of Political and Social Sciences* 515: 88–103.

Preston, Michael B. 1987. "The Election of Harold Washington: An Examination of the SES Model in the 1983 Chicago Mayoral Election." In *The New Black Politics: The Search for Political Power*, edited by Michael B. Preston, Leoneal J. Henderson Jr., and Paul Puryear, 139–71. New York: Longman.

Raboteau, Albert J. 1997. "The Black Experience in American Evangelism: The Meaning of Slavery." In *African-American Religion: Interpretive Essays in History and Culture*, edited by Timothy E. Fulop and Albert J. Raboteau, 89–106. New York: Routledge.

Randolph, Lewis A. 1998. "The Civil Rights Movement in Richmond, 1940–1977: Race, Class, and Gender in the Structuring of Protest Activity." *Proteus* 15, no. 1 (Spring): 63–72. Special Issue: The American Civil Rights Movement in Global Perspective.

Randolph, Lewis A., and Gayle T. Tate. 1995. "The Rise and Decline of an African American Political Power in Richmond: Race, Class, and Gender." In *Gender in Urban Research: Urban Affairs Annual Review 42*, edited by Judith A. Garber and Robyne S. Turner, 136–54. Thousand Oaks, Calif.: Sage.

Range, Ross Peter. 1991. "Playboy Interview: L. Douglas Wilder—A Candidate Conversation." *Playboy* 38, no. 9 (Sept.): 61–81.

Redding, J. Saunders. 1943. "A Negro Speaks for His People." *Atlantic Monthly* 171, no. 3 (Jan.– June): 58–63.

Reed, Adolph. 1988. "The Black Urban Regime: Structural Origins and Constraints." In *Power, Community and the City. Comparative Urban and Community Research*, vol. 1, edited by Michael P. Smith, 138–89. New Brunswick, N.J.: Transaction Books.

"The Republican 7." 1921. *Richmond Planet*, Sept. 10, front page.

Robertson, Claire. 1996. "Africa into the Americas: Slavery and Women, the Family and the Gender Division of Labor." In *More than Chattel: Black Women and Slavery in the Americas,* edited by David Barry Gaspar and Darlene Clark Hine, 3–40. Bloomington: Indiana Univ. Press.

Robinson, Armstead. 1991. "Introduction: Reassessing the History of the Civil Rights Movement." In *New Directions in Civil Rights Studies,* edited by Amstead Robinson, 1–7. Charlottesville: Univ. of Virginia Press.

Robnett, Belinda. 1996. "African American Women in the Civil Rights Movement, 1954–1965: Gender, Leadership, and Micromobilization." *American Journal of Sociology* 101, no. 6 (May): 1161–93.

Russell, Jeroline E. 1970. "She Cites Reasons for Backing Holt." *Richmond Times-Dispatch,* June 2.

Rustin, Bayard. 1965. "From Protest to Politics: The Future of the Civil Rights Movement." *Commentary* 39, no. 2 (Feb.): 25–31.

Sidbury, James. 1997. "Saint Dominique in Virginia: Ideology, Local Meanings, and Resistance to Slavery, 1790–1800." *Journal of Southern History* 63, no. 3 (Aug.): 531–52.

Standley, Anne. 1993. "The Role of Black Women in the Civil Rights Movement." In *Women in the Civil Rights Movement: Trailblazers and Torchbearers, 1941–1965,* edited by Vicki L. Crawford, Jacqueline Anne Rouse, and Barbara Woods, 183–202. Bloomington: Indiana Univ. Press.

Stone, Clarence N., and Carol Pierannunzi. 1997. "Atlanta and the Limited Reach of Electoral Control." In *Racial Politics in American Cities,* edited by Rufus P. Browning, Dale Rogers Marshall, and David H. Tabb, 163–200. New York: Longman.

Tate, Gayle T. 1991. "The Political Consciousness of Black Women in the 19th Century." *Third World in Perspective* 1, no. 1 (Fall/Winter): 1139–57.

Terborg-Penn, Rosalyn. 1978. "Discrimination Against Afro-American Women in the Women's Movement, 1830–1920." In *The Afro-American Woman: Struggles and Images,* edited by Sharon Harley and Rosalyn Terborg-Penn, 28–42. Port Washington, N.Y.: Kennikat.

Walker, Ruby C. 1990. "A Place at the Table." *Style Weekly,* Feb. 20, 75.

Walton, Hanes, Jr., Leslie B. McLemore, and C. Vernon Gray. 1990. "The Pioneering Books on Black Politics and the Political Science Community: 1903–1965." *National Political Science Review* 2: 196–218.

Watkins, Ralph. 1990. "A Reappraisal of the Role of Voluntary Associations in the African American Community." *Afro-American in New York Life and History* 14(2): 51–56.

Weems, Robert E., Jr. 1995. "African-American Consumer Boycotts During the Civil Rights Era." *Western Journal of Black Studies* 19, no. 1 (Spring): 72–79.

White, Deborah Gray. 2000. "Let My People Go: 1804–1860." In Kelley and Lewis, *To Make Our World Anew,* 169–226.

Williams, Gwynn. 1960. "The Concept of 'Egemonia' in the Thought of Antonio Gramsci: Some Notes on Interpretation." *Journal of the History of Ideas* 21: 586–99.

Williams, Juan. 1991. "One-Man Show." *Washington Post Magazine,* June 9, 13–37.

Woods, Barbara A. 1993. "Modjeska Simkins and the South Carolina Conference of the NAACP, 1941–1965." In *Women in the Civil Rights Movement: Trailblazers and Torchbearers,* edited by Vicki L. Crawford, Jacqueline Anne Rouse, and Barbara Woods, 99–120. Bloomington: Indiana Univ. Press.

Worrell, Bill. 1983. "Curtis Holt: Man Who Fought City Hall and Won." *Richmond Afro-American and Richmond Planet,* Jan. 29, 2–3.

Wright, Gavin. 1991. "Economic Consequences of the Southern Protest Movement." In *New Directions in Civil Rights Studies,* edited by Armstead L. Robinson. Charlottesville: Univ. of Virginia Press.

Newspapers

Liberator
New National Era
New York Tribune
Norfolk American Beacon
Norfolk Journal and Guide
North Star
Richmond Afro-American
Richmond Dispatch
Richmond Enquirer
Richmond Free Press

Richmond News Leader
Richmond Planet
Richmond Republic
Richmond State
Richmond Times and Compiler
Richmond Times-Dispatch
*Virginia Gazette and
    General Advertiser*
Wall Street Journal
Washington Post

Unpublished Material

Alexander, Ann Field. 1972. "Black Protest in the New South: John Mitchell, Jr. (1863–1929) and the Richmond Planet." Ph.D. diss., Duke Univ.

Dickinson, A. J. 1967. "Myth and Manipulation: The Story of the Crusade for Voters in Richmond, Virginia." Scholar of the House Paper (bachelor's thesis), Yale Univ.

Holton, Dwight Carter. 1987. "Power to the People: The Struggle for Black Political Power in Richmond, Virginia." Honors bachelor's degree thesis, Brown Univ.

Kimble, Greg. 1992. "Race and Class in a Southern City: Richmond, 1865–1920." Paper presented at the Organization of American Historians (OAH) annual conference, 1–32.

Lee, Lauranett. 1993. "More than an Image: Black Women Reformers in Richmond, Virginia, 1910–1928." Master's thesis, Virginia State Univ.

Mason, John. 2000. "A Crown Is More than a Hat." Lecture, Livingston Campus, Rutgers Univ., Nov. 16.

Randolph, Lewis A. 1990. "Development Policy in Four Cities." Ph.D. diss., Ohio State Univ., Columbus.

Williams, Oscar R. 1990. "The Civil Rights Movement in Richmond and Petersburg Virginia During 1960." Master's thesis, Virginia State Univ., Petersburg.

Index

Entries in *italics* refer to illustrations.

Abbreviations:

CRA = Civil Rights Act
CRM = civil rights movement
JD = Justice Department
MR = massive resistance campaign
RCC = Richmond Civic Council

RCV = Richmond Crusade for Voters
RF = Richmond Forward
RUL = Richmond Urban League
VRA = Voting Rights Act

Rights for a **Season**

was designed and typeset on a Macintosh computer system using QuarkXPress software. The text and display type is set in Stone Serif. This book was designed and typeset by Bill Adams and manufactured by Thomson-Shore, Inc.